FROM THE HOUSE OF WAR

John Simpson in the Gulf

ARROW BOOKS

Published by Arrow Books Limited
20 Vauxhall Bridge Road, London SW1V 2SA

An imprint of Random Century Group

London Melbourne Sydney Auckland Johannesburg
and agencies throughout the world

First published 1991

5 7 9 10 8 6 4

Copyright © 1991 by John Simpson

Set in 10½/12 Sabon by Speedset Ltd, Ellesmere Port

Printed and bound in Great Britain by
Cox & Wyman Ltd, Reading

ISBN 0 09 996670 0

Contents

To
Nick della Casa,
who remained with me in Baghdad when the war came;

to
Charles Maxwell,
who died beside him in Northern Iraq in
March 1991;

and to
Rosanna della Casa,
who was with them there, and has not been found.

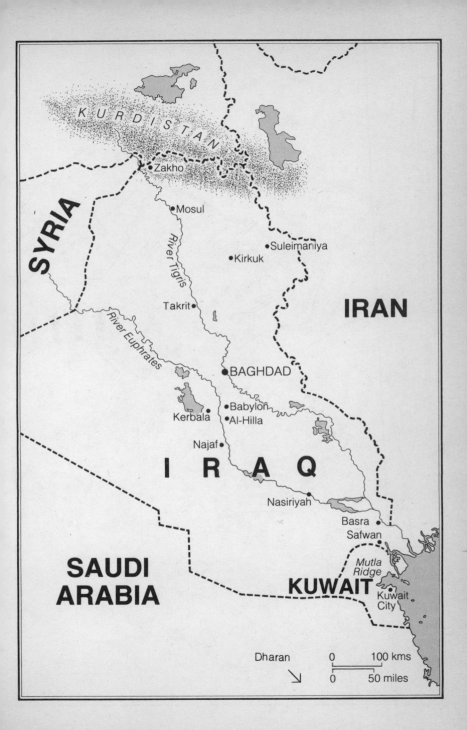

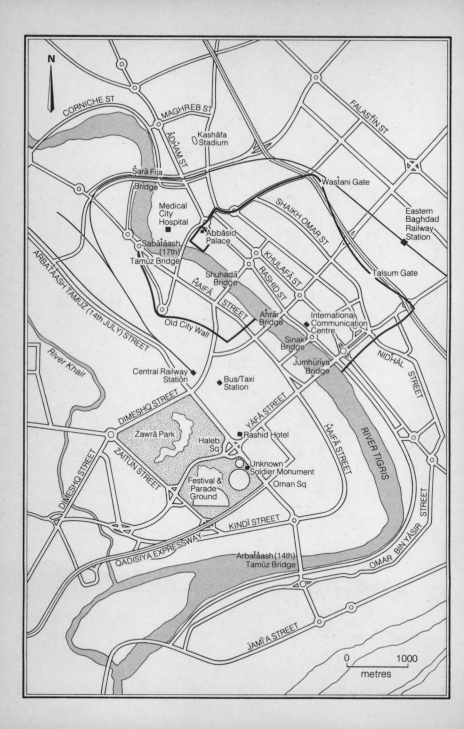

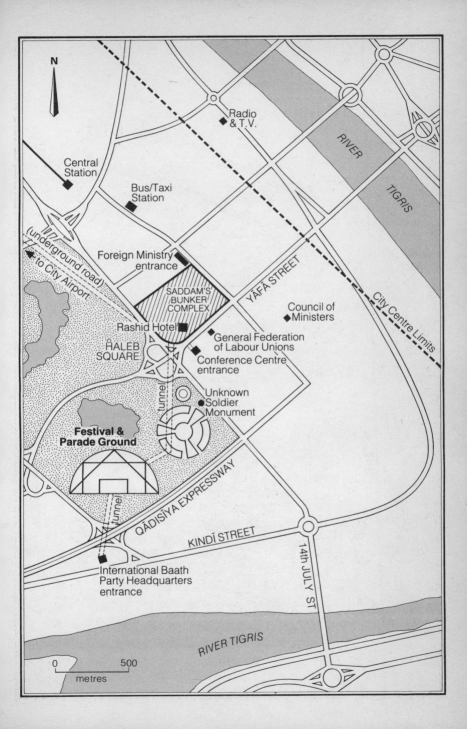

Introduction

On a rainy June morning a thousand soldiers, sailors and airmen marched through the City of London in celebration of Britain's part in the Gulf War against Iraq. Planes of the RAF flew overhead. The march-past after the Falklands War had followed the same route. Indeed, it was roughly where all England's victory marches have taken place, back to the time of Agincourt and no doubt before. There can have been few as muted as this, though. Unlike the victory parades a few days earlier in Washington and New York, where nothing but superlatives were used, the British commemoration was a modest affair; suitably so, since all the British ground forces put together only equalled the number of women soldiers in the American contingent.

There were many things for the British to be proud of: their professionalism, their courage, and the absence of bloodlust. The pilot of a British Army Lynx helicopter said privately that at the end of the ground offensive against the Iraqi troops in Kuwait he and his colleagues would circle over the Iraqi tanks as a warning to the crews. The Iraqis could escape before their tanks were destroyed. 'That way,' said the pilot, 'we could feel at peace with ourselves. We had total superiority, but we didn't use it.' Yet not everyone approved of the way the war had been fought: at least five British officers resigned their commissions after seeing the effects of cluster-bombs and fuel-air explosives on Iraqi soldiers. When the parade was over, the Prince of Wales made a speech at Guildhall in which he praised the achievements of the British contingent, but added that he suspected most people had nothing but sympathy for the Iraqi soldiers.

I spent almost six months in Baghdad from the early days of the crisis in August to its unsatisfactory conclusion: more than any other Western journalist and, I suspect, longer than any Western journalist had spent in Iraq for a good twenty years. My time there gave me a great affection for the people, and showed me what was not always appreciated by those who paid the usual swift visits to Baghdad: that there was as little enthusiasm for Saddam Hussein among ordinary Iraqis as there was for Nicolae Ceausescu among ordinary Romanians or for Erich Honecker among ordinary East Germans. The system of reward and punishment obliged people to come out onto the streets and go through the motions of hero-worship with enthusiasm, or face the consequences. In Iraq the consequences were even more severe than they were in Romania or East Germany.

The subject of this book is the extraordinary fraud which Saddam Hussein tried to perpetrate upon the entire world. The dictator of a smallish country in serious financial trouble, he invaded his much smaller and much richer neighbour on a sudden whim, and then attempted to convince some of the most powerful countries in the world that he was strong enough to take them all on and beat them. It is hard to think of a bigger bluff since Hitler's men entered the Rhineland in 1936 in relatively small numbers, lightly armed, and with orders to withdraw at the first serious show of resistance by the far superior French forces. Saddam Hussein based his bluff on the notion that his people worshipped him and would fight to the death to defend him; and that if the outside world took him on it would suffer heavily. It is surprising how many otherwise sensible people were taken in by this.

Even though Iraq and Saddam Hussein himself were at the heart of the whole affair, few people in the West seemed to want to know very much about either; and now that the war is over, not many people seem interested in finding out what really happened. Much has been exaggerated. This book will attempt to show, among other things, the extent to which we took Saddam Hussein at his own estimate of himself; how Mrs Thatcher encouraged Kuwait to resist any compromise with Iraq, and how Saddam's resulting fury led to his sudden decision to invade; how his ally, Yasser Arafat, ensured that Saddam's threat of worldwide terrorism came to nothing; how the West persistently overestimated the size and capability of the Iraqi ground forces, and how, when the long-awaited offensive finally came, the Allied forces probably out-numbered the Iraqis by two or even two-and-a-half to one.

Iraq's casualties were often exaggerated too. This was a new kind of war. Perhaps for the first time since 1918, a major conflict was fought by concentrating on the destruction of the opposing army, not on civilian morale. A well-known British MP has talked of up to 200,000 civilian deaths; the Iraqis themselves have suggested a figure of 2,000. Because Iraq is a closed society, people treat it as a wonderland about which just about anything can be said. I do not, however, wish to suggest that Iraq got off lightly: the deaths of several hundred women and children in the shelter at Amiriyah was as terrible in its way as anything that has happened in modern warfare.

The figure for the number of Iraqi soldiers who died is still unknown. Many people have put it at 100,000 or even twice that number. My own impression is that it too was much lower: maybe thirty thousand killed, and fifty thousand wounded, though this can only be a guess. Even the Allied figures are a little vague: 126 members of the Coalition armed forces died, but the number of injured is uncertain. In the ground offensive there were fewer casualties than in many NATO training exercises. Forty-seven Allied planes were lost, thirty-two in combat.

It seems to me that the Allies owe a great debt to the Iraqi people. If they had supported their leader, if they had felt the slightest enthusiasm for his posturings, if they had shared his hostility towards the West or his exaggerated notions of national honour and dignity, then they would have made Iraq a formidable opponent. Thousands of Arab, Islamic and Western soldiers would have died. They did not, and the Iraqi people deserve our gratitude as a result.

This book has no pretensions to be a history of the war. It is rather like an account of a football match written from a seat near one of the goals. Whenever the play was down at my end I had a superb view of it. But when it moved to the far end of the pitch I only knew what was happening when I heard the crowd roar. I have tried to make up for this inadequacy by talking after the match to other spectators, and some of the players. But mine is mostly the viewpoint from Baghdad: the viewpoint, I feel, which was much neglected in Britain and Western Europe, and which was scarcely acknowledged in the United States.

I have not attempted to be a fly on anyone's wall. This book contains no unsourced accounts of conversations between the leading characters of the 'Dammit, Tariq, tell those bastards they can't fool with me' variety. I have tried to indicate a source for everything I have written, and when there is no source except my own conjecture I have fallen back on the good old journalistic stand-bys – expressions like 'presumably' and 'seem to'. I have done my level best to ensure that the things I say are facts.

I was extremely fortunate throughout the writing of this book to have been helped by Bridget Harney, a researcher and editor with wide experience of the Middle East and of the military side of things. She supplied me with vast quantities of facts, interviewed all sorts of people, kept an eye on what I wrote and reined back some of my wilder plunges. It was a big challenge to write a book with as wide a scope as this in a short time, and if Bridget had not been there to help my courage might have failed me.

Tira Shubart was as always generous in her help, enlivening in her wit, and quick and certain in her judgment. Several libel cases were no doubt headed off by her shrewdness, and she too helped me by interviewing people. Neil Belton, my editor at Hutchinson, was tactful and well-informed. Richard Cohen, my former editor, was also most kind. Mike Robinson, chief news editor of BBC Television, helped me in all sorts of ways, for which I am most grateful. The *Panorama* programme gave me the fruits of some of its research. Eamonn Matthews from 'Newsnight', who had stayed in Baghdad when the war began, helped me greatly with accounts of his other adventures. So did Steve Anderson and Mark Urban from the same programme, and Jeremy Bowen from BBC News. Robert Fox, a friend from our days as despised sub-editors together, was generous with his information and advice. Bob Simpson, whom the Iraqis used to think was my brother, helped me with information and allowed me to use a mildly scandalous but delightful anecdote about himself. Anthony Wood, who worked with us in Baghdad at the start of the war, sent me his amusing reminiscences of life under fire with the BBC. Vaughan Smith, one of the ultimate heroes of the entire war, took the risk of telling me his adventures. Richard Schofield, the acknowledged expert on boundaries in the Middle East, helped with details of the dispute between Iraq and Kuwait. Anoushiravan Ehteshami, lecturer in Middle East politics at Exeter University, was a regular and generous source of ideas and information. Henry Dodds of Jane's Information Group supplemented my ignorance of military matters with great kindness. Caroline Wells, Librarian at the International Institute of Strategic Studies, was most helpful, as were the delightful staff at the library of BBC Monitoring at Caversham and the no less delightful people at the BBC World Service library at Bush House. I benefited greatly from talking to Dr Ahmad Chelabi, Adel Darwish, Malcolm Switzer, Stephen Solarz and Professor Fred Halliday (who, I found, had come closer than almost anyone else in forecasting when the war would begin). I had advice and assistance from people in the PLO and the British, French, Israeli, Saudi and United States governments, none of whom would want me to mention their names. I have received immense help from a large number of people in Iraq, but do not intend to say who they are either. My hope is that one day they will not have anything to fear from allowing their names and their stories to be made public. That day is not yet, however; and the reason for that, too, is something this book will endeavour to explain.

AFTER THE WAR

There he remained, eyes wide open, a flower brushing lightly against his cheek. There wasn't a single sound in this little corner of the world.

He heard nothing, saw nothing, but felt by a kind of sixth sense two boys silently rushing towards the château. It happened so quickly that at first he thought he was dreaming. He didn't want to call out for fear of waking the other sleeping boys. He got up, brushed the grass and flowers off his cassock and headed for the château. The thick lawn hid the sound of his footsteps. He remembered now he had noticed one of the shutters had been badly secured and was slightly ajar. Yes, he was right! The moon lit up the front of the house. One of the boys was pushing the shutter, forcing it open. Before Philippe could shout at them to stop, a stone shattered the window and there was a rain of glass. The boys, as lithe as cats, leapt inside.

'Oh, you little brats! Just wait till I sort you out!' Philippe said to himself.

Hoisting up his cassock, he followed them through the window, and found himself in a drawing room with furniture covered by dustsheets and a large, cold parquet floor. He groped about in the dark for a few moments before finding the light switch. When he turned the lights on he saw no one. He hesitated, looked around (the boys were hiding or had run off): the sofas, the piano, the winged bergère chairs covered by billowing sheets, the flowered chintz curtains at the windows – all made good hiding places. Seeing some fabric move, he walked towards a bay window and yanked back the curtains. One of the boys was there. He was among the oldest, almost an adult with a blackish face, rather beautiful eyes, a low forehead and a strong jaw.

'What are you doing here?' said the priest.

He heard a noise behind him and turned round; another boy was in the room, standing right behind him; he too was about seventeen or eighteen. He had thin, contemptuous lips and his yellowish face looked wild, as if he were possessed. Philippe was on his guard but they were too fast for him. In a flash they attacked; one tripped him and knocked him down, the other grabbed his throat. But he managed to fight them off, silently, successfully. Catching hold of one of them by the collar, he tightened his grip so much that the boy was forced to let go. As the boy pulled away, something fell out of his pocket and rolled along the ground: it was some silver.

'Congratulations, you've moved fast,' said Philippe, half choking, sitting on the floor, thinking to himself, 'The main thing is not to make a big thing of it, just get them out of here and they'll follow me like little puppies. Then we'll sort it out tomorrow.'

'That's enough, now! Enough of this nonsense . . . get going.'

He had barely finished speaking when once again they threw themselves on him, silently, desperately, savagely; one of them bit him, drew blood.

'They're going to kill me,' Philippe thought in amazement. They hung on to him like wolves. He didn't want to hurt them, but he was forced to defend himself; they punched him, kicked him, he fought them off and they came back at him even more violently than before. They no longer looked human, they were demented, animals . . . Philippe would have proven the stronger in spite of everything but they hit him on the head with a pedestal table with bronze legs; he fell down and as he fell he heard one of the boys run to the window and whistle. He saw nothing else: not the twenty-eight teenagers suddenly waking up, running across the lawn, climbing through the window; not the rush towards the delicate furniture that was being ripped apart and thrown out on to the grass. They were frenzied, they danced around the priest as he lay sprawled on the floor, they sang and shouted. One of the youngest, with a girlish face, jumped with both feet on to a sofa whose old springs creaked under the weight. The older ones had discovered a liquor cabinet. They dragged it into the drawing room, kicking it to move it along; when they opened it, they saw it was empty but they didn't need liquor to be drunk: the carnage was enough for them. They felt a terrifying kind of joy. Dragging Philippe by the feet, they threw him out of the window, so he fell heavily on to the lawn. At the edge of the lake, they swung him like a bundle . . . 'Heave-ho! Kill him!' they shouted in their harsh, high-pitched voices, some of which still sounded childlike.

When Philippe fell into the water he was still alive. Out of a sense of self-preservation, or a final burst of courage, he managed to remain at the edge of the lake; he clutched the branch of a tree with both hands and tried hard to keep his head above water. His battered face was red, swollen and grotesque. They were throwing stones at him. He held on at first, clinging with all his might to the branch that was swaying, cracking, giving way. He tried to get to the other shore but he was being bombarded.

Even our level of destruction is different from the rest of the world. It is bad, but it is an expression of our potential. The potential of the Iraqis is unique even in terms of destruction.

President Saddam Hussein, during a visit to the Al-Dora refinery in southwest Baghdad, 14 April 1991

I stood close to the edge of the 14 July Bridge and looked down into the waters of the Tigris: they were as thick and brown as the tea in a workman's café in London. The bridge wasn't a bridge any longer. During the airstrikes on Baghdad the Royal Air Force had turned it into a kind of dam. Branches, reeds, old clothes, chunks of styrofoam, spirals of oil, wads of grey scum had gathered along it. Other parts of the bridge stuck up out of the water like a half-submerged and flattened W, and the Tigris could only flow freely in the places where the W had sunk below the surface.

It used to be a suspension bridge and I had always liked it for its elegance and faithfulness to late nineteenth-century design. Now the suspension had gone. The iron teeth of the grid which had once connected the section where I stood with the rest of the bridge stuck out into the air like the perforations of a torn-off postage stamp. Two bombs had struck its middle section and the destruction was as neat as the bridge itself had been. In the middle of the river the roadway stuck up at absurd angles, the tarmac folded over the breaks as carefully as a surgeon folds the skin over an amputated stump. 14 July, which the bridge commemorated, was the day in 1958 when the Iraqi royal family, too pro-British for its own good, had been

3

overthrown and murdered. I was looking for symbolism; this would do as well as anything.

My colleagues filmed the bridge while I stood and watched. Beside us a soldier and a plainclothes security man looked on admiringly. A few months earlier I had been arrested for merely standing on this bridge and looking across the river at the forbidden sites opposite: Saddam Hussein's presidential palace and the barracks of the special troops who guarded it. But the palace wasn't visible now. It had been hit more often than any other target in the war and seemed to have evaporated. As for the barracks, the security man asked us politely not to point the camera in that direction since it was still in use. Otherwise we were free to film what we wanted. It was refreshingly sensible after the months of mindless control. The attitude now seemed to be that anything of interest or importance had already been bombed, so there could be no reason to stop us filming it.

When we had finished one of my colleagues offered the soldier and the security man a cigarette each. They took them in the polite Iraqi way, placing their hands on their hearts and bowing slightly. 'Hello mister, thank you very much, hello, hello,' the security man said in his best English: 'hello' being the word Iraqis have perversely adopted to mean 'goodbye'. As we walked away he called out: 'A British pilot bombed this bridge.' It was said half ruefully and half in admiration, as though beings from another planet had swooped down and manifested their superior powers here.

If Iraq had bombed Hammersmith Bridge in London, or the Pont Alexandre III in Paris, any Iraqi television crew which came to film the result might expect to be thrown in the water or lynched. In Baghdad, by contrast, people came to examine the damage, watched us film it, smiled or shook hands with us and wandered off. There was no more personal animosity than there had been before the war started. At first I thought it was because the war – and the death and destruction which it had brought with it – seemed like some vast natural calamity, for which there was no point allocating blame. Gradually, though, I realized it was more than that: it represented a form of passive resistance by ordinary Iraqis to Saddam Hussein's dreams of supremacy and the ferocity with which he pursued them.

After the war I finally managed to return to Iraq in April 1991. During the months I had spent there as the crisis unfolded I had had the overwhelming impression that no one I met or knew had any stomach for the confrontation, from the men who played backgammon or cleaned my shoes in the Baghdad teahouses to most of the government officials I dealt with. In private, no one said anything to me in praise of Saddam, in favour of the Baath Party, or in defence of the invasion of Kuwait; just as none of them seemed to think an Iraqi victory was remotely possible. Yet the repression in Saddam's Iraq was so savage that no one went beyond this purely negative form of resistance. There was no avoiding the public show of support for Saddam; all you could do was to go through the motions with as little enthusiasm as you dared.

'I feel,' said a friend of mine in the days before the war began, 'as though someone had tied me to the front seat of a bus and pushed it down a mountain. No brakes, no horn, no steering wheel, no chance of getting free.' Coming back to Baghdad after the war was over, it was hard to avoid the feeling that people saw things like the destruction of the 14 July Bridge as the inevitable retribution for Saddam's hubris. In the days immediately before the war another friend of mine had got excited. 'Fuck Saddam!' he bellowed. 'I hope the bombs come and destroy everything, so we will be free of fucking Saddam!' After the war he was quieter: 'Iraq deserved this,' he said, as we passed one of the bombed sites in Baghdad.

The country as a whole did not suffer as seriously as most people in the West assumed. There was no 'carpet bombing', either in the cities or in the countryside. According to unofficial estimates in Baghdad, approximately 2000 civilians died in the air war. A government official assured me that only 29 buildings had been destroyed in the capital. I counted them, as best I could, and felt he was right. The bombing of the air raid shelter at Amiriya by the US Air Force, in which several hundred people, including women and children, died, seemed to me to be as unforgivable as any of the crimes committed by the Iraqis; but it was an exception, not a commonplace.

Elsewhere in Baghdad, it was clear that buildings had been attacked night after night, long after they were thoroughly destroyed, because of a shortage of other targets. At the headquarters of the Baath Party, a three-piece suite in red plush hung crazily out of a window. In the grounds below the tomb of one of the Party's founding fathers, Michel Aflaq, was utterly destroyed, much to the quiet pleasure of the Iraqi who told me about it. The telecommunications centre at Al-Alwiyah in the eastern suburbs was reduced to nothing more than a network of mangled girders and the confetti from what had once been customers' accounts lay as thick as a new fall of snow on the ground about it. Yet the Agadir Hotel immediately opposite looked untouched. There was something rather distasteful about the boasting that went on in the United States and Britain about precision bombing; but it worked. The infrastructure had been severely damaged and there was a serious danger of disease as a result of the destruction of power supplies and water purification; though by the middle of April power was slowly being restored.

When I was in Baghdad during the bombing most of us assumed that the city was getting off lightly in comparison with other Iraqi cities. This, we thought, was because of the presence of foreign journalists whose reports of heavy damage or loss of life might sicken public opinion back home. But when I returned and travelled round the country to Basra, Kerbala, Najaf, Amara, Mosul, Samarra, Takrit and elsewhere, the picture was the same as in Baghdad. For the most part damage was limited to a few clear targets in each city, though I did visit a hospital in Basra which had been hit by an Allied bomb. In town after town two or three individual buildings, usually on the outskirts, would be in ruins from the bombing; but as I drove in towards the centre the serious damage would always have been inflicted by Saddam Hussein's army as it recaptured the place from Shi'i or Kurdish rebels. According to a senior figure in the Baath Party, four times as many people lost their lives in the uprisings against Saddam as in the war against the Allies.

There had obviously been heavy casualties among the Iraqi armed forces: tens of thousands must have died, at least. One

American estimate put it at 65,000, and from what Iraqi government ministers said after the war, that number might be right. Western assumptions may have put the figure much higher than it actually was. Allied claims about the number of tanks destroyed were hopelessly inflated. The Iraqi army was not drawn into battle and destroyed; it melted away. Men deserted in great numbers when the Allied bombardment was at its height. Often they simply headed back to their homes. There was heavy loss of life on the road to Mutla Ridge, halfway between Kuwait City and the Iraqi border, where several hundred trucks, armoured vehicles and hijacked cars were attacked and destroyed. Yet even here the best estimate is that about four hundred Iraqi soldiers died.

The manner of this attack was not pleasant. Apache helicopters five miles away lined up their sights as though they were in an electronic games hall, liquidating some vehicle and its occupants whom they couldn't see and who couldn't see them. The disparity in force levels between the western forces in the Alliance and the Iraqis was enormous. At Mutla Ridge, the victims were mostly what the American troops called REMFs, 'rear echelon motherfuckers' who had stayed behind to loot and then made their escape as best they could. It was very far from magnificent, and it certainly wasn't war. Awareness of what the television pictures of all this might do to public opinion at home played an important part in President Bush's decision not to pursue the Iraqi troops any further, and certainly not to take the war to Baghdad.

The wrecked lorries, the bodies sprawled under blankets, the litter of loot and of personal belongings in the sand haunt the memory, like the sepia photographs of the battlefield at Omdurman. As at Omdurman, the battle for Kuwait pitted the discipline and weaponry of the West against a Third World army, and the Iraqis were mown down as they ran. 'It was like stamping on ants,' said a helicopter pilot. 'Every volley with the guns brought down 50, 100, 500,' said one of Kitchener's officers at Omdurman in 1898, where 10,000 Sudanese died at a cost of 28 British lives.

> Jest send in your Chief an' surrender – it's worse if you fights or
> you runs:
> You may hide in the caves, they'll be only your graves, but you
> can't get away from the guns!

Thus Kipling on the efficacy of the screwgun against tribes-
men. There is, fortunately, unlikely to be a poet of the cluster-
bomb or of the anti-tank missile, whose long-rod penetrator
turns everything inside its target to metal ash or powdered
bone.

Western public opinion had scarcely started to register
anxiety about the way the war had ended when a new phase
began. As the defeated Iraqi troops withdrew into southern
Iraq, the Shi'i majority there rose up against Saddam Hussein's
régime. Almost simultaneously rebellion broke out in the
Kurdish towns and cities of the north. There was no co-
ordination between the two groups of insurgents, and not
much between one Shi'i city and the next, or between one
Kurdish town and another. Each uprising was a spontaneous
attempt to use the opportunity of Saddam's defeat to get rid of
his régime.

The revenge was savage. We saw – as we drove through –
that town after town had been attacked by Saddam's tanks.
The holiest shrines of Shi'i Islam, artistic as well as religious
centres, bore the marks of shells and heavy calibre bullets.
People had died in large numbers in these shrines. The
buildings around them had been levelled by tanks and
bulldozers in order to widen the fields of fire. There was
terrible destruction in the Kurdish towns and cities of northern
Iraq, too. When Western troops took over the area they found
torture chambers, execution sites, burying grounds. The Shi'i
and Kurdish populations had taken Western leaders at their
word and tried to overthrow Saddam Hussein. This was their
reward. His army might have failed on the battlefield, but it
had achieved the tasks it was best equipped for.

I had always expected that elements in Saddam's army
would turn against him after his defeat, but he had prepared
himself against that too carefully. The officer class stayed loyal
to him and most of their men followed. They used methods of

8

considerable savagery against the rebels and some of those in Western Europe who had been most critical of the war against Saddam Hussein now attacked the Allied countries because they wouldn't intervene militarily to save the Kurds. In Western countries there was little awareness of or sympathy for the even greater sufferings of the Shi'i people in the South.

Before the war it was customary for journalists and academics writing about Iraq to take some at least of the carefully marshalled demonstrations of love and support for Saddam Hussein at their face value. 'He inspires great fear and equally great adulation,' said a British television documentary on Iraq as late as February 1991. 'The majority of Iraqis had appeared to agree with the progressive nationalist ideology of the Baath as long as it was primarily centred on Iraq,' runs the slightly more careful last sentence of an American scholarly history of Iraq written in 1985. If these things were ever true – and that must be open to serious doubt – they certainly no longer applied by 1990. Among western academics specializing in Iraq, Peter Sluglett of Durham University and Marion Farouk-Sluglett of the University College of Wales were in a minority when they questioned whether ordinary Iraqis provided Saddam with anything more than lipservice. People endured the regime because if they did not, they and their families were liable to disappear for good.

The war showed Saddam's pretensions to be empty and absurd. Even though he recovered power, to the extent that he defeated the uprisings against him, his position seemed critically weakened. When he appeared on television he was no longer the familiar Saddam, portly and tough. Now he was shrunken and diminished. In the old days there was no popular nickname for him because it would have been too dangerous to pass it on. After the defeat people started calling him 'The Yes-man', because he said yes to everything President Bush demanded of him. It is hard to think of anything more insulting to his self-image as 'the one who confronts' – the only Arab leader with the courage to stand up to the West. He went around Baghdad hidden in an armoured personnel carrier and escorted by a dozen police cars with sirens blaring. He was obliged to appoint a Shi'i prime minister and to negotiate a

deal with the leaders of the Kurds which was deeply unfavour-
able to him. He promised to hold elections and the newspapers
became much freer to criticize the Baath Party and the way the
country had been run. The greatest change, however, was in
people's attitudes. Before the war the principal rule in Iraq was
never to say publicly what you really felt about the régime. On
my return I saw the full extent of the change.

A group of officials whom I had known as meek and loyal
servants of the government were standing round in a circle.
'General Schwarzkopf didn't go far enough,' said one in a loud
voice. 'He should have come to Baghdad and finished the job.'
The others nodded. They didn't seem to care any longer
whether anyone heard them. In the south Shi'i officials would
tip us off about the damage that had been done to their cities by
the army. 'Tell your country what Saddam has done to us,' one
of them said. 'You must tell people that we really tried to
overthrow Saddam – otherwise they will go on thinking we are
outcasts,' an expensively-dressed woman said. I knew her
from my previous visits; she had always been far too timid to
say anything political before. Face to face with a security man,
one of the various drivers we had used said, 'Donkey, donkey,'
in a voice loud enough for the man to hear. It seemed to me that
something had snapped in Iraq, and that it could never be put
back exactly as it had been.

One night, after pushing the censors further than ever before
with one of our reports, I elected to walk back to the hotel from
the Ministry of Information rather than take a car. I always
like walking through a city at night: it seems to talk more
plainly to you then. In the past I had been arrested several times
for wandering through the streets of Baghdad after dark. Now
everything seemed so lax I was sure I wouldn't run into any
problems.

It was the night of Eid, the first day after the fasting month of
Ramadan. Normally the streets would be full of cars hooting
and people celebrating, but this year there was little enough to
celebrate. There was no electricity in this part of town and the
streets were mostly silent. A grubby cat shot into the bushes in
front of me; the loudest noise around. The air that night was
thick and heavy as the crescent moon of Eid dropped closer to

10

the rooftops. Crickets sang. There was a smell of flowering bushes and sewage in the air. Absently I scratched an old mosquito bite. In Baghdad every bite seemed to come up in a great lump because of the dirty conditions, and the oily rainclouds which hung over the city almost every day originated from Kuwait, where five hundred oil wells were still burning, pumping soot and chemicals into the air. People complained of sinus problems and hayfever without realizing where it all came from and why.

I passed the charming little mosque beside the river, glad that although the buildings close to it had been reduced to heaps of mud-coloured brick the mosque itself had apparently survived intact. From somewhere near the river, beneath the palms outlined against the night sky, I could hear the twiddling of a wooden flute playing some quiet, meandering tune. There were occasional handclaps in time to the intricate rhythm. I badly wanted to go over and join this subdued little celebration, but the mud from the previous night's thunderstorms clogged my shoes and defeated me.

A family of five, a man, woman and their three young daughters, sat on the front doorstep of their house as I passed. It was too hot to stay indoors and it represented a concession to what should have been a sociable evening. They hadn't yet started to mend the windows which must have been smashed when the bombs landed opposite. They sat round their oil lamp and ate little cakes, their faces golden in the light as though they had been painted by de la Tour. I wished them good evening and they waved to me enthusiastically to join them. I smiled and thanked them but explained I had to get back. I could still hear their cheerful voices and see the afterglow of the golden light for some distance down the dark, uneven street.

In a gloomy modern building the standard portrait of Saddam hung crookedly on the wall. It wasn't hard now to imagine it lying smashed on the ground, stamped on by triumphant demonstrators, its eyes poked out like the portraits of the Shah in Tehran in 1979, horns on its head and blood dripping from its fangs like those of Ceausescu in Bucharest ten years later. It had happened in Basra and every other Shi'i and

Kurdish town and city, but not in Baghdad. For now, the portrait continued to hang in its proper place, and there was no saying when, or if, it might be taken down. As time went on, it seemed more likely to remain in its place. Inside the building four uniformed soldiers lounged around on armchairs. They sat up sharply as I peered in, but when I waved their hands dropped from their pistols and they sank back again.

I reached the corner. To my left, faintly outlined against the sky, was another broken bridge – the Jomhuriya. An elderly Toyota sped out of the gates of a security base close to the end of the bridge and two lounging traffic policemen in the middle of the road stood to attention. The car's yellowish headlights swung around and picked me out like a plane in a searchlight beam, throwing my shadow onto a dry fountain and new-looking picture of Saddam Hussein. Two soldiers in red berets walked towards me and stopped as I headed past them. They seemed to be debating whether they should ask me who I was and where I was going. Then they moved on. What, in these conditions, was the point of trying to catch British or American spies? The spies knew everything anyway.

Near the Al-Rasheed Hotel, where so much had happened to me over the previous few months, the electricity supply was working. A bus crammed with people singing and playing trumpets careered past. Here, at least, Eid would be celebrated tonight. They were the guests at some wedding ceremony, and the guests would be gathering tonight at the Al-Rasheed, the first wedding party to be held in the hotel since before the war. The brassy, unconvincing notes of the trumpets and the insistent beating of small drums was coming from the gateway to the hotel. The humid wind rattled the ropes against the 80 steel flagpoles which were once to have carried the standards of the countries of the Non-Aligned Movement at their summit in Baghdad: it would have been Saddam's great diplomatic triumph of the early 1980s, except that clever Iranian diplomacy succeeded in having it held elsewhere.

Opposite the hotel was a large and unfamiliar portrait of Saddam. I went and looked closer: it was painted on canvas and had been nailed over another portrait. I had heard stories of people throwing paint at this picture and even emptying their Kalashnikovs into it. 'Individual acts of vandalism,' said a senior government official airily when I asked about it. But if Saddam's portraits could be vandalized in the very centre of his capital then things must have been distinctly shaky for him. I stood back and looked at the new portrait. It had been painted in a hurry and didn't look much like him. He wore a light green suit and a loosely knotted silver tie and his shoulders were badly out of proportion with the rest of him. His stubby fingers, interlaced, were the size of an ornamental rosebush.

The whole thing was lit from below, which gave it a strange, hovering, eerie look, as though Saddam were not of this world. Somehow the old arrogance in his appearance no longer had the same effect. He was The Yes-man now; he would never seem invincible again. Even if he survived, as he might well do, everyone would remember those splashes of paint and the holes from the Kalashnikov bullets. Standing there in the unearthly light reflected by the replacement Saddam, I thought of Shelley's 'traveller from an antique land', and the inscription on the two shattered legs of stone he had seen in the desert:

> 'My name is Ozymandias, King of Kings;
> Look on my works, ye Mighty, and despair!'
> Nothing beside remains. Round the decay
> Of that colossal wreck, boundless and bare
> The lone and level sands stretch far away.

I turned and headed in the direction of the crass, happy music of the trumpet and the drums at the gates of the hotel.

THE HOUSE OF
ISLAM

The Man from Takrit

Be sure, my comrades, that our hearts quake at the thought of unnecessary violence, no matter how slight. At the same time, we have the strength of character to behead those who betray their nation and conspire against their people, no matter how many.

Saddam Hussein, speaking at a meeting of the Revolution Command Council, 1978

As the road from Baghdad to Mosul approached the town of Takrit, hundreds of tanks and armoured personnel carriers were drawn up in the fields on either side of it for mile after mile. I had never seen so much armour in one place before. The war for Kuwait was over, yet perhaps as many as four armoured divisions of the Republican Guard were positioned around Takrit. They had turned it into a rallying point in case of an attack on Baghdad by Shi'i rebels, or a coup by disaffected elements in the army.

Throughout the war Saddam Hussein had kept the divisions here, just as he had during his war with Iran. In the final analysis the survival of his régime was more important to him than the outcome of the war, and the best tanks and the most reliable units had been assembled here to ensure it. The year before, Saddam Hussein had produced a picture of the executed Nicolae Ceausescu at a meeting of the Revolution Command Council to show his closest colleagues that what had happened in Romania could happen in Iraq as well. Ceausescu, chased out of Bucharest by the angry crowds, had nowhere to escape to. Saddam Hussein had Takrit.

I had tried several times in the past to get permission to film

17

there, but without success. Now the war was over, however, the atmosphere had changed a little. On a trip north from Baghdad I asked our minder if we could stop off in Takrit. He was uncomfortable about it but found it hard to think of a reason why not. And so we became the first foreign television team to enter Saddam's city. It proved to be a condensed version of everything he had striven to build up in the country as a whole. At the entrance was a remarkable portrait of the President, his smiling face forming the iris of an enormous eye. This made him the apple of the town's eye; it also meant he had his own eye on everyone and everything. Just as I had never seen so many tanks as those drawn up outside Takrit, so I had never seen so many security men as there were inside it. As we drove slowly in I saw two men on a street corner checking the papers of everyone we passed. Another noted our number plates and pointed them out to his colleagues. When we stopped, so did at least one other car and three men walked across from shops nearby.

Saddam Hussein had turned Takrit into his notion of a model city. Its wide avenues were crossed by pedestrian bridges equipped with unfinished escalators. Until the 1960s the town's main industry had been growing melons and sending them down the Tigris to Baghdad. Now it was devoted to serving the army. The streets were packed with soldiers, walking hand-in-hand, climbing on and off buses, eating kebabs or drinking tea. There were more men in uniform than in civilian clothes. Every shop in the town, as far as I could see, had its own picture of the great benefactor over the door. And of course there were great portraits of him everywhere, smiling his contented smile, his eyes like obsidian pebbles giving nothing away.

As we filmed it all we were approached by men in uniform and men out of uniform, by military security, by special police security, and by the Mukhabarat, the most unpleasant of all. They would take our minder to one side and he would explain who we were. While they questioned him others would watch us: men in cars, on motorbikes, strolling across the road, sitting on the neat park benches which Saddam Hussein's generosity had provided, or hanging around us a little too

18

closely. Slowly we moved up the security hierarchy, from the footsoldiers to the officers. At last we were approached by a superb figure in a lightweight grey pinstripe who trailed a string of amber beads in one hand and a walkie-talkie in the other. Even his sunglasses had an expensive name on one of the lenses. As our minder went off with him I smiled and waved at the two men in the car which had parked behind us and at the pleasant-faced older figure wearing a well-laundered shirt and a Levi Strauss belt buckle on his jeans. He returned my smile, then made a sign to someone across the road. None of them seemed to notice that our cameraman had been discreetly filming the latest exchange with security. The minder came back across the road, sweating slightly, his lips thin and grey. 'Must we stay here any more?' he asked.

On our way out we passed the site of Al-Ouja, the hamlet where Saddam was born. Joseph Stalin, who had a miserable childhood not unlike Saddam's, allowed the humble cottage where he was born in the Georgian village of Gori to be turned into a shrine to his memory. Saddam Hussein often referred with pride to his humble origins, which set him apart from the intellectuals in the Socialist Baath Party. Yet although he missed few opportunities to commemorate himself, there is no monument to him at his place of birth. The memories represented by Al-Ouja seem to have been too painful to be recalled. As Takrit had grown, it has subsumed Al-Ouja completely. The site of the mud brick hut where Subha Tulfah gave birth to a son on 28 April 1937 and called him with considerable prescience 'The fighter who stands steadfast' now lies somewhere under the dreary collection of newly-built barns and garages on the edge of town.

According to Israeli government ministers, the Israeli intelligence agency Mossad estimated that Saddam Hussein had killed 22 people with his own hands by the time of the invasion of Kuwait. The number of named individuals he ordered to be killed may well run into thousands. It includes some of the people who must have felt they were closest to him.

There are many stories – all unverifiable – about the people he murdered; such stories abound in Baghdad. Among others they involve his health minister (who supposedly argued at a cabinet meeting in favour of a ceasefire in the war with Iran, and was taken next door and shot), two members of the National Assembly (one of whom passed a note to the other, both being killed by successive shots from Saddam's revolver where they sat), and his defence minister, Saddam's cousin and brother-in-law (who was said to have remonstrated with him about an extra marital affair and died in a helicopter crash soon after). It may well be that none of these are true, but since his childhood Saddam Hussein has inhabited a cincture of violence in which such tales are at least plausible; and he expanded this cincture until it included the whole of Iraq.

The story of Saddam's unhappy boyhood has become a familiar one. His father, Hussein al-Majid, died before he was born, and his mother soon remarried a man called Ibrahim al-Hassan, who beat the boy unmercifully. In the village the other children taunted Saddam with accusations that he was illegitimate and his political opponents used this claim against him later in life. In the last meeting between Kuwait and Iraq before the invasion on 2 August 1990, the Kuwaiti prime minister shouted across the table that if the Iraqis were so poor that they needed the revenue from Kuwaiti oil wells, they should send their wives and mothers out onto the streets to earn money for them. It was intended as a personal insult to Saddam.

The savagery of his treatment from his stepfather and the feeling that everyone was against him must have had the most far-reaching effects on the character of the young Saddam: a predilection for compensatory violence; a sense that no one, however close, could be trusted; the urgent requirement to reassure himself that in spite of everything he had experienced in his formative years he was better, braver, more intelligent, more valuable than everyone around him. A clinical psychiatrist, faced with the symptoms indicated by Saddam Hussein's behaviour, might well diagnose the condition known as malignant narcissism: a paranoid approach to those around him; an almost total self-absorption; a lack of interest in or awareness of the suffering of others; the absence of anything that might be called conscience in the pursuit of his own drives and impulses.

It became commonplace among politicians and journalists in the months that followed the invasion of Kuwait to accuse Saddam Hussein of being mad. Yet there is nothing 'mad', in the sense of derangement or wild, irrational behaviour, about a sufferer from malignant narcissism. It can be a highly dangerous personality configuration, but it does not necessarily involve loss of control. On the contrary, the sufferer will often show control and rationality in a high degree – but in pursuit of his own paranoid ends. Saddam Hussein in person is serious and thoughtful, and can be mildly jovial. His eyes are hard and cold and they lock onto yours at the beginning of your meeting in a way that many people find unnerving. When he begins to talk, however, his eyes dart around the room continually, as though he is making sure that no one in the room is planning to attack him. His voice is harsh and he is inclined to ramble from one thought to another, talking without pause for fifteen or twenty minutes at a time. (This, of course, is mere habit; no one with any sense interrupts Saddam when he is in full flight.) He is not given to sudden outbursts of rage; his anger is slow-burning and considered. If he is frightening, it is because he is rational, rather than irrational.

Visitors to Saddam Hussein in the months before the war, men like Willy Brandt, Edward Heath and Yasuhiro Nakasone, came away reassured by his balance and his common sense. After meeting him Heath said: 'The whole of our conversation was conducted in an atmosphere of the utmost calm. . . I was very impressed by the extraordinarily detailed knowledge he showed on the subjects we were discussing.' Brandt's view was similar: 'This is a man whom, in spite of the burdens he has to bear at present, has a mind which goes well beyond the present crisis. I was impressed by the intensity of his engagement.' Nakasone too praised Saddam's breadth of vision.

All three men were implicitly defending themselves against the charge that they had come to Baghdad to negotiate with a madman. All the same, the quality of Saddam Hussein's intellect was not the issue: what was in question were the ends to which it was directed and the means he used to those ends. In this sense at least the tired comparisons with Hitler and

Stalin are relevant. Yet far from examining the comparison to see what light it might shed on Saddam Hussein, politicians in the West used it merely as a form of insult. 'Summary executions, routine torture – Hitler revisited,' said President Bush at a formal dinner in the autumn of 1990. He was referring to the behaviour of Iraqi troops in Kuwait, though he had never publicly condemned Saddam Hussein's régime in past years for carrying out the same policies in Iraq itself.

Many people have endured brutal upbringings and exhibited paranoid symptoms as a result. Saddam Hussein, however, put these symptoms in the service of a cause. If his stepfather's beatings distorted the young Saddam's character, his mother instilled in him the beginnings of nationalism and political radicalism. According to his official biography she told him stories about her brother, Khairallah Talfah, who took part in the pro-Nazi uprising headed by Rashid Ali al-Qaylani in 1941 against the British presence in Iraq. Some members of the family were, she told him, killed by the British and their houses burned down. Other members of the family had supposedly been involved in earlier rebellions against Turkish rule. It seems likely, too, that she told him how Saladin, the greatest warrior of the medieval Arab world and the man who defeated the Third Crusade, had been born in Takrit in 1138 – 799 years before his own birth there. Saladin featured heavily in Saddam's speeches before the war with the Allies, though the fact that he was a Kurd was not mentioned.

Saddam's cousin Adnan, Khairallah Talfah's son, went to school in Takrit and boasted of his ability to read and write. (More than 40 years later, it was Adnan who, as Saddam's defence minister, was supposedly murdered in the helicopter crash. After his death a notoriously inaccurate missile was named after him.) At the age of eight Saddam insisted that he, like Adnan, wanted to go to school. Although his mother and stepfather objected, he ran away to the house of some other relatives – possibly his uncle Khairallah himself – who sent him to school by car and, Saddam later said, gave him a pistol. This, in the hands of an eight-year-old, meant that no one called him a bastard to his face again.

A year later Khairallah Talfah, settled in Baghdad, and with him went his son, Adnan, and his nephew, Saddam. At school in Baghdad, Saddam's need to compensate for the cruelty and shame he had suffered in Takrit showed itself in more violent behaviour. He had to give up the pistol, but he carried an iron bar around with him everywhere. A former school-fellow, Dr Ali al-Hakim, who now lives in exile, says the headmaster wanted to expel his violent pupil:

> When Saddam heard about this he came to the headmaster's office and threatened him with death. He said, 'I will kill you if you don't withdraw your threat.' Why did the headmaster want to expel him? Because he was troublesome at school.

The threat worked and Saddam was not expelled. It must have been as important a lesson for him as anything else he learned at school.

Saddam Hussein settled with Khairallah and Adnan in a working-class area of Baghdad called Takirte, after all the other Takritis who had settled there. Nowadays it has lost its connection with the town and is just another run down district with grimy, grey brick buildings draped with electrical cables and heaps of rubbish by every lamppost. But in the 1950s it was a natural home for the small-time crooks and thugs who had broken away from the bands of dacoits operating around Takrit. Hassan al-Alawi, who was in charge of the presidential press office under Saddam from 1975 to 1980 before leaving the country, says that the future president's penchant for cruelty was obvious even at this stage:

> He used to collect firewood and burn it. Then he would put an iron bar on the fire and make it red hot, and when he saw an animal passing he would run out and stab it in the stomach. I believe this story is true. Saddam grew up thinking that only his iron stick would protect him. He used to take it everywhere.

In this atmosphere of brutality and lawlessness the young Saddam turned to political activism.

As a country Iraq had been inherently unstable since its creation. After the defeat and break-up of the Ottoman empire in 1918, most of its former territories were divided up between

23

Britain and France in a series of Allied peace settlements. Throughout World War I Britain and France had intrigued to obtain a postwar division of spoils which would serve their own strategic interests. In May 1920 Britain was awarded a League of Nations mandate over the territories of present-day Iraq, and following much administrative infighting between the Colonial office in London and the Imperial government of India it was decided that Iraq should take in the former Turkish provinces of Baghdad (which was Arab and part Sunni Muslim), Basra (which was Arab and Shi'i Muslim) and Mosul (which was Kurdish and Sunni). Winston Churchill, as colonial secretary, was more concerned with cutting British expenditure in the Middle East than with the longer-term issue of Iraq's viability. He accepted the proposal for which the writer Gertrude Bell had argued and intrigued: that the new country's boundaries should take in a population divided between Sunni Arabs, Shi'i Arabs and Kurds, as well as smaller groups of Christians.

King Faysal, the leader of the Arab revolt against the Turks, was installed as monarch of the new nation by the British on 27 August 1921. Eleven years later, in October 1932, the British mandate was formally ended and Iraq became independent. The newly independent state was always nervous about the minority groups within its borders. Less than a year later the army carried out the widespread slaughter of the Assyrian Christian community. Many Assyrians had served as auxili- aries with the British Army – in the Iraqi Levies and other units – and this had made them greatly hated. King Faysal was opposed to the idea of a pogrom but his government supported the army's action and its chief of staff, General Bakr Sidqi, became a national hero. The British, who had relied heavily on the Assyrians when setting up the mandate, did little to protect them. In 1936 Bakr Sidqi staged a coup, the first in the Arab world, though the new king, Ghazi I, remained on the throne. Nine months later, in August 1937, Sidqi was assassinated by an army faction. During the four years that followed, this faction engineered more coups and supported the premiership of the pro-British, Nuri al-Said, who was to dominate Iraqi politics for the next two decades.

Heavy-handed British control during World War II stabilized the political situation but weakened the monarchy and the pro-British line it took. By the mid-1950s the régime was nominally headed by Faysal II, the cousin of King Hussein of Jordan. Educated by British tutors in Baghdad and at Harrow, Faysal had been crowned at the age of 18 in May 1953. There was a continual struggle for power between the former regent, Crown Prince Abd al-Ilah, and the prime minister, Nuri al-Said, both closely associated with the British domination of Iraq.

In the early hours of 14 July 1958 a group of senior officers took control of the radio station. Their overall leader, who remained at Jalawla northeast of Baghdad, was Brigadier Abd al-Karim Qassem. The Crown Prince, together with the King and the rest of the royal family, tried to escape through the kitchen door of the palace. They were spotted and were all shot dead. Nuri al-Said escaped but was recognized the next day in the street, disguised as a woman. He was shot then and there. In the days that followed, wild crowds of demonstrators dug up and mutilated the bodies of the Crown Prince and Nuri al-Said, before dragging them through the streets and hanging what remained. The scenes that followed the revolution gave Iraq a reputation for savagery which it has never lost.

Saddam Hussein grew up, then, in a country where violence was endemic. It appealed to his character. A former Iraqi diplomat, Mustapha Karadaghi, met him soon after the revolution:

> He was very aggressive. He kept talking about how to overthrow the Qassem régime, and shoot everybody, wipe them out, and make the streets of Baghdad a lake of blood. He used that phrase, a lake of blood, frequently.

Saddam had already been called on to show his toughness: he went back to Takrit to kill an enemy of his uncle's in 1956. The following year he was recruited to the Baath Party by a low-ranking civil servant, Abd al-Khalik al-Samarra'i. The Baath Party (Baath means renaissance) had been founded in Damascus in 1944 by a group of eight young Arab nationalists, including Michel Aflaq, a Christian Syrian schoolmaster.

Baath ideology came to be based on two fundamental beliefs: that all Arabs belonged to a single nation, which should be politically united; and – though this came a little later – that only radical social change could free the Arab lands from colonial power and bring down the old hierarchies. By April 1947, when it held its first congress, the Party had a membership of several hundred. Its teachings reached Iraq in 1949 and the first organization was set up in Baghdad two years later.

In some ways the Baathist movement owed a good deal to Marxism-Leninism. It was organized in cells, which gave it a conspiratorial flavour and made it very hard to eradicate. Its nationalism, however, brought it into regular conflict with the Communists and, although the two movements sometimes formed a tactical alliance, they remained fundamentally hostile. Baathism was a strange fusion of Arab nationalism and Stalinism, which aimed to create a 'new man', just as the Soviet Union had done in the 1930s. This new man was to be a servant of the Arab state, a willing sacrifice for the future of the wider Arab nation. He was to have no feelings other than love for his leader and for the political entity which included him. He was a tiny component of the Arab masses, a Muslim perhaps, but first and foremost a political and cultural conformist, obedient to the vision of the Baathist founders. It is hard to think of any nationality less suited to this concept than the individualistic, family-conscious Iraqis with millenia of sophisticated urban existence behind them. But there were some Iraqis, rootless, embittered super-nationalists, who found the notion of the 'new man' distinctly attractive. Saddam Hussein was one.

Saddam Hussein moved slowly up the Party structure, beginning as a mere bully-boy, an enforcer, and being given more responsible tasks as he showed his abilities. At each step he, like every other Party worker, was carefully vetted. The Party trusted no one. Its internal discipline and its under-ground character meant that the Baath was always much more than just another extreme nationalist movement. There was nothing at this stage to lead an outsider to suppose it would ever take power, but like Hitler in the undistinguished

National Socialist Party of the 1920s and like Stalin in the faction-ridden Social Democratic Party before World War I, Saddam Hussein had backed an unexpected winner.

The Baathists had supported the 1958 coup on the grounds that it would rid Iraq of British influence. But the new President, Brigadier Qassem, was not a serious pan-Arabist, nor did he introduce the kind of radical social change the Baathists wanted. The party quickly went underground. Saddam was heavily engaged in political activities at Baghdad University where he was studying law. Some months after the coup he received orders to go back to Takrit and murder a senior government official there. The official was duly murdered and, although it later became unacceptable to say that Saddam Hussein was responsible, he was certainly arrested and put in prison. As with the previous murder he had committed in Takrit, it was an important part of his apprenticeship. When he was released the Party leadership approached him and asked him to take part in an assassination attempt on President Qassem.

A museum was later dedicated to the incident, which occurred on 7 October 1959. It is old and musty and scarcely anyone goes there, except for occasional groups of school-children. The custodian grumbles a little as he unlocks the door: he regards his job as something of a sinecure and doesn't like to be disturbed. 'It's unusual to find people just turning up here,' he says. Inside, the room is dominated by a vast elderly black limousine: the car in which Qassem drove down Rasheed Street, in the bazaar area of Baghdad, that afternoon. Round the walls are stills from a melodramatic film which was made about the affair after Saddam took over the Party leadership, together with photographs of the eight men who took part in the attack. Saddam's has pride of place.

The official accounts make out that Saddam played the central role, though in fact he was simply there to give covering fire to the men who had the job of shooting Qassem. According to dissident Baathists Saddam panicked and opened fire blindly before escaping without knowing whether Qassem was dead or not. He was slightly injured, having been struck in the shin by a spent bullet which lodged under the skin. Saddam cut it out with a razor blade and a leading Baathist, Dr Tahsin Muallah, cleaned and dressed the wound. Now in exile, Dr Muallah insists that the wound was a very minor one. The official account, however, turns Saddam's flight into an epic of self-sacrifice and suffering. He spent the next three years in Cairo, where he was a figure of some importance because of the Iraqi Baath Party's loyalty to President Nasser. He was also, according to Hussein Magid, the owner of the café he frequented, still inclined to violence:

> He was rowdy with the customers and the waiters. He would sit by the pavement and tease the girls who passed. Once he had a fight with some Yemenis, and he hit one of them with an axe. When I called the police they sided with him, because he was under Nasser's protection.

This was not youthful high spirits. Other people who knew him at this time called him silent and unsmiling. He seemed dedicated to his political work.

In February 1963 the Baathists succeeded at last in toppling Qassem in a violent coup which cost several hundred lives, including that of Qassem himself. His body was shown on television to prove that he really was dead. The new prime minister was an ex-officer who had been in Qassem's government, Ahmad Hassan al-Bakr. This was Saddam Hussein's greatest piece of luck – the factor that turned a small-time gangster and ward heeler into a potential leader. Al-Bakr came from Takrit and was a distant relative of Saddam's mother. In the clan politics of Iraq, Saddam Hussein was certain of a job. He came back from Cairo and was employed at the Central Agricultural Office. This, however, was a cover for a much more important task: that of heading al-Bakr's security department. Other Takritis were being assembled around them: it was the start of a new dynasty.

At first, however, the Baathists split between moderate and radical factions, and the army backed the moderates. As the situation degenerated into near civil war, Saddam's twin talents for violence and political manoeuvring made him indispensable to his new boss. He now had the personal support of the founder of the pan-Arab Baath Movement,

28

Michel Aflaq, who recommended him to the Regional (ie Iraqi) Command of the Party when he was still only 26. At the age of 29 he was made deputy general secretary. His enemies tried several times to kill him and in the cold officialese which he later adopted he described his difficulties with rival elements in the Baath Party as 'obstacles. . . placed in the way of those comrades who wanted to work along proper Party lines.' His solution was a characteristic one. Saddam Hussein, according to his officially approved biography, 'was to have entered the conference room, where the civilian and military leaders were meeting, and machine-gunned them all'.

Instead he was arrested and imprisoned. As always with his prison sentences, he was treated lightly while his companions were beaten up or tortured. People who were in gaol with him said he used to read books about Hitler, Stalin and Mussolini to find out how they came to power, how they kept power and how they got rid of their opponents. Eventually he and all his group escaped and the 1968 coup was carried out with none of the bloodshed Saddam had earlier envisaged.

Blood was shed later, though. Saddam now had responsibility for national security and established a series of witch-hunts for Israeli agents which resulted in prolonged periods of torture for hundreds – perhaps thousands – of people and the public execution of several dozen in Independence Square. Two thousand political prisoners were executed or simply disappeared in the first three years after the coup.

Saddam told Sami Ali, a journalist who later took refuge in London: 'We are different from the former régime. We are going to clean Iraq of all the weak people, all the people we don't want. We have a plan, and we are going to do it.' The plan was heavily influenced by the KGB, which advised Saddam on his reorganization of Iraq's intelligence services into three new groups: the Mukhabarat, or Party intelligence, which was the most important; the Amn, or internal security; and the Estikhabarat, or foreign intelligence service. He followed standard Marxist-Leninist and fascist practice by using Party members to supervise the activities of everyone in their apartment block or street. They were expected to inform the Mukhabarat of anyone who criticized the Party or the government or who failed to conform in other ways.

Children were used to inform on their parents, and teachers were under instructions to ask them questions which would reveal any irregularities in their family lives. In an address published in 1977 Saddam wrote:

> To prevent the father and mother dominating the household with backwardness, we must make the little one radiate internally to expel it. Some fathers have slipped away from us for various reasons, but the small boy is still in our hands and we must transform him into an interactive radiating centre inside the family through all the hours he spends with his parents ... You must place in every corner a son of the revolution, with a trustworthy eye and a firm mind that receives its instructions from the responsible centre of the revolution.

There were many instances where children whose parents preferred not to watch the undiluted diet of Saddam Hussein on television told their teachers they were not allowed to watch 'Uncle Saddam'. If the teacher was decent, he or she would warn the parents rather than report it; but that put the teacher in some danger too. A story that was going the rounds in Baghdad in 1990 was unverifiable, but perfectly likely: Saddam, on one of his frequent, unscheduled trips around the country, stopped in a village and took a child on his knee. 'Do you know who I am?' he asked jovially. 'Yes,' said the child. 'Every time you come on television my father spits on the ground and switches it off.' According to the story, the entire family, including the child, disappeared.

Iraq was a country where children became old and responsible before their time; where nothing could be said without being thought about in advance; where only your closest friends and family could be trusted. The Party, under Saddam, sought to weaken the natural links between parents and children, brothers and sisters, husbands and wives, because they provided a refuge for those who privately dissented from the official worship of Saddam.

Where necessary the Party was capable of behaving with the greatest savagery within the family unit. I know a man in

Baghdad whose brother was caught up in one of Saddam's purges. Most of the family were convinced Baathists, which made the brother's offence – if indeed he had really committed any offence – all the worse. Immense pressure no doubt including promises as well as threats was used on my friend to inform on his brother. When he did so, no doubt it was because he allowed himself to believe that the brother would obtain some kind of immunity. He didn't, of course. The only immunity was obtained by my friend: he was not required to be there when his brother was executed. But the security police, at gunpoint, gave weapons to the father and the other brothers and made them shoot the erring member of the family, to cleanse both it and themselves of the guilt of not loving Saddam Hussein. In Saddam's Iraq, you cleanse yourself of guilt by washing in the blood of others.

Hassan al-Alawi, Saddam's press spokesman in the late seventies, became a strong critic of the Baath Party's methods. He believes the rot set in immediately it seized control in 1969 and that the blame lay with Saddam himself:

> The curious thing is that when the Baath Party came to power, its secret organizations remained secret even though they no longer needed to be. One wonders why the Party needed to remain secret when it was in power. Here we should take into account the psychology of Saddam Hussein – a man who is afraid of society, who doesn't trust his neighbours. These features have left their mark on Iraq since the Baath Party came to power. The state doesn't trust its neighbours, the Baath Party doesn't trust its members, the government doesn't trust its ministers. All this reflects the atmosphere of fear and terror in which Saddam Hussein has always lived.

The new President, Ahmad Hasan al-Bakr, was a colourless, uninspiring character who always seemed slightly in awe of his distant cousin at the big public occasions at which they both appeared. Where al-Bakr was stooped and elderly, Saddam was upright, energetic, good-looking. Still only in his thirties, Saddam was already the force behind the régime. His photographs were everywhere, alongside al-Bakr's own. Yet the time was not ripe to thrust the older man aside. Instead, Saddam's energies were directed towards establishing the Baath Party permanently in power.

Saddam's experiences since the 1963 coup led him to believe that the army was not to be trusted. From the day the Baathist régime was formed, Saddam worked to purge the military: in the first instance of senior officers who were not members of the Party; later, of men whose loyalty was to al-Bakr. The purge was not a large one: only thirty-five names all told. But sixteen of them were generals and one was the former minister of defence, Hardan al-Takriti. He was exiled in October 1970 and Saddam Hussein went on board the plane to kiss him and say goodbye. The following March four gunmen murdered al-Takriti in Kuwait City.

By the early summer of 1979 Saddam had stripped away Ahmad Hasan al-Bakr's last remaining support and it was time to push the old man aside. 'It has never happened before,' said Saddam on 17 July at a specially-convened meeting of the Baath Party, 'that two leaders have been in power for eleven years within one command, without. . . their relationship ending in one of them driving the other out.' The fiction of a harmonious succession was maintained by al-Bakr's speech:

> For some time now I have been telling my comrades, and especially my dear comrade Saddam Hussein, that my state of health no longer permits me to carry the responsibilities the Command has honoured me with, and I have asked them to relieve me of the responsibility.

Afterwards, his house arrest in a pleasant-enough residence near the presidential palace was explained away as the result of ill-health: it was, according to the official version, his own wish to stay within the confines of his house and garden.

Beneath the decorous appearance an ugly struggle for power had gone on, leading to the first and bloodiest of Saddam's purges. Six days previously, on 11 July 1979 the news that al-Bakr was to step down was given to a meeting of the Revolution Command Council, the highest level of the Baathist hierarchy. The Council's secretary, Muhyi Abd al-Hussein Rashid, stood up and demanded a vote. 'It is inconceivable,' he said to al-Bakr, 'that you should retire. If you are ill, why don't you take a rest?' Saddam Hussein was visibly angered, but when the vote was taken no one joined Muhyi Abd al-Hussein and al-Bakr's resignation was approved. The following day, 12 July, Saddam was elected president and Muhyi Abd al-Hussein was arrested. In the words of the approved biography, Saddam also 'decided to keep under observation those leaders who had looked worried or distressed after the Regional Command had decided that Muhyi Abd al-Hussein should be taken in for questioning'.

This was characteristic of the new president. Saddam trusts his instincts about people implicitly and believes he has the power to read people's characters from their looks. Each time he meets a person for the first time, he peers deeply into their eyes: an unnerving experience, in the circumstances. 'I know that someone will betray me before they know it themselves,' he has said; as an indictment, it is completely unanswerable.

Those who were not Saddam's supporters must have known what would happen and their opposition had now achieved the status of a plot. As his biographer puts it,

> The participants in the plot tried so hard to act naturally while the questioning of Muhyi Abd al-Hussein was going on that they made themselves conspicuous. . . . Muhammed Ayesh behaved in an increasingly guilty manner, and he was arrested on 16 July. Ghanem Abd al-Jalil's behaviour was also suspicious, although he had not been investigated, and so too was Adnan Hussein's . . .

At a dinner the following night Saddam asked everyone present to write a detailed report on any meetings they had had with the supposed plotters.

On 22 July there was an extraordinary regional conference of the Party in Khald Hall in Baghdad, an unremarkable modern building which was to be the setting for an ugly piece of business strongly reminiscent of Stalin's show trials. On Saddam's orders the proceedings were videotaped. It was his intention to ensure that Baathists everywhere should know the new force which now existed in Baghdad. Copies were sent to Party organizations throughout Iraq and to Iraqi student groups in Britain, France, Germany and the United States. It is badly shot in black-and-white and the sound quality is poor, but nothing can hide the dramatic nature of what is taking place.

The proceedings are opened by one of Saddam's strongest supporters, Taha Yasin Ramadan, a man with curiously Asiatic features. He announces the discovery of the plot and says that all the traitors are present in the hall. There is genuine consternation and shock in the audience at this. Then Muhyi Abd al-Hussein, walking slowly and speaking with apparent difficulty, makes a lengthy confession in which he condemns himself in grovelling terms and accuses four other members of the leadership, including his closest friend and ally, Muhammed Ayesh, of plotting against Saddam. The plot was sponsored by President Assad of Syria, he says, and its purpose was to unify Iraq and Syria on Syria's terms. At last he comes to the end of his speech. He looks about him for a moment or two, then takes his seat among the audience. It is plain that he has been made to sit well apart from the loyal supporters of Saddam, men like Ramadan, Tariq Aziz and Izzat Ibrahim. They, at least, are safe.

Throughout the confession Saddam has been sitting alone at a table on the platform, slumped in his chair and smoking one of his favourite eight-inch Havana cigars: the smoke wreaths around him as he listens. In the cutaway shots the delegates are disturbed and nervous, shifting in their seats and no doubt trying to decide how precisely they should react. Then it is Saddam's turn to make a speech. He has put out his cigar and stands very straight at the lectern, hands behind his back, speaking without notes. Long silences punctuate his phrases.

> We used to be able to scent a conspiracy, before we even gathered the evidence. Nevertheless we were patient. And some of our comrades blamed us for knowing this but doing nothing about it.

His cousin, Ali Hassan al-Mejid, who is later to become governor of Kurdistan and, after the invasion, of Kuwait, stands up and shouts out: 'What you have done in the past is good, and what you will do in the future is good as well. But there's just one small point: you're being too gentle and merciful now.' Saddam Hussein frowns. 'Yes, that's true,' he says. 'People have criticized me for that. But this time I will show no mercy.' There is a storm of nervous applause and before it is over Saddam begins to read from a list of names. The clapping dies away instantly. The first conspirator is named and he stands up, looking bewildered. The camera crash-zooms into a shambling figure whose arm is being taken quite gently by one of the security men standing around the sides of the hall. Saddam continues smoking his cigar. Another name is called out, another crash-zoom reveals a man in a light-coloured suit being guided towards the door at the back. The audience pretends to be enjoying it now: they are clapping and smiling and leaning across to congratulate each other on Saddam Hussein's wisdom. But hysteria isn't far away and soon individual delegates are getting up and screaming their praises of Saddam. A large man, his face streaked with sweat and his tie crooked waves his arm in the air: 'Long live the Party! Long live the Party! God save Saddam Hussein from the conspirators!'

Saddam works through a list of more than 60 names. There is a box of tissues next to him and when he reads out the name of one of the plotters, Ghanem Abd al-Jalil, tears come to his eyes and he pulls at a tissue, wiping his face thoroughly with it and blowing his nose loudly. But his cigar is still burning in the ashtray and when he gets up he takes it and the tissue with him. He goes down into the audience to sit with his faithful colleagues. Tariq Aziz, later to be his foreign minister and then deputy prime minister, beams at him. Saddam sinks down into the seat beside the strange, skeletal figure of Izzat Ibrahim, still wiping his tears from his eyes. Ibrahim comforts him, but he too seems to be smiling.

That same day a special court found 55 men guilty: 22 of them were sentenced to death by 'democratic execution', a method undoubtedly of Saddam's own devising. This means that senior members of the Party had to take part in the firing squads. Like my friend whose father had to execute his own son, the guilt of the family was expiated by participation in another form of guilt – the shedding of blood. Once that is done, there is no going back: responsibility is spread. By 1

August 1979, two weeks after the new president had taken office, something like 500 senior members of the Party were weeded out for 'democratic execution'. A beginning had been made.

America Changes Sides

We do not reject alliances in politics. Temporary alliances for a definite goal existed even in the time of the Prophet Muhammad. I fully realize the power and the capacity of the United States, and I am not against establishing an honourable relationship with that nation if it will serve our interests without the USA exploiting our region for its purposes alone.

Saddam Hussein, interviewed by Fuad Matar in August 1979

Baghdad has never been a beautiful city: its flatness and the mud-coloured brick from which it is mostly built make sure of that. All the same, the decrepit buildings along the river Tigris with their ricketty wooden balconies and their overhanging eaves are delightful when they are allowed to go unnoticed. The *souqs*, a few of them dating back to the rebuilding of the city after its destruction by the Mongols, still have something of the feeling of the Baghdad of Haroun al-Rasheed who wandered round in disguise with his vizier Jafar al-Barmaki and his executioner Masrur, doling out gold *dinars* and silver *dirhams*, searching for entertainment. In the teahouses, merchants and mere dealers slam down their dominoes and play five types of backgammon – Adi, Mahbous, Gulbaha, Chesh-besh, and another whose name I never caught – throwing the dice with a tremendous flourish and making a series of moves which the uninitiated can scarcely follow, let alone emulate. The fans turn slowly overhead, the flies settle on patches of spilt tea, the hubble-bubbles are passed from hand to hand with relish, the gotch-eyed waiter darts around delivering new orders, metal tray high in the air, the old shoe-cleaner who calls everyone 'Lord' bashes away with his brushes in the shade of the courtyard tree. And outside the grimy, crazed windows the Tigris carries the mud of the fertile Mesopotamian plain sluggishly down towards Basra and the waters of the Gulf.

Saddam Hussein sees himself as the embodiment and the culmination of the Iraqi past: as Nebuchadnezzar (whose Babylon he rebuilt from scratch, to his own design), as al-Mansour and al-Rasheed, as Saladin. Baghdad, which only forty years ago was still the dusty, unpaved place the Ottomans had known, has received the best and most expensive attentions of the city-planners. There are pedestrian precincts, overpasses, underpasses, blocks of flats, public statues in Saddamist style combining Arabian Nights fantasy with socialist realism, and flowers planted down the central divisions of the urban motorways. It is a great deal cleaner than most Middle Eastern cities: which makes it cleaner also than parts of London or New York. In a newspaper article I wrote of it as being like the dormitory town of Basildon in southeast England. Basildon's local member of parliament, not a familiar face or name, immediately attacked me as some sort of far-left iconoclast, but the fact is that, like Basildon, Baghdad has been redeveloped out of any real character; and such character as it has you have to look for in the backstreets.

Aside from these few enclaves, Saddam Hussein has made the city his own, filling it with exercises in self-celebration. No street, no government building, is free of his picture: he smiles or looks serious, he embraces children, he pours water, he plants grain, he wears panama hats and dark glasses, he carries a hunting rifle, he smokes his eight-inch cigars; outside the law faculty of the university he grips the scales of justice in one hand and, meaningfully, a sword in the other. Hospitals, schools, stadia, barracks, the main airport and an entire suburb bear his name. He is an inveterate builder of testimonials to himself. The Shaheed Monument to the martyrs who fell in the war with Iran has simplicity and beauty, but most of the others lack the first rudiments of good taste and are merely large. The Allies took the decision not to attack any of Saddam's monuments during the bombing, since they were anxious not to anger public opinion in Iraq unnecessarily.

Tactically this was probably a mistake; few things would have demonstrated the destruction of Saddam's power better.

The most characteristic monument is the least tasteful of all, celebrating his victory over Iran. Until the war with the Allies, each night's television news was preceded by pictures of Saddam riding on a white horse along the parade ground near the presidential palace, passing under one of the two pairs of arms which hold aloft enormous scimitars to form arches. The arches were designed to be higher than the Arc de Triomphe in Paris and the arms and hands which hold the swords were modelled on those of Saddam himself. The original concept of the crossed scimitars was his. So was the idea of hanging from the hilt of each sword a net, shaped like an enormous tassle, containing hundreds of Iranian helmets gathered from the battlefields. Most of the helmets have been holed by bullets or shrapnel. The conception makes the Fountain of Blood at Behesht-e-Zahra cemetery in Tehran look positively restrained. Not all the helmets are in fact Iranian: to make up the numbers Iraqi ones have been added. When the Mongol leader Hulagu destroyed the Baghdad of the Abbasid Caliphs in 1258, he built a mound of skulls to celebrate his victory. This is Saddam Hussein's mound of skulls. He also had dozens more helmets set into the surface of the roadway under each of the arches to enable him to ride over the heads of his enemies.

The war against Iran was also a kind of personal memorial to Saddam Hussein. It showed exactly the same combination of opportunism and overconfidence he demonstrated ten years later – almost to the month – against Kuwait. On 17 September 1980, counting on the weakness of the new Islamic Republic after the Iranian revolution, Saddam abrogated the agreement on the Shatt-al-Arab waterway which he had signed with the Shah in 1975. Five days later on 22 September he launched a massive series of attacks across the border into Iran.

The outside world was thrown into immense confusion by this. There was probably not a single government anywhere which wanted to see Ayatollah Khomeini's Islamic Republic survive. Western countries had little reason to admire Iraq, though at this stage it still seemed no more than another averagely unpleasant police state, supported by the Soviet Union. Saudi Arabia and the Gulf states were frightened by the revolution in Iran and were pleased to see an Arab leader doing something to snuff it out. As a result, there was a high degree of hypocrisy about the international reaction. The UN Security Council neither condemned Iraq for aggression nor demanded the withdrawal of its forces; Resolution 479 merely called for a ceasefire. For years afterwards, one of the most sensitive issues was to be whether Iraq had begun the war in the first place or whether the Iranians had provoked it by their actions on the Shatt-al-Arab. Western governments tended to go along with the Saudis in suggesting that the Iranians had been partly responsible, while in Tehran the authorities used to latch gleefully onto any acknowledgement that the whole unnecessary conflict had been sparked off by the Iraqi invasion: as it clearly had.

Saddam Hussein's estimate was that a blitzkrieg of four days duration would achieve total victory. The aim was to conduct a mainly demonstrative war which would overthrow the new Islamic regime and thereby safeguard his own Shi'i population from the religious influence of Iran and make himself the most powerful leader in the Gulf. At first the Iranians, enfeebled as Saddam had expected them to be, were indeed crushed. Then they regrouped and began to counterattack. Saddam's troops were not the Panzer divisions he perhaps imagined: their only combat experience had come from fighting Kurdish rebels and burning down their villages. Ineptly led and quickly demoralized, Saddam's troops were unable to match the ferocity and determination of the Iranians and quickly fell back. The war became static. Iraq dug itself in behind immense defences, Iran threw hundreds of thousands of troops against the moats and walls and minefields, unable to match the technology which Iraq bought in bulk from the West. In June 1982, close to defeat, Saddam announced a unilateral withdrawal from Iranian territory. Ayatollah Khomeini lacked the will to compromise and failed to take this opportunity of ending the war on his own terms: he wanted nothing less than total victory. Instead, the war dragged on for a further six years and ended with another Iraqi blitzkrieg. This time it was a real one.

On 17 April 1988, having spent most of the war on the defensive and refusing to attack even when the opportunity arose, the Iraqi army stormed the Faw Peninsula which two years previously had been captured by Iran. The Iranian positions were thinly manned by old men and reservists; it seemed remarkable at the time that the Iraqis, whose intelligence had never been very good, should have chosen their moment so well. In May the Iraqis recaptured land around Basra which had cost Iran 70,000 casualties during three weeks' bitter fighting the previous year. Again the Iraqis chose their moment with extraordinary perception and the battle lasted only seven hours. On 25 June Iraqi troops regained the Majnoon islands after a few hours. Here too the Iranian garrison proved to be weak. A fourth battle took place around Dehloran and Iraq's victory there meant that Iranian troops could no longer threaten Baghdad. Finally the Iraqis advanced forty miles into Iran in the region of Kermanshah. Altogether it was a stunning victory. On 18 July 1988 Khomeini issued his famous statement, though he was too anguished to read it out in person: 'Happy are those who have departed through martyrdom. . . Unhappy, am I, that I should still live and have drunk the poisoned cup.' He died eleven months later.

Iran's will to carry on fighting had clearly snapped. Yet to those of us who had seen the two armies fight, the outcome of the war was an astonishment. I had been with the Iranian troops in northern Iraq as late as March 1988 and had been able to contrast their fighting spirit with the excessive caution of the Iraqis. Even when several Iraqi ground attack aircraft had us at their mercy, they stayed out of range of the feeble rifle fire of our escorts and flew back to base. It seemed to me inevitable that the political system in Iraq would collapse under the strain of continuing the war and that Iran, where there was a genuine long-standing bitterness against Iraq for starting the conflict and where the government had more popular support, must eventually be victorious. In a matter of weeks I was comprehensively proved wrong.

With hindsight the turning point had been reached much earlier in February 1986. It came about as a result of an Iranian victory, part of a much bigger offensive which mostly failed.

Soldiers of the Iranian Revolutionary Guard had attacked the Faw Peninsula by water and had captured it against great odds. I was with a group of western journalists who were taken there a few days later; one of our number died in an air attack which the Iraqis launched because they knew we were coming. The plane which had taken us there was shot down on its way back to Tehran. The Iraqis wanted to show that even if they had lost the Faw Peninsula they could still make it difficult for Iran to boast of its victory.

The repercussions of the capture of Faw were considerable. Until this point the outside world had mostly stayed aloof from the war. Companies in the United States, Britain, West Germany, Sweden, Switzerland and elsewhere sold equipment of different kinds to the two sides, but most governments insisted that they were neutral. The Soviet Union supplied weapons, technology and military advisers to the Iraqis and the defensive system of moats and waterways around Basra was completed with Soviet assistance at a cost of a billion dollars. France gave Saddam Hussein diplomatic and military assistance and when I told one of the most senior figures in the Quai d'Orsay that I had just come back from the Faw where it looked as though Iraq was losing, he looked alarmed and said: 'Impossible! It is the French policy to support Saddam Hussein.'

What changed things was the geographical position of the Faw Peninsula. Iranian troops were only 25 miles from Kuwait; western governments perceived Iran's Islamic fundamentalism as a serious threat to their interests in the Muslim world, especially in those Gulf states which, like Kuwait, had sizeable Shi'i populations. Alarm bells rang particularly loudly in London, where the Gulf was an area of special postcolonial interest, and in Washington, where the humiliation over the American hostages in Tehran was still felt deeply. Both governments jumped to a series of conclusions: first, that Iran was planning to act on the wilder rhetoric of the less important fundamentalist clerics in Tehran and Qom and start the 'liberation' of the Gulf states by moving into Kuwait; second, that Iran would soon be in a position to move up the Faw Peninsula and capture Basra; third, that western interests would best be served by tilting towards Iraq in the war. It was a critical mistake, which opened the way to the Iraqi invasion of Kuwait five years later.

Israel made no such mistake. It had long before sorted out its strategic priorities and knew that a far greater long-term threat to its interests was posed by Saddam Hussein's ambitions than by the fundamentalists in Tehran. Israeli diplomats and intelligence officers tried to convince the Americans that they were wrong. For some months in 1986 American policy was unsettled: it warned Iran not to move against Kuwait – something the Iranian leadership had no intention of doing anyway – but the Reagan administration pushed ahead with its opportunist plan to buy the freedom of American hostages in Lebanon with supplies of weapons. For a brief period in the summer of 1986 the strategy, which became known as Irangate when news of it filtered out in Beirut, worked. Robert McFarlane, the president's national security adviser, paid a ludicrously ill-arranged visit to Tehran with Colonel Oliver North, an adventurer who had a job in the Reagan White House. American public opinion had become so accustomed to thinking of Iran as the main enemy in the region and the Reagan administration had so often spoken with apparent sincerity of its refusal to negotiate with terrorists, that the deal, when it was exposed, seemed like the worst kind of betrayal. Ronald Reagan found it hard to give coherent answers to questions about the affair and never regained the level of popularity he had enjoyed before it occurred.

There were no such problems in the strange but perfectly logical relationship between Israel and Iran. It was natural for each of them to look for tactical help to the country that lay on the other side of its main enemy. Each felt its entire future was at stake. Israel skilfully supplied Iran with untraceable weapons, intelligence and training. Iran allowed Israeli jets to attack the Osirak nuclear plant from its territory in June 1981. As long as Iran carried on fighting, the Israelis had nothing to worry about from Saddam Hussein. Israel could not, however, persuade the United States to stay on the sidelines. Once the

Irangate deal had collapsed the Reagan administration felt obliged to restore the balance after Iran's success at Faw by tilting more obviously towards Iraq.

The United States rarely tilts gently. It had always sided with Iraq to a limited extent: Operation Staunch had been an American attempt to stop the flow of arms to Iran while permitting arms to Iraq. The Americans had also increased their purchases of Iraqi oil – encouraging their allies to do the same – while cutting back on oil from Iran. But as a result of the capture of the Faw Peninsula and the atmosphere of gloom and approaching disaster in Baghdad, the United States took a number of radical steps to help Saddam Hussein. These steps have remained secret until now.

By the beginning of 1987, if not before, American satellite and radar intelligence was being handed to Iraq in considerable quantities and the United States had become an active if secret partner in Iraq's battle against Iran. American intelligence officers plotted the movements of Iranian troops and planes and passed the information on to Iraq. According to an officer who served with them, two American warships, the USS *Stark* and her sister ship *Coontz* had the task of radioing the coordinates of targets which American intelligence officers themselves recommended to the Iraqis and guiding them onto the attack. On 17 May 1987 two Exocet missiles from an Iraqi Air Force Mirage homed in accidentally on the radio beam from the *Stark* which was directing the pilot to his target. Following the beam down, they struck the *Stark* amidships, killing 37 American crewmen and injuring dozens of others. The incident was not allowed to interfere with the strategic decision to help Iraq in its war with Iran. Saddam Hussein wrote President Reagan a fulsome letter of apology and cooperated in full with an American board of inquiry. The rumour in Baghdad was that the unfortunate pilot was executed. The Reagan administration did not even ask Iraq for compensation, since it understood perfectly well that the incident had been an unfortunate technical accident. Instead it issued a fierce warning to Iran, which had not of course been involved, that it should do nothing which might invite American retaliation.

Iran regularly accused the United States of siding with the Iraqis and providing them with satellite intelligence, but the authorities in Tehran, as so often, were their own worst enemies. They had made so many accusations against the Americans in the past that even objective-minded people failed to take them seriously. Indeed, this is the first time that the true cause of the *Stark* incident has been made public. Yet it is clear now that Iraq was receiving extremely accurate information about troop strengths behind Iranian lines in the summer of 1987. It must be a fair assumption that when Saddam Hussein and his generals planned their offensive for the spring and early summer of the following year they were still receiving American satellite intelligence. In other words, they knew precisely where the weak points were in Iran's defences. If this is so, it would explain how they managed – so unexpectedly – to break through in 1988 with such effect.

By the late summer of 1987 Iran's planners thought they might have to face an open attack by the United States. The seven ships which the US Navy was deploying in the Gulf at the time of the attack on the *Stark* had been reinforced tenfold: there were now nearly eighty of them. American naval ships were escorting Kuwaiti oil tankers which had been reflagged with the Stars and Stripes. There was heavy western protection for tankers and other shipping against Iranian attack, but the Iraqis were able to carry on attacking ships and oil installations as they chose. On the night of the Iraqi attack to retake Faw, a US naval force distracted the planners in Tehran by staging a show of strength further down the Iranian coast. On 3 July 1988, when the Iraqi offensive was at its height, the USS *Vincennes* shot down an Iranian Airbus which had just taken off from Bandarabbas on its way to Dubai. All 290 people on board were killed. It was clearly a mistake – a video camera which was running throughout the incident caught the crew's reaction when news came through that they had destroyed a civilian airliner – but the Iranians were convinced it had been done deliberately as a warning. The United States offered compensation but refused to apologize. Vice-President George Bush, speaking at the United Nations, made it sound as though it was the Iranians' fault, even though the flight had been a scheduled one and the plane was on time and on course: 'They allowed a civilian aircraft loaded with passengers to proceed on a path over a warship engaged in battle. That was an irresponsible and a tragic error.' Afterwards the Pentagon agreed that the crew of the *Vincennes*, lacking combat experience, had been at fault. But Hojatoleslam Ali Akbar Rafsanjani, the most powerful politician in Iran, was looking for a way to end the war with Saddam Hussein and used the Airbus tragedy in his arguments. It showed, he said, that the United States would soon launch an all-out attack on Iran in alliance with the increasingly successful Iraqis. Faced with such an attack, he said, the structure of the Islamic Republic itself might be destroyed. He persuaded Ayatollah Khomeini to accept the United Nations call for a ceasefire – something for which, it seems, Khomeini never forgave him. On 18 July 1988 the UN secretary general, Javier Perez de Cuellar, received Iran's formal acceptance of Resolution 598. Saddam Hussein had been rescued from defeat and could claim to have won a victory. It would not have happened without the very considerable help he received from the United States.

The Americans, like the British, had made a serious error of judgment. The Israelis had understood that Iran was their natural strategic ally against radical, pro-Soviet Iraq: without some kind of relationship with Tehran, no matter how indirect and secret, it was impossible to achieve any proper balance for western interests in the region. There was a fundamental lack of understanding in the West of Iran's ambitions. When Iran captured the Faw Peninsula in 1986 it had no intention of threatening Kuwait or the other Gulf states. The State Department and the Foreign Office took Iranian rhetoric at face value and assumed that the Islamic Republic represented a serious regional threat. In fact, as I discovered from making a number of visits there between 1986 and 1990, Iran and its clerical rulers were obsessed with their own internal affairs. By 1986, when Faw was captured, the Islamic revolution had already run out of ideological steam and the electrifying effect it had had on the Shi'i populations of other countries in the Middle East was beginning to fade.

For the West, rescuing Saddam Hussein from defeat was an

error. Helping him on to victory was an equally bad decision. It was clear by 1986 what sort of man he was and no democratic country should have given him the help that France, the United States and, to a lesser extent, Britain, were all prepared to give him. The Israelis had been warning Washington for at least three years that if he won his war with Iran Saddam would be a danger both to them and to the region. The Americans took no notice. They were convinced that Iran was their main enemy. The British believed with equal firmness that they had to safeguard a former colonial possession from Iran and its militant fundamentalism. From 1986 onwards, both London and Washington tilted decisively in favour of the one country which really would present a threat to Kuwait.

On 21 March 1988 I landed at Mehrabad airport in Tehran. Usually it took four hours or more to get through the immigration and customs controls. This time my producer, Tira Shubart, and I emerged from the airport only an hour after landing, even though we had no visas. For once the Iranian government actively wanted us to be there and was prepared to help. 'Bombaran', said a notice in Farsi by the passport desk. 'Bombaran' meant bombing. We had been invited to report on an incident that had taken place four days earlier, on the northern front.

As the details became clearer, they seemed to me to be subject to the usual degree of official exaggeration: it hardly seemed likely that several thousand people could have died in one incident. I resigned myself to one of those unpleasant tugs-of-war one goes through with Middle Eastern officials on such occasions, when to question the literal truth of their claim causes great anger. The next morning we were flown to the border by plane, then taken by helicopter to the site of the bombardment. Our destination was some way into Iraq, in territory which had recently been taken over by the Iranians. There was a certain vagueness about how this had happened, until gradually it became clear that the main role in liberating the towns and villages here had been taken by the Kurdish

47

Peshmurga guerrillas, who had then handed them over to the Iranian troops. It had been a remarkable victory: 4000 prisoners taken, several hundred tanks, more than 100 officers over the rank of major. We had not, however, been brought here to see the victory, but to see Saddam Hussein's response to his defeat.

Our helicopter headed over mountains and green hills into Kurdistan. In the distance lay a lake and, beyond that, a medium-sized town. 'That is Halabje,' shouted our guide over the noise of the rotor blades. I was still uncertain of the name and took the precaution of jotting it down. The Peshmurga had captured the town on 15 March 1988. The following day Iraqi planes and artillery had attacked it for several hours with chemical weapons. There were many casualties, but I still assumed the number had been ritually exaggerated. Our helicopter came in to land on the outskirts of the town and we walked towards the centre.

The first thing I noticed was the stench, then the bodies of sheep and cows starting to bloat and swell. Out in the fields there were occasional shapes under blankets, shepherds whose bodies had not yet been taken away. As we approached the streets of the town we found that many – though not all – of the bodies had been left for us to see. By now they had been dead for five days. A street we turned into was full of them. No one had touched them since they had run out of their homes, hoping to get away from the houses and streets where the gas would collect. Some of them had shrapnel wounds but it wasn't the shrapnel that killed them. There was a strange waxiness to their faces, an absence of fear or pain. Many of them lay with their eyes open and, even after five days out in the open, they seemed much more human than the usual bundles of dead flesh in old clothes which you find after massacres.

There was the boom of shells not far away; the Iraqis had not given up their efforts to recapture Halabje. Our Iranian escorts produced an old man who had witnessed the attack and survived. He wore a black and white Kurdish turban and seemed to enjoy our attention.

I heard the planes coming over, and then I saw the bombs starting to fall. White smoke came out of some of them. I was near the concrete shelter, so I went down into it and waited. I was too frightened to come out for a long time. When I did, it seemed as though the whole town was lying dead. People I knew, just lying in the streets, or lying inside their houses. It was a dead place, this town.

How could he be certain the planes had been Iraqi ones? someone asked. Couldn't they have been Iranian ones, just as well? The Iranian officials standing beside us shifted irritably. The old man cackled. 'What, you think the Iranians came and bombed our town the day after their men had come in here? That would be very stupid, wouldn't you say?' He cackled some more. I looked away to a group of bodies lying near me: a young woman, aged perhaps twenty, in a magenta and orange dress, holding a baby in her arms. The mother could have been sleeping, but the baby's eyes were white and dead. Its clothes were continually fluttering in the slight wind. Chance had taken them and left the wizened old man with his self-satisfied cackle.

We wandered round the houses. Most of them still had people inside. I went into one where a rocket had come through the roof. Part of it was still lodged in the ceiling of the room. There was a sound of buzzing: flies were at work on the food the family had been eating when the attack began. There were six of them around the table. A child had rolled out of his chair and lay on the floor, face down. A man and woman were hunched down in their seats: I couldn't see their faces. An older man, the grandfather, lay with the side of his face on the table, his hand to his mouth, his jaw still clamped on a piece of flat bread which he had been in the act of biting when the rocket came through the roof and filled the room with poison gas.

A couple of shells landed nearby, one 100 yards away and the second one only 50. I sniffed the air: mustard gas smells of sewage; nerve gas has a much more pleasant smell, like chocolate according to some people and new-mown hay according to others; cyanide gas supposedly smells like almonds, though if you take a single breath of it you are likely to die. According to the Iranian doctor who accompanied us it was cyanide which had killed the old man eating his bread and the mother with the child in her arms. All over in a second or two, he said. The others were really bad. Nerve gas strangles you from the inside and takes a long time to do it. The contorted bodies I saw later on the edge of town must have died that way. Mustard gas kills only 3 per cent of people on average, but condemns a good 50 per cent of the others to an ugly half-life of chest and throat pain, of huge blisters which can erupt 10 or 20 years later, of serious damage to the eyes and the nasal passages. Let it be cyanide, I thought, as I waited for the third shell. There was another explosion, but it was farther away and there was no cloud of gas rising from it. I had never thought I would be grateful for simple high explosive.

There was a terrible Goyaesque moment as three donkeys, two grey and one white, crazed with the fear of the bombing, galloped wildly across the fields beside us, trying to bite each other with grass-green fangs. As they lunged forward, teeth bared, they trampled over a pile of dead bodies which broke out into brutal eructations as the gases were forced out of them, and then lay twisted and broken as the donkeys ran on, braying, biting and trampling. These were the big piles of bodies, gathered together for burial in a mass grave but left there for the moment so that everyone would know what had happened, that it wasn't as I had assumed, just an exaggeration in the mind of a government official. A Belgian doctor who was taken to Halabje the day after the attack said he counted about 5000 bodies.

We went on. More bodies, then an entire truck full, four or five deep: dozens of women in bright-coloured clothes, dozens of old men and children. The stench was more than I could stand and the sight of those calm, grey-white faces was beginning to haunt me. I went back to the centre of the town. A man wailed and ran, his arms in the air: he had just come back from a journey and had no idea what had happened. Dead pigeons lay on the ground; I hadn't noticed them before. The television cameramen were trying to film the bodies in such a way as not to offend the delicate sensibilities of people at home. My eyes met those of a child that lay on its back, dropped by a woman as she herself had fallen dead.

I couldn't get that face out of my mind afterwards. On the anniversary of Saddam Hussein's attack on Halabje a photograph of the same child appeared on posters in London advertising a protest march. One was pasted up on the Victorian-Ionic pillars of a house near mine in London and I used to pass it all the time. Over the weeks and months the poster became more and more tattered. In the end all that remained were the child's empty, white eyes looking out at me and a few letters: 'REMEMBER HALAB . . .' I only wish I could forget it.

In September 1988, Washington again seemed to change its attitude to Iraq completely and without the slightest warning. Tariq Aziz, the Iraqi foreign minister, went to Washington on 8 September for what he clearly expected to be a friendly and relaxed meeting with Secretary of State George Shultz. Two hours before the meeting took place, Shultz made a public declaration condemning the latest use of chemical weapons by Iraq against Kurdish rebels about two weeks before. The next day the US Senate unanimously voted a series of sanctions against Iraq which the chairman of the Senate Foreign Relations Committee, Claiborne Pell, described as the strongest in decades. (As it happened the sanctions were not imposed. They were appended to a bill which lapsed on a technicality before the House adjourned and by that time the Senators' minds had shifted to something else.)

The US administration's attitude remained firm, however. The difference between its response to Iraq's newest use of chemical weapons and to Halabje was noticeable. The State Department had condemned the attack on Halabje, but not as strongly as it condemned the one in August. And yet tens of millions of Americans had seen the television pictures of Halabje for themselves, whereas in August the only evidence for the chemical attack, though it certainly took place, came from Kurdish refugees who had fled across the border into Turkey and told their story to officials of the US Senate Foreign Relations Committee. This time there were no pictures and no visible bodies.

George Shultz, normally an undemonstrative, cautious man, was certainly not inclined to take a sudden new tack purely on the basis of moral disapproval. As Ronald Reagan's secretary of state he had supported the Contras in Nicaragua, Noriega in Panama and a number of other unpleasant figures in a variety of countries. The change which took place in US foreign policy in September 1988 was directly linked to a new perception of Iraq's position in the Middle East.

Until August 1988 Saddam Hussein's only real concern had been the war against Iran. All his military efforts were directed eastwards. From the moment the ceasefire came into effect Iraq became the dominant military power in the Muslim world. Its income from oil, 70 per cent of which had at times been directed to the war effort, was suddenly liberated for whatever purpose Saddam might choose. His modified Scud missiles, bought either from the Soviet Union or from any other country willing to supply them, could reach Tel Aviv, Damascus, southern Turkey and northern Saudi Arabia. He ended the war with a million men under arms and more than 5000 tanks. He could afford to forget about Iran, prostrate after the ceasefire and in no mood to fight on.

The Israelis were aware of all this. Early on they had disapproved of American policy in the war, realizing that it would lead to precisely this conclusion. Now, it seems, they put heavy pressure on Washington to stop Saddam Hussein from acting on his old promises to deal finally with Israel. It is likely that the Israeli government threatened to take its own action against Iraq, as it had done against the Osirak atomic plant in 1981, unless the United States undertook to do something itself. Not long after this information started to emerge in Israel that Saddam Hussein was beginning a crash programme to develop his own nuclear warheads. It is fair to assume that only a threat of some urgency would have been enough to have persuaded the United States to shift its entire approach towards Iraq almost overnight.

Three days after Shultz's brutal reception of Tariq Aziz in Washington the Iraqi government gave its first, characteristic response. On 11 September 1988 more than 100,000 people obediently demonstrated outside the American embassy in

Baghdad, the first such demonstration against the United States since the Six Day War in 1967. In November the head of the embassy's political section, Haywood Rankin, was expelled. Several days later an unidentified Iraqi diplomat was expelled from Washington as a reprisal. Saddam Hussein, who had such trust in his ability to scent plots against his own life, now scented an American-Israeli-British plot against his efforts to turn his country into a regional superpower. On 11 April 1989, Foreign Minister Tariq Aziz said:

> Israel wants to attack Iraqi industrial and scientific sites to maintain the balance of power, which has changed . . . When an Arab country achieves [technological advances] then the whole fuss comes, the comments, suspicions and attempts to discredit the image of the Arab country.

From this point on, Iraq felt it was on a collision course with the West.

The Road to Confrontation

They attack us from different directions. They said we shouldn't hang the spy, Farzad Bazoft. But what they really want is to control Iraq and make it a backward place where all the spies can go free and Iraq will be destroyed from within. And then they will just take Iraq's strength away.

Saddam Hussein, speaking at a conference of Islamic clerics in Baghdad, 8 May 1990

I always made a point of telling government officials in Iraq that he had been a close friend of mine. It seemed like a proper tribute to his memory in the country where he had been murdered. But it wasn't really true. We had known each other, but long before his death we had lost contact. I was always meaning to write and congratulate him on his newspaper reporting. Somehow I never got around to it.

We first met in 1983. At a reception of some kind he came over to talk to me, a smart, good-looking man of 24 in a blazer and a carefully knotted tie. I could see at once that he was a Persian. He was kind about my coverage of the Iranian revolution four years earlier, then he introduced himself: 'My name is Farzad Bazoft.' There was something a little overeager about him, perhaps, but he was well mannered and amusing. He wanted very badly to be a journalist. He wondered if there might be any jobs going at the BBC. I said the noncommittal things one does on these occasions. He rang me not long afterwards. Was I interested in information about Iran? He had been in touch with some well-connected friends in Tehran. I listened and the information was quite good: good enough, after some checking and confirming, to use in a broadcast.

We met several times after that. He became noisy and boisterous as we knew each other better and was inclined to be boastful. It was only the boastfulness of a young man compensating for his self-doubt, however. He was also generous spirited and witty and I enjoyed his company. There was no pattern and often no great importance to the information he gave me. I paid him little enough for it, but it pleased him greatly. Farzad Bazoft wanted status, and being on someone's payroll gave him a modicum of that. Still, he knew he had to earn the money and I soon realized he was dishing up unverifiable and often rather old Tehran gossip. He assured me twice that Ayatollah Khomeini had died – this would have been in 1983 and 1984 – and when I said I didn't believe him he was hurt and offended. I grew tired of the connection and told him that there was only one thing I was interested in now: he should try to find a way of getting me into Iran as after the revolution I had been put on a blacklist for visas. He promised he would be able to do it but I could tell it wouldn't happen. So be it, I thought, it's a way of saying goodbye to him. The phone used to ring from time to time after that and my secretary would say 'It's Farzad' in an embarrassed way. Sometimes I would speak to him, sometimes not. It's easy, if you have a secure job with a well-known organization, to be effortlessly cruel to an outsider who wants to make his way in the profession but can never quite break through.

Then he started working for the *Observer*. He didn't have a staff job there either, but you could tell he was trying hard to earn one by producing bigger and better exclusives about Iran and the war with Iraq. Some were good, some a little dubious. I noticed that he was spending time in Baghdad. It was brave of him to go there, I thought, given that the Iraqis would know perfectly well that he still had Iranian nationality and that the British authorities had only given him temporary travel documents. It is easy to accuse people like Farzad Bazoft of spying and I thought it was a sign of some maturity on the part of the Iraqis to allow a man with an Iranian background to visit their country in wartime.

After he had been executed for visiting the site of an explosion at the Al-Qa'qa weapons plant outside the town of

Al-Hilla south of Baghdad, news emerged that Farzad Bazoft had a criminal record in Britain. It looked as though it had been leaked deliberately, to counter accusations that the British government had failed in its handling of the case. This may be too tidy an explanation and it may simply be that people who knew about Farzad's past had kept quiet about it until he could no longer be damaged by the revelation. The British tabloid press, most of which could be relied upon to support Mrs Margaret Thatcher no matter what she did, gave great prominence to the news. Many people who read the headlines the next morning must have reflected that Farzad Bazoft was a shady character whom it would have been unwise to defend too strongly.

The facts of the case are that in June 1981 Farzad owed £260 in rent to his landlady in Banbury, near Oxford. He had no money to pay it because his allowance from Iran had not been getting through. He walked into the Heart of England building society in the Northamptonshire village of Brackley carrying a parcel which he placed on the counter. It was, he said, a bomb. He demanded money. He escaped with £475 and was arrested two streets away. There was, of course, no bomb and it would be hard to think of a more incompetent crime. Farzad was gaoled for 18 months and the judge recommended that he should be deported on completing his sentence. When he was released a year later, the Home Office accepted that his life would be in danger if he were returned to Iran and he was allowed to stay.

Farzad Bazoft had first come to Britain in 1975 and studied at the North Oxfordshire Technical College. The couple who took him in said later that he could be overenthusiastic, very gullible and naive, but they liked him and virtually adopted him into their family. He developed a reputation for lavish spending in these years of sudden oil wealth in Iran. For a time he received generous cheques from his father, a middle-ranking executive in the Iranian oil industry, but after the revolution in Iran the money dried up. Concealing his criminal record, he decided to offer his services to the small newspapers published by Iranian exiles in London and, among other organizations, to the BBC. He also offered information to

Scotland Yard, though not, it seems, for money. The things he told them were never followed up and were sometimes absurd: once he claimed to have information about Lord Lucan, who had disappeared some years before. Scotland Yard paid no further attention when it became clear that Farzad wanted money to travel to Switzerland to carry out further investigations. His contacts with the police may well have been little more than attention seeking.

Not long after Farzad's execution, I visited Baghdad for the first time. While there I interviewed Deputy Foreign Minister Nizar Hamdoun, an intelligent and cultivated man. For 20 minutes or so he defended his government and his president in answer to my questions about the various issues of the moment, including Farzad's execution. We came close to shouting at each other, but he had been trained in television interview technique in the United States, where he had been Iraq's ambassador to the UN; he knew how to switch the emotions of anger and outrage on and off at will.

At the end of the interview, when the business of filming two-shots and cutaways was finished, I sensed that Hamdoun had something more to say to me. We sat there facing each other in silence. Then he said quietly: 'It's strange and very sad to think that Farzad Bazoft was sitting exactly where you are, only a few months ago.' I said nothing, but waited intently for him to continue. As the cameraman and sound recordist packed away their gear, Hamdoun spoke again: 'He came to me to ask if I would help him get to the Al-Hilla site, where the explosion had been. He said the Ministry of Information was useless – that they kept promising him that they would take him, and then never did. And then, of course, after he went to Al-Hilla he was arrested.'

I sat forward. 'You mean to say you knew in advance that he wanted to go there?' Hamdoun nodded and looked down at his hands, which were folded in his lap. 'Then he told me he was planning to go by himself if he couldn't get anyone from the ministry to go with him.' I could feel the anger mounting inside me. Hamdoun had just said during our interview that it was beyond doubt that Farzad was a spy. 'What kind of a spy is it that tells a government minister and the Ministry of

Information beforehand that he's going spying?' There was no answer. We said our goodbyes and left. Some days later the British embassy in Baghdad told me that Farzad had tried to call Nizar Hamdoun as a witness at his trial, but that he had not appeared. Either the application was rejected or Hamdoun refused to give evidence on behalf of a man whom the Iraqi security service had already decided was a spy and whom the Iraqi president was determined to execute in order to show his independence from the West. In fact, during this period Hamdoun travelled to London to be the guest speaker at a conference on the future of his country. The prevailing mood was one of goodwill and optimism for Iraq, and the care of Farzad Bazoft, whose trial had just ended, was not mentioned. Only two speakers, one from the BBC and the other an academic, were critical of Iraq, and Hamdoun himself was charming and eloquent. He presumably knew as he was speaking that Farzad would be executed the following day. Indeed, it is quite likely that Farzad's execution was delayed to allow him to speak.

Farzad Bazoft was precisely what he claimed to be – a journalist looking for a good story. He had visited Iraq five times in the two years before his arrest and the Iraqis had always asked him back. He had good contacts with the Iraqi embassy in London and with the People's Mujaheddin, the Iranian opposition group based in Iraq which was working for the overthrow of Ayatollah Khomeini's régime. There was a double risk in being an Iranian and a western journalist in Baghdad, but when he left London for the last time he had every reason to be confident that his trip would go well.

At this time the Iraqis allowed western journalists into the country at infrequent intervals and in small numbers. Journalists would be invited in to report on something specific and would then have to leave. The subjects were rarely of much interest to the outside world and in the case of Farzad's ill-fated trip it was a set of carefully-restricted elections in Kurdistan. The trick was to take the opportunity of getting in and then try to do some genuine reporting. It was clear this time what the subject would be.

On 17 August 1989, less than three weeks before Farzad

Bazoft left London, a huge explosion had taken place at the weapons manufacturing plant of Al Qa'qa and 700 people were said to have been killed. The plant covered an area of several square miles and was defended with anti-aircraft guns and radar. It was known that missiles were stored there and the possibility existed that somewhere in this immense complex chemical weapons or nuclear warheads – perhaps even both – were assembled. News of the explosion leaked out on 6 September – the day Bazoft and the other western journalists on the trip left for Baghdad. All of them must have had hopes of finding out what had happened.

Al-Hilla is only about 60 miles from Baghdad, a little further along the main road which leads to the ruins of ancient Babylon. Babylon is easy to get to, but later reports of Farzad Bazoft's activities made the excursion sound much more difficult and dubious than it was. Several other journalists who were visiting Iraq on the same facility made the trip down to Al-Hilla. Three members of a camera team from the British company Independent Television News, for instance, reached the town and climbed over the wire surrounding the place where they thought the explosion had taken place. They were arrested, their video-cassettes were taken from them and they were questioned for several hours before being released. Their equipment was returned to them and they went back to Baghdad.

Plainly it was tricky but not, apparently, dangerous to get to the plant at Al-Qa'qa and find out something of what had happened. That evening, after their adventure, the ITN team met Farzad Bazoft and a British nurse working in Baghdad, Daphne Parish. They all laughed about it. It might have been worrying at the time, but it seemed clear the Iraqis wouldn't do anything serious against western journalists. The following day Bazoft asked Mrs Parish if she would drive him down there. He was an attractive man with a highly persuasive manner and she agreed.

Farzad explained to her that he had asked the Ministry of Information for help in getting there and they hadn't turned him down. At one point he had even been told to expect an official car but it never came. He had then made his request to

Nizar Hamdoun who agreed to put in an official request. Farzad told him he would go anyway. He was confident that if he got into trouble his friends in the various government ministries would help him out. It did not seem an unreasonable risk to take. In such circumstances I and many other journalists who have worked in Iraq would certainly have done the same thing.

There was no question of secrecy. He telephoned the *Observer* in London and told them openly what he was planning to do, knowing that all foreign phone calls were monitored by the Iraqis. After his execution there was a persistent story that Farzad had been disguised as an Indian doctor. It was completely untrue; he wore a sports shirt and jeans that day. Daphne Parish told the hospital transport office where she was going and the route she would take and the two of them travelled in a four-wheel drive car with the hospital's name on the side. After a good deal of searching they found a place they assumed to be the weapons plant and Bazoft noticed a pile of ash beside the road. He decided he wanted to come back the next day to take samples and Mrs Parish agreed to drive him again.

The following day, again dressed informally, he took a camera and two medicine bottles which Mrs Parish gave him. In full view of a group of soldiers guarding the entrance Bazoft jumped out and scooped up some of the ash and a rock. Then he found an old shoe and picked it up, which annoyed Mrs Parish. As they left he took three photographs: one of the fence, one of the general area and one of the sign giving the name of the suburb where the Al-Qa'qa plant was situated – Iskanderia. It was all rather naively done and he collected samples because a well-known television journalist had done the same thing in Kurdistan. His plan was to ask the *Observer* to have them analysed for evidence of what had occurred at the plant three weeks earlier.

Bazoft was booked on the next morning's flight to London. He drove to the airport with an Arab journalist and the usual Ministry of Information minder to help them through the red tape. On the airport road their car had a puncture. Three security men were following them and came and stood by

Bazoft as he waited for the tyre to be changed. It made him understandably nervous. At the airport the minder saw him through passport control and into the departure lounge. None of the other journalists who were on the flight saw what happened to him after that, but there is a small office on one side of the lounge which the security police use to interrogate passengers they have arrested. One of the journalists had the presence of mind to contact the British embassy.

It was more than a month before the Iraqi authorities admitted that Bazoft was accused of espionage, though the Baghdad newspapers had already trumpetted his guilt. One, *Al-Iraq*, accused him of spying for Britain, though when he appeared on Iraqi television on 1 November 1989, he confessed to being an Israeli spy. It was clear he had been maltreated. He had a bruise on his right temple, part of his moustache had been pulled out and there were heavy bags under his eyes, no doubt caused by stress and sleep deprivation. A man in a blue suit sat beside him and with what appeared to be a script in front of him. He asked questions from it and Farzad gave what were presumably the pre-arranged answers:

Question: Did you face any kind of pressure or assault when you were arrested or during investigation?
Answer: The treatment I have received so far I can say is much better than the treatment one would receive in a detention centre or institution in the UK.

Later, in the months that led up to the war, I used to see Farzad's questioner in the Al-Rasheed hotel. He was a pleasant-looking man who wore a studious pair of glasses and well-cut suits. He had been educated in Britain and used to like meeting western journalists, particularly women, so that he could practice his English. Some people talked to him. I never did, for fear I might not be able to control my temper.

Daphne Parish was picked up soon afterwards. She realized she had to resist her interrogators' demands to confess, though they blindfolded and threatened her. At other times they tried to tempt her. 'We'll send you back tonight,' they said. 'All you must say is that you work for the British government. If you're not prepared to say that, just give the name of someone who works at the British embassy.' Mrs Parish refused to tell them what they wanted. They kicked her and pulled her hair and threatened her with a knife, but they never used it.

Farzad believed the promises. When they were interrogated together he tried to convince her to confess, as he had done. He also told her they had used, or threatened to use, electrical torture on him. 'Look,' he said, 'we'll probably be flying out of here in a day or so if we get these last points sorted out.' She wouldn't give in. She was 53, a strong-minded woman with the maturity and wit to look after herself. Farzad was 31 and remained what he had always been: an innocent with a strong desire to please.

It turned out that the Iraqi security agency, the Mukhabarat, had been watching Farzad for years. After his death they produced pictures they had taken of him photographing empty shell cases at the Faw Peninsula and invested them with sinister meaning. When he applied to go to the site of the explosion at Al-Qa'qa they watched him even more closely. After that they had more evidence: the ash samples, the shoe, the photographs he took when he was with Mrs Parish. They also found the name of a former senior officer of Mossad, the Israeli intelligence service, in his contacts book.

Jacob Nimrodi, the ex-Israeli agent, had become an arms dealer. It is as unlikely that a genuine agent would carry around the name of his Mossad controller as that he would tell everybody that he was going on a spying expedition. The Iraqis were looking for anything that would hang Farzad, however. Later the editor of the *Observer*, Donald Trelford, explained that he had himself introduced Bazoft to Nimrodi, as part of an investigation into Israeli arms sales to Iran. Iraqi embassies in the West issued photocopies of Farzad's handwritten confession. 'YES,' said one sentence, in capital letters to make it easier to read, 'I DO WORK AND DEAL WITH ISRAELIS AND BRITISH SPECIAL BRANCH (SECRET POLICE).' It was stilted and unconvincing, full of official Iraqi phraseology, referring for instance to the Iraqi Air Force's 'great and glorious role in the liberation fight'.

The trial was an unpleasant piece of business. Farzad

Bazoft's Iraqi lawyer was shown the details of the prosecution's case just a few hours beforehand. Now that it was too late, Farzad claimed his confession had been a fabrication. The judge said angrily he wasn't interested. When he asked Mrs Parish if she pleaded guilty or not guilty she replied: 'Guilty of what? What is the charge? I haven't been formally charged so far.' She had not been allowed a private interview with her lawyer.

At the end there was further pointless, cruel confusion: neither Mrs Parish or Bazoft was told what the sentences had been. Bazoft asked if the judge said he was to be hanged. The interpreter laughed and told him the judge had said he wouldn't be hanged. Mrs Parish was told that she would be freed. It was only when she was taken to another prison that she found she had been sentenced to fifteen years. She was released after ten unpleasant months when President Kenneth Kaunda of Zambia, at the request of the *Observer's* owner, 'Tiny' Rowland, asked Saddam Hussein for clemency.

Farzad Bazoft's death sentence created an international outcry. A number of Arab governments privately tried to intercede for him, though in public they supported Saddam Hussein. As for the Arab world's newspapers, they were almost unanimous in siding with an Arab government against a western journalist. The Kuwaiti press was particularly strong in its condemnation, one paper affirming that he had been working for an air strike against Iraqi military installations. The British tabloid newspapers were no more moderate. They screamed their hatred of 'The Butcher of Baghdad', a man who had rarely attracted their attention when he was carrying out much worse butcheries. Margaret Thatcher and her government took a strong line in public, when perhaps they should have dealt more quietly with the affair.

On 15 March 1990, five days after the trial, Robin Kealy, number two at the British embassy, was summoned to the Abu Gharaib prison outside Baghdad, where the executioners are said to be on duty round the clock. He was told that Farzad was to be hanged that morning. Kealy is a thoughtful, sensitive man, and the memory of the occasion still affected him when he told me about it a month later. He was shown into the prison governor's office. Farzad was there, unshaven and wearing a dirty white *dishdasha*. He looked thin and ill. He started telling Kealy of his hopes that international appeals would pressure Saddam Hussein to free him and – as naive as ever – that he might be given the chance to put his case to Saddam in person. Kealy saw that although the room was crowded with officials, no one had told Farzad that he was to be hanged directly the meeting ended.

Farzad took the news reasonably well. He sent his love to his parents, his sister and brothers and to the girlfriend with whom he had broken up before going to Baghdad the previous September. He remembered Daphne Parish: 'Tell Dee I'm sorry.' He denied once again that he was a spy or that his confession was genuine. He asked for forgiveness from anyone he had ever hurt. Then he gave Kealy a message: 'I hope the world will decide, after I'm gone, what kind of person I have really been.' The meeting was over. Kealy was told to leave. They took Farzad out a minute or two later and hanged him.

Some months afterwards, in Baghdad, I talked to a senior government man about the case. I made a point of discussing it with the more important officials there. I was certain that they knew as well as I did that Farzad had been innocent of the crime he had been hanged for. I told the man aggressively: 'If I had been here when Farzad was, I would certainly have gone down to Al-Hilla and tried to find out about the explosion. Would you have hanged me?' The official shook his head. 'Why not?' 'You are British. You would have got ten or fifteen years and been released quietly later. He was Iranian. It's as simple as that.'

In his last meeting with Robin Kealy, Farzad asked that his body should be brought back to his adoptive country, England, and buried in Highgate cemetery. His grave lies close to the towering tomb of Karl Marx. It is still reasonably well kept, with a few flowers that someone – a friend, a relative, or perhaps a passerby – has left beside the headstone. After his coffin had been lowered into the grave his brother said: 'Remember him as a happy man. Now let him rest in peace.' No one said he had died because he was not a European.

'I have no doubt in my mind,' said President Kaunda after Mrs Parish had been released and was in Zambia, 'that if it had not been for that vicious attack on him and on Iraq by the British authorities and press, that man might have lived, might have been here with Daphne together.' Iraqi officials insisted afterwards that if the request to let Farzad Bazoft live had been made more diplomatically Saddam Hussein would have agreed to it. That may be true, though given the public mood in Britain and Europe – the United States, as always, was scarcely concerned with a case that did not involve American citizens – it might not have been possible anyway.

The importance of the Farzad Bazoft case is that it marked a new mood of belligerence and confrontation in Saddam Hussein's approach to the West. It is clear from talking to his ministers and officials that he saw the incident as a personal challenge. Mrs Thatcher called his decision to execute Bazoft – and everybody knew it was his decision – 'an act of barbarism deeply repugnant to all civilized people'. Saddam Hussein often referred in his speeches to Iraq's 4000 year history, its position as the birthplace of civilization. To be called un-civilized and by a woman must have been intolerable to him. His embassy in London sent him each new noisy accusation made by the *Sun*, the *Daily Mirror*, the *Daily Mail* and the rest, which seemed to vie with one another in inventing new insults. The Foreign Office in London tried to point out that no one told the British press what to say, but this meant nothing to a man who believed that newspapers only existed to say what political leaders wanted. The tone between Baghdad and London became openly insulting. 'Mrs Thatcher wanted him alive. We gave her the body,' said Saddam's minister of information.

The change in British and, to a lesser extent, European attitudes seemed to parallel the change in American attitudes which Saddam Hussein had already noted. 'To a mind like Saddam's,' said an American diplomat in Baghdad at the time, 'everything forms a pattern.' The pattern was certainly different now. Britain, like France and West Germany, had always been prepared to put financial and trade considerations before moral ones in dealing with Iraq. Suddenly, for the sake of an individual who wasn't even British, the attitude was completely different. It would not have been easy for Saddam to understand the concern about Farzad; he would scarcely have taken the same attitude himself. Britain must therefore have adopted the US view that Iraq was becoming too strong, too independent.

Britain bulks larger in the Iraqi political imagination than its standing in the world might indicate. As the nation which ran Iraq's political destinies until 1958, it is believed by most Iraqis to have retained powerful behind-the-scenes influence. In Iran it is still widely believed that while the United States appears to be the major power, Britain, the old imperial fox, still has the decisive influence. In Iraq people assume that Britain's role is to supply the knowledge of Arab affairs that the United States so conspicuously lacks. Everything, to a country of intelligent, supple-minded people who have known nothing but colonialism for several hundred years, is part of an overriding conspiracy. Nothing can be merely what it seems.

The Farzad Bazoft affair came at a time when Saddam Hussein was just starting to exercise the new power that his apparent victory over Iran had given him. Financially Iraq was in difficulties and had been obliged to stall its creditors and mortgage its oil revenues, even though it was thought to be only a matter of a few years before the fall in military expenditure made up the deficit. Saddam was anxious about the future reliability of the Soviet Union as an arms supplier. The day before Farzad Bazoft was executed, Alexandr Golytsin, a senior diplomat in London, said Moscow was reassessing its policy on human rights, and that these issues, rather than strategic ones, would be taken into consideration when dealing with Iraq in the future. It was one of a number of signals to Saddam Hussein that he should look elsewhere for the supply of arms.

He was also looking for short cuts to military superiority. On 28 March 1990, while the bitterness over the execution of Farzad Bazoft was still at its height, a joint operation by the American and British customs services trapped a group of Iraqis who were trying to smuggle 40 American-made capacitors – high voltage electrical triggers for detonating nuclear weapons – into Iraq. It may not have been a coincidence. There were signs that the British authorities hoped to bargain the release of the Iraqis for Mrs Parish, perhaps for Farzad Bazoft as well. The operation came too late for that.

Two weeks later, British Customs seized some high precision steel pipes made by the British company Sheffield Forgemasters which were intended for assembly into a long-range weapon designed by a Canadian, Dr Gerald Bull, and christened 'the supergun' by the British press. At first people were reluctant to believe in such a thing and the supergun was the subject of endless jokes and cartoons in Britain and Western Europe. In the days and weeks that followed, however, more parts for the guns were discovered in countries across Europe. It also became known that Dr Bull had been murdered in Brussels on 22 March, though at the time his death had been largely ignored by the newspapers. Israeli intelligence was instantly accused of the crime, though an alternative suggestion was that the Iraqis themselves had murdered him, either to keep him quiet or to punish him for having informed the British of the supergun plan.

This sudden burst of activity seemed to Saddam Hussein to be deliberate, whether or not it really was. To his mind, always inclined to see plots against himself, it was part of a large-scale pattern of conspiracy by the United States, Britain and Israel to defeat his effort to turn Iraq into a regional super-power. He gave the impression he was building up an elaborate arsenal of sophisticated weapons. In December 1989 Iraq announced it had launched a three-stage rocket capable of putting a satellite into space and that it had tested missiles with a range of 1200 miles. While the West remained sceptical of these achievements, as 1990 went on there were to be increasing anxieties about the capabilities which Iraq was developing. Although Saddam's nuclear programme proved to be largely a matter of rhetoric, there was a sudden new wave of anxiety in Israel and the United States that Iraq might be close to producing its own nuclear weapons once again. The Osirak raid of 1981 had, it was said, simply delayed the nuclear programme, not stopped it. The Israelis in particular had not forgotten what Saddam had said in an interview in 1979:

Science must always be based on solid foundations. I do not believe nuclear weapons can be used for peaceful, scientific purposes in an underdeveloped, bedouin society. Money alone does not mean that a state possesses the key to the correct use of nuclear weapons for peaceful purposes . . . However, I think that if you ask any person in the world whether he would like to possess a nuclear bomb, he will tell you that he would.

Israel was worried that Iraq was renewing its efforts to build nuclear weapons, and it tried to convince the United States that this was so. Nevertheless, the best indications are that Iraq had no nuclear weapons at the time of the invasion of Kuwait, though its nuclear infrastructure and research programmes were well advanced, thanks to the expertise from France, Germany, Argentina and Brazil.

At the same time Saddam seemed to believe that it was possible to balance Israel's own suspected nuclear capability with 'the poor man's H-bomb' – chemical weapons. The rhetoric was characteristically vague, but most western observers believed that Saddam was referring to conventional missiles, possibly filled with chemical warheads, when he told the General Command of the Iraqi Armed Forces on 2 April 1990:

The West is deluding itself if it imagines it can protect Israel if Israel comes and strikes at some metal industry factory of ours. By God, we will devour half of Israel by fire if it tries to do anything against Iraq.

And he added,

[Foreign agents] used to come every day to ask us, 'Don't you want enriched uranium to make an atomic bomb?' We used to say, 'Leave us alone, keep your evil away from us and take your bags with you . . .' We do not need an atomic bomb, because we have sophisticated binary chemical weapons.

Though Saddam's strategy was simply to talk up Iraq's potential, this was enough for him to make his enemies uncomfortable and to satisfy his friends: he didn't need to be too specific. He was almost as concerned with the appearance of power than with its reality. He no doubt believed that once Iraq behaved like a country with the self-confidence of a super power, the reality would follow. That in turn required a willingness to stand up to the political influence of the United States and its allies; something which the circumstances of Farzad Bazoft's execution and the events which followed were leading him to anyway. Saddam knew that this approach would be highly popular in large parts of the Arab world. The new atmosphere of democracy which had arisen in Algeria, Tunisia and Jordan and was starting to spread to other countries increased the support Saddam enjoyed. To challenge the West and its culture, to rail at its leaders, would only increase that support. Farzad Bazoft's execution did not create the conditions for Saddam Hussein to confront the West, but it gave him an excuse to do so. And it showed him the potential benefits.

It is impossible to ignore the double standards which both Britain and the United States employed towards Iraq. Neither country liked Saddam Hussein, yet neither wanted to see the lucrative contracts it offered go to others. On 12 April 1990, Senator Robert Dole and five other American senators met Saddam Hussein in Mosul. They stressed the dangers of his chemical, nuclear and biological warfare capabilities, but in other ways their attitude was unpleasantly close to grovelling. They blamed many of the problems between their two countries on the American press, and made it clear they wanted further profitable grain contracts with Iraq, as most of them came from the states which produced grain. In the embarrassing transcript which the Iraqis later issued of the meeting there was of course no mention of Farzad Bazoft; but then he didn't hold an American passport.

Britain also found it hard to speak with one voice towards Saddam Hussein. Six months after condemning the chemical warfare attack on Halabje, Britain doubled the trade credits it was making available to Iraq. After the execution of Farzad the British ambassador was temporarily recalled, ministerial and trade visits cancelled, and six Iraqis on Ministry of Defence courses were sent home. That was all: there were no economic sanctions, no severing of diplomatic relations. Iraq was too valuable a market for Britain to relinquish. With the Americans and British prepared to put up with almost anything, and the Germans and the French prepared to sell him the most dangerous technology, Saddam Hussein was understandably contemptuous of the western democracies: as he said in one of his interviews during the crisis, western governments were really only interested in money. Everything else was just a slogan, which they didn't really mean. When, finally, they were serious he found it hard to believe them.

By the time I paid my first visit to Baghdad in May 1990, the pattern of confrontation was settled. There were daily demonstrations outside the British and American embassies complaining about the alliance the two countries had, according to the demonstrators, struck with Israel against Iraq. We drove up to the embassy and found the Association of Arab Lawyers marching towards it: neat gentlemen in lightweight suits who stopped politely at the embassy gate and handed in a message of complaint. In their view, said a spokesman in excellent English, it was a violation of human rights for Britain to withhold the technology Iraq required for its development. What technology was that? I asked. The technology to defend itself, said the lawyer, a little uncomfortably. He meant the barrels for the supergun (which Iraq denied was a gun of any kind) and the nuclear capacitors.

That evening our television report was censored as it was being satellited to London: I had referred to the fact that we were being followed everywhere we went. I did not mention that when our engineer tried to fix up the telephone for me to transmit a radio report to London he found ten different wires in the socket. Our Ministry of Information minder had worked with Farzad Bazoft and described him as a very bad man who caused a lot of problems. This no doubt explained why he was intensely nervous of us and kept asking me what we were planning to do next. When we went to the *souqs* to film, people looked through us as though we didn't exist. No one tried to get into conversation with us or sell us anything. Western journalists, it was clear, were dangerous. No one wanted to be associated with a spy. I felt like the carrier of some conspicuous, contagious disease. Wherever we went, men would slouch behind us, stopping when we stopped and moving on when we moved on. I came to recognize one or two of them and gave them a wave. It wasn't returned. In the hotel lobby, in the street, they were always there. In the privacy of our hotel rooms we sensed their presence.

Much to the nervousness of the omnipresent security men we stationed our camera at the entrance to the big new hall where Saddam's conference on international Muslim solidarity was taking place. It was an attractive hall in many ways. I discovered several months later that it was also one of the principal points of access to the main command bunker which lay deep under the roadway between the Foreign Ministry, the Al-Rasheed Hotel and the conference centre itself. People came streaming up the main access road towards the entrance to the hall and we stopped them one by one and asked them for their views.

Algerians, Palestinians, Egyptians, Sudanese, Pakistanis or Malaysians all believed the same thing: 'The West is trying to punish Iraq, because it has dared to raise its head.' 'The West doesn't want to see an Islamic, Arab nation showing its strength. It will do anything to stop it.' 'I am a Maronite Christian from Lebanon, but I want to say I support Iraq in its struggle.' 'Saddam Hussein is fighting a battle for us all. He is doing what every Muslim nation should do: stand up for itself, and attack Zionism. And of course he is suffering for it as a result.' Some of the delegates were hostile to us, but most were rational and pleasant enough. They had been excited by Saddam Hussein's threat that if Israel attacked Iraq he would burn half of Israel. His stand seemed to have a liberating effect on them: someone, at last, was saying the things they had always wanted a political leader to say. 'He is the new Nasser,' said an old, bent figure in spotless white, stopping by our camera and leaning on his carved walking stick as he talked. 'You will see. They destroyed Nasser, but they will not be able to destroy Saddam.' He flourished his stick at us jovially and hobbled into the conference.

When Saddam Hussein himself appeared, we were not

allowed to be there. We merely watched it on Iraqi television. It was a bravura performance which played on all these emotions in his audience. He roused them by talking angrily about the campaign against him in Britain and the United States and listed the elements in this campaign beginning with Farzad Bazoft and finishing with the seizure of the nuclear capacitors. Then came a moment of theatre which brought them to their feet, clapping and laughing and cheering. 'You see this?' He held a small metal object high in the air. 'This is what they're making all the fuss about. It's one of the things they call a capacitor. It looks rather like a lighter. They say it can be used for an atomic bomb. This is the American capacitor that they say Iraq has imported.' A pause, then he waved something else. 'And this is one that was made by our students at the technical university in only five days. This is the American one, and this is ours.' As he held the two objects up, there was a wild storm of applause, laughter and cheering. Iraq and, by extension, the Muslim world were on a par with the West. All that was required was to stand up for yourself.

It was a characteristic speech: full of unspecified threats and get-out clauses, denying on the one hand that Iraq had or wanted nuclear weapons, yet giving everyone in the hall the clear impression that it did want them and would be able to make them itself if necessary. 'We don't like talking too much,' he said, untruthfully, 'and we don't want to fight anyone else. But where there's no choice but to lose our Arab land and our rights, then we must fight.' That brought the loudest cheers of the entire occasion. His rhetoric was meant mostly to build up support for himself, but he was already showing signs of being trapped and pulled along by it. If the atmosphere of confront-ation provided him with such support, it stood to reason that the support would wane if he allowed the tension to relax. He had become a prisoner of the easy laugh, the vague promise, the uncritical standing ovation.

We were in Baghdad for a week. We worked hard and got some interesting pictures to take back with us to London and build up a short documentary on Saddam's growing mood of hostility. Then I made a mistake. I recorded an interview about the situation as it appeared in the streets of Baghdad and I felt obliged to talk about the surveillance and control which we saw all around us. That too was censored. 'You have been doing bad things,' someone from the Ministry of Information told us. We submitted all the video-cassettes we had shot to the Ministry for vetting. The process took a long time but it seemed to be a purely bureaucratic delay. We agreed in the end that the rest of us should leave on the appointed day and that the producer, Eamonn Matthews – who will appear again later in this story – would stay and argue for the release of the pictures.

Eamonn wasn't on the next plane out. There were problems, he told us over the phone. It sounded worrying. He had realized there was no hope of getting the cassettes out and had gone to the airport to catch the flight he was booked on. The Mukhabarat had picked him up in the departure lounge, just as they had picked up Farzad Bazoft. They held him for questioning for some time, then took him to a different hotel from the one where we had been staying. As they were walking into this new hotel, another group of security men brought out a Swedish businessman of Iraqi birth. He had been arrested for black-marketeering and was later executed.

Eamonn was escorted to the airport the following morning. They interrogated him roughly again. He was found to have $100 less than he could account for. When he arrived in London, hours later, he was still showing signs of the strain he had been under. We lost all our cassettes, not simply the mildly surreptitious filming we had done in the streets, but the long interviews with impeccably pro-Saddam delegates to the conference and the full rushes of the interview we had recorded with Nizar Hamdoun. I decided that it would be a long time before I went back to Baghdad. It had been altogether too close for comfort.

The Unloveable State

We wanted to tell our brothers in Bahrain and Kuwait that [Iranian] forces will be powerless to attack the sovereignty of any Arab land or people. As long as we are in a position to fight back, we shall do so. Iraq's geographical position may not enable it to place its armies to face the Zionist entity, but it is certainly capable of positioning its forces against any threat aimed at Bahraini or Kuwaiti sovereignty, and at the Gulf in general.

Saddam Hussein, interviewed in November 1979

Kuwait City is everything Baghdad is not: neat where Baghdad sprawls; tidy where Baghdad crumbles; small, educated and advanced where Baghdad struggles; extravagantly wealthy where Baghdad's money has been squandered on more than a decade of pointless warfare. If the people of Baghdad are essentially urban tenement dwellers, Kuwait's inhabitants are by instinct commuters from suburbia, living in carefully aligned square houses, two storeys high, each with its garden, its rose bushes and – where space and money allow – its swimming pool. A great deal of highly expensive city planning has gone into Kuwait. Its urban motorway system is as sophisticated as anything in Western Europe or the United States. Its appetite for construction has kept western and Middle Eastern architects and artists employed for three decades. Per capita income in Kuwait is approximately three times that of Iraq. When Kuwaiti gross domestic product is divided by citizenship rather than population, the figure is one of the highest on earth.

Kuwait is also the most unpopular of all the Arab states as

far as other Arabs are concerned. It employs people from throughout the Middle East and treats them all with an equal lack of esteem. 'Who said there are only two superpowers?' proclaimed the Kuwaiti foreign minister at a Gulf summit meeting in 1989. 'There are three – and Kuwait is the third.' It was, perhaps, meant as a joke. No one laughed. The people of Saudi Arabia, who are regarded as overbearing by the Arab world and beyond, themselves find the Kuwaitis arrogant.

Those Kuwaiti residents who were of traditional Kuwaiti stock – and who alone had the right to citizenship as the descendants of specified families living in the country in the 1920s – were rarely involved in directly productive activities, except as the locally-appointed directors without whom no business could legally operate. Most work in prewar Kuwait was done by expatriates. Europeans and Americans, Palestinians, Indians and Pakistanis carried out management and consultative tasks; Filipinos, Egyptians, Sri Lankans, Sudanese and Iraqis did the manual labour. The expatriates had no permanent right of abode, could never hope to achieve citizenship and had only limited rights in law. There is ample testimony that Kuwaitis were not regarded as good employers, firstly from a Filipino housekeeper:

They locked me in the house when they went out in the evenings. They said I had to look after everything. Once when I was ill they said 'No, you can't go to see the doctor. Who will look after the house? The doctor will come here.' But he never came.

An osteopath from southern Europe:

They said I was wonderful and did miracles. The wife – she was the one I told you about, who beat the old servant with a stick because she said he had been stealing – she said she would never let me go, that I must stay there always. I didn't like her but I liked her husband a lot. He was a gentleman. They promised me a Mercedes and a house of my own but they never gave them to me. In the end they even forgot to pay me, so I left the country. But I had to be careful when I got out. After all, they were al-Sabahs.

75

The wife of a British engineer:

> We were always trying to find Kuwaiti friends. We liked the
> place, and we certainly liked the money, and we thought, here
> we are – it's not right just seeing expats all the time, we've got to
> make some friends in the place itself. But honestly, every effort I
> made was repulsed. Sometimes they were really downright
> rude. I honestly think it was racist – they didn't think
> somebody European matched up to their standards.

A Palestinian doctor:

> I gave some of my best years to that place. I stayed on there
> when the Iraqis came. Partly it was because I had all my money
> there, but also I felt I had got a lot out of Kuwait, I should stay
> there when it's in trouble. I nearly starved there, and I helped
> everybody I could, even the Resistance. And then, when it was
> all over, they called me a filthy collaborator. I either had to get
> out or face the kind of threats they were making all the time.

Despite all this, Kuwait was a highly profitable place to be.
The economies of Jordan, the occupied West Bank, Egypt,
Sudan and Yemen all benefited considerably from the money
which their citizens working in Kuwait sent back home. No
one in Kuwait paid income tax. Housing, electricity, the
telephone service and water were all heavily subsidized by the
state. Some of the most important things – social security,
education, health – were free. Government salaries were high
and every time there was a recession the state would buy land
at inflated prices in order to pump its oil revenues back in the
economy.

This high level of state expenditure created problems during
the various economic downturns of the 1980s. While providing so much for so little, the Kuwaiti government was
always looking for ways to limit its munificence to fewer
people and to protect the longer term interests of the country.
Citizenship was defined so narrowly as to limit it to 1.2 million
people out of a total population of 3.45 million.

By the time of the Iraqi invasion Kuwait received rather
more of its income from overseas investment than from oil: a

shift from the semiproductive to the totally nonproductive. In 1976 a policy was introduced of setting aside 10 per cent of all state revenues to safeguard the standard of living of future generations. There was an intermittently intensive campaign to increase Kuwaiti self-sufficiency in food production. The Kuwait Investment Office, which had been based in London since the days when Kuwait had been a British possession and its oil wealth had been an important support for sterling, bought heavily into property in Britain when the market was depressed. It purchased Kiawah Island, off the Atlantic coast of the United States, in order to turn it into a holiday resort. Kuwaiti money bought a sizeable number of properties on the Champs-Elysées and Kuwait became the biggest foreign investor in Spain. The KIA purchased 22 per cent of the stock in the newly-privatized British Petroleum in 1987, but the British Government insisted the holding be reduced to below 10 per cent, much to the anger and hurt of the Kuwaitis themselves. Subsequently, also following signs of hostility in the United States to further Kuwaiti investment, the KIA directed its money more towards Western Europe in the years immediately preceding the Iraqi invasion.

The reaction in most western countries to the notion of being 'bought up by the Arabs' – which in practice usually meant the Kuwaitis – is instinctively hostile. Recently, however, it has been more restrained than during the period of the big oil price rises of 1973–5 when individual Arabs were the victims of physical or verbal attacks in the streets of New York and London. There was more than a tinge of racism to these attacks. Yet Kuwaitis often epitomized the type of Arab most disliked in the West: heavy-drinking, gambling, driving the most expensive cars and hiring the most expensive prostitutes. An entire industry grew up in London and Paris to service visiting Kuwaitis. The fact that the great majority who spent time in the West were peaceable, law-abiding and paid their bills on time did nothing to alter the stereotype.

As the 1980s wore on, the atmosphere in Kuwait itself changed. Fewer people took holidays to countries where they might not be welcome. Vast entertainment centres grew up to cater for them at home. More and more Kuwaitis built houses along the coast. It became fashionable for families to camp out in the desert, taking generators to operate the microwave ovens, the air conditioners and the video recorders. Having thoroughly destroyed the old Kuwait City, with its mud brick walls, its narrow streets and its *souqs*, most of which were swept away in the 1960s, the government unveiled a project before the invasion to build a replica of the old city in south Kuwait. The houses, instead of being large, unattractive boxes made of concrete and cooled by air-conditioning, were to be of mud brick and built around a central courtyard. The estimate was that it would cost nearly a billion dollars to recreate what had been pulled down three decades earlier.

For 200 years the al-Sabah family has governed Kuwait as a personal fiefdom, but not in the sense that the Ceausescus ran Romania or the Marcos family ran the Philippines. On the contrary, Kuwait has had the money to enrich all its citizens and the al-Sabahs made health care and university education possible for people who would never have obtained them elsewhere in the Middle East. Yet government has been a family business and a majority of ministers has always come from within its ranks. Partly as a result of this, life in Kuwait was heavily controlled. The war between the country's two big neighbours, Iran and Iraq, was used as an opportunity to close down the already restricted National Assembly and to impose tight censorship.

Before this Kuwait was the only Arab state in the Gulf to have an elected parliament. There are very few countries elsewhere in the world with so highly educated a population where civil liberties are as restricted as in Kuwait. The government often dealt fiercely with those of its citizens who criticized it. They could expect arrest, brutality, sometimes exile. It wasn't a police state, but it wasn't a free society either. A few weeks before the Iraqi invasion a man was arrested, taken to a police station and tied to a bench. Over a period of six hours a couple of policemen beat the soles of his feet with broomstick handles. All the bones in his feet were broken. The police did not deny having caused these injuries; they merely said he was suspected of having committed a crime and that they were trying to get him to confess. The man himself maintained that his crime had been to demand freedom of expression and a multiparty democracy. His feet were so badly damaged that he would never be able to walk again.

Even when the war between Iran and Iraq ended there was no loosening of control. At the end of 1989, the year of revolutions in so many countries with far less wealth and scope than Kuwait, a petition asking for the recall of the National Assembly was signed by 40 per cent of the country's voters, 25,000 people. The Emir, Shaikh Jaber al-Ahmad al-Jaber al-Sabah, played for time until a series of demonstrations, not all of which passed off peacefully, obliged him and his prime minister, the Crown Prince, to come up with some proposals of their own. These were made public in April 1990. One third of the 75 members were to be appointed, not elected, and the National Assembly's main function would be 'to study the reasons for the problems which arise between the executive and legislative arms of government, in order to find ways of avoiding them in future'.

Unlike the more nervous rulers of the United Arab Emirates, the al-Sabahs possess admirable self-assurance. As owners of 10 per cent of the world's oil reserves they knew they could count on diplomatic and, even, military support from the United States and Britain, as well as other countries; yet the confidence seemed to come from within. The Emir may not have been an arrogant man himself. He lived in moderate style and occasionally wandered round the city in disguise. But what seemed to be arrogance in his subjects was transmuted by him into considerable toughness. After the outbreak of terrorism in Kuwait in 1983, he consistently refused to give in to the blackmail of kidnapping and hijacking. Seventeen Shi'i fundamentalists who had been gaoled for earlier attacks remained in prison in spite of two hijackings, one in 1984 and one in 1988. In the second, three members of the al-Sabah family were held prisoner, but the Emir did not give way. Neither would he allow Terry Waite, the Archbishop of Canterbury's envoy, to come to Kuwait to discuss the possibility of exchanging western hostages being held in Lebanon for them. There was an attempt on the Emir's life in 1985 when a suicide bomber crashed a car into his motorcade. Other acts of terrorism, seemingly the work of Iranian agents or sympathizers, continued until the ceasefire between Iran and Iraq in July 1988.

The end of the war came as a huge relief to Kuwait. For eight years it had subordinated everything to the need to keep itself secure from the two belligerents, especially Iran. It had supported Iraq solidly and loyally throughout the conflict, joining the other Arab states in giving financial and diplomatic help. With the war over it became possible for Kuwait to expand its economy again. It was already producing an average of just under 2 million barrels of oil a day and at the 1989 OPEC summit it negotiated a formal increase in its quota in order to regularize the position. The other members of OPEC were not enthusiastic, but since Kuwait's real production was already well over its agreed quota there was little that could be done.

At this same summit the Iraqi delegate expressed reservations about Kuwait's behaviour, but not in particularly strong terms. Kuwait's oil revenues for the first half of 1989 rose by more than 50 per cent compared with the first half of 1988. The government celebrated by raising the wages of all state employees and significantly increasing public expenditure. There cannot have been a single person in the entire country who thought that within a year this would have become Saddam Hussein's excuse for invading Kuwait and turning it into Iraq's nineteenth province.

When in 1914 the British established a protectorate over the country, the state of Kuwait was little more than a port with a desert hinterland. Its borders could scarcely have been less precisely defined. In 1923 Britain's political agent in the country, Major More, marked the frontier between Iraq and Kuwait by putting up a noticeboard in the desert, approximately one mile south of the most southerly palm tree at Safwan. In 1939 it was discovered that Iraqi police patrols had moved the board and the political agent of the day was told to replace it. He did so, but moved it several hundred yards into Iraqi territory. The Iraqi police moved it again. By 1946 the picture was further complicated by the realization that there was a new southernmost palm tree at Safwan: the Iraqis had planted some more.

In this featureless desert, the absence of any precision about the border had always been troublesome. In the 1913 Anglo-Ottoman Gulf settlement the line, such as it was, was defined by a red semicircle, 40 miles in radius from Kuwait City. This included the islands of Warba and Bubiyan, little more than large sandbanks. Under the same agreement a green line marked the rather wider area where the al-Sabahs could levy tribute. In December 1922 Sir Percy Cox, British high commissioner in Baghdad and stepfather to the new country of Iraq, recommended that the border with Kuwait should now be drawn with precision. The British high commissioner in Baghdad and the British political agent in Kuwait agreed it between them, but it was still vague, based as it was on palm trees and noticeboards.

In 1932 the British Colonial Office decided it was necessary as part of Iraq's request to join the League of Nations that it could show its frontiers were well defined. Iraq was unhappy with the position as it was and the government in Baghdad openly advocated the annexation of Kuwait. Iraq wanted to improve its access to the waters of the Gulf and believed that Britain had deliberately used its powers to define the border as a way of cutting down on Iraqi ambitions. (A Kuwaiti government minister, years later, likened Iraq to 'a big garage with a very small door'.) This does not seem to have been the case. The British, having a responsibility to Kuwait as well as to Iraq, seem rather to have created a compromise between them. However, a combination of vague wording in the 1932 delineation and the absence of good maps compounded the problem.

In 1938 the Iraqi foreign minister repudiated the division outlined six years earlier, arguing that Kuwait belonged by right to Iraq and should now be incorporated into its territory. Britain rejected this on the basis of the Treaties of Sèvres and Lausanne in 1920 and 1923 respectively, by which Turkey formally gave up its claims to former Ottoman territory. The argument reverted to one over border lines, with such definitions as:

> The 'point just south of the latitude of Safwan' shall be the point on the *thalweg* [depression] of the Batin due west of the point a little to the south of Safwan at which the post and noticeboard marking the frontier stood until March 1939.

During the mid-1950s it seemed as though the two countries might agree to a demarcation which was favourable to Iraq. Under this, Kuwait would have granted Iraq a 99-year lease over the most northerly part of its territory, together with the island of Warba. Iraq was to guarantee supplies of fresh water to Kuwait in exchange. At the last moment the Emir rejected the idea, worried that by abandoning control over his country's water supplies – especially to a state which had in the past claimed the right to annex Kuwait – he was providing a future government in Baghdad with a powerful instrument of blackmail. Indeed, if Saddam Hussein had had such an instrument, he would undoubtedly have used it in July or August 1990.

In 1973 there was still no proper agreement on the border when the Iraqis carried out a brief attack on the Kuwaiti border post of al-Samta, resulting in the deaths of two Kuwaiti frontier guards. Baghdad's attention then shifted to the issue of the islands, particularly Warba. From this time onwards the Kuwaitis became increasingly defensive about the islands and border points and many shops, cafés, businesses and oil tankers were named 'Warba', 'Bubiyan' and 'al-Samta'.

Any further attempts to resolve the problem came to a halt during Iraq's war with Iran, though the subject was raised by Kuwait within days of the conflict ending. Ever since the 1970s Iraq had claimed that Kuwait had effectively shifted its borders northwards by moving its chief customs post from the Mutla ridge to Abdaly, 75 kilometres to the north but still just inside the internationally-recognized border on the road from Basra to Kuwait City. This was patently untrue, but the Kuwaitis had undoubtedly encroached by a matter of a few hundred yards at certain points along the border. However trivial it might seem,

Iraq's heightened notion of national sovereignty and Kuwait's determined refusal to give way ensured that bad blood would persist between them.

Ever since its creation after World War I, Iraq had always had a general feeling – for most of the time nothing more than that – that it ought to own Kuwait. It was not an equivalent conviction to, say, Spain's claim to Gibraltar, or Argentina's claim to the Falkland Islands, or Jordan's claim to the Occupied West Bank. Text books in Iraqi schools did not teach children that Kuwait was a natural part of Iraq. Maps printed in Iraq showed a clear border between the two and listed Kuwait as a separate entity. President Saddam Hussein himself, as the quotation at the head of this chapter shows, referred to Kuwaiti sovereignty as something that had to be defended against outside attack. He did not sound like a man preparing the ground for a merger at some later stage. Nevertheless there had been a general, unfocussed sentiment among Iraqis that, if justice were done, then Kuwait would belong to them.

Before the establishment of British protectorate status, Kuwait nominally belonged to the Ottoman Empire, like the rest of the region. The Ottoman Empire, however, was a languid affair. Its rulers did not bestir themselves to put their stamp on every single territory they owned. Kuwait was supposedly run from Basra, but Basra let Kuwait go its own way. In 1752 the leaders of the nomadic tribes who inhabited the area chose Shaikh Sabah to be their leader. When he died, his youngest son was elected to succeed him: a pattern, and a dynasty, had been established. There were pressures from the interior – what is now Saudi Arabia – but in the nineteenth century Kuwait established itself as a thriving port with its own fleet of *dhows* trading all along the northern and southern coasts of the Gulf and into the Indian Ocean. A considerable pearling industry also developed.

In 1871, Turkey gave the al-Sabah of the day the title of provincial governor after he had committed troops to a joint expedition. The intention, however, was to ward off British influence, not to incorporate Kuwait into the Ottoman Empire. Twenty-five years later Mubarak, the greatest and most extrovert head of what has historically been an intro-verted and unobtrusive dynasty, came to power determined to safeguard Kuwait's independence by allying his country with Britain. After initial reluctance the British changed their minds. In 1898, at almost the very moment when Lord Curzon, the 38-year-old advocate of imperial expansion and the protection of the route to India, was appointed India's Viceroy, Turkey granted a Russian company the right to build a railway from the Mediterranean to the Gulf, passing through Baghdad and terminating at Kuwait.

Curzon was obsessed with the Russian threat to India from the northwest. This development seemed to present a new angle of attack. The government of Lord Salisbury took up Mubarak al-Sabah's offer of an agreement with some speed. Just as it did so, a German company approached the Ottomans with a rival proposal to extend the Berlin-Constantinople railway to Baghdad and Kuwait. The British felt the agreement with Mubarak came just in time and it took control of Kuwait's foreign policy. Nothing more was heard of either railway proposal.

Following the terms of the agreement Kuwait's borders were delineated in 1913 after negotiations between Britain and Turkey, though the settlement was never ratified. After World War I the creation of an independent Saudi Arabia and Iraq meant that the borders had to be renegotiated with these new states. Britain, having called them into existence, found itself having to protect Iraq from the increasing power of Saudi Arabia. Sir Percy Cox, the British high commissioner in Baghdad, imposed a solution under which Kuwait became the double loser: part of its land was allocated to Iraq and part to Saudi Arabia.

The interwar years were largely taken up with disputes between Britain and the United States about access to Kuwaiti oil which were settled in Britain's favour. Eventually, however, the terms would favour Kuwait's future development. By the 1950s there was genuine nationalist demand for independence from Britain, heightened by the 1956 Suez campaign. By 1960 the Macmillan government in Britain decided that the best way to ensure that sterling would continue to have the support of Kuwaiti oil resources was to give Kuwait effective independence. Britain undertook to defend Kuwait from attack if requested to do so.

Between the wars Iraq had often stated its claim to sovereignty over Kuwait and the Baghdad press now returned again and again to the subject. Yet not even the succession of military régimes in the late 1930s and early 1940s had envisaged doing anything about it. Directly the agreement between Britain and Kuwait was cancelled and Kuwait became fully independent on 19 June 1961, the claim was renewed. Six days later President Abdul Karim Qassem, who had seized power in 1958 when the royal family were murdered, declared that Kuwait had always been part of Basra province under the Ottomans and that it must now therefore belong to the successor state, Iraq. It was unclear whether Qassem planned to invade Kuwait, but the Emir, Shaikh Abdallah al-Salem al-Sabah, appealed to Britain for support under the new friendship treaty.

The first British troops arrived within 48 hours and eventually numbered 8000. By August they were replaced by a much smaller force from four Arab League countries: the United Arab Republic (made up of Syria and Egypt), Jordan, Saudi Arabia and Sudan. Qassem was overthrown in February 1963 and the threat to Kuwait was over. The following October the new régime in Baghdad recognized Kuwait's independence. The régime was to change its political make-up the following month by a coup-within-the-coup; but when it accepted the existence of Kuwait as a sovereign country it was still Baathist.

For the following 27 years the Baath Party does not appear to have made any formal mention of Iraq's claim to Kuwait. In the official handbook *Iraq 1990* – the year when Saddam Hussein incorporated Kuwait into Iraq on precisely the historical basis declared by President Qassem in June 1961 – there is no mention whatever of the claim. The handbook is expensively produced and occupied the efforts of the Ministry of Information in Baghdad for months. Great care went into preparing the historical section. (History in Baathist Iraq can be as sensitive as it was in the Soviet Union before glasnost.) However, in the passage about the Ottoman empire there is no reminder that the province of Basra had once included Kuwait. The references to the creation of an independent Iraq are equally bland:

> Britain exploited the issue of demarcating Iraq's borders as a bargaining chip to serve its interests, particularly exploration for oil. In 1932 the League of Nations admitted Iraq to its membership and ended the British mandate. The pre-independence period was marked with the desire to establish Iraq's borders and complete its institutions.

The only mention of Kuwait is in the section on Iraq's geographical position, where it is simply listed as one of the states bordering Iraq. There was no careful, slow preparation for the forcible integration of Kuwait into Iraq. Indeed, there was no preparation of any kind.

Within months of the publication of the Kuwaitless *Iraq 1990*, the Ministry of Information produced a booklet entitled *Kuwait – Historical Background* intended to give the evidence for Saddam Hussein's claim that Kuwait had always been an integral part of Iraq. The booklet was obviously put together in a hurry. It is expensively yet poorly produced, and has not been properly proofread. Above all, the details of the claim are rambling and inconsequential:

> Lorimer ['Gazetteer of the Gulf, Oman and Central Arabia', 1981] admitted in 1775 [sic] that he considered Kuwait as part of Basra. It is known that Lorimer relied on documents of the British East India Company.
>
> In 1876, Major Bride and the British Commissioner said that Kuwait, Qatif and Aqir were Turkish ports on the Gulf.
>
> In 1911, the Ottoman Government honoured Mubarak [al-Sabah] with the Majidi medal of the first class.

Moving from one vague assertion to another, missing out

points which might have suited Iraq's case better, the booklet settles down to the more congenial business of attacking the al-Sabahs for 'Subervience [sic] to Imperialism' ('In 1914 a charitable institution was set up in India . . . to raise money to help the wounded in the British army which took part in occupying Iraq. Mubarak [al-Sabah] contributed with 50 thousand Rupees') and 'Aggressive Attitudes that Harm Iraqis and the Arabs' ('Mubarak al-Sabah also sent a telegram to the British Government congratulating her on the advance of British troops on Baghdad in 1917').

To justify action which would lead to the deaths of hundreds of thousands and uproot millions before it was over, Iraq produced in evidence a medal, a charitable donation and a telegram of courtesy. The haste and inattention in the way the claim is presented matched the more general haste and inattention with which Saddam Hussein and his government approached the invasion. It had all the hallmarks of something done on the spur of the moment, almost on a personal whim.

The Whim of Iron

A law is a piece of paper on which we write one or two lines and sign underneath it, 'Saddam Hussein, President of the Republic'.

Saddam Hussein speaking on Iraqi television, 1980

As the spring of 1990 gave way to summer, Saddam Hussein's sense of being caught in a trap intensified. As he saw it, Israel was preparing for an attack on Iraq while the British and Americans were combining to prevent him from importing the technology he required to defend himself. Worse, Iraq's economic problems were intensified by Kuwait's decision to produce more than its OPEC oil quota, lowering the value of Iraqi oil exports.

Slowly, Kuwait became the focus for much of Saddam Hussein's anger and frustration. During his war with Iran he had relied heavily on money and assistance from both Kuwait and Saudi Arabia, perhaps amounting to $15 billion each year for eight years, a rough total of $120 billion. Three-quarters of that was provided by the Saudis, the remaining $40 billion coming from Kuwait. Part of Kuwait's loans had been in oil, some of it from the southern Rumailah field that lay in Kuwaiti territory which Iraq largely claimed. There was no pressure on Iraq to pay these debts, but while the Saudis were prepared to commute a good proportion of them to outright gifts, the Kuwaitis were not. Saddam did not forget this. He took such things personally.

From this point on, the most important events all took place within the narrow confines of Saddam Hussein's office. The history of the crisis becomes the history of Saddam's growing anger and frustration. The best political intelligence available indicates that there was no plan, no blue-print; that, as always, he moved from one position to the next on the basis of instinct and feeling, with no one to hold him back. Most international crises are the result of interacting forces and influences: this time the overriding force was Saddam Hussein's personality.

Absolute power can have something of the same effect as enormous wealth: it frequently leads its possessor to hide from the world. Stalin lived and worked in a couple of rooms in the Kremlin or in his small dacha; Ceausescu indulged himself and his family, insulated from Romania's poverty by secret police; Kim Il Sung leads the life of a recluse in North Korea. This was never Saddam Hussein's way. He was an extrovert who enjoys parading in front of his people. He is vain about his appearance, one reason why his picture was on display everywhere. Towards the end of the war with Iran he ordered the entire nation to diet and exercise, even publishing the weight of his ministers in the newspapers. They had instructions to keep their stomachs as trim as his. It was one of the clichés of Iraqi political life that women were strong supporters of Saddam because of his virile good looks. Even though he was still a young man by the standards of international politics, his public portraits usually kept a few years behind the original.

He selected the pictures of himself that he wanted to appear in the following day's newspapers. His personal photographer, Hussein Mohammed Ali, a large, gloomy man with a Clark Gable moustache and a taste for double-breasted suits with plenty of shoulder padding, had worked with him continuously since 1970. Every afternoon he would spread out the day's contact sheets and Saddam went through them with him. If the President hadn't appeared in public or met anyone of importance that day, the newspapers merely chose a stock shot from their library. During the crisis the same picture was used day after day. No newspaper appeared without a photograph of the President on its front page.

Saddam Hussein was also a role-player. Iraq's long history

provided him with large numbers of incarnations to adopt, from Hammurabi the Lawgiver to King Faysal I, whose horseback statue he had placed in the redeveloped centre of Baghdad. The roles he found congenial were the great builders and achievers of Mesopotamian history. I walked bemusedly through the ancient ruins of Babylon during my first visit to Iraq. 'From Nebuchadnezzar to Saddam Hussein', said a poster in the gift shop, 'Babylon Invokes Its Glories'. The southern palace, where the Hanging Gardens had once been, was completely rebuilt by Saddam, the new Nebuchadnezzar.

The place was entirely empty, just yellow brick walls 25 feet high crowned by fantastic machicolations. There was no roof. It was also silent and when the pigeons were disturbed and burst into the air the noise was alarming. An occasional group of Vietnamese nurses would giggle as they took each other's photograph beside the crude statue of a lion straddling a prone victim: a representation of the curiously sexual power of ancient Babylon. A single *agent provocateur* lurked out of sight, darting forward to try to persuade the unwary into buying a Babylonian cylinder seal of clay, a serious crime which would render the purchaser liable to a prison sentence or (no doubt) heavy blackmail from the vendor.

There was something not quite right at the base of one of the walls. I went over to inspect it. The tidy new brickwork gave way to three courses at ground level which were crude and irregular. They proved to be the original mud bricks of Babylon and in the bright new reconstruction they looked badly out of place. It requires a special brand of self-confidence to take a major archeological site like Babylon and rebuild it – against the advice of the country's more courageous archaeologists – along the lines of an uncompleted supermarket. Saddam Hussein of Iraq does not lack self-confidence. At irregular intervals, inscribed bricks appeared in the new walls:

In the Name of the Victorious Saddam Hussein, President of the Republic, Protector of the Great Iraq and the Renewer of its Civilization, this Palace – built by King Nebuchadnezzar II, who reigned from 605 to 563 before the modern era – has been rebuilt at different stages, the second ending in 1986.

On a hill overlooking the ancient palace a new palace was going up, bigger in conception than anything in Baghdad. We were asked not to point our camera in that direction. The new Nebuchadnezzar was planning the grandest of all his residences – like Nicolae Ceausescu, he has one in every province of the country – and the rumour was that when it was completed he would make his permanent home here. It didn't sound likely. Saddam is not a man to hide himself away in the provinces. He wants the kind of attention he can only get in a capital city.

If Saddam based his architectural ideas on Nebuchadnezzar's, he constructed his self-image along the lines of an early Abbasid Caliph. Just as al-Mansour and Haroun al-Rasheed held open court where their subjects could seek redress for injustice, so Saddam nurtured the fantasy that anyone could approach him. In the early 1980s an American correspondent visited Baghdad and was given an interview with Saddam. With the necessary degree of caution, he approached the question of human rights. Wasn't it true that people lived in considerable fear in Iraq? Saddam, visibly irritated, asked him where he had heard this. The correspondent, greatly daring, mentioned Amnesty International. There was an explosion of rage and the correspondent thought he was a dead man.

'Come with me. I want to show you something,' Saddam shouted. He grabbed the correspondent by the arm and pulled him, scarcely resisting, into the palace courtyard where several Range-Rovers stood, together with a number of Saddam's personal bodyguards. The correspondent was certain he was going to be shot, but Saddam yelled an order and jumped into the driving seat of one of the Range-Rovers, indicating to the correspondent to get in. The bodyguards threw themselves into the escort cars as Saddam roared out of the courtyard, tyres screaming. They drove at speed towards the centre of Baghdad, while cars and frightened policemen pulled out of their way.

Eventually the motorcade came to Rasheed Street and Saddam screeched to a halt. The other Range-Rovers slithered into place behind him and the bodyguards threw themselves out and gathered around. He pushed them impatiently aside

91

and lunged into the crowd of passersby who were too shocked to make their escape. The American correspondent watched as Saddam settled on one unfortunate and pushed his swagger stick into the man's chest: 'This foreign journalist thinks I'm unpopular in Iraq. What do you say to that?' The man said everything he could possibly think of: how everybody loved and respected Saddam, how he was the only leader who could keep the country together, how he had made everybody wealthy. Saddam nodded approvingly. At length the swagger stick was removed from the man's chest. 'You see?' said Saddam to the journalist. 'Of course the people love me.' He laughed uproariously and jumped back into the Range-Rover. The interview continued as before.

Just as Haroun al-Rasheed secretly wandered the *souqs* of Baghdad to discover and act upon the complaints of his subjects, Saddam Hussein liked to descend on towns and villages without warning to show himself among his people. On the spur of the moment – partly for security reasons and partly because this was how he did everything anyway – he would head out into the countryside. Often the local Mukhabarat would have only half-an-hour's warning. One such meeting was shown on Iraqi television late in 1990. Saddam descended on the house of a half-blind villager who had been a soldier in the period before the royal family was overthrown. Saddam was acting out an Abbasid convention in which the old man was supposed not to recognize who the visitor was. In spite of the army of bodyguards, the fleet of Mercedes escorted by armoured personnel carriers, in spite of the two camera crews in military uniform, the old man stuck faithfully to the fiction that this was just any visitor asking questions of him.

Saddam (*squatting down in front of him*): Is your old age pension big enough for your needs?

Old Man: Yes, thank you sir. Nowadays it's much bigger than it used to be and we count ourselves very lucky.

Saddam: Who was it that raised the level of your pension? Who do you have to thank for that?

Old Man: Why, our leader, President Saddam Hussein, of

course. We're very grateful indeed for everything he's done for us, I can tell you.

Wife (*appearing suddenly from house, ululating*): Look who it is, husband! Don't you recognize him?

Old Man (*startled*): Me? No! Who is it, then?

Wife: It's our wonderful president, Saddam Hussein himself, that's who!

Old Man (*shouting and crying*): Oh God! Let me kiss your hand, sir.

And so on for about half an hour. This was the lead story on that evening's news bulletin, which in consequence lasted for an hour and three-quarters.

Saddam Hussein's activities were always the lead item and the report tended to last as long as the event itself, since no one wanted to edit anything the President said or did. As for the meeting with the old man, it takes an unusually high degree of self-regard to want to stage a scene with dialogue like this, especially when it is so corny and transparent. The President's officials maintained that things had to be kept simple in a country with so many peasants, yet all the peasants I have come across in Iraq are perfectly well aware of the realities of life, including the possibility that if Saddam descends upon them they have to play to his lead with all the apparent sincerity they can muster.

Before the war over Kuwait a large proportion of each night's television was about Saddam Hussein (it lessened slightly after the war, when his unpopularity could no longer be ignored). There was always a strong personality cult around Saddam but it intensified in 1982 when Ayatollah Khomeini challenged Saddam's political legitimacy by pointing out that whereas the President of Iran was elected by a majority of the people in a moderately free – though highly restricted – vote, Saddam was completely unelected. Saddam's response was not to hold elections but to organize a Day of Allegiance. On 11 November 1982 the Mukhabarat and the Baath party exerted all their efforts to get people out, and 11 million supposedly took to the streets to show their love for their President.

Following the Day of Allegiance a kind of variety programme was introduced. Each night on television until the war with the Allies began in 1991, crooners would sing his praises and poets would declaim verses in his honour:

> All evil people fear your sword, Saddam.
> It has already been tested.
> You are the Father of good things,
> And with you we will challenge
> All the aggressors who have built up their power.
> We beg God to keep you well and happy,
> And to maintain your appearance
> Shining on us all the time,
> So we can have pride in you
> Above all others.

There was no one to suggest to Saddam Hussein that his personality cult might have gone a little over the top. On the other hand he did occasionally listen to advice or complaint. In 1983 he visited a village where the farmers complained about the creation of a local cooperative: he declared it abolished, then and there. In 1983 he even listened to the pleading of two of his generals who said that his personal conduct of the war against Iran was costing dangerously large numbers of men and would end in Iraq's defeat. Although the generals succeeded in persuading him to hand back control to the military men, they suffered for their boldness.

Essentially, though, prior to the invasion of Kuwait Saddam governed Iraq alone. President Turgut Ozal of Turkey said presciently when the Kuwaiti crisis arose that the most difficult thing about dealing with Saddam would be his lack of advisers: there was no one who could be contacted quietly nor influenced, no channel through whom it would be possible to pass messages. Saddam was President of the country, chairman of the Revolution Command Council, prime minister, secretary general of the Baath Party and commander-in-chief of the armed forces. In all but name he was as absolute a monarch as history could show.

The highest governing body in Iraq before the invasion was the Revolution Command Council, constructed roughly along the lines of a Politburo in a Marxist-Leninist state. Each time it met, Saddam's military camera crews would film the occasion

94

and the silent pictures would be broadcast that night on television, dubbed with music by Vivaldi or Bach. The members would stand as Saddam, dressed in his olive-green party uniform, came in and sat down.

Half the high-backed chairs at the table were always empty. The Revolution Command Council had begun life with seven members after the 1968 coup and had then moved steadily upwards to 12. Inexorably, as accidents – or what seemed like accidents – befell some of its members and others were eased out less violently, the number fell. Somehow, though, the chairs remained, each of them as accusingly empty as Banquo's place at Macbeth's feast.

Violent things had happened in the past at Revolution Command Council meetings. When Saddam was vice-president, he and Hardan al-Takriti, the defence minister, had pulled their guns on one another during an argument in 1970 about Iraq's failure to help the Palestinians during Jordan's Black September. Nine years later, when he became President, Saddam held the families of eight members of the Revolution Command Council hostage while he forced its members to vote and sign documents as he demanded. All eight were then shot, together with many of their relatives. Nothing like that ever happened nowadays. The Council members became totally subservient to Saddam's will, their only function being to agree with him and to work out how to put his wishes into effect.

The Council members were a strange group: Saddam's deputy, the tall and painfully-thin Izzat Ibrahim, with his bright red hair and undertaker's manner; Taha Yasin Ramadan, a close associate of Saddam's since the 1960s; Tariq Aziz, the foreign minister, a Christian yet a profound national-ist whose jovial appearance belied an alarming temper. Only Ramadan appeared to have the personality to be a leader rather than a follower of orders and, since that was the most dangerous characteristic to possess in Saddam's Iraq, he obeyed orders as enthusiastically as the rest.

I was in the coffee shop of the Sheraton Hotel in Baghdad in

May 1990 when there was an announcement over the intercom. The people around me, mostly delegates to the Islamic conference, burst into spontaneous applause. What was it? I asked my neighbour. Saudi Arabia, he told me, had just announced it would attend the Arab League summit which Saddam Hussein had offered to host in Baghdad at the end of the month. It seemed a clear diplomatic victory for Iraq.

The ostensible purpose of the summit was to condemn the large-scale emigration of Jews from the Soviet Union to Israel. Saddam, however, was planning to use it as part of his diplomatic counterattack to the international conspiracy he believed he had detected. By now he appears to have been certain in his own mind that it involved the Gulf states, the US, Britain and Israel and that the aim was to sabotage the Iraqi economy.

In January 1990 Iraq had announced it would devote $9 billion to reconstruction that year and between $4 and $5 billion for debt repayment. After the plans had been announced, it became clear that the oil price was dropping alarmingly because of overproduction by Kuwait and the United Arab Emirates. Government ministers began to realize that as well as being unable to carry out their spending plans, the country wouldn't have enough money to import all its basic needs. A number of ministers began to share Saddam's view that the economy was being deliberately undermined. The Arab League summit was part of his attempt to fight back. Its aim was to recruit Arab support for his case, and to isolate Kuwait and the UAE in the hope of forcing them to reduce output. The United States sent Saddam a message through its ambassador, April Glaspie, requesting him in moderate terms to avoid insulting attacks on American policy during the summit. Saddam made the details of the request public and attacked American policy as well.

King Hussein of Jordan had never liked Saddam Hussein personally and had opposed Iraq on various issues in the past. Now, though, the King felt he had no alternative but to back him. Virtually all of Jordan's oil came from Iraq at preferential rates and he couldn't afford to lose those supplies. He also believed – or claimed to believe – that Israel was planning to strike at Iraq through his territory. On both counts, supporting Iraq was a necessary form of self-protection. At the summit he criticized the West for what he called its campaign against Saddam and drew the line almost as clearly as Saddam himself between those Arab leaders who supported him and those who did not.

The Palestine Liberation Organization also supported Saddam. The United States had recently cut its links with the PLO, which found itself uncomfortably isolated after making some delicate compromises over its attitude to Israel. The PLO leadership believed the best way to oblige the US to negotiate with it again was to take a harder line on other Middle Eastern questions, so it naturally swung behind Saddam Hussein when his dispute with the West came to a head.

At the summit in May King Hussein did some of the talking on Iraq's behalf. As the summit's host, Saddam could not always be quite so open. Saddam provided the invective against Israel, a safe enough subject; the King took on the pro-Western states around the table. In particular he challenged the Gulf states to help his own country and Iraq now that they were both facing danger from Israel. The leaders of the Gulf states sat there, stony-faced and embarrassed, and said nothing. Given the climate of suspicion it wasn't hard for Saddam Hussein at the head of the table to believe that they were acting on American and British instructions. At the end of the summit Kuwait, whose overproduction had depressed oil prices while increasing its own revenues by half and paying nothing to help Iraq, was clearly singled out:

> Wars can be started by armies, and great damage is done through bombing, through killing, or attempted coups. But at other times a war can be launched by economic means. To those countries which do not really intend to wage war against Iraq, I have to say that this is itself a kind of war against Iraq.

In speaking like this, Saddam showed that by the end of May 1990 he had already identified Kuwait as an enemy. It was in a position to help him and yet it was refusing to do so: for him, that was enough. The worse Iraq's economic position became, the more intensely Saddam felt deserted by Kuwait and the more determined he was to force it to do what he wanted. Iraq, Foreign Minister Tariq Aziz claimed, had protected the countries of the Gulf and Kuwait in particular from the dangers of Iranian fundamentalism. To do so had cost Iraq dear and the help Kuwait had provided had been nothing like enough to pay its debt.

Eight years of war against Iran had done terrible damage to the Iraqi economy. Iraq's earnings from oil in 1989 were roughly $13 billion. Its expenditure that year was approximately $24 billion. Foreign debt stood at $80 billion. There was an urgent need to begin the task of reconstruction, but that, western economists estimated, would take 20 years, even if the entire national oil income was devoted to it. The cost of the war which Saddam Hussein had casually launched against Iran in 1980 on the assumption that it would last four or five days, was almost incalculable. Now it seemed about to wreck the country's entire future.

Throughout June the dispute continued, as Iraq waited for the Kuwaitis to make some offer of help. None came. The Emir was mostly concerned with patching up diplomatic relations with Iran, having supported Iraq throughout the war. Knowing that he had the support of Saudi Arabia and the United States, he showed no sign of giving in to Saddam's demands, just as he had always refused to give in to the demands of the Shi'i fundamentalist groups when they hijacked planes and carried out bombings.

Saddam had no alternative but to press on with his demand. In June 1990, anger over Kuwaiti overproduction led to a specific demand: the Revolution Command Council agreed that Kuwait should be asked for an amount of money equivalent to the income from the oil wells at Ratga, the Kuwaiti end of the large Rumailah oilfield which straddled the border between Iraq and Kuwait. There is in fact some question as to whether Ratga, which lies a few kilometres from the Iraqi border, really is an extension of the Rumailah field as the geological structure is uncertain. But if the experts were unsure, the Revolution Command Council was not. It maintained that the oil from Ratga had been stolen by Kuwait, since by right the entire area belonged to Iraq.

Typically, Iraq had done nothing to prepare the ground for this. Kuwait, as its finance minister pointed out the month after the invasion, had been taking an average of 10,000 barrels of oil a day from Ratga since the late 1970s, yet Iraq had never previously advanced any claims. Day by day, hour by hour, Saddam Hussein was making up his strategy as he went along.

The Rumailah claim represented an important new stage in the crisis, though Saddam himself may well not have realized it. From now on, if Kuwait refused to help Iraq financially, the logical next step would be for Iraq to claim land in lieu of money.

The best information in Baghdad is that until 17 July at the earliest Saddam Hussein had no thought of invading Kuwait. On 16 July Foreign Minister Tariq Aziz came out with the accusation that Kuwait had deliberately engineered a lower price for oil in order to damage the Iraqi economy. This strategy, according to Aziz, had begun as early as 1981 and had cost the Arab world as a whole $500 billion in revenue. Iraq's share of this loss in income he estimated with remarkable precision at $89 billion. The oil 'stolen' from Iraq in the Rumailah oilfield was worth $2.4 billion. The conviction that Kuwait, with Saudi and American encouragement, was out to damage Iraq was reinforced by the interception of a telephone conversation on 9 July between King Fahd of Saudi Arabia and the ruler of Qatar, one of the United Arab Emirates, about the increase in Kuwait's production and the serious effect it would have on Iraq's economy. The purpose, according to Saddam Hussein later, was to 'disturb the relationship existing between the [Iraqi] people and their leadership'.

Ever since the end of the war with Iran, the Saudis – like the Israelis and the Americans – were worried that Iraq would now be too powerful. In the version of the phone call as made public later by Iraq, King Fahd indicated that he would back Kuwait diplomatically and financially if Kuwait produced more oil than its OPEC quota, thus lowering the oil price and cutting the value of Iraq's own oil production.

The 17 July was critical. It was the anniversary of the Baathist seizure of power in 1968 and as usual Saddam marked it with a speech on television. He took Tariq Aziz's argument of the previous day a stage further. If Kuwait had deliberately robbed Iraq, it was because there was a conspiracy between Kuwait and the United Arab Emirates on the one hand and imperialism and Zionism on the other. Iraq wouldn't, he said, put up with this situation much longer. It was better to be dead than lose the means of earning a living. Then he made the threat which formed the basis of Iraq's invasion 16 days later:

If words do not give us sufficient protection, then we will have no option but to take effective action to put things right and ensure that our rights are restored.

According to political analysts in Baghdad, Saddam did not envisage a full-scale invasion at this stage. He hoped this vague threat would be enough to make the Kuwaitis give in and agree to help with Iraq's serious economic situation. If it did not quite achieve that, then it could oblige the other oil-producing countries to fix a more favourable price. Failing all this, he would be obliged to take the effective action he had hinted at: the seizure of the part of the Rumailah oilfield that lay in Kuwaiti territory and the establishment of his troops along the line of Mutla Ridge, a third of the way down the map of Kuwait. Perhaps, too, he would take the opportunity of putting his men onto the islands of Warba and Bubiyan which Iraq had long claimed. There was, the analysts say, still no thought in his mind about capturing Kuwait City.

To the Kuwaitis and their supporters in Saudi Arabia this did not seem like the right moment to settle as to do so would be to allow Saddam to drive too hard a bargain. They rejected his demand in a letter to the secretary general of the Arab League, using the kind of language which has earned Kuwait its reputation for arrogance:

The sons of Kuwait, in good times as in bad, are men of principle and integrity. They will not yield to threats or extortion under any circumstances.

Saddam was left with only two options: either to back down and accept that he would not be able to get any money from the Kuwaitis, or else to press ahead. Everything in his make-up would have urged him to press ahead. He was an inveterate political gambler, whose response to every challenge was to raise the stakes. On 21 July, three days after the Kuwaiti response, his troops moved towards the border.

In Washington and London, as well as in the Gulf states, people assumed they knew what all this was about. There was to be an OPEC meeting in Geneva on 27 July and Iraq would use the threat of force and disruption to win agreement for a higher benchmark price. When the meeting started Iraq proposed that the benchmark should be raised from its current level of $18 to $25. After long hours of negotiation a deal was struck: $21, the highest price the Saudis would accept, and a limit on production of 22.5 million barrels per day. The crisis seemed to be over. Saddam had got what he had really been after the whole time.

Yet American satellite pictures showed that the 20,000 men he had moved to the Kuwait border were still there and had in fact been reinforced. Saddam had assured President Mubarak of Egypt that he would not take action against Kuwait unless all the diplomatic options had been exhausted, but a higher oil price was clearly not enough to buy him off. Now, it seems, he wanted redress for the insult Kuwait had offered him. The only conceivable redress would be payment of the money Kuwait 'owed' him.

On 25 July, with Iraqi troops still in position along the border, the American ambassador April Glaspie went to the presidential palace to see Saddam Hussein. Although she had been posted to Baghdad two years before, this was the first time he had seen her alone, his usual practice being to meet foreign diplomats only in groups. Their meeting became part of the folklore of the crisis. In the United States, where there was little understanding of the character of the Iraqi President and a considerable desire to find someone to blame, many newspapers and politicians blamed Ms Glaspie for failing to explain to Saddam Hussein the full consequences of invading Kuwait. The State Department appeared to do little to defend her. Yet at the time when she met Saddam, he had no clear idea in his own mind what he would do and indeed assured her that there would be no invasion. Ms Glaspie and the Bush administration might well have felt justified in believing that the Iraqi troops were merely on the border with Kuwait in order to put extra pressure on the Emir and to ensure that the OPEC meeting in Geneva two days later would take the decisions Iraq wanted.

There was a considerable degree of confusion on the American side in the days immediately before Ms Glaspie's visit to the presidential palace. Officials in Washington insisted that the United States had no defence commitments to Kuwait, while on 24 July the US announced a joint military exercise in the Gulf at the request of the UAE. The purpose of the exercise was to act as cover for the sending of American surveillance planes to the UAE as a precaution in case of Iraqi aggression. Saddam Hussein summoned ambassador Glaspie to demand an explanation.

On 11 September the Iraqis took the unusual step of leaking a transcript of this meeting to the western press. The transcript was edited in a way to make it deliberately misleading and it contained no mention of their conversation's most important element: Saddam Hussein's assurance that he would not invade Kuwait.

The transcript is mostly a record of Saddam's monologue, which went on altogether for about an hour and a half. Much of it was concerned with the notion of a plot against himself:

> It was clear to us that certain parties in the United States – not necessarily the President, I mean, but certain parties who had links with intelligence and with the State Department, and I don't necessarily mean the Secretary of State himself – did not like the fact that we had liberated our land [from Iran]. Some parties began to prepare papers entitled 'Who will take over from Saddam Hussein?' They began to contact Gulf states to make them worried about Iraq, so they wouldn't give economic aid to Iraq. We have evidence of these activities . . .
>
> We do not accept threats from anyone because we do not threaten anyone. But we say clearly that we hope the US will not suffer from too many illusions, and that it will look for new friends rather than add to the number of its enemies.

Saddam went on, according to the transcript, to complain about the things the American media had said about him and Ms Glaspie hastened to agree with his criticisms of a free press. It was an unedifying moment:

> I saw the Diane Sawyer programme [about Saddam Hussein] on ABC. And what happened in that programme was cheap and unjust. And this is a real picture of what happens in the American media – even to American politicians themselves. These are the methods that the western media employ. I am pleased that you add your voice to the diplomats who stand up to the media . . .

Grovelling to a man like Saddam Hussein on the issue of freedom of expression is unlikely to have earned Ms Glaspie the President's respect, any more than did the British MP Tony Marlow, who visited Iraq while Farzad Bazoft was in prison there, and wrote that Iraq was the victim of a 'vociferous and unrepresentative minority that affects to believe that our way of life and system of government is [sic] the measure by which all other countries should be measured'; or the American Senator Alan Simpson who told Saddam 'I think the troubles you have are with the western media, not with the American government. The press is full of itself . . .'

The section of the Iraqi transcript which later attracted attention came when Ms Glaspie said:

> I admire your extraordinary efforts to rebuild your country. I know you need funds. We understand that, and our opinion is that you should have the opportunity to rebuild your country. But we have no opinion on Arab-Arab conflicts like your border disagreement with Kuwait. . . We hope you can solve this problem using any suitable methods via Klibi [the secretary general of the Arab League] or President Mubarak. All we hope is that these issues will be solved quickly.

To her critics in the United States, these did not sound like the words of a woman who was firmly warning Saddam Hussein that any move he took into Kuwait would be met with force. She kept silent for many months, granting only one

103

newspaper interview, before giving evidence to the House of Representatives Foreign Affairs Sub-Committee on Europe and the Middle East on 21 March 1991.

Ms Glaspie maintained that about a fifth of the content of her interview with the Iraqi president was distorted, falsified or cut. She said that she had repeatedly warned him against using violence. 'I told him our policy was that we would defend our vital interests. We did not realize he would be so foolish as to ignore our repeated and crystal-clear warnings. . . I don't take comfort that everybody else that I was working with in Baghdad, including the Arab ambassadors, came to that same wrong conclusion.' She went on:

> He railed against what he believed we were threatening . . . He complained to me for one hour about fleet movements and American neo-imperialism and militarism. . . [He had clearly] decided on that day or the day before, for the first time, that we really would fight if we had to. Saddam had no question in his mind. I'm absolutely sure of that.

Then, however, Saddam Hussein left the room to speak to President Mubarak of Egypt on the telephone. They talked for half-an-hour and agreed that the Kuwaiti Crown Prince should meet Saddam's deputy, Izzat Ibrahim, in Jeddah. The Kuwaitis had agreed. Saddam 'came back and in effect said "We're not going to do it. It's all over."'

Representative Hamilton:	[D]id he say specifically he would not use force . . . or invade Kuwait?
Ambassador Glaspie:	Yes, sir.
Representative Hamilton:	And that was not a conditional statement of any kind. It was just a flat, clear, plain statement: we will not invade Kuwait, is that correct?
Ambassador Glaspie:	There certainly is no question [of conditionality] about it.

Saddam had obviously decided that by agreeing to the meeting in Jeddah the Kuwaitis were signalling a willingness to back down. Not surprisingly this section was cut from the version which the Iraqis leaked. They had no wish to show the lack of clear purpose which Saddam was showing at this time. Ms Glaspie, in her evidence to the Sub-Committee, went on to say that not only she but also President Mubarak and King Fahd had reached identical understandings with Saddam. She added that two different Iraqi ministers had said to her flatly, on 28 and 29 July, 'We are not going to use troops.' No doubt at the time they meant it.

Three months later, two reporters from the American television organization Cable News Network (CNN) inter-viewed Saddam Hussein in Baghdad. At this stage it was not generally known that Saddam had assured Ms Glaspie that there would be no invasion and the interviewers still assumed the issue was whether she had given Saddam a clear enough warning of the consequences of any invasion. The President's answer is interesting:

> I did not inform her that we would be entering Kuwait, in order that she could have told me that she would bring 200,000 [American soldiers], more or less. The important thing here is that we entered Kuwait and you [the US] have brought over, what you have and will be bringing more. . . And even if we assume that we had told one of your ambassadors that we would be going to Kuwait under the circumstances explained in the communiqué on sending troops at that point, could an ambassador decide how to confront our forces – unless the United States had previously decided to send troops to the Gulf region and the ambassador knew of this plan before 2 August, which is a different issue?

Saddam believed strongly that the Americans were planning to put US Marines into Kuwait in early August, much as Britain had put Royal Marines into Kuwait when President Qassem threatened it in 1961. A senior source close to the PLO leadership suggested later that Benazir Bhutto, then prime minister of Pakistan, had warned Saddam that the Americans had this plan in mind. Two weeks earlier, Ms Bhutto had visited Baghdad and Kuwait in an attempt to mediate. The source claimed that the United States, furious at the tip-off, gave the green light to the Pakistani president to dismiss the government of Ms Bhutto. She was forced to step down only four days after the Iraqi invasion.

Ms Bhutto did not, however, tell Saddam Hussein this; though she may have told him that Kuwait would ask the United States to send in the Marines. Since Saddam feared this would happen, he now had to decide whether to send in his own troops before the Americans could comply with any Kuwaiti request. As for Ms Bhutto, her dismissal came five hours after the US ambassador in Islamabad, Robert Oakley, met President Ishaq Khan. Washington was the first foreign capital to endorse the new government, and it seems certain that Oakley made it clear the US would like to see Ms Bhutto out of office. The reason, however, seems to have been Ms Bhutto's deep reluctance to send troops to join the Allied force in Saudi Arabia.

There was a curious lassitude in Baghdad in the last days before the invasion. Tariq Aziz later told 'The New Yorker':

> We expected an American military retaliation from the very beginning. . . . As foreign minister, I was convinced that in April [1990] the Americans had stopped listening to us and had made up their minds to hit us . . . We felt fatalistic. That is the mood that governed our judgment here.

Given the expectation that the Americans would attack Iraq no matter what he did, Saddam Hussein characteristically decided to take over the whole of Kuwait rather than just the northern strip which Iraq claimed. His interest in the efforts of people like Benazir Bhutto to negotiate a settlement was minimal.

Another concerned leader was the PLO Chairman, Yasser Arafat. He was worried that an outright conflict between Iraq and Kuwait might endanger the Palestinian cause. He is by nature a man who prefers deals to confrontation, and the PLO under his leadership has often been praised by the Arab world for its ability to broker agreements between hostile governments. Now he offered his services as peacemaker, and together with King Hussein of Jordan and the Saudi foreign minister, he flew from capital to capital looking for ways to end the impasse. His relations with both sides were good. Saddam Hussein seems not to have liked him personally, but nonetheless regarded him as a close ally. Arafat's relationship with the Emir of Kuwait was shaky to say the least, but he had good reason to be friendly with the Crown Prince. In September 1970, when King Hussein fought his war with the radical Palestinians, the Crown Prince saved Yasser Arafat's life by smuggling him out of Amman dressed as a woman, and flew him to Cairo.

As Yasser Arafat sat in the Crown Prince's office now, he advised the Kuwaitis not to say yes or no to Saddam Hussein's demands, but to say they would look into them. He believed a peaceful settlement was possible, if only Kuwait were less aggressive in its responses. The Crown Prince listened carefully, and Yasser Arafat had the feeling that he took the point. Then he was called away to the telephone in another room, and Arafat was left alone. When the Crown Prince came back, Arafat was aware that something had changed. The Crown Prince told him that the call had been from Margaret Thatcher, and that she had told him to stand firm and not yield an inch to Saddam's demands. Britain and the United States would back Kuwait to the hilt if he did, she said.

Saddam Hussein believed he had to act fast. It quickly became clear that the Jeddah meeting between Ibrahim and the Kuwaitis might not, after all, settle anything. It was scheduled for 28 July but was almost immediately postponed because the Iraqis issued a statement saying they expected their 'legitimate rights' to be met by Kuwait. These were an undertaking for Kuwait not to exceed its OPEC quota, to hand over the southern part of the Rumailah oilfield, to pay Iraq $2.4 billion, to write off Iraq's debts and make some additional form of compensation.

Eventually the meeting in Jeddah took place on 31 July. It changed everything, but not in the way Saddam had earlier assumed. The final Iraqi team was composed of three men: Izzat Ibrahim, vice-chairman of the Revolution Command Council, whose daughter was married to Saddam's eldest son; Sa'doun Hammadi, the deputy prime minister, a quiet and courteous man; and Saddam's cousin Ali Hassan al-Majid, the local government minister who was later to be appointed governor of occupied Kuwait. The Kuwaiti side was dominated by the Crown Prince who is also the prime minister, Shaikh Saad al-Abdallah al-Salem al-Sabah, a normally rather friendly man whose looming frame and staring eyes – the result of an incurable disorder – belie his easygoing nature.

It was clear to the Iraqis from the start that Saddam's assumption – that the Kuwaitis were looking for a way out of the crisis – was wrong. They themselves seem to have had instructions to be as flexible as possible, but they found the Crown Prince arrogant and unyielding. Kuwait, he said, had the backing of the United States, Britain, and Saudi Arabia and had no need to pay blackmail to Iraq. His real opponent was Ali Hassan al-Majid, himself an aggressive man with a violent record. The meeting lasted all through 31 July and resumed on the morning of 1 August, when the atmosphere was, if anything, more poisonous than it had been the previous day.

According to well-informed observers in Baghdad, al-Majid once again put forward the argument that Iraq had defended Kuwait against the threat from Iran and deserved some recompense. 'Why don't you just drink the sea?' the Crown Prince shouted. Things were so bad that it looked as though a fight would break out and the security guards whom the Saudis had stationed outside the room had to come in and hold the two men apart. Then came the last, unforgivable insult. When al-Majid said that the Iraqis were impoverished because of the war and scarcely had enough money now to feed themselves, the Crown Prince said loudly 'Why don't they send their wives out onto the streets to earn money for them?' Everyone round the table knew what he was referring to: the old stories from Takrit which had made the young Saddam's life miserable about his mother and about his illegitimacy.

The meeting broke up and the Iraqi team returned to Baghdad. Saddam was wild with anger when he heard what the Crown Prince had said. Sources say he gave the order then and there that the Iraqi troops should move into Kuwait, but that they shouldn't stop at the Rumailah oil-field or Mutla ridge: they should take the entire country.

Later, sources in Baghdad told me that until quite late that

108

evening only four men knew of Saddam's hasty decision: the future governor of the 'nineteenth province', Ali Hassan al-Majid; his son-in-law, Hussein Kamil al-Majid, the defence industries minister; his half-brother, Sabaawi Ibrahim, the head of the Mukhabarat; and the Commander of the Revolutionary Guard. The defence minister, an elderly man put into the job as a figurehead, was not informed until the operation had begun. The generals commanding the various Revolutionary Guard divisions were under the impression until the last minute that it was just an exercise. In the early hours of 2 August 1990, as the tanks crossed into Kuwait, Saddam said to his four closest associates: 'The Emir will not sleep in his palace tonight.'

THE HOUSE OF
WAR

Invasion

Kuwait has been returned to the fold of its motherland, Iraq, from which it was long severed and usurped, like an infant separated from its mother. It will never be separated again.

Saddam Hussein, speaking on Iraqi television, September 1990

'I suppose it was the tanks I heard first, that horrible growling, grinding noise they make. I'd never heard a tank in my life before, but I knew there was something very wrong when I heard that noise. I shook my husband and said, "Wake up, Steve, something's going on out there." It certainly was. When we looked out of the window – it was already light – there were dozens of the horrible things coming along the road, past our block of flats.' Mrs Susan Jenkins and her husband were British expatriates who lived and worked in Kuwait. What they saw that morning was the start of a terrible few months for the western community of around 8000 and for nearly half a million workers from the Third World. As for Palestinians who lived there and for the Kuwaitis themselves, there is no foreseeable end to the troubles that started on 2 August.

The tanks – 300 of them, together with 100,000 troops – began the invasion of Kuwait at 2am local time. The invasion plan had been improvised in a matter of a few days, but it was well enough thought out. At the last moment it had been extended to take the tanks and troops down to Kuwait City instead of the border area. The great majority of the tanks were carrying minimal quantities of ammunition, so they could get to Kuwait City as fast as possible. Some had no ammunition at all. It didn't matter: Kuwait's armed forces, which totalled

113

only 16,000 men, did nothing to stop them as they crossed the border. A statement from the Kuwaiti defence ministry broadcast at 6am local time called on Iraq to stop 'this irresponsible action' and said Kuwait reserved the right to defend itself 'with all the ways and means that will eliminate this aggression'. It was just rhetoric.

Nevertheless the ministry did achieve one very important success. In the two hours which it took for the first Iraqi tanks driving at their top speed of 50 mph to reach Kuwait City, the officers on overnight duty alerted the defence minister. He then warned the Emir and went the rounds of his colleagues in the government, waking them and getting them to pass the news to others. It was clear from the tone of Iraqi propaganda that there would be no room either for the Emir or the leading members of the al-Sabah family in the new régime which the Iraqis intended to set up in Kuwait. The assumption among officials and political analysts in Baghdad whom I spoke to later was that they would have been imprisoned or, in the case of the Emir and the Crown Prince, shot 'accidentally' during the takeover of the palace.

This was the way the Emir's half-brother, Fahd al-Ahmad al-Sabah, died. He was a bluff extrovert, very different from his quiet elder brother, and he was the manager of Kuwait's national football team. Rather than escape with the others he took up his position on the steps of the Dasman Palace with the soldiers who had been detailed to guard it. The palace was attacked from the air and surrounded. There was heavy fighting, but the defenders stood their ground for nearly an hour. Finally the Iraqis charged the building. Shaikh Fahd was last seen standing on the steps, gun in hand. Then he was shot down where he stood.

The Emir and the Crown Prince, whose intemperate language had caused so much trouble, escaped in their armour-plated Mercedes. So did all the members of the government. During the early hours of the morning limousine after limousine drove southwards towards Saudi Arabia, well ahead of the Iraqi tanks. On board the ministers kept in touch with one another and with the outside world by carphone. It proved to be of considerable importance in the propaganda

114

war that the Kuwaiti government should have got away intact. During the weeks and months that followed, the Emir set up his government in exile in the Saudi summer capital, Ta'if, rallying support, a vivid and constant reminder of the crime that had been committed against his country.

The first news of the invasion seems to have been passed to the outside world by means of the ministerial mobile phones. The news became public, however, only in a broadcast on Voice of the Masses radio from Baghdad which was monitored at 04.10 Greenwich Mean Time (7.10 am in Iraq and Kuwait):

> God has helped the free and honest men of Kuwait to depose the traitor régime in Kuwait, which is involved in Zionist and foreign plots. The free sons of dear Kuwait have appealed to the Iraqi leadership for support to prevent any foreign interference in Kuwait's affairs . . .
>
> They have urged us to restore security, in order to protect the sons of Kuwait from harm. The Revolution Command Council has decided to respond to the request made by Kuwait's free provisional government and to cooperate with it on that basis, leaving the citizens of Kuwait to decide their own affairs by themselves.
>
> We will withdraw when the situation becomes stable and when Kuwait's free provisional government asks us to do so. This may not exceed a few days or weeks.

The statement was, typically of the operation, made almost on the spur of the moment. Nothing had been done to give it even a veneer of authenticity. The 'free and honest men' who had supposedly overthrown the Kuwaiti régime never existed.

For the next 12 hours or more some of the braver inhabitants fought the Iraqis in the streets. Contrary to later assumptions, the resisters at this stage were by no means all Kuwaiti citizens. A British woman who later passed through Baghdad on her way to England told me her experiences that morning:

> My children and I were in our kitchen, because that seemed the safest place – it was at the back of the block of flats and there were tanks and soldiers in the front. We were lying on the floor, I don't mind telling you. Then I heard a noise outside the

kitchen window and a man was standing out there on the fire escape, trying to attract my attention. I was frightened, but I could see he had a gun, so I thought I'd better let him in. I didn't know who he was, but he was just in a shirt and jeans, not in uniform, so I didn't think he was an Iraqi soldier.

He was quite polite and asked if two of his friends could come in too. They were all Arabs and they all had guns – goodness knows where they got them from. Then they went into the other room and I could hear them shooting down at the Iraqi tanks. I was petrified, but for some reason the Iraqi's didn't fire back. Thank God for that, anyway.

They didn't stay long – maybe ten minutes altogether. I offered them a cup of tea and they laughed, but they didn't say yes. I asked them, 'Who are you?' They wouldn't really say, but one of them said he was a Palestinian and that one of the others was his brother and the other one was an Egyptian friend of theirs. Then they said they had to go and find somewhere else to shoot from and they climbed out of the window again. Extraordinary, really.

At the airport, a British Airways jumbo jet, flight 149, en route to Delhi from London, landed after the invasion had begun. The airport was closed and it was unable to take off. The 301 passengers, many of them Indian, and the crew and relief crew of 77 were taken prisoner. All the other key Kuwaiti installations – the television station, the power stations, the port – were taken over. The British and American embassies were surrounded and the Iraqi soldiers sprayed both of them with bullets.

At 9.05 GMT BBC Monitoring picked up a station calling itself Radio Kuwait and broadcasting on five shortwave frequencies used in normal times for transmissions from the Kabd area, southwest of Kuwait City. It called for help from the Desert Shield force of the Gulf Cooperation Council:

How can Arab blood be shed by Arab hands? How can Arab honour be trampled on by Arabs? How can an Arab occupy the land of his Arab brother? Arab Kuwait . . . which has never abandoned its pan-Arab duty, today appeals to the Arab conscience everywhere. God is above the aggressor.

116

Sometimes the radio went off the air for long periods. Then the BBC monitors would hear it again, broadcasting patriotic music and exhortations: 'O citizens, defending the homeland is a duty', 'O citizens, defending the soil is essential.'

Condemnations were starting to come in from abroad: from the United States, which called for an immediate Iraqi withdrawal, and announced that the aircraft carrier, USS *Independence*, was heading for the Gulf with a battle group; from Britain, which said the invasion was a threat to peace and stability in the area; from China; from the Soviet Union; from Iran, Morocco and Algeria; from France. An emergency meeting of foreign ministers of the Arab League was summoned in Cairo that afternoon and the Iraqi ambassador walked out although the deputy prime minister, Sa'doun Hammadi, agreed to stay under protest. Baghdad Radio broadcast the details of three communiqués from the 'Provisional Free Kuwait Government', deposing the Emir, dissolving the National Assembly, promising elections after stability had been restored and imposing an indefinite curfew. Explosions and gunfire throughout the day showed that resistance was not yet over.

At the request of Kuwait and the United States, the United Nations Security Council went into emergency session. After several hours of discussion it passed Resolution 660 by fourteen votes to none; Yemen, which had a seat on the Council, abstained. The Resolution

Condemns the Iraqi invasion of Kuwait.
Demands that Iraq withdraw immediately and unconditionally all its forces to the positions in which they were located on 1 August 1990.
  Calls on Iraq and Kuwait to begin immediately intensive negotiations for the resolution of their differences and supports all efforts in this regard and especially those of the Arab League.

The crisis found many key figures away from their desks. The American ambassador in Baghdad, April Glaspie, had left on holiday and would not return to Iraq for the rest of the crisis. The British ambassador, Harold Walker, was also on

117

holiday, as were Foreign Secretary Douglas Hurd and President Mitterrand of France. James Baker, the US Secretary of State, was visiting Outer Mongolia; he asked his Soviet opposite number, Eduard Shevardnadze, to halt arms deliveries to Iraq and Mr Shevardnadze agreed. President Bush was not yet at his holiday home in Kennebunkport on the coast of Maine, but was just about to go; the crisis did not stop him. Mrs Margaret Thatcher, who rarely took holidays, was in Colorado in the western United States in order to give a speech; she made immediate contact with Washington.

No one had foreseen the possibility that Saddam Hussein might order the invasion. It came out of the blue, much as the Argentine decision to invade the Falkland Islands had, eight years earlier, and for much the same reason: it was virtually a spur of the moment response, combining frustration with opportunism. Stories emerged later in Washington that the CIA had suggested the possibility of an invasion. If they were true, not merely an exercise in departmental in-fighting, the suggestion had not been taken seriously. Neither Israel's Mossad nor the British SIS, it is said, spotted the signs; nor did the KGB or French intelligence who both had much better contacts with the Iraqis. Given the secrecy and last-minute nature of Saddam Hussein's decision, it is scarcely surprising that the foreign ministries and intelligence organizations of the outside world picked up no hint of what was about to happen.

The first reaction in Washington was one of shock and dismay. There was serious anxiety for the safety of the 2500 Americans living and working in Kuwait and the 600 in Iraq. There was also the fear that Saddam's move might just be the first in a general attack on pro-western régimes in the region, starting with Saudi Arabia and continuing along the coast of the Gulf to Bahrain, the United Arab Emirates and even Oman. There were serious anxieties that in other pro-western countries – Egypt in particular – political and religious radicals would come out onto the streets in support of Saddam and weaken or even overthrow the government.

Even that first day, though, there were signs that President Bush and some of his officials realized that the crisis contained opportunities as well as dangers. Saddam Hussein was a disturbing influence on the Middle Eastern scene who might have to be dealt with at some stage. Now he had put himself firmly in the wrong and the near-unanimous Security Council vote showed he had few, if any, friends to back him. Among the dangers and uncertainties, it may be that Mr Bush saw some advantage too.

The American media, with their alarming herd instinct, had helped to make a big issue out of the so-called 'wimp factor', which had never been anything more than a reaction to the way Mr Bush looked and spoke. As vice-president, Mr Bush had seen how President Reagan had benefited from two clumsy and questionable military operations: the invasion of Grenada on 25 October 1983 and the bombing of Libya three years later. This would be a bigger business altogether, but if it succeeded Mr Bush's reputation would be unassailable. It would also make a reality of something he had begun to speak about in the wake of the revolutions which had swept through Central and Eastern Europe and the virtual collapse of the Soviet Union as a superpower: the new world order.

In Moscow the news came at a time of industrial unrest, particularly in the Donetsk and Donbass mining areas, nervousness about the intentions of the Soviet Army (the self-appointed head of a soldiers' and officers' union said there was clear evidence that a coup was being planned) and continued disturbances in the republics of Central Asia and the Baltics. An international crisis involving Iraq contained potential embarrassment and potential opportunity, in roughly equal amounts. It offered a chance to demonstrate to the United States and Western Europe – the only places with the financial muscle to seriously help the Soviet Union out of its economic troubles – that it was now a dependable partner in international affairs. And so it was that, from the unlikely direction of the Mongolian capital Ulan Bator, James Baker asked for a halt to Soviet arms supplies to Iraq and Eduard Shevardnadze was happy to agree.

On the other hand it was plain that this approach would cause problems with the very military whose allegiance seemed (wrongly) to be in question: Iraq had been a dependable ally for the old pre-Gorbachev, pre-glasnost superpower which the

Soviet Union had once been. Over the next few months the more conservative voices would condemn Gorbachev and Shevardnadze for letting their friends down. Before the crisis was over, conservative pressure would do near-fatal injury to Gorbachev and destroy Shevardnadze's political career within the Soviet system.

In Britain, the invasion came as the political system was closing down for its summer break. Britain was bound by its colonial past to aid Kuwait and was anyway involved more deeply than it wanted in the continuing and bitter argument over Farzad Bazoft and the supergun affair. On the other hand it was still Iraq's biggest overseas customer with the largest number of westerners – more than 700 – living in Iraq. This was on top of 4000 people in Kuwait, again the largest number of western expatriates.

All this might have been expected to encourage caution. The British prime minister Mrs Thatcher had however made a political career out of not being cautious. Her main concern in foreign policy seemed to be to ally herself as closely as possible with the United States. In a speech three days later at the Aspen Institute in Colorado she maintained that the crisis provided the United Nations with an opportunity to fulfil the role for which it had been created, precisely the approach President Bush had adopted. Those British newspapers which always supported her unquestioningly gave the impression that Mrs Thatcher was the real force behind the London-Washington axis, making certain that President Bush did no backsliding. There was, in fact, no need but the message was picked up by the government in Baghdad which soon identified Mrs Thatcher as their real enemy. The government newspaper *Al-Iraq* reported a week or so later:

> This is the lady who is encouraging enemies and vomiting poison like a spotted serpent, attempting by all means to inflict harm on Iraq to make up for the inferiority complex that she has because of the proud Iraqis and their unique leader, Saddam Hussein, who has dealt the most violent and strongest possible political blows to the ugly British face.

For months to come the Iraqi government and media found

it hard to decide whether Britain was leading the United States ('this lowly buffoon is urging the United States to use the military option') or vice versa ('What a miserable and lowly role is being played by old Britain and the circus act and corrupt lady, Thatcher, who is playing into the hands of US politics'). Whichever way it was, they were obsessed with Mrs Thatcher. Even after her fall from power in November Saddam Hussein and his newspapers were reluctant to give up attacking her.

In France there was intense debate within the government about policy towards Iraq. President Mitterrand himself instinctively supported Israel, which made him an equally instinctive opponent of Saddam Hussein. He had followed a more pro-American policy than his predecessors and was inclined now to join the United States and Britain in punishing the invasion. Nevertheless France, like Britain, had important economic interests in Iraq. Saddam Hussein's only visit to a western country was to Paris in 1975 during Valéry Giscard d'Estaing's presidency. Saddam negotiated with the government of prime minister Jacques Chirac to buy a 70-megawatt nuclear reactor, which the French called Osirak. Chirac had visited Baghdad the previous year and his successor as premier, Raymond Barre, also made the trip in 1977. After an international outcry against the deal, France provided Iraq with 24 kilos of highly enriched uranium, instead of the 72 kilos originally promised. Saddam was annoyed but still praised France's willingness to act independently of the influence of the United States. He even thought he saw ideological similarities between Gaullism and Baathism. Again during the 1980s he had strong reasons to be grateful to France for its military and diplomatic support in his war against Iran. After the Soviet Union, the French supplied most of Iraq's weapons: it bought Mirage fighter aircraft from Dassault, Alouette, Gazelle, Super Frelon and Puma helicopters from Aerospatiale; Crotale-7 surface-to-air missile systems; Magic R-550 air-to-air missiles and Exocet missiles from Thomson CSF – plus large quantities of defence electronics.

From all this a division of interests arose within the French government. The defence minister, Jean-Pierre Chevènement, was a strong advocate of Iraq and did what he could to propose solutions which he thought Saddam could accept without humiliation: a redrawing of Kuwait's borders in exchange for an Iraqi withdrawal, for instance. By contrast the foreign minister, Roland Dumas, supported the much stronger line of the United States and Britain. At the beginning of September, for instance, Dumas supported the principle that anyone who harmed the foreign hostages in Iraq and Kuwait should be liable to prosecution for war crimes. Chevènement lacked any great support within the French cabinet and failed to prevent France from taking part in the air war against Iraq. Finally he resigned on 29 January 1991, but his rearguard action throughout the crisis meant that France rarely spoke with a single voice.

Germany, by contrast, scarcely spoke at all. It too had supplied weapons to Iraq and had a few large contracts there. But throughout the 1970s, the biggest period of growth in Iraq, Germany's diplomatic links with Israel had made it hard to enter into too many agreements with Baghdad. Nevertheless, a number of German companies had helped supply Iraq with the chemicals it wanted for use against Iran and against those elements in its own population who might cause trouble for Baghdad. There were, nevertheless, about a thousand Germans in Iraq and Kuwait.

Germany's experience throughout the crisis was a difficult one. Chancellor Helmut Kohl was in the process of losing the popularity he had gained through the smooth political union of East and West Germany due to the much more painful process of economic integration. In Germany, too, the revolutions in Central and Eastern Europe had bulked larger than they had in Britain or France, and there was a certain impatience about the way other western countries were behaving in the Middle East, especially since the West German constitution specifically forbade sending troops abroad to fight.

'You British,' said a young woman near the newly-opened Brandenburg Gate in Berlin, where I was reporting on the reunification ceremony in October, 'you just want to get back to the sands of the desert and wear your solar topees. But that's all in the past, don't you understand? Here, we're trying to think about the future.' It was sincerely meant, but to the British and the Americans who were preparing for the possibility of war it seemed like mere selfishness and isolationism. As the crisis in the Middle East developed and political problems within Germany increased, the government of Chancellor Kohl seemed diminished by it all. By the summer of 1991, Germany's standing was nothing like as considerable as it had been a year before, when reunification seemed to make it unquestionably the most potent nation in Europe.

Japan also was forbidden by its constitution to become involved in military adventures abroad, and it too seemed diminished by the unfolding of a situation in which Japanese wealth, business expertise and manufacturing excellence could play no part whatever. The Japanese cabinet, stung by criticisms in the United States, proposed to send troops in a peace-keeping role though it is unclear what, if anything, they might have done. In any case, the opposition parties united to block the plan. For the most part Japan too would be an observer, its attention fixed on the problems of 200 of its citizens who left their place of refuge in the Japanese embassy in Kuwait and were held hostage in Baghdad. The Gulf supplied Japan with three-quarters of its oil, but without the ability or will to protect their own interests, the Japanese had to rely on the actions of others.

From the very start it was clear that a crisis involving a country as belligerent as Iraq would create some new and unlikely alliances. Part of the new alignment was obvious: Saudi Arabia, the other Gulf states and Egypt had no alternative but to oppose Saddam. The strong condemnation that came in the first few hours from Iraq's former enemy Iran made it look for a few days as though the government in Tehran, too, might join the growing anti-Saddam front. But President Rafsanjani had a more complex plan in mind: to keep his weakened country out of any hostilities, to use the crisis to reach a formal end to the state of war with Iraq while strengthening Iran's relations with western countries whose help it required in the reconstruction of its economy. Before the crisis was over Iran attained each of those objectives and the radical fundamentalists who wanted to join Iraq in a *jihad* against the United States were badly discredited. It proved an important success for Rafsanjani.

President Assad of Syria, who ran a régime in many ways just as unattractive as Saddam Hussein's, took a different approach. The Syrian Baath Party, of which he was the head, regarded the Iraqi Baath Party as its natural enemy. There was no ideological difficulty for Assad in aligning himself with the western powers, with Egypt and, in a sense, with Israel, though it required a certain amount of lateral thinking. The dreadful state of the Syrian economy, with electricity supplies often cut to as little as four hours a day, made the leap of imagination a great deal easier. Assad, however, had to go even further than Iran in proving his good faith. Nothing short of committing troops to the general undertaking would be enough for the Americans and British to accept him as someone with whom they could do business.

Jordan moved in the opposite direction. In private, King Hussein had no liking for Saddam and felt that the invasion of Kuwait was a disaster. But he recognized that this crisis could bring him down, just as the aftermath of the Suez crisis had brought down his young cousin, King Faysal II, in Baghdad in 1958. What was more, the introduction of a limited degree of democracy in Jordan gave ordinary people a new voice in the handling of affairs, and there was no doubt what ordinary people felt. On 12 August 1990, 10 days after the invasion, Saddam Hussein took the advice of Yasser Arafat and the PLO and publicly linked an offer to withdraw from Kuwait with Israeli withdrawal from the occupied territories, American withdrawal from Saudi Arabia and Syrian withdrawal from Lebanon. It was probably the cleverest thing Saddam Hussein did throughout the entire course of the crisis and it won him support throughout the Muslim world, if not with governments, then in the streets. It seemed to give dignity and strategic importance to what had previously looked like a smash-and-grab raid. For King Hussein the pictures of Saddam which were put up all over the Jordanian capital Amman and throughout the country were a signal that it would have been extremely dangerous to ignore.

All this, however, was in the future. On the afternoon of 2 August Iraqi soldiers were taking over the centre of Kuwait City, building by building. In the early stages many of them clearly had orders to behave politely and, although there were roadblocks, it was possible to move around in many parts of the city without too much difficulty. The great majority of people stayed indoors, however. Statements from what was called the 'Provisional Free Kuwait Government' were broadcast at great length on the radio, which early in the operation had been taken over by Iraqi troops. Communiqué number 1 was a long and rambling defence of the action Iraq had taken, accusing the al-Sabahs of gross corruption and of being imposed on the country by Britain. The messages were supposedly being written and broadcast by men who were themselves Kuwaitis, though many people who heard them said the accents were recognisably Iraqi:

> O citizens and dear sons of Kuwait, things have reached an unbearable level. Our people could no longer tolerate that degree of injustice, corruption, counterfeiting and conspiracy. The national forces, which rejected tyranny, despotism and corruption and resisted the régime, which is connected with imperialist and Zionist circles, have decided (relying on God and the people's free will and the good representatives of the people) to assume responsibility and topple the tyrannical, corrupt régime.

One of the primary national aims of the Provisional Free Kuwait Government would, it said, be to rectify the harm and aggression which the former government had carried out against 'our people and brothers in Iraq'. Communiqué number 2 announced a curfew with immediate effect and until further notice.

The shooting that had gone on during the first seven or eight hours of the invasion had died away by late afternoon. The tanks in the second and third waves of the invasion ground their way down the city streets, their tracks cutting deep furrows in tarmac softened by the intense summer heat. The racket of their engines and the thick grey smoke from their exhaust filled the air. They positioned themselves at all the main crossroads and outside every major building, then switched off. As the afternoon wore on the city became more and more quiet.

In London and Paris the governments moved fast that day to prevent Iraq from gaining the benefit of Kuwaiti's enormous investments. In Britain all Kuwaiti assets were frozen. In France the same measure was also applied to Iraqi assets. In Washington the Iraqi ambassador suggested that the military operation in Kuwait might take a few days or weeks. This gave rise to a view which gained widespread support: far-reaching though it was, the invasion was simply being done for political effect and a withdrawal would at some stage follow once the point was made. In fact the hectic and unplanned nature of the whole affair meant that the ambassador had been unable to contact anyone in Baghdad and was saying this because, lacking any clear briefing from his ministers, he hoped it would turn out that way. The first hint of what would afterwards become an action involving the forces of 30 countries came in a joint statement from Mrs Thatcher and President Bush: it called for a collective international effort which would force Iraq to withdraw from Kuwait if it did not do so voluntarily. In Saudi Arabia there was deep anxiety that the Iraqi move was the beginning of a much deeper thrust at the city of Dhahran or perhaps even the capital Riyadh. By late afternoon the deeply-nervous Saudi government had still allowed no mention of the invasion to be made on Saudi television or radio, as though the crisis would have no power to harm the country if it were not referred to. Members of the Kuwaiti government were meanwhile beginning to gather in the safety of Dhahran. Some of them, fatigued by the heat, had stopped off at their chalets along the coast for a siesta before moving on to the Saudi border. Radio Kuwait was still broadcasting patriotic songs and announcements, the most frequent of which was that the only legitimate government of Kuwait was the one headed by the Emir. A recorded message from the Crown Prince said Kuwait was facing 'a brutal aggression by the enemies of love and peace' and appealing to everyone to rally behind the Emir. Later one of the speakers asked 'How long will the world remain a spectator while peace is being slaughtered in the land of Kuwait, the land of peace?' The radio station continued to broadcast through the evening and night, but went off the air the following day just after broadcasting another appeal to the world to help the people of Kuwait. It ended with the words, 'Hurry to their aid'.

In Baghdad the government announced that it was mobilizing the Popular Army, a million or so reservists, all of whom had served in the war with Iran. 'The order,' it said, 'shall come into force as of today.' Later there were two more announcements:

In the Name of God, the Compassionate, the Merciful: Communiqué number 1 issued by the Armed Forces General Command.
    In accordance with the requirements of the public interest, it has been decided to close the land borders and airspace, and restrict air traffic movement according to regulations which will be issued in due course.

A few minutes earlier the Presidential Office had announced:

It has been decided to ban the travel of Iraqis outside the country. The Interior Ministry is empowered to regulate the travel of non-Iraqis in the light of instructions which will be issued later by the Presidential Office.

In the welter of statements, condemnation, advice and pleas flowing out of almost every capital in the world, this last sentence, on a dispatch from the Iraqi News Agency, scarcely attracted much attention. It was, however, the first indication of one of Saddam Hussein's most serious tactical errors: the decision to hold foreign citizens hostage.

In Kuwait that evening, as it grew dark, Susan Jenkins felt a sense of desolation and anxiety worse than anything she had ever experienced before:

It had all been so far beyond anything we'd ever known or thought about. Maybe if we'd had a bit of time to prepare ourselves for the idea of an invasion it would have been

127

different. I was putting the children to bed that night and trying to tell them everything would work out all right and they mustn't worry about it, and I thought, this is exactly what I was doing last night, in every way. And yet everything was incredibly different, and we couldn't think what was going to happen to us.

Outside, she could hear the rattle of gunfire once again. The invasion of Kuwait had been accomplished, but it had not been accepted as quietly as the invaders had hoped. Resistance was continuing.

Approaches to Baghdad

> When we come to the Arabs, we will find a large number of
> Arab states are on our side, and we are on their side because the
> issue is one. If you ask Arab citizens you will find that the
> majority of them support this position. But if you consider the
> corrupt ones, who are discarded by their people, – anyone who
> takes these people as the criteria will be making a mistake.
>
> Saddam Hussein, speaking to Austrian reporters, August 1990

The Iraqi ambassador navigated a way through the overblown
gilt furniture and switched on the television. 'I prefer this,' he
said, with a confidential nod towards me. '*Jamais, jamais de la
vie,*' a well set-up blonde was shouting from the screen. A tall
man with Jacques Chirac's patent-leather hair seemed to be
trying to quieten her so the servants wouldn't hear. It was one
of the soap operas set in expensive chateaux which the French
put on after lunch.

Inside the embassy there was no other way of telling that it
was the afternoon. The thick, expensive curtains were drawn
across windows which were themselves high enough for a
chateau. The ambassador, a tough, short, stocky man with a
handshake like a martial arts expert, found his way back to the
desk and sat down. He said something that sounded welcoming, though over the noise of the argument in the chateau I
couldn't be entirely sure.

Abdul Razzak al-Hashimi, Iraq's ambassador in Paris, kept
his credentials beside him on the desk: a large photograph of
himself with President Saddam Hussein. People said he was
close to the President and, although Saddam was rarely seen

with anyone below the rank of minister or general, it may well have been true. During the crisis al-Hashimi certainly proved himself one of the most able of his country's spokesmen abroad and his English was excellent. Any television programme in Britain, France or elsewhere in Europe which wanted someone to put Saddam Hussein's point of view rang al-Hashimi's office first. He must have faced dozens of interviews with television presenters and anchors who wanted to show their toughness. He usually won.

I was there to smooth over any ruffled feathers from a BBC interview of the previous day. The interviewer had strayed beyond the bounds of good manners and I was anxious that the BBC shouldn't slip into the habit of being rude or insulting to people simply because their government had done something our government disapproved of, including the brutal invasion of a small neighbouring country. There were, I felt, enough insults to be found every day in large sections of the British press: there was no need to add to the number. I reread the guidelines which the BBC's Board of Governors had issued in World War II, among them that broadcasters should 'address even individual Germans as an Englishman or a Frenchman would speak to them, if they could meet in a neutral café'. Above all, the guidelines said, there was 'no room for ranting'.

If that were the case during a war in which Britain's very existence as a nation was at stake, there was even less room for ranting in a crisis where, however it turned out, our future was not threatened and we would almost certainly win. Sitting in al-Hashimi's stuffy office, with the television going full blast in the corner, I explained that whatever our private views might be of the action his country had taken in Kuwait, it was our intention to maintain a decent civilized tone towards the representatives of Iraq. He seemed to notice, though, that I had not gone as far as apologizing for what my colleague had said to him the previous morning.

At that moment the telephone rang. He listened for a long time, putting in an occasional question in Arab. Finally he hung up and beamed at me. 'We have just received information that a well-known member of the Saudi royal family . . . lost 6 million French francs at the gambling table in Nice last night.' He gave instructions for the man's name to be passed around the Arab journalists in Paris. It seemed an auspicious moment to ask al-Hashimi if he would heip me to get a visa to Iraq. He beamed again. 'Why not?'

Only later did I discover that 'Why not?' was the Iraqi official's standard formula for deflecting a request which he either could not or did not want to do anything about. Nevertheless I had also seen that my rather empty title – foreign affairs editor – had had its effect. Civil servants are impressed by titles: they spend their lives working for better ones. I had the distinct impression that the ambassador was obscurely flattered by the idea that the BBC might want someone with a title to cover their side of things.

I had already decided that in a world crisis with so many centres, Baghdad was the best place to be. My experience three months before had shown that it would be difficult to get there and even more difficult to stay for any decent length of time. I acknowledged to myself that I was more likely to fail than to succeed and that it could be quite unpleasant; but like an old gourmet sated with the usual delicacies, I felt I needed something a bit spicier than Saudi Arabia, Turkey, Washington or Egypt could supply. If there were to be peace, it would be planned and announced in Baghdad; if war, Baghdad would be a major target. Assuredly, Baghdad was the place to be.

I glanced once more at the television: a brunette was having breakfast in bed as the man with patent-leather hair put on a dressing gown. Al-Hashimi laughed. 'Who can hear us while that is on?' he asked. I agreed. I had barely been able to hear him myself. We exchanged another martial arts handshake, and his press secretary, a saturnine man with a scar on his cheek who spoke English superbly and French, if anything, better, showed me downstairs. He had the looks and the *hauteur* which could have got him a part in the chateau soap opera. In the months to come, when he was expelled from France and I was a long-serving resident of Baghdad, he and I would have a great deal more to do with one another, when he became senior official at the Ministry of Information.

On 4 August 1990 the Iraqi News Agency announced the formation of a cabinet in Kuwait, headed by a Colonel Ala Hussein Ali as prime minister, commander-in-chief of the armed forces, defence minister and minister of the interior. It soon became clear that all nine members of the new cabinet – far from being Kuwaitis as they claimed – were just Iraqi army officers. No genuine Kuwaitis had been found who would do the job. After the announcement of his appointment and a reference to a meeting with Saddam a few days later, Ali and his ministers disappeared from the unfolding events. Perhaps it was simply another spur-of-the-moment move designed to give the impression that Saddam was serious when he spoke of withdrawing Iraqi forces from Kuwait.

That idea, too, soon came to nothing. The day after the invasion the Soviet foreign minister, Eduard Shevardnadze, said that he had received assurances from Iraqi officials – he meant Iraqi's ambassador in Moscow – that Iraqi forces would soon be pulled out. A group of Iraqi journalists, some of them working for western news agencies, were even flown to Kuwait City to witness the withdrawal. They watched large numbers of Iraqi tanks driving off along one of the city's ring roads, their crews waving. After that the tanks took up positions somewhere else. Few of the Iraqi journalists had the courage to report the truth about what they had seen. Their reports, combined with pictures of this non-event which Iraqi television gave to the outside world, added to the confusion about Saddam Hussein's intentions.

Despite the confusion it was plain that the Iraqi president was failing to comply with the terms of the Security Council's Resolution 660, passed on the day of the invasion, requiring an immediate withdrawal from Kuwait. On 6 August 1990, at the urging of the United States and Britain, the Security Council adopted a Resolution 661 imposing sanctions on Iraq. The voting was 13 to nil with Cuba and Yemen abstaining. The wording of the Resolution, in which the United States, Britain and the Soviet Union played an important part, was all-embracing. The Council, it said

Decides that all states shall prevent the import of products from Iraq or Kuwait.

132

Decides that all states shall prevent the sale of any commodity to Iraq or Kuwait including military equipment but excluding medical supplies and, in humanitarian circumstances, foodstuffs.

Decides that all states shall not make available any funds or economic resources to the Iraq government, except payment for medical supplies and, in humanitarian circumstances, foodstuffs.

Calls on all states to protect the assets of the legitimate government of Kuwait.

These were sanctions as fierce as the United Nations had voted against Rhodesia after its unilateral declaration of independence in 1964. The difference this time was that no one was likely to break them. The following day, in spite of an urgent visit from Taha Yasin Ramadan, Iraq's deputy prime minister, President Ozal of Turkey announced that it would comply with Resolution 661 by stopping the flow of Iraqi oil carried across Turkey by pipeline. Iraq's economy was switched off with almost the same speed and ease.

Saddam Hussein's strategy, ill-conceived as it was, had no chance whatever of succeeding with all five permanent members of the Security Council against him. At their talks in Moscow on 3 August, James Baker and Eduard Shevardnadze had reached almost total agreement on the need for Iraq to withdraw. It was the first big test of the new Soviet policy of cooperation rather than confrontation with the US. Even though the Soviet Union still had many ties with Iraq and a sizeable number of military advisers on contract there, it was essential to its new interests to demonstrate to the United States and Western Europe that Moscow was a reliable partner. Saddam Hussein seems to have calculated that the Soviet Union would ultimately have to swing round and support him. It showed a lamentable ignorance of the changes that had come about in world politics. Six or more years earlier the Soviet Union would indeed have been forced to take Iraq's side, no matter how reluctantly. The arrival of Mikhail Gorbachev had altered all that. Without Soviet support, Saddam was irredeemably condemned to failure.

By the end of the first week of August it was still unclear how

133

far Saddam planned to go: was he going to stop at Kuwait, or did he also intend to attack Saudi Arabia and the other Gulf states? On 6 August he promised to honour his treaty of non-aggression with Saudi Arabia, but it was impossible by this stage to have confidence in his assurances. Most commentators and diplomats believed he meant it and would go no further; President Bush, perhaps disingenuously, maintained that there was a threat and used it to justify his build-up of forces in the Gulf and in Saudi Arabia itself.

The aircraft carrier USS *Eisenhower*, a fifth of a mile long, elderly, slow, yet immensely powerful, moved with great stateliness under nuclear power down the Suez canal in the direction of the Gulf, and whatever might await her there in the way of action. Her upper works shimmered in the immense heat of summer, seeming to melt and liquefy in the sun. Her radar scanners evaporated into mirage and back to reality as they turned. On her decks lay her greatest strength: a jumble of folded wings and fuselages which represented 60 of the world's most advanced fighter aircraft. They were parked as close as cars on a ferry.

It was 8 August. As the *Eisenhower* moved down the canal with his full knowledge and permission, President Hosni Mubarak of Egypt was giving a press conference. It proved to be a splendid performance. He waved his arms about energetically, his face taking on a series of exaggerated expressions: alarm, anxiety, reassurance, innocence. There are few more entertaining spectacles than a crafty man showing the world how honest he is, and each time his face registered a new emotion and he reinforced it by his gesticulation the press photographers, crouched in the front row, shot off more stills. His face gleamed in the stark light of their flash bulbs.

It was a difficult press conference for Mubarak and he carried if off impressively. Some western commentators were already forecasting that he would be one of the victims of the crisis: that the people of Cairo and Alexandria, stirred up by the fundamentalists of the Muslim Brotherhood, would come out onto the streets in support of Saddam Hussein and threaten Mubarak's government and his entire policy of peace with Israel and alignment with the West. He had given the United States various private assurances about sending troops to Saudi Arabia, but it did not suit his purpose to be so direct about it in public. His first concern, as he presented it, was maintaining Arab unity. He did not want to be seen as taking the lead against Saddam Hussein.

> It shouldn't be assumed that I am on the side of Kuwait against Iraq, nor that I am going to support Kuwait. We are neutral in this. . . We have a brotherly relationship with Saddam Hussein. I asked him [before the invasion] if any of his troops would move southwards. He said what was happening was just a routine exercise, 60 or 70 miles from the Kuwaiti border. 'Is it,' I asked, 'your intention to intervene?' 'I have no intention to intervene,' he said to me . . .

Mubarak wanted to establish himself an alibi, to show that he was trying to keep the dispute within the Arab family. If he failed, it would be Saddam's fault, not his. He also wanted to appear a passive spectator, independent of the western powers.

> I'm afraid that Iraq will be subjected to a very severe threat. Don't think the foreign powers won't act. It's just my own opinion, mind you – I haven't heard this from anyone else; but it's obvious to me that there's going to be aggression. It'll be horrible and destructive. The British, the French, the Americans will come here and impose their own solution. Wouldn't it be more honourable for us to solve the problem under an Arab umbrella, without humiliation? . . .
> Naval forces are already passing through the Suez canal. I can't stop them. I don't want to get involved – don't put me in a critical position. I'm trying to uphold Arab dignity, but there's nothing I can do.

Someone asked him the most important question: Was he planning to send Egyptian troops to join the western force in Saudi Arabia?

> People say I already have troops there. I don't have any troops

there. I tell you this frankly – I'm not going to join a foreign force.

When President Mubarak tells you something frankly, it's time to watch the words he is using very carefully.

The Egyptian leader ended his press conference with a call to the rest of the Arab world to attend an emergency meeting of the Arab League in Cairo, 'before it's too late'. Although he was presenting it as a way of preventing western interference, it was clear his plan was to isolate Saddam Hussein and make it easier to cooperate with the West. The summit was to take place in the great Conference Hall in Nasser City on 9 August. That in itself was not without irony: Saddam Hussein was consciously using the issue of Kuwait as Gamal Abdel Nasser had used the issue of the Suez canal – a way of restoring his country's economic fortunes, at the same time as making a declaration of independence against Western postcolonial interests. The slogan 'Saddam is the New Nasser' had already appeared in Jordan.

If President Mubarak seemed cautious, King Fahd of Saudi Arabia was infused with a new determination, overmastering the nervousness which Saudi statesmen usually showed at times of crisis. 'This is the ugliest aggression in modern history,' he announced before leaving for Cairo. He maintained that the presence of western forces on his soil would be purely defensive and temporary, but his spokesman said later that Arab troops – he didn't specify which nationality – would be joining American troops in Saudi Arabia the following day.

There was then a hitch. Difficulties arose over the fact that the Emir of Kuwait was to be there as well as Saddam Hussein's deputy prime minister and foreign minister. Two delegations were delayed and Mubarak seems to have been worried that this postponement might favour the Iraqis. Yasser Arafat, the PLO leader, began lobbying the other members of the Arab League in support of a compromise by which Kuwait might lease the islands of Bubiyan and Warba, and a deal would be struck on the question of Iraq's debt to Kuwait and the oil from Rumailah. Eleven days before, when the two sides were preparing for their meeting in Riyadh, a compromise along these lines might have been possible. Now, after the invasion and the murder of the Emir's brother on the steps of the palace, it was unthinkable.

During the evening the Iraqis took the offensive. They announced that they weren't prepared to sit at the same table as the Emir of Kuwait since, they maintained, no such country existed any longer. They also insisted that the summit meeting should deal with what they called 'the American threat to the territory of an Arab country'. By the following morning a deal had been struck and the Arab Salvation summit, as, with some cynicism, it was starting to be called, opened 15 hours late. The two Iraqis, Taha Yasin Ramadan and Tariq Aziz, took their seats after all. The Emir of Kuwait sat apart from the rest of the Kuwaiti delegation, clearly an important part of the overnight compromise which had made it possible for the Iraqis to turn up.

In the meantime, Yasser Arafat had tried and failed to get a peace proposal accepted by the other members. His idea was to assemble a group of six Arab leaders from delegates at the conference to go to Baghdad and persuade Saddam Hussein to leave Kuwait on whatever terms that might be arranged. He argued that Saddam would not be able to withstand such moral pressure. Mubarak skilfully waved this idea aside. Arafat believed this showed that the Egyptian leader, with the encouragement of the Americans, was determined to force Saddam out of Kuwait in a way that would be humiliating to him. He was convinced that the Americans, the British, the Saudis and the Egyptians were intent on defeating Saddam and had disregarded any attempt to reach a peaceful solution.

Opening the session President Mubarak insisted that the summit was not intended as an arena for apportioning blame, then immediately said it was unacceptable for one country to use force against another – something, he said, which represented a danger for the whole Arab world. Egyptian television, which was broadcasting the opening session live, cut to Taha Ramadan at this point. He laughed and scratched his nose and the director quickly cut away from him. There were no pictures of the Emir at all, since the Egyptians didn't want to humiliate him by showing him sitting apart. Soon afterwards he walked out. Mubarak had managed to get everyone round the table just long enough to manoeuvre the Iraqis unquestionably into the wrong.

When a vote was taken on a motion to send a pan-Arab force to Saudi Arabia, and calling for the withdrawal of Iraqi troops from Kuwait, 12 countries voted in favour and there were only three votes against: Iraq, Libya and the PLO. Algeria and Yemen abstained and Jordan, Sudan and Mauritania expressed reservations. The final vote foreshadowed the broad alliance of the future, and for the first time in years it brought Syria into a pro-American grouping. It was a bravura performance by Hosni Mubarak, one of the greatest diplomatic triumphs of the crisis.

The next day the first contingent of Egyptian troops arrived in Saudi Arabia. Morocco, Syria, Bangladesh and Pakistan (where the government had just been changed by a constitutional coup) announced they would be sending troops to join them. Syria would follow later. The Arab contingent was lining up with an increasingly powerful western force. The USS *Eisenhower* would soon be joined in Gulf waters by other American and British naval vessels. Over a period of weeks ships from France, Canada, Belgium, the Netherlands, Italy, Spain, Germany and even Argentina also arrived. The Royal Air Force was already starting to assemble planes in Saudi Arabia. President Mubarak's achievement had been to make it possible for Arabs and Muslims to ally themselves with a western force; and the political and ethical difficulties lessened as time went on.

It was a matter of principle for Saddam Hussein to strike back if he were himself struck at. When it became clear that the Security Council was about to pass Resolution 661 imposing sanctions on Iraq, the foreign minister in the phantom government which had been installed in Kuwait, Walid Saud Muhammad Abdullah (a lieutenant-colonel in the Iraqi army), warned that counter-action would be taken against any country which joined in the sanctions. Lieutenant-Colonel Abdullah said governments should remember that they had interests and citizens in Kuwait.

Over the next five months the hostage issue brought European countries which might, under other circumstances, have remained neutral into the fray. In countries like Egypt, which had anticipated problems at home for joining the alliance against Iraq, the government found its position strengthened by the way its citizens were treated in Iraq and Kuwait. The taking of hostages gave extra credence to President Bush's attack on Iraq as 'international outlaws and renegades'. The taking of hostages was strictly contrary to international law and began as early as 4 August, when a group of British army and RAF officers were arrested at their homes in Kuwait and taken to Baghdad.

At first a number of foreigners in Kuwait found it relatively easy to get away across the desert: if they could get hold of the right kind of vehicle there were plenty of Iraqis who would guide them. There was uncertainty among the officials at Iraqi border crossing points which made it possible for some people to leave officially. Sometimes would-be escapers ran into Iraqi patrols and were turned back or, occasionally, arrested. Often the Iraqis would simply let them continue on their way. On one occasion, 11 August 1990, they shot and killed Douglas Croskery, a British man who was trying to escape. There was no pattern to it at all.

No one knew what the Iraqis' intentions were towards those who stayed. It is likely that Saddam Hussein himself did not know what should be done with them, beyond a general sense that they might have to pay a price for the action of their governments. It became apparent that the Iraqis were sending anyone whom they were obliged to deal with – the passengers and crew from the stranded British Airways flight for instance – to Baghdad. Then on 16 August a decision seems to have been taken. All British and American citizens in Kuwait were ordered to assemble at the Regency Palace Hotel in Kuwait City.

The British ambassador, Michael Weston, was told that the move was intended to protect the British community better. If the British community did not move voluntarily, Weston was told, they would face 'difficulties'. The Foreign Office minister in London, William Waldegrave, described the order as 'grave and sinister'. 'I hope,' he said, 'these reports and the storm of protest that will break around the head of Iraq if she pursues any policy of interning people will make her draw back, even at this late stage.' The Iraqi ambassador in London, called in to hear a formal protest, was visibly taken aback by the news; Baghdad had not informed him of the instruction.

The Regency Palace had 400 rooms and there were ten times that many British citizens in Kuwait. At first the Foreign Office advised people to go there with minimum clothing but as much food as possible. It proved to be an error of judgment: American citizens were not advised by their government to assemble at the Regency Palace and suffered no 'difficulties'. Those British people who obediently turned up at the hotel found that no one was expecting them. They drifted back home and there was no trouble as a result. Nevertheless it seemed obvious that this was an ill-planned rehearsal: any time the Iraqis decided to take action against the Westerners in Kuwait or in Iraq itself, they could do so without difficulty. Kuwait's Iraqi foreign minister, Lieutenant-Colonel Walid Abdullah, said meaningfully on Baghdad's Voice of the Masses radio station: 'These countries should not expect us to behave honourably when they are conspiring against us.' A threat from Abdullah was a threat from Saddam himself.

A heavy palm slapped the wall map of the Middle East four times: Iraq, Syria, Jordan, Egypt. The Israeli minister was thinking aloud about the sudden new political possibilities which were opening up for his country. He had a good mind and it was like listening to an enthusiastic history lecturer. Then he looked at our camera.

'Is that thing running?'

It wasn't since the meeting was off the record. A pity: it would have made excellent television, watching a member of the Israeli government thinking aloud in the briefing room which his fellow ministers use at times of crisis. The events in the Gulf didn't seem to worry him. On the contrary, he saw them as offering a new beginning, a chance to break out of the

140

regional stalemate. 'It could bring a new order and a new realism,' he said.

During the previous 10 months he had watched the breaking of blocs in Europe; now it seemed to be spreading eastwards. It was still only mid-August, but even at that stage the minister believed the chief benefit of the crisis would be the smashing of Iraq's military potential.

The Israelis were full of talk about the parallels with the 1930s: how important it was to act against a new Hitler. The phrase everyone was using was 'red line': 'A red line must be drawn in Jordan to ensure that Iraqi troops won't be sent there.' The Palestinians were full of talk about the parallels with 1956 and the new Nasser who had stood up to western pressure. I wandered around the Arab quarters of old Jerusalem looking at the slogans on the walls – 'Saddam Our Leader', 'Unite For Action', 'Arise!' Some had been blotted out with black paint: those were the ones the Israeli soldiers had found most offensive.

It was very quiet in the Arab areas. More often than not the shops were closed for the latest strike which no shopkeeper wanted and no shopkeeper felt able to break. The Israeli parts of the city, by contrast, seemed to have a new bustle to them. On both sides of the divide, though, people were expecting something to happen, and both thought it would benefit them and harm the others. 'We have to have pride in ourselves,' said a rather gloomy Palestinian shopkeeper I knew. He was no great supporter of Saddam, but he believed as strongly as anyone else that Saddam would give him this elusive quality.

I went down to Jericho. In the folds and valleys of the wilderness on either side of the road from Jericho to Jerusalem, Bedouin had pitched their tents and were tending their goats, as they always had. Above them, strategic hilltops had been taken over by the developed world: blocks of white apartments, like fortified yuppy estates, showed where the settlers had staked their claim to Eretz Israel. We drove past the sign that points towards the place where Jesus was baptized. Something had happened here not long before: the streets were still buzzing with excitement.

'What's going on?' I kept asking. No one would tell me.

Instead they just made vague gestures down the street, as though it was a private quarrel. A bored Israeli soldier made my Palestinian driver wait for a long time. He put up with it and said nothing. Being Palestinian in Israel is like being black in pre-de Klerk South Africa: the only choice you have is between open resentment and meek obedience.

For a place so numinous, the Allenby bridge, which crosses the river Jordan and links the road from Jerusalem with the road to Amman, is remarkably unimpressive. Metal, ricketty and small, the Allenby's unfixed timbers rattle under your wheels as you cross a reed-clogged river the width of the Cam at Magdalene. Yet it marks a great frontier, not just between Israel and the Arabs but between the developed world and the Third World. The no man's land is lined with rusty wire and sown with mines. The dry limestone hillocks and the empty plain beyond are as colourless as a David Roberts drawing.

On the Israeli side of the bridge, in the shade of a eucalyptus grove, a soldier glanced at my passport. Someone has ordered them to be polite, at least to non-Arabs. They are bigger and tougher-looking than the weedy Jordanian soldiers, and a great deal more effective. Things are just as slovenly, as rusting, as dirty and unpainted on the Israeli side of the river, but you feel it's because the Israelis concentrate on the things that count, like military efficiency. Jordan is a nicer country to be in, but it has a thousand reasons and excuses for being ineffective.

Amman, I found, was in a high state of excitement. Saddam Hussein's face glared or smiled at me from almost every shop window and the back window of every taxi. His 12 August offer to link withdrawal from Kuwait to an Israeli withdrawal from the Occupied Territories – which owed everything to Yasser Arafat and the PLO – had electrified the Palestinian population of the city.

'This is our opportunity,' said a Palestinian friend of mine with a heat I had not previously associated with him. I asked him how he, a man of honour and decency, could think it was possible to build a Palestinian state on a foundation of aggression and piracy. Hadn't the Kuwaitis now lost their land in something of the way the Palestinians had lost theirs?

Wouldn't the very soil of a country gained by such means have a taint to it for ever? He told me I was wrong, but didn't explain how.

The western journalists quoted to each other the articles on the editorial page of Amman's English-language newspaper. They were written by a rather excitable man in not very good English who rambled a good deal:

> Those who come here from the West in search of fame will only find it if they learn the ways of the camel, this extraordinary ship of the desert, with big, fat, ugly feet − supported on veritable cushions made by the hand of God himself. The Middle East does not work like a microwave oven. Arabia is not Arkansas.

Everything was somehow the fault of the United States and Britain; and the United States and Britain had to act, and act fast, to make up for the wrong they had done: to Jordan, to the Palestinians, to the children of Iraq, to the Third World in general.

At first glance it seems to be strongly supportive of the line taken by Saddam Hussein. On closer inspection, however, it is the very opposite of what he was saying and doing. The *Jordan Times* writer, like a great many Palestinians and Jordanians, felt the western powers had a duty to undo the wrongs they had done; there could be no justice and no peace until that happened. Saddam's approach was far more radical: Arabs should take matters into their own hands and stand up to the western powers, not sit around waiting for them to do something. The one was the attitude of postcolonial dependence, still looking to the old imperial power for everything; the other was something far bolder and more aggressive.

The name and telephone number of the *Jordan Times* writer appeared on everyone's contacts list. Many of the western journalists seemed to feel he must represent the views of King Hussein, and when they couldn't see the King they read articles in the *Jordan Times* instead. A good deal of unnecessary harm was done to Jordan's reputation, particularly in the United States, by this means.

I laboured up the hill to the King's palace in the August heat and spent time with the King's officials while he was away. They did not blame everything on the United States and Britain, but they were extremely glum about the future.

'We all hope His Majesty will come out of this reasonably well,' said a youngish man in a superb blue double-breasted suit, glancing at a picture of the King as he spoke. A large overhead fan thrashed around as he spoke. His tone reminded me of talking to a similarly-dressed young man in the Shah's palace in Tehran in August 1978. Neither he nor his colleagues seemed to think Saddam Hussein had provided them with an opportunity.

'There is nothing we can do but go along with it, though,' said an older man. The younger ones nodded seriously. Some of them had not even been born in 1958, when their King's cousin had been overthrown and murdered in Baghdad.

Part of my reason for spending time at the palace was to ask the King to use his influence with Saddam Hussein to get me a visa to go to Baghdad. I did not realize at that point how little influence the King had on Saddam. I applied at the Iraqi embassy in Amman, which was constantly besieged by Jordanians and Egyptians who also wanted visas to go to Iraq. The only way to enter the building was to trick the doorman into opening the door. A well-placed foot kept it open and a little pushing was needed to get one's entire body inside. But once in it was useless. The press attaché, when I asked him if I could have a visa, merely asked: 'Why not?' My strategy of trying to cover the crisis from Baghdad was looking increasingly ill-chosen.

The only other contact I had made was with the Iraqi press attaché in London, a charming and amusing man with great appetites and a stoical view of the world. His office, like the Iraqi embassy in Paris, was pretty dark: the windows had been smashed early on in the crisis and the police, who seemed not to be very interested, suggested it was the work of football hooligans (Naiel Hassan, the press attaché, is something of a football fan and was able to tell the police how far it was to the nearest football ground: a long way.) He had promised to see if he could get me a visa, but as the days passed all he could tell me down the phone line to Amman was that he was still negotiating with Baghdad.

And then Tariq Aziz came to Amman and gave a press conference. He put a pleasant-seeming face on everything, especially the hostage question:

> First, they are not hostages. I am sorry the president of the United States should have used a wrong word for the situation of these people. We really meant that we would like to keep them as guests for a while and live with our own people. And then, living with our people in the places where they live, they might contribute to peace – they might prevent the dangerous policies of the US administration.

The conference room was very hot and very full. At times Tariq Aziz showed his anger at the questions. I asked him a couple, more to allow my face to register with him than anything else. Then, when he was leaving, I managed to force my way through the crowd of reporters and security men and slipped out of the building with his party. I planted myself in front of him and the Iraqi ambassador in Amman as they were about to get into their car.

'Would it be possible for the BBC to visit Baghdad?'

'Why not?'

For once it didn't seem like a fend-off and I told the ambassador I would be in touch with him. The next day, through the combined influence of the ambassador to Jordan and of Naiel Hassan in London, our visas came through from Baghdad. Without my being certain how, the right combination of buttons had been pressed at last.

Silent City

Ladies and gentlemen; dear children: I know that you are pained because your relatives are not allowed to leave Iraq. I am just as pained as you are... [A]ll of us are sorry for what happened, which was not of our making but was the outcome of the will of certain people who acted arbitrarily and deviated from the will and teachings of God.

Saddam Hussein, open letter to the families of foreigners in Iraq, August 1990

I was nervous. A friend of mine, high up in the Foreign Office, rang twice to advise me not to go. Another friend, who had known Iraq well during the worst times, was even more insistent. The decision to hold foreigners hostage, for purposes which were still unclear, had disturbed everyone. So why did I still insist on going? Partly it was a spirit of contrariness, no doubt, but there was also the feeling that something which had taken so long to achieve couldn't be discarded now that it had been obtained. I opened my passport and looked at it for the twentieth time: a green and red sticker on page seven, with a heraldic yet mildly caricatured eagle at its head and a few carelessly entered details:

Embassy of the Republic of Iraq in: AMMAN
No.: 2/44/4
Date: 22/8/90 (this in Arabic numerals)
Type of visa: ANTRY
Holder is permitted to enter Iraq until: 3 MONTH
Number of journeys: ONES

Underneath was a blue stamp:

> Visitors who expect to stay in Iraq for more than 30 days
> should contact the Residence Directorate in Baghdad during
> their stay. Those who fail to do so will be liable to Prosecution.

This, however, was scarcely likely to be our big problem.

I was fortunate in my companions. It seemed a good idea to go with as few people as possible in case something unpleasant happened. There were four of us: Ray Gibbon, a friend and colleague for many years, whom I had first worked with when he volunteered to work in Lebanon in the 1982 war. He was a tough terrier of a man, keen and enthusiastic no matter what happened, who looked and acted a good deal younger than his 50 or so years. He was witty and quick-minded and would be good company. In addition, he wasn't the type to blame me if everything went wrong.

Dave McDonald was Ray's opposite physically, tall and rangy with a wispy little beard like General Custer. Dave's quiet drawl placed him as coming from the northern part of the United States and he was as laid back as you might expect of someone who had studied at the University of Colorado in Boulder. He worked for the television agency Visnews, the BBC's closest ally, and had all the skills you develop if you have to do everything yourself: he was producer, cameraman, picture editor all in one. Having grown up in the Gulf, he also spoke Arabic.

The fourth member of the team was the most famous. Mohammed Amin had been born in pre-Independence India but had grown up in Kenya. He was a cameraman too, working for Visnews. His pictures of the Ethiopian famine in 1984 when he was working with the BBC correspondent Michael Buerk had touched the conscience of everyone who had seen them. But Mo was mostly an entrepreneur, working on books and documentaries, fixing deals, pulling strings. His contacts with the general in charge of Pakistan's security service had once helped me greatly in Afghanistan. He knew everybody it was necessary to know. All in all, then, my three companions were the kind I could trust and have an amusing time with: the only criteria which really matter.

Friends shooks hands with me with a special intensity when

we left the InterContinental Hotel and a couple of photographers took snaps of us, just in case. A cameraman filmed us loading the gear onto baggage carts at the airport. Someone threw a few questions about why we were going. It felt like marching up to the front line past a freshly-dug mass grave: very sensible, no doubt, but it's hard not to think about the purpose it'll be put to. 'Before leaving on his last, ill-fated journey,' Simpson said . . .' I made my answers as flippant as possible.

The plane was full of Iraqis returning home. There was only one way to fly to Baghdad now that the UN Security Council's sanctions had come into force: a single daily Iraqi Airlines flight from Amman. I had assumed we would have problems with our fellow passengers but that was because I didn't understand the situation. It proved to be an important lesson.

'BBC, eh?' said a member of the Iraqi Airways crew as he handed me a glass of flat cola. 'Everyone in Baghdad listening to BBC.' He looked round and said, in a quieter voice: 'Is the only way to find out what happen. Even in Iraq.'

The man sitting behind me heard part of the conversation and dug me in the back with a powerful forefinger. 'Welcome,' he said before putting his head back into his in-flight magazine. Every time I looked round, the other passengers would smile at us, even the ones who had been moved so we could sit together.

The flight attendants let us leave the plane first. Only Ray Gibbon seemed unaffected by the nervousness of the moment. We emerged into the arrivals hall and a large group of security men, not expecting us so soon, scattered like snooker balls to the outer edges of the hall as we came through the door. Two of them sat near us, not saying anything, looking at the wall in front of them with unfocussed eyes. The Iraqi passengers waited quietly for their luggage, aware that they were back in a country where everyone was under permanent observation.

Our Information Ministry 'minder' melted away once the job of meeting us and ushering our equipment through customs was over. We were on our own. We pushed our way through the airport doors and the savage heat wrapped round us like a hot towel at the barber's: 42 degrees centigrade, the pilot had told us on the plane. Too hot for flies, which was a comfort. It was also too hot for taxis. We stood looking at the empty road for some time until despair made me jump out in front of a passing orange-and-white cab and offer him serious money to drive us into town. A little later we were lucky enough to hijack another on the approach road.

The motorway from the airport was entirely empty, except for some buses which the driver said were going to the airport to pick up returning Iraqi prisoners from the war with Iran. Otherwise nothing: no cars, no trucks, no buses, not even a bicycle. 'Welcome to Baghdad, Capital of Arab's Saddam', said a notice beside the road. Arab's Saddam was also much honoured in portraits along the middle of the road. The driver explained that the official rate for the dollar, which had always been artificially high, was now close to ruinous. When I had been in Baghdad the previous May, three beers, a Pepsi-Cola and a pot of tea had cost the equivalent of $100 at the official rate. Now it was three times as bad as that.

The temperature inside the taxi was stifling, so I opened the window. It was like being blasted in the face with a blowtorch and I shut it fast. The taxi driver, a gap-toothed, ill-shaven character, snorted his amusement.

We reached the centre of town. Things had changed here too: the great gateway leading to the presidential palace now had a couple of anti-aircraft guns on top of it. The gunners peered down at us; cars were rare enough to warrant a second look. I knew what Ray and Mo must be feeling in the car behind me and I hoped very hard that they would not give way to the temptation to film the gates and the guns.

It was Tuesday evening and the streets of Baghdad should have been filled with people enjoying the evening and getting ready for the weekend. Instead, things were strangely quiet. We drove along Rashid Street, where Eamonn Matthews and I had come during our visit in May in search of watches with Saddam's face on them, as worn by Baathist enthusiasts and sycophants. Now it was mostly empty and many of the shops were closed. A few men sat outside drinking tea from small glasses. Their heads turned to watch us drive past. An armoured personnel carrier was parked in a side street, its gun pointing towards us. Soldiers stood on every street corner, tough-looking characters who looked as though they knew how to use their guns. Were they expecting the Americans or the British to attack this early? Or were they there to make sure the citizenry remained loyal? The more I watched them, the more I thought it must be the second. Saddam didn't want any unscheduled awkwardness in the streets.

We arrived at the Sheraton. It was silent and almost empty, except for the kind of men lounging around who could only be working for the Mukhabarat. A notice on the reception desk warned us not to try paying with credit cards. I remembered the man and woman behind the desk from last time. If they remembered me, they were careful not to show it and kept their eyes away from mine. It was all rather disturbing. I sat down in my room and started ringing round the people I had met before. One man put the phone down when he heard my voice. At the British embassy a security man said 'Which organization do you say you work for?' and was unable to help. It didn't seem to upset him greatly; it never does at British embassies.

We were the first British journalists to arrive in Baghdad since the invasion of Kuwait and we had beaten our competitors thoroughly on one of the things that mattered most to us and to them. Teams from the American networks CBS and ABC had been allowed in earlier in the week for a couple of days and had been bundled out again. I was determined to get a report out as quickly as possible and went to the business services office in the hotel because I remembered that they had put me through to London very quickly the previous May. I also remembered that Farzad Bazoft had used this office and evidence from his phone calls and telexes had featured at his trial.

The women who worked there, dark and heavily beautiful, were all Assyrian Christians with good English, brought up no doubt on stories of past pogroms. They were deeply nervous of me, yet their upbringing made it impossible for them to be anything except pleasant and helpful. I felt like the carrier of a plague bacillus: my actions could end in their disappearance or imprisonment. Now, though, they were more frightened about the likelihood of war.

'Will things be very bad?' one of them asked with a touching anxiety. I tried to reassure her. 'Please remember,' she went on, as though I had the power to stop the air raids, 'that it isn't our fault.'

A big portrait of Saddam Hussein kept watch on me from the wall as I read over my report, uncensored, about the strange atmosphere in Baghdad. The Assyrian girls looked at one another nervously. There were strange noises on the line just as I was finishing and the line went dead. The girls smiled as pleasantly as they could, but the whole episode had worried them.

We had an appointment with the minister of information, together with the CNN team who had travelled into Baghdad with us. As we walked out into the early evening heat a group of taxi drivers leaped up: the word had gone round that the empty hotel had guests again. One stood out from the shambling, sleepy-looking crowd: a short man with a face the colour of a Sam Browne belt and a distinctly military bearing. His hair was as black and as plastered across his head as the character in the French soap opera I had watched in the Iraqi embassy in Paris. He seemed ancient but wiry; I learned afterwards he was only four years older than I was. His car was a large red Toyota Crown, the limousine of the Middle East, and I took to him at once.

'Name Mr Hattam,' he said, coming close to saluting. He never referred to himself, I found, in the first person. It was always 'Mr Hattam wait here, six o'clock in morning,' or 'Mr Hattam very tired. Have two wives.' One of the cornerstones of my future in Iraq had been laid and his smooth driving and his air-conditioned car cemented it.

We were shown into the office of the director general of the Information Ministry. He came round from his desk with an ironic smile on his face. 'Mr Simpson. Welcome, welcome.' He was a pleasant-looking, highly-westernized man who could have been French or even British. Not everyone found him as charming as I did; after an exchange with him some time later, a *New York Times* man took refuge at the American embassy and slept his remaining four nights in Iraq on an office floor.

I liked Naji al-Hadithi from the start, because his grasp of English was extremely good and he was a confirmed Anglo-

151

phile. He had a well-developed sense of humour and never minded what jokes I made to him. He reminded me a little of some witty, feline official trained at the Sublime Porte under the Ottoman Empire. It is easy to think that, because you have good relations with senior people in a government, you will be protected when things go wrong. But as Farzad Bazoft had found, in Iraq you are on your own. Your highly-placed friends can do nothing more than shrug their shoulders and give that apologetic smile.

Together we entered a large room with a sofa and chairs in one corner and an Iraqi flag behind them. We were about to meet another of the stock figures of my time in Baghdad, Latif Nsayef Jassim, minister of culture and information. It was Jassim who had said of Farzad: 'Mrs Thatcher wanted him alive. We gave her the body.' It was also Jassim who, at an international television film festival held in Baghdad during the Iran–Iraq war, had announced in his opening speech that to celebrate this auspicious moment a dozen Scud missiles had been fired at Tehran. Most of the Arabs in his audience stood up and cheered.

Jassim proved to be a dapper little man in his tailored olive-green Party uniform, with a display handkerchief sticking out of the top pocket: a revolutionary travelling business class. He had a pleasant, open face and meat-grinder English which I and others shamelessly flattered him into using. I always thought it was rather brave of him: a slip in a language of which he was not master could have landed him in serious trouble.

Jassim was undoubtedly close to Saddam Hussein. There were pictures of them with their arms around each other on the walls of the corridor linking the lifts to the interview room. Although he was not a clever or inventive man (and perhaps for that very reason) it was safe to assume that he had Saddam's backing for everything he said. Now he explained to us that there was no reason to worry about the hostages: they were the guests of Iraq and no harm would come to them. Why, anyway, must we insist on calling them 'hostages'?

The news began on Iraqi television as we were moving from one room to another. I stood in front of the set in Naji al-

Hadithi's office, balancing my notebook awkwardly and trying to take down his rapid translation as he went along. In these curious conditions there would be no chance of checking back on anything that had been said. Saddam Hussein was visiting a camp or installation where British hostages were being held. We saw pictures of children playing chess and kicking a football around. Then we were indoors. Saddam Hussein was sitting on a chair at the end of the room and a group of nervous-looking British people were answering his questions. Saddam beckoned and a boy of about 10 walked unwillingly over to him. His name, he said, was Stewart. Saddam draped his arm over Stewart's shoulder in a way that set my teeth on edge.

'Are you getting your milk, Stewart? And your cornflakes too?'

Stewart, standing very stiff and embarrassed as though he could scarcely bear the touch, said he was.

'I don't think all Iraqi kids can get cornflakes now. So please forgive us, because we, like you, have our own children, like Stewart and Ian [Stewart's brother], and we have our own women like you, and have our own families. We know how you feel, but we are trying to prevent a war from happening.'

There was something very wrong about the whole exchange, but not perhaps in the sense that most people in the West who saw these pictures would have assumed. Iraq is a culture where it is regarded as perfectly normal for men to touch children who are not their own; in Britain it is emphatically not. The stiffness of Stewart's reaction made it seem far worse, although this was probably just the result of shyness and embarrassment. But there was something more unpleasant underlying the episode, which derived from Saddam's willingness to take this opportunity to make propaganda. It was a reminder to Iraqi viewers of his propaganda claim that their children were going short of milk while these British children, whose government was responsible for cutting off the milk supply, were enjoying the best of everything. The whole interchange was deliberately phoney: the effect was to stress the difference between the suffering of Iraqi children and the little boy whose shoulder he was clasping. The body language of the two, though misread in the outside world, nevertheless pointed to a deeper accuracy.

The Iraqis certainly wanted to show that the hostages were being well treated; that too was an important part of the propaganda line. Saddam Hussein talked at some length to the parents:

> Ladies, how are you passing the time? I am an Iraqi, and I realize that if I were in your shoes I would rather be at home in Iraq. But sometimes one is forced to do things that are not one's own choice. Your presence here and in other places is meant to avoid the scourge of war; in Arabic we would say 'preventing danger'.

When he found that one of the boys in the group, Alan Barnett, was on his own and had simply been visiting a friend in Iraq, the President gave orders that he should be allowed to go home. At the same time he made it clear that if Iraq suffered so would the other hostages:

> In the past few days I've come across articles published in western newspapers, so-called democratic papers, in which the writers urge President Bush to actually strike at Iraq and Baghdad, despite the fact of your presence here. And they talk about human life and humanitarian issues!

Jassim, the information minister, seemed delighted with the whole spectacle, believing that it had shown Saddam to the West in a sympathetic light. On the contrary his willingness to release a single prisoner on a whim demonstrated clearly that he could release everyone if he chose and his concern for their welfare seemed hypocritical. When we broadcast all this the reaction was a strong one: the British Foreign Secretary, Douglas Hurd, called it sickening; it was roundly condemned in the United States, the Soviet Union, France and Germany. The British ambassador, Harold Walker, placed it in a less emotive context when I spoke to him the next day:

> It's right out of our tradition, and it really makes one feel a bit nauseated. But also here one's very conscious that it's part of a

very successful propaganda campaign which may be having an effect in some parts of the Arab world.

He also tried to calm some western fears:

The Iraqi authorities have always assured us that although our people might be detained, and although we might not have any access to them, and not even know where they are, they would be 100 per cent safe. I've always believed that. I think perhaps the President wanted to show it visually.

The television station, from which we had to satellite our report, seemed an ill-omened place that night. In the hot darkness soldiers patrolled the empty roadway. No car would stop nearby for fear of them, so Mr Hattam had to drive past and park in a side road. An armoured personnel carrier sheltered in an entrance; another was parked on the pavement at the far end of the building. The APCs were not there to protect against an Allied attack: they were guarding the natural first objective of any coup attempt.

Nothing had been easy for us and we had arrived with only five minutes to spare before our satellite booking. The link would last for only 15 minutes and we had doubts about the ability of Iraqi Television to cope with the precision of western satellites.

The soldiers inside the entrance did not share our sense of urgency. We had no written permission to enter the building and there was no answer from the office of the powerful woman who ran the television news department, the only person with the authority to let us enter. Dave McDonald remained relaxed, slumped in a chair. I paced up and down, sweating, waving away the sleepy flies with the cassette that had our report on it. The soldiers joked about me while the clock ticked into our satellite time. Later that night, when we satellited for a second time, I found that if I wrenched the door open and ran through in spite of them they wouldn't shoot me. On this first visit we were less certain.

At last the woman in charge came walking across the courtyard with exaggerated slowness. I shouted at her angrily and we headed off. In the darkness of the courtyard there was a smell of sewage and my foot caught on the broken pavement. Feral kittens playing in an abandoned oil drum squeaked and scattered. Dave and I ducked under a tree, an apparently live wire and an air conditioning unit before following her through a door and along a corridor. I took a sideways glance at her in the artificial light: Madame Awatif was in her forties, handsome and dark, her hair tied back like Eva Peron's. She had an unpleasant way of imitating what you said while her face took on a sneering expression. She had great power over us and many western television people came to loathe her. I regarded her with respect and even liking. Unlike some of her colleagues, she was both incorruptible and hard-working. Although our first satellite was a disaster, she made sure everything worked properly when we reappeared a couple of hours later.

Madame Awatif was, however, a brutal censor. 'Take that out!' she bellowed the next day, as an innocuous shot of the Baghdad skyline appeared We had filmed it at Naji al-Hadithi's suggestion, from the window of his office. That cut no ice even though he was her boss. 'I will not allow this,' she snapped as pictures of a woman carrying something on her head came onto the screen. When she saw our shots of the awful crossed swords of Saddam's monument to the war with Iran she hissed: 'Quite impossible.' If her objection had been aesthetic it would have been easier to take. It can scarcely have been on grounds of security, since the swords featured prominently on television each night before the news. Why, then?

'No discussion,' said Madame Awatif, her mouth shutting like a mousetrap.

It seemed clear that Saddam Hussein was becoming unsettled about the policy of holding hostages. On 25 August, two days after we arrived, the President Kurt Waldheim of Austria flew into Baghdad with a group of journalists. It was a curious move. Dr Waldheim had never managed to make himself internationally acceptable after the disclosure of his wartime record. It seemed as though he was trying to buy himself some popularity at home by coming to Iraq to plead for the release of the 80 or so Austrian hostages in Iraq and Kuwait. It was not regarded in London or Washington as a good idea and he was much criticized. In fact he set a precedent which was followed by a number of other politicians who came to Iraq for different reasons and were mostly rewarded with the release of some, at least, of their nationals.

As UN secretary general Dr Waldheim had played a part in an effort to end the Iran–Iraq war and was accorded a good deal of respect in Baghdad. While the West mostly saw his decision to go there as a further sign of his general unacceptability, it was greeted in Iraq as a sign that the outside world was starting to come to its senses. Watching the proceedings on Iraqi television, it seemed as though Dr Waldheim was being a little embarrassing in his praise of President Saddam Hussein and Saddam reciprocated. There was a lengthy press conference, at which the Austrian television correspondent had the quickness of mind to ask Saddam if she could stay in Baghdad for a few days. He agreed and said that all the Austrian journalists were free to stay. Many of them, however, turned the opportunity down. That evening Dr Waldheim and the 80 Austrian hostages took off for Vienna.

King Hussein of Jordan saw this as an opportunity to get other hostages released. He appealed to Saddam to free the families of the American diplomats in Kuwait who had been told that they and the staff of all the other embassies there should close down and leave. The Soviet Union closed its embassy, saying this did not constitute recognition of the Iraqi takeover. Most of the western embassies, however, had elected to stay. A convoy of more than 50 American women and children left Baghdad in an operation which the American chargé d'affaires in Baghdad, Joe Wilson, tried unsuccessfully to keep secret. A group of women and children, the dependents of German diplomats, reached the Turkish border but were turned back by the Iraqis. The wife of a French diplomat in Kuwait was taken off a plane at Baghdad airport as she tried to leave. There seemed to be no clear policy.

The only principle behind it all was the growing realization that holding the hostages was turning into a serious political liability. On the evening of 28 August, in one of the interminably extended news bulletins that always began with Saddam's activities that day, we saw him meeting a group of British, Japanese and American hostages. It started off in much the same way as the earlier meetings, and seemed intended purely as an exercise in reassurance. 'Sometimes,' he told them, 'even unpleasant circumstances open the way for good relationships and happy encounters.' But soon his mood changed and he said that any attack on Iraq might cost the lives of western women and children – people like themselves. 'If it were just a matter of you who are here with me now,' he said, 'I'd be glad to let you go free. But it's wider and more complicated than that.'

Finally, sounding like a chat show host, he said: 'I'm told we've got one little lady here with a birthday. Happy birthday, Rachel.' Apparently on the spur of the moment he said that Rachel and her mother could leave. Some of the British women began asking him questions and at the end he again said, with no pause for thought, that all women and children could leave. Most western commentators afterwards believe it was simply another charade, that he had decided already to release them because of the embarrassment the hostage issue had caused, and that he chose to announce it in this way. To those of us watching it seemed like another of his sudden changes of mind, of the type that had induced him to invade the whole of Kuwait in the first place. Certainly no one at that stage had done any planning for an exodus which involved several hundred people.

Even during the brief time we were there, less than two weeks, I could see the changes that were taking place. When we first arrived, Saddam Hussein – judging, perhaps, by what he himself would do in such a situation – was still expecting a sudden attack by the Allies. In the first few days of the crisis, according to Yasser Arafat, he had even forecast the possibility of a nuclear attack on Baghdad. The great archaeological treasures were taken from the museums and kept in safe places: the Assyrian bulls, the Sumerian jewellery, the Akkadian cuneiform texts. And Saddam being Saddam, he included in the great national treasures, to be protected at all costs, the thousands of photographs of himself, most of them taken by Hussein Mohammed Ali, his personal photographer. The entire gallery at the Saddam Art Centre was emptied and closed down, so that posterity would be certain of having enough photographs of Saddam Hussein.

Slowly, however, that first sense of fear and tension faded. No one seemed to think that the crisis would continue to develop; it was more natural to assume that a deal would be done, a compromise reached. Everyone in Baghdad I spoke to, from the most loyal of officials to the Kurdish woman who told me in much too loud a voice of her hatred and contempt for Saddam, forecast a settlement under which western forces would withdraw from Saudi Arabia, Iraqi troops would withdraw from Kuwait, and the way would be open for a settlement of the Palestinian question, very much along the lines of Saddam's 12 August offer.

By the beginning of September there was a new and easier atmosphere in Baghdad. We were by no means the only westerners there now: more and more news organizations were being allowed into Baghdad. There was a brief moment of concern when Mo Amin was prevented from getting on a plane bound for Amman (some private concern called him away halfway through our trip). The difficulty was soon sorted out and it was clear that he would be allowed to leave the country without hindrance. We even noticed that the security surveillance of us was becoming much lighter; there had never been so many foreign journalists in Iraq before and the Mukhabarat must have had problems coping with us.

I was slowly coming to another view of Iraq, a view which bore little relationship to the usual western picture of the place and none at all to the increasingly excitable views in the British and American tabloid press. We had spent part of one day filming at the offices of the British Council. There were at least a dozen people there, reading quietly in the library or drinking tea in the café. The staff said they had had no problems from anyone: no threats, no attacks, no demonstrations. On the contrary, more and more people were coming in to thank them for staying open during this time of crisis. I was struck, too, by the general absence of hostility to us. The newspapers were full of bitter condemnation of the crimes that Britain and the West generally were supposedly committing against Iraq. And yet I had not found anyone who, in private, justified the invasion of Kuwait or had any criticism to make of the western powers. People were frightened and worried, but not hostile.

One evening, after finishing our satellite feed, we drove along the east bank of the Tigris, past dozens of restaurants and cafés. Rationing had already been introduced, though apart from queues at the bread shops and reports of a rice shortage there were no serious problems. It wouldn't be long before most of the restaurants would be closed by law but for the moment they were open, and doing good business. People were eating their kebabs and rice down one side of the road, while on the other, the river side, they were eating the Baghdad speciality, *mazgouf*: a rather mushy fish barbecued in front of a giant fire in traditional style. There was plenty of alcohol around: Iraq had never been a strict Muslim society and Saddam Hussein's increasingly religious rhetoric would not turn it into one. As the appetizing smell of wood smoke and fish swirled around them, the diners sat back and enjoyed themselves.

At our hotel, too, a strange transformation was taking place. The atmosphere of gloom and surveillance gave way for a few hours to something more endearing. There was a skirl of trumpets and a woman in a large white wedding dress came in on the arm of a man in a white dinner jacket. Both were sweating in the evening heat. I saw them later on, walking around shyly together down a corridor, hand in hand, in more sensible clothes. Downstairs, meanwhile, there were sudden bursts of ululation as other newly-weds headed for the Semiramis Lounge or the Sheherezade Room for their reception. Wars are good for the wedding industry. That night, as I listened to the faint noise of revelry downstairs, I found my ideas changing. For a moment Baghdad had lost its atmosphere of threat and anxiety. I had caught a glimpse of something timeless, more attractive and much more sympathetic than the angry speeches of Saddam Hussein.

The Rape of Kuwait

Q: How can you justify the atrocities committed by Iraqi troops in your name? . . .
A: What is certain is that I have not heard of any such acts. It is possible that. . . the western media is trying to fill the minds of people everywhere, every day, with lies about the situation. . . it is also possible that some false reports may come out of Kuwait, claiming the sort of things you have described.

Saddam Hussein, interviewed by Trevor MacDonald for ITN, November 1990

It was early evening and we had finished our work for the day. It had been quiet enough: nothing more than a demonstration by children carrying heart-shaped cardboard placards with a wide selection of peaceful slogans:

Iraqi Children Love Their Leader Because He Cares For Childhood
The Evil Forces Do Not Love Saddam Hussein Because He Loves Peace
Mr Bush Do Not Flex Your Muscles On Iraqi Children
Children Of The World, Prevent Your Fathers Killing Us
Saddam Hussein Is The Symbol Of Our Love And The Defender Of Our Dignity
Saddam, We Are Yours For Ever

A nasty-looking fat boy harangued the audience – the demonstration was being held in the theatre of Baghdad University – about the evil that the United States and its allies were doing in singling out the children of Iraq for their special hatred. His gestures were reminiscent of Mussolini's. A little girl yelled out a message in English: 'Yes, yes to peace, no, no to war.' She did it with great earnestness, beating her fists on the lectern for emphasis. A cameraman working for one of the American networks, a pleasant, thoughtful man, was standing beside me.

'Guess they really mean all this peace stuff. Makes you think: hey, suppose they're right and we're wrong?' He shook his head. 'I mean, like everybody wants peace. And who wants to kill these kids? I sure don't.'

We put the pictures into a story about Iraq's propaganda aims and there were the usual problems with the censor. For once there would be no more satellites that night. For the first time in three weeks it was possible to think about eating a decent meal at a respectable time, instead of foraging from tins at midnight. I changed and wandered back along the corridor to the room we used as an office. The door was shut. I hammered on it loudly. When someone opened it the television set was on too loud, braying music in praise of Saddam. Everyone in the room seemed strained and I couldn't work out what was going on. A couple of men I hadn't seen before were sitting side by side, looking up at me nervously. It was only when we were introduced that they settled back in their chairs and went on talking. The flow of their story seemed stilted for some time after that and I saw that I had put them off.

Gradually they warmed to the subject again. One was Irish, the other was a Dutchman who had been based in Ireland. They had just arrived from Kuwait where they had been in hiding. One of the men had been the director of a big catering company and he was still bristling with anger. On their way in to the Al-Rasheed Hotel they had spotted one of his delivery trucks, stolen from Kuwait and repainted, standing in the hotel car park. He had run his fingers over the letters of his company's name underneath its new disguise of paint.

'152 Mercedes-Benz trucks I had in Kuwait. All of them stolen by the Iraqis. We used to prepare 145,000 school meals a day and deliver them to the schools. And that's all gone too.'

The other man was a management consultant. Both had been wardens of the small Irish community in hiding in Kuwait, keeping tabs on everyone each day, sorting out problems with health or food, finding out if they had news of anyone else in the community. They called it 'positive feedback'. Most of the foreign groups in Kuwait operated a similar system. They were helped by the fact that the Iraqis had been unable to work the sophisticated phonetapping system which a British company had installed for the Kuwaiti government, in which any one of thousands of keywords in 51 languages would automatically trip a recording machine. And because the Kuwaitis had always billed their foreign customers at their offices, the Iraqis never found out which telephone number applied to which private house or flat.

Now the two men, the Dutchman and the Irishman, were free to leave: Saddam Hussein had declared that all hostages could go. But they were very nervous. They had with them, hidden away, evidence of various crimes carried out by the Iraqi forces in Kuwait. They were worried that when they left the following morning these things would be found on them. They wanted to talk to us before they went, in case something happened to them. I promised that we would go with them to the airport the next day and make sure they caught their plane. After that they brightened up a little and continued their story.

We had heard plenty of rumours in Baghdad about what had been going on in Kuwait, but nothing certain. When Vice-President Dan Quayle, quoted the American wife of a Kuwaiti as saying she had watched Iraqi soldiers bayonetting a pregnant woman, it was hard not to remember propaganda stories in World War I Britain about German soldiers spitting babies on their bayonets and murdering nuns. There was no doubt that serious crimes had been committed as loot from Kuwait was everywhere in Baghdad: vast supplies of frozen food in the shops; new police cars with the Kuwaiti markings painted out; the latest BMWs and Mercedes, unregistered, being driven by the playboy sons of generals; there were 14,000 new buses in circulation in Baghdad and elsewhere which had been stolen from Kuwait. But there was a major difference between looting and bayonetting pregnant women.

I listened to the Irish-accented voices, rational and pleasant, describing the kind of things they had seen and experienced during the previous four and a half months:

It was on 5 August, just three days after the invasion. They came bursting into my apartment and held me and another man at gunpoint. There were three women in the apartment at the time as well. They raped all of them, including one who was seven months pregnant. I saw them do it. Four men raped her, in front of her little son, who was four years old – my godson. They were Republican Guards, you could tell them by their red berets. One of the officers made the youngest soldier do it – he was hanging back, like he was afraid. He just pushed him forward and made him do it. Afterwards we took the three girls down to one of the big hotels, but they would only take one of the girls in. The American who was the manager there said if they allowed everyone to have their relatives and friends there, they'd be inundated.

Gradually the stories began to flow from them both.

I happened to be looking out when a car with soldiers in it crashed into another car. Maybe it was their fault, maybe it was the Kuwaiti's. I don't know. Anyway, they pulled him out of the car and started beating him up. Then one of them ran over to a roadworker who was standing there and took his shovel off him, and swung it at this poor fellow's leg. And he almost cut it off with one swipe. He just lay there in a pool of blood with his leg hanging off, and they got in the car and drove away.

Death became a familiar sight, so familiar no one did anything much about it. On one of the main bridges in the centre of the city, the Dutchman said, he noticed a body lying in the roadway. It was a Kuwaiti who had been shot by the Iraqis. People just drove over it. The head, the hands and the legs were all right, but the rest of the body had been flattened by the passing cars, like a dead animal. Life in Kuwait had become too savage to do anything about a single dead person.

By now the two men were reminding each other of people they knew and cases they had heard of.

There was that women, was her name Karbazed? Her son was shot in the street in front of her, and they told her not to touch the body. She couldn't bear it, she was crying hysterically, and they grabbed her head and rubbed it in his blood.

Then there were the al-Awtabis, they were a big family, very famous. They shot the son in front of the father, so he would know his line had ended, then they shot him too.

Abdullah al-Darmi was tortured and shot because they found a copy of the resistance newsletter in his flat. Someone had just pushed it under his door – that was how they delivered them. But they shot him.

I knew a doctor, Dr Hisham al-Obudan I think his name was. He worked in the Al-Sabah Maternity Hospital. They caught him leaving one night with a piece of saline tube in his pocket. They thought he must be going to help some foreigners, or maybe someone in the resistance. Anyway, they shot him in the back of the head in front of the kitchen staff. It turned out he was taking it home for someone in his family who needed a saline drip.

In the Salmeer Mosque the mullah, Mahmoud al-Jassam, had his beard torn off with pliers, then they beat him and shot him and threw his body into a garbage container in the street, because that's what the resistance did when they shot an Iraqi.

Halfway through November they killed a couple of Kuwaitis, poor fellows. Hung them up by their shoulders and cut off their genitals and let them bleed to death. I didn't see this myself, but a lot of people did. They just did these things out in public, you know, to frighten everybody.

They caught me once as I was going for a haircut. I lived on the seafront then. A couple of men in plain clothes drove up in a stolen car with no number plates. They said was I English? (They were arresting the English and Americans then.) No, I said. Were there any English people in the building where I lived? No. Did I know any English people? No again. You can see my papers, I'm Dutch, I work here. They weren't looking for anyone else then, just Americans and English. So I got away.

That led the two of them back to the subject of looting: how, when the Iraqis found a house that was empty they would paint a red cross on the door and come back with a truck or a van and take everything out of it. In the block where one of our informers lived the Iraqis kicked in the doors and took everything, not just the furniture and the ornaments but the sinks, lavatories, the doors, the lightbulbs and the light switches. 'I saw soldiers shooting other soldiers for loot,' one of them said. Most of the time the Iraqis seemed to be very badly fed, and they went round foraging for food. They had also had very little training in the use of their guns: the Irishman saw a soldier asleep in a doorway with his rifle resting on his stomach, pointing at his chin. He watched another Iraqi spend half an hour trying to get a stolen electric kettle through a metal grille.

> I'll tell you, though, some of them must have a sense of humour. There was a big shopping centre, the Matana, full of shopping malls and three levels of car parking. We watched them going right through that place, taking everything with them. In one shoe shop, it had been completely stripped bare of everything, one of the soldiers left his old pair of boots on the stand in the middle of the window.

The two expatriates had compiled a list of the equipment they knew had been taken. In an empty city, where everything that could be moved had been stolen, it seemed scarcely necessary, almost obsessive. They had done it, they said, because they wanted the outside world to know the scale of what had happened. It was their way, perhaps, of creating a kind of order in a disordered universe, an inventory, neat and precise, of the chaos that had suddenly engulfed a couple of pleasant, well-to-do, well-organized lives. They went through the list of things that had been taken, but they stressed that these were only the things they had been able to confirm:

28 of the 40 dental units – table, light, drill, chair – from the main hospital;
  – a total of 12 other dental units from the other hospitals;
  – all 16 of the children's mobile dentistry units in Kuwait;
  – 7 of the 9 ambulances at the Amiri Hospital;
  – 100 out of 120 ambulances at the Subham depot;
  – all the hearses and the mechanical diggers at the three main cemeteries;

– all the equipment from the city's three main sports centres. The equipment had, they said, been the best they had ever seen anywhere. The empty centres, with their showers, cubicles and overhead beams, had been used as torture centres;

– hundreds of tons of medical equipment and medicines from the main medical centre;

– the entire library and records from the Kuwaiti Medical School;

– the entire library of Kuwait University;

– all the equipment and records from the Institute for Scientific Research. This, they said, had been done intelligently, overseen by men who were themselves scientists. 'They knew what they were looking for. They didn't let the soldiers loose on that';

– equipment and a new crane from the communications tower;

– at the civil airport, all emergency fire equipment, all navigational equipment, including one of the most advanced instruments-only landing systems in the world, all unloading gear, all flight and maintenance simulators, all machine-shop tools;

– from Failaka Island, two ferries. These were later seen in use in Basra;

– from the National Bank of Kuwait, the largest private bank in the country, everything in the building was taken: safes, desks, chairs, bookshelves, computers, hat stands, soap dispensers, towel rolls. Several big 20-wheel trucks were required to empty it. The bank's mainframe computer was taken, but it was smashed as they were lifting it out;

– most of the experimental sheep at the Kuwait Livestock Company, which had taken 15 years to rear;

– many of the animals at Kuwait Zoo: the soldiers would kill them for sport or for food;

– the big Matana shopping centre required 10 days' continuous looting before it was emptied of everything. The soldiers clearly had orders to clean out all the personal computers they could find, but they tended to throw them into the backs of the big lorries they used and many of them must have been broken;

– air conditioning units were taken from the roofs of thousands of houses and blocks of flats, though the looters often forgot to take the chiller units that went with them.

The Iraqi soldiers found it hard to open the big metal shutters that many shopkeepers had installed in Kuwait City. The forklift trucks they had stolen were used to pull the shutters out, but many were too strong even for that and the forklift trucks would sometimes topple over and have to be abandoned. All the frozen sheep and beef carcasses in the vast storage plants in the city were taken. Kuwait was the storehouse for much of the rest of the Gulf. For several months, room service in the Al-Rasheed hotel served Pepsi-Cola and 7-Up in cans marked with the name of the main bottling plant in Kuwait and their date of manufacture: 1.8.90.

On the day before the two men talked to us in our room in Baghdad, Amnesty International issued a report on human rights violations in occupied Kuwait. The tone was, as always, measured and cool. There were no angry accusations, no moral posturings, no use of emotive words like 'evil'. The report allowed the facts Amnesty had obtained speak for themselves: Kuwaiti Red Crescent workers arrested and their organization merged with their Iraqi counterpart after they had raised the cases of people who had disappeared; round-ups of innocent people; detention under cruel conditions; torture and ill-treatment in any of 38 listed ways, including the use of electricity, extracting fingernails and toenails, plucking out beards and moustaches with pliers, cutting out tongues, blinding by gouging or pouring caustic liquids into the eyes, and various forms of sexual abuse; random shootings, often in the street; widespread executions by shooting or hanging.

In his interview with the British television company, ITN, in November 1990, Saddam Hussein defended his country's record:

A number of Iraqis from the province of Baghdad, or they may have been from the province of Basra or maybe from other provinces, were executed because they stole from the homes of

168

the people in Kuwait. This has happened. Why does the British press not talk about this? Because it reflects the just aspect of our position.

There were indeed a number of executions for looting, but several people told Amnesty they had recognized some of the victims. A university lecturer, for instance, was quoted as saying:

> They showed their photographs on television. I saw four or six of them. One of them was an Egyptian national employed by the Kuwait Oil Company. A maternal cousin of mine recognized him, but I don't recall his name. On 18 August they showed on television the photograph of another of those executed. He was a Kuwaiti from the al-Hajiri family . . . .

Not every atrocity story turned out to be true. An employee of the Regency Palace Hotel said a British Airways stewardess had been raped on board a bus outside the hotel, but this turned out to be an invention. Nevertheless, there was reliable corroborated evidence of widespread violence by the Iraqi forces against the Kuwaiti population. A doctor working for the Red Crescent said an average of four or five bodies would be brought to their centre every day, often as many as 10. Many would have been shot in the back of the head at point blank range. The usual pattern, he said, was that the Iraqis would arrest someone, usually torture them, then take them home for their family to identify. Then they would shoot them in front of their family. Almost all the victims were young men, picked up because the soldiers thought they might have something to do with the resistance. There were various cases in which women were said to have been 'executed' as well.

The testimony collected by Amnesty was, as always, checked and crosschecked carefully. There is a terrible sameness about the stories people told of the careless, arbitrary way in which people were killed, the impersonal, routine torture:

> My relative could not control himself. He started shouting at the soldier, saying: 'You have ruined our lives, why did you come? The Iraqi soldier shot him dead then and there, in front of everybody.

As he was reaching for his wallet, one of the Iraqis pushed him and pulled it out. They found Kuwaiti currency, 150 dinars. 'You've got that dog Jaber's money [referring to the Emir of Kuwait].' The Kuwaiti was going to explain when the soldier pushed him hard, making him stumble, and then he sprayed him with bullets from his machine gun.

On average, about 20 or 30 bodies were found daily in the period starting beginning of September. In each district I covered I would find five or six bodies.

After a while there were so many bodies that there was no more room at the morgue of the nearby Mubarak Hospital. We began putting some of the bodies in the large hospital refrigerators normally used for food. Families would come looking for missing relatives in the morgues and refrigerators.

At some hospitals they no longer admit Kuwaitis, only Iraqis. Many Kuwaitis are afraid to go to the hospitals anyway.

At Al-Razi Hospital there was a young Kuwaiti man who was wounded and his condition was critical . . . I noticed that his oxygen supply had been cut off. So I switched it on again and he began to improve. I made a protest about his treatment, so one of the Iraqi doctors took me aside and [warned me against saying anything]. The following day the young man died because the oxygen supply had been switched off again.

The officer then said, 'We are here to help you with the uprising.' When I replied that there had been no uprising, the officer standing by the door hit me on the head with his rifle. I was immediately taken to another room where I was subjected to torture for about one hour. They applied electricity to my fingers and genitals and I was beaten with sticks.

I hid the traces of torture on my body in order to avoid being executed, because anyone who has clear traces of torture on his body or is suffering from permanent damage is executed.

A student of 19 who was arrested on 11 September was held for two weeks at a private house in Al-Jahra. They beat him and interrogated him under torture. They asked him about weapons they had found at his home and about any foreigners, diplomats, members of the armed forces or members of the al-Sabah family whom he might know. He only knew of one major in the Kuwaiti army and he didn't tell them about him. At 2.30 on the morning of 24 September an officer came in and said that Saddam Hussein had ordered the release of all detainees. They were to be released, he said, in groups of 12.

The student's group was blindfolded and handcuffed and he was put in a car with two others, Samir and Muhammad. Eventually they were taken to Samir's house and told to get out. He and Muhammad asked why, since they didn't live there. Then he realized they were going to be shot. It was just after dawn prayers. The first two bullets were fired and he heard Samir fall. Two more were fired and both of them grazed his skull. He too fell down. Two more bullets and Muhammad fell on top of him. The soldiers took off the blindfolds and handcuffs and went away. They assumed they were all dead.

When they had gone the student crawled out and tried to revive Samir, thinking that he was pretending too. Then he realized that both of the others were dead. His head was bleeding badly, but he dragged their bodies to one side and recited a short prayer for them. Then he started walking. Someone took him in and gave him refuge for three days. Then he called his family and his father came to collect him. The father had bribed an Iraqi officer who had told him the son had been executed. The father had gone the rounds of the hospitals looking for the body. When the son got home he found that friends and relatives were still coming round to give their condolences on his death. Soon afterwards he escaped from Kuwait.

The Iraqis went to great lengths to hunt down foreigners in Kuwait, yet scores of them remained hidden for the entire length of the occupation. There were regular house-to-house searches and sometimes foreigners were beaten up or shot when they were arrested. For the most part, though, Europeans and Americans were not treated badly. For Filipino and Indian women, who worked in large numbers as domestics, it was a different matter. It was routine for the Iraqi soldiers to rape them when they took over a house.

As it turned out, there was no real need for Europeans to hide; when they were captured they were taken to Baghdad and then eventually released and allowed to leave for home without being harmed. At the time, of course, there was no way of knowing this. It was natural for them to assume that their lives would be in the greatest danger if they were captured.

Many foreigners received help and food from Kuwaitis and Palestinians, who ran tremendous risks. In some cases, the penalty for helping foreigners was death. This put great strain on everyone, yet there were few examples of anyone being betrayed. This British woman's experience was more common:

We had been hiding for several weeks in the flat underneath ours. It was empty and my husband, who was always a handyman, got into it and fixed up a kind of hidey-hole under the stairs. You could never tell, if you didn't know. It just looked as though the flat was completely empty. Once some soldiers came, but they just looked round and thought there couldn't be anyone there. The sound-proofing was so good they couldn't have heard us, not even when we listened to the BBC.

Our big problem was not being able to go out. There were roadblocks everywhere and we knew they were looking for Brits in particular. So we couldn't buy ourselves any food and we soon ran out of supplies. There was a Palestinian family in the building and they knew we were around. They came and asked us very early on if they could help us and they brought us food two or three times a week. Every time they came I would say, 'Are you sure you can carry on doing this?' And they always said, 'We're your neighbours, of course we're going to help you.' Sometimes I thought they might be getting too frightened to go on, but they always did, right up until the time we left. They were wonderful. What can you do to thank people who risk their lives for you, just because they live in the same building? However can you thank them enough?

Throughout the Iraqi occupation the resistance kept up its activities. On most nights in Kuwait you could hear shooting and, although much of it was done by the Iraqis, there was a continual low level of sniping and assassination. No clear figures ever emerged of Iraqi soldiers killed and wounded, but some resistance sources claimed the total was well over 100. In a small city with a shortage of hiding places that would represent a high level of operation. For the most part, though, the resistance demonstrated its existence by the no less dangerous methods of passing round leaflets containing information and advice for the population. A member of the resistance would get into a big apartment building and slip copies of *Sarkha* (The Cry) and *al-Samud al-Shabi* (The People's Resistance) under the doors of each of the flats before slipping away unseen.

Other resistants painted slogans on the walls, going out into the empty streets at night in defiance of the curfew:

LONG LIVE FREE KUWAIT!
IRAQIS, YOU HAVE NO RIGHT HERE!
THE KUWAITI PEOPLE ARE FREE!
LONG LIVE SHEIKH JABER!
IRAQIS, WE WILL NEVER SURRENDER AND NEVER FORGIVE!

Many people, whether from the resistance or not, pasted up photographs of the Kuwaiti royal family on walls and the unsmashed windows of empty buildings. Another method of resistance – which almost everyone was able to practice with less risk to themselves – was simply to go out onto the roof-top and shout '*Allah-u Akbar!*' ('God is most great!') A Kuwaiti housewife described one of the beneficial aspects of this to Amnesty International:

> The children were in a permanent state of fright. Many of them developed a stutter and could not talk normally. Others began suffering from uncontrolled urination. We tried to cure their stutter by taking them up to the rooftops with us where we shouted '*Allah-u Akbar!*' in protest at the Iraqi invasion. At first the children had difficulty in getting the words out, but we urged them to shout at the tops of their voices. After several attempts, some of them regained normal speech.

Perhaps the greatest of the resistance's successes was the

recovery of the body of the Emir's half-brother, Fahd al-Ahmad al-Sabah, who had died on the steps of the Dasman Palace in the first hours of the invasion. It was kept under guard for four weeks but, at the beginning of September, a detachment of resistance workers slipped into the morgue where it was being held and took it away for secret burial. It was an important coup and when the news was passed around by word of mouth and by pamphlet it had a considerable effect on morale.

When the war ended and many Kuwaitis who had fled the country returned, there were indefensible acts of cruelty and brutality towards Palestinians and Iraqis who were subjected to very much the same treatment as the Kuwaitis themselves had endured. It was noticeable, however, that those who had stayed in Kuwait and worked with the resistance rarely acted in this way. For one thing, they knew which Palestinians had collaborated with the Iraqi forces and who had, at serious risk to their lives, identified with the Kuwaitis and even belonged to the resistance themselves. For another thing, those who remained had nothing to prove: they had reason to be proud of the way they had behaved.

The morning after the Irishman and the Dutchman had come to see us in our office we went with them to Baghdad airport. A pleasant and efficient Indian woman was travelling with them. It took me a little time to realize that she was one of those who had been raped in Kuwait. There was a good deal of tension as they made their way through the complexities of the airport system. One of them was taken off to a side office because he was found to have Kuwaiti dinars on him. We waited outside the door, in full view, until he was allowed out. The papers they had amassed – the lists of crimes and looted equipment – were not discovered. I last saw them as they left the departures lounge to board the plane to Amman and safety.

We drove back to the centre of town. I felt at home here now. Not safe, exactly, because in a country like Iraq no one, especially not a journalist, can feel entirely safe, but certainly relaxed. But I looked at the people I knew in a slightly different light: our drivers, the minders, the people at the hotel, the people in the *souq*, the other friends I had made. They came from the same background as the looters, the executioners, the torturers, the officer who had ordered the youngest recruit to take part in the gang rape of the pleasant, dignified Indian woman to whom I had just said goodbye, the man who had hacked off the leg of a passing motorist after a traffic accident, the doctor who had switched off the oxygen supply to a sick man in hospital because he was a Kuwaiti.

I remembered too the demonstration by Iraqi children the previous day: 'Iraqi Children Love Their Leader Saddam Hussein Because He Cares For Childhood.' It required great cynicism to present the whole crisis as an attack by the outside world on the children of Iraq, when the children of Kuwait were reduced to stuttering and incontinence by the ferocity of Iraq's soldiers: 11 years of Saddam Hussein's rule had engendered some ugly propensities in a nation which otherwise seemed to me so peaceable and easygoing.

I glanced at yet another vast portrait of him, grinning down on his people and holding out his hand in a way that seemed more imperious than inviting. They would never, I thought, be able to come to terms with what he had done to them, any more than the people of Kuwait would. Like Stalin, like Hitler, like Ceausescu or Pol Pot, he would damage the lives of the people permanently. Whatever happened, whether there was a war or not, whether he survived or was overthrown, his spirit would be in them, working away, for the rest of their lives. 'Saddam, We Are Yours For Ever', another of the placards at the children's demonstration had said. They would be.

Sinking Deeper

The people of Iraq have expressed their view through their demonstrations when they took to the streets in roaring waves protesting against what Bush said in his television message to them. They came out immediately after the broadcast of his message in every town and village in Iraq.

> Saddam Hussein, broadcasting to the American people on 26 September 1990, in reply to a message broadcast by George Bush to the Iraqi people

From a height of 15,000 feet Baghdad was a darker stain on a horizon the colour of mud brick. I leant back in my seat and asked the attractive flight attendant if I could have another glass of champagne with my smoked salmon sandwich. This, we kept telling ourselves, was the way to do it. I was coming back to Iraq only nine days after the end of my first visit and, for a brief moment before the insurance rates went up, it was actually cheaper to charter a small HS-125 executive jet from Amman than to fly with Iraqi Airways. This time we had the right number of people and all the right equipment; and I was suffering from none of the anxieties which had afflicted me earlier.

Saddam International Airport was as silent as a foreclosed scrapyard. Planes in the green and white livery of the national airline were parked untidily everywhere. Nothing moved. The one solitary flight from Amman would not be landing for hours. An empty 7-Up can rolled across the tarmac in the sudden blast of air from our engines, like tumbleweed in a ghost town. Across the empty arrivals hall stalked a white and yellow feral cat; there weren't even any secret policemen to spy on us. 'Welcome in Baghdad,' said a voice in the silence. I jumped. An Information Ministry 'minder' whom I had met in the past was standing there, his hand extended. He was wall-eyed and the hand pointed a little to one side of me.

When I had shaken it he explained that there was a change from last time. We would not be staying in the Sheraton Hotel, which was privately owned. We would be staying in a very special hotel for government guests, the Al-Rasheed. 'You will like very much,' he enthused, obviously worried we were going to make a scene. I looked across at the most prominent of the illuminated advertisements on the wall: 'The Al-Rasheed – It Is More Than A Hotel.' I hesitated. I had come to like the Sheraton, where it was easy to identify the spooks and the rooms which were bugged; the Al-Rasheed was known to be bugged through and through. But my colleagues, new to Baghdad, had no preferences, and somehow I found the advertisement irresistible: how much more than a hotel could it be?

On the other side of the customs and immigration formalities stood Mr Hattam, well turned-out in a dark suit and well-polished black shoes. We exchanged three whiskery kisses: for all his smartness, it was not yet time for his weekly shave. With him was an older, hang-dog figure, with one shoulder lower than the other and the general air of an old soak. He wore loose-fitting trousers and shirt and a pair of sandals. 'This Mr Hattam friend, Mr Ramadan,' said Hattam. Mr Ramadan, leaning at a slight angle, gave a little bow. A faint, attenuated smell hung around him. It might have been his aftershave, except that he hadn't shaved either. I thought I could detect the distinctive flavour of Johnny Walker. Still, his English proved to be better than Hattam's as he had at least mastered the personal pronouns. In the months that followed we decided he drove marginally better when drunk than sober, though it was a fine distinction. There were also few enough opportunities to make the comparison.

The Al-Rasheed, being more than a hotel, had the atmosphere of an institution. There was a high wall around it, set with watch towers. A solitary gate was protected by men half-hidden behind the tinted, bulletproof glass of a guard-room. The high entrance was set with stained glass, like a crematorium or a Mormon temple. At the top of the steps stood a magnificent figure much taller than me – I am six feet two – with a turban and an immense robe. Throughout my months in this place he always addressed me in French, though he knew I was British and spoke perfectly good English himself.

'*Bonjour, monsieur.*'

A team of Sudanese porters sweated in the 90 degree heat as they hoisted our 27 cases of equipment up the steps.

Inside it was cool and high and rather dark. Minders sat at the receipt of custom in the hallway, reading newspapers or chatting to journalists. Further in, the reception desk ran the full length of the lobby. In armchairs opposite sat a whole range of people: brides on a Friday morning, their eyes fatigued, yet still registering surprise at what had happened the night before; public relations men for the Iranian People's Mujaheddin, a now-declining opposition group with a campaigning fervour equal to that of the Moonies; mullahs from surrounding countries, guests of the government; people who had come to Baghdad to press for the release of their countrymen and women; stooges of different kinds, who fawned on their hosts; peace activists, some quiet and thoughtful, some flamboyant refugees from the 1960s with beards and bells and t-shirts with messages on them. And there were the young men who sat in the same place for hours at a time and read the same newspaper over and over, fingering their Saddam moustaches and looking away when your eyes met theirs.

It was solidly built, the Al-Rasheed. A marble plaque inside the door recorded the fact that it had been opened by His Excellency President Saddam Hussein. Saddam had intended it to house the delegates to the Non-Aligned Movement summit which he had hoped to host when the war with Iran was at its height, though without success; it had therefore to be proof against Iranian missiles. Outside, there were angled concrete baffles over every window to protect them from anything falling from the sky. The glass in the windows themselves was three inches thick and set in frames of strong steel. The doors

178

and panelling were of the best teak. You could hold a party in your room – we often did – and not be heard in the corridor or the neighbouring suites. The wood made the corridors very dark, but there was reassurance in the solidity of everything.

On each floor by the lifts there were little pulpits of teak for security men to sit and guard the approaches to particularly important guests. Two little cameras overhead watched all the comings and goings. The rooms were certainly bugged, probably from one of the two overhead sprinkler devices, though the Romanian Securitate and the East German Stasi, both of whom acted as advisers to the Mukhabarat, also favoured putting microphones in the electricity plugs and (of course) the telephone handsets. Directly we moved in we insisted on changing the rooms we had been assigned. Three men came to our new accommodation and changed the light bulbs and did various little tasks around the room we used as our office and living area.

Many rooms were equipped for video as well. I met a man who played a part in negotiating the contract with a Swedish firm – Swedes, Swiss and Austrians do many of the nastier but more lucrative jobs in the Third World – to install tiny television cameras inside the television sets in some of the rooms. The sets would watch you as you watched them; and after you had stopped watching them, they would continue watching you. We took one set to pieces and failed to find anything, but there were always stories in the *souqs* that the Mukhabarat offered for sale, as a profitable spin-off, the black-and-white cassettes of wedding night scenes at the Al-Rasheed.

In these early months of the crisis, when it was safe for people to come to Baghdad, the Al-Rasheed was pretty full. There were sometimes as many as 200 journalists and television people staying there, as well as all the other visitors. Then there were the Kuwaiti families who had been obliged for some reason to come north. Their children raced up and down the corridors and they lived an expensive, room service existence. They always had good reasons why they were there rather than in Saudi Arabia. One plumpish man in a white dish-dash, who had a room next to mine, explained:

We thought it too dangerous to drive across the desert, especially with all my children. My wife prayed me not to go that way. So I thought we come here to Baghdad, then fly away. But now is very difficult to get a plane. We have been here one week already. No, I do not hate the Iraqis [this accompanied by a gesture to show that my question was inopportune, and that he might have another opinion if asked somewhere where there were no microphones]. The Iraqis are our Arab brothers. That is why I come here with all my family. [Final anguished look, then the door closes.]

Every time you entered one of the infuriatingly slow lifts at the Al-Rasheed you could see the intensity of the hatred the Kuwaitis had for Iraq: a suppressed rage which erupted when they were alone which made them scratch the walls with their initials, with messages and, sometimes, just with angry gashes.

Outside the confines of the hotel, Baghdad seemed to have settled relatively easily into its phoney war: in particular, coming to terms with sanctions. Many of the more expensive restaurants were shut and there were longish queues at the bread shops which we were allowed – but not encouraged – to film. Our minders and censors could never quite decide whether it was a good idea to show the outside world that Iraqis were suffering as a result of the United Nations embargo, or a bad idea because it would give the impression that they were unable to cope properly. It was all a little irrelevant, since for one thing people in Middle Eastern countries usually queue outside bread shops at baking time in order to get their bread as fresh as possible; for another, most Western diplomats estimated that Iraq had sufficient food supplies for five months – which, by coincidence, was roughly the length of time before the ceasefire brought the war to an end.

Nevertheless, television teams were always making the trip out to film the bread queues and some newspaper journalists still continued to write stories about the growing hardships, because that was what their editors at home were demanding. I was fortunate in working for an organization which was prepared to let me say what I found in Baghdad, rather than to tell me what I was to look for. Perhaps because it was enemy territory, many newspapers and television and radio stations seemed deeply nervous about sending their correspondents there in the first place and fiddled around a good deal with what they reported.

Naji al-Hadithi at the Information Ministry selected the people who came to Baghdad with great care. From Britain, the BBC and ITN were almost always given visas, as were the serious newspapers. His years in Britain had convinced him, though, that there was no point in letting in the tabloids, with the solitary exception of the up-market *Evening Standard*. 'None of your tabloids tell the truth about anything,' he said, 'and they will only come here looking for scandal.'

The French newspapers and television were almost always given visas. The Iraqis recognized their importance and hoped to be able to influence France to stay out of the coming war. There was usually a journalist or a television crew from Italy, which was also playing a significant part in the Alliance. In the case of Germany, a country which was playing little part in the military build-up and which the Iraqis regarded as lacking international influence, visas were available much less often. Spain was favoured because of the traditional feeling that it was almost a part of the Arab world itself. There were occasional Dutch and Nordic journalists and, once or twice, some from South America. The Japanese tended to come in waves and then go away again.

The absence of Americans was noticeable. As early as September, Saddam Hussein's attention was directed towards CNN. Information Minister Latif Jassim told him with great enthusiasm about the pleasures of being interviewed by CNN and then seeing the result broadcast straight back to Iraq. Soon there were CNN sets in most government ministries, and in the palaces and private houses where Saddam spent the night. It gave him – and them – a sense of knowing what the enemy was doing. Over the years the Iraqis had become used to the other American television networks and they too were allowed in on a regular basis, much as the BBC and ITN were.

The big American newspapers and magazines were different. *The New York Times*, *Washington Post* and *Los Angeles Times* were given visas early on in the crisis, as were *Time* and

Newsweek. The results, from Iraq's point of view, were not worth the effort. *Time* and *Newsweek* were probably the worst, putting out variants of the stories about Saddam Hussein which everyone had known about but had found difficult to check months before. The newspapers were scarcely impressive either, reporting things which the Iraqis maintained, with a certain justification, were little more than wilful propaganda. I sat in Naji al-Hadithi's office as he went through one article.

'What is the point of letting these people come here, when they could write things that are just as biased back home in the United States? They have learned nothing by coming here.'

I make a point of not agreeing with the officials of unpleasant dictatorships when they criticize a free press; somehow, it seems bad for business. In this case I only just managed to avoid concurring. The article I was reading upside down on Naji's desk looked like a rather boring form of propaganda to me: a rehash of the stories that journalists told one another about Saddam Hussein's misdeeds. From what I could see the journalist in question had grasped nothing serious about the situation. Perhaps, however, this was merely because he did not seem to agree with me on what was rapidly becoming my obsession: the belief that the population of Iraq as a whole had no interest in Saddam's holy war and simply wanted to be left alone to get on with their lives in peace. It seemed to me that far too many journalists were taking all the carefully-organized demonstrations at face value and assuming that people were enthusiastic supporters of Saddam.

It was a demonstration outside the British embassy which first suggested this to me. We rarely had any warning of these occasions: they happened almost daily were well-organized and invariably peaceful, lasting only for a matter of minutes. For this particular demonstration, however, the Information Ministry had told us in advance and we had left the hotel early. Mr Hattam, now promoted to the rank of Number One Driver, took the cameraman and sound recordist. Mr Ramadan was required to stay at the hotel for other duties, which was a good thing because at eight o'clock in the morning he was already showing definite signs of swaying. My colleague and namesake from BBC Radio, Bob Simpson, offered me a lift in his car.

Bob Simpson is one of the heroes of this book. He remained excellent company throughout the months that led up to the war, then stayed on when it began. A tall, rangey, balding man, infuriatingly attractive to women, well-read and of a literary cast of mind, he was almost exactly the same age as I was – three months separated us – and the Iraqi minders had terrible difficulties in telling us apart. This morning it was plain that he too had had a rough night and was looking, if anything, more wrecked than Ramadan. He winced in the bright sunlight as we walked out through the crematorium entrance of the Al-Rasheed and stood on the top step. I acknowledged the 'Bonjour' of the doorman. Bob looked in the direction of the car park and said: 'Where is the large, fawning, prune-shaped idiot?'

I knew whom he meant. His driver, Hassan, was a Kurd who had worked most of his life for British companies and spoke good English. He was short and broad and seemed to have no neck at all. Bob complained that he always drove too close to the car ahead, was inclined to cheat on financial arrangements and made up for it with an unrequired generosity in the way of food: he would appear in our room with fruit and kebabs and bread which we rarely wanted and made us all feel guilty. He also had the traditional Iraqi habit of showing respect by kissing our shoulders or hands, which was unsettling. On balance, I liked him. Bob detested him.

Hassan was a superb batman. When we reached the British embassy that morning he set us down, then bustled over to a nearby watchman's hut and demanded tea for us both. He came back within a couple of minutes with two small glasses of very hot, sweet tea. Even Bob felt better after that. We had just set the glasses down and Hassan had obsequiously gathered them up and taken them back to the hut when we heard the sound of chanting and banging in the distance. The camera crews at the embassy gate stood up and got ready. Along the avenue came a long line of schoolchildren, headed by a group of a hundred or so wearing the strange blue camouflage of the Baath Party's youth wing. 'They wear that so they can take up positions in swimming pools and not be noticed,' Bob said.

The children were chanting the usual things:'Down, Down, Bush' and 'Our souls and our hearts' blood for Saddam'. For them it was a pleasant morning off school. They carried empty milk cans which they waved at the cameras: a reference to the Iraqi propaganda claim that the United Nations embargo meant that children were dying from lack of the right kinds of milk. This was much repeated and believed all over the Middle East, but although doctors at a number of hospitals assured us it was true they were never able to show evidence for the claim that children were dying as a result. Before the end of the year other subjects for propaganda arose and the issue of children's milk was forgotten: not something you would expect to happen if children really were dying.

The noise of the children's voices squeaking in unison was deafening now. They had been joined by teenage girls who exchanged meaningful glances with Bob and turned away to giggle with their friends then look back at him again. The teachers gathered importantly round the gates, holding up banners: 'THATCHER YOU ARE ALSO MOTHER TELL BUSH OUR CHILDREN DYING' and 'BRITAIN + USA = DEATH'. A couple of the teachers read little speeches, then they made their way through the side gate into the embassy grounds.

Waiting there politely for them was the second secretary at the embassy, James Tansley, a man in his mid-twenties with a gravitas well beyond his years. He had evolved a method of receiving these daily demonstrations, especially the ones which concentrated on the question of children. He listened to the prepared speech, took the written protest which the teachers handed them, then suggested to them in good Arabic that since they were so interested in the welfare of Iraqi children they might like to look at some pictures he happened to have with him. He pulled out several photographs of Kurdish children killed by chemical weapons in Halabje. The effect of this was usually instantaneous: the protesters would hurry away as though they had been exposed to some infectious disease. Tansley was expelled from Iraq for this two months later, but the delay seems to indicate that most of the people he showed the pictures to were too nervous even to report what they had seen.

Outside the embassy a small group of teachers waited, keeping an eye on the demonstrating children. I wandered over to talk to them. Like most Iraqis, they were pleasant and welcoming. Did I like Iraq? Did I know Nottingham, where the brother of one of them had studied? Or Edinburgh? The others turned away as the order came to line the children up and march them away. One, slight and dark with deep-set eyes, stayed. What did I think was going to happen? I gave the standard answers.

'You must realize,' she said, 'that no one here supports Saddam. No one wants this war to happen. No one wants Kuwait.' She saw me looking over at the demonstrators, still chanting 'Down, Down, Bush' and 'Down, Down, Thatcher'. She guessed what I was thinking. 'We are only here because we have to be. No one wants to demonstrate. You must understand that.' She turned and her slight figure was lost in the crowd of school uniforms and blue camouflage.

No one in Baghdad had spoken quite so openly to me before, though there had been plenty of hints. Perhaps I should have been more sensitive to the feelings and behaviour of those around me; but from that point on I understood with increasing certainty that what she had said was right: there was almost no genuine feeling or emotion at any of the demonstrations that took place. There was never the slightest danger to embassy property or to those of us who looked on. The entire country, with very few exceptions, was going through the motions. People did what they were told, because they had no alternative. It was very wrong to take these peaceable, unenthusiastic occasions in the way that many foreign journalists did – as evidence of a powerful national will to defy the world and fight to the death for Saddam Hussein, or for what was now formally declared to be the nineteenth province of Iraq.

We just managed to get a shot of the American chargé d'affaires, Joseph Wilson IV, carrying a large can of videotape down the road to his car. Joe Wilson was a general unfavourite in Baghdad. I turned up once at the US embassy after he had tipped off the American television networks that he would be coming out of the embassy at a certain time. The Americans sent word to him that everybody was stationed outside a particular door. He emerged from a different door saying 'I can't understand what you're all doing here – I've got nothing to tell you.' Joe Wilson regarded himself as a figure of the 1960s, moulded by the antiwar movement, though he seemed to have no reluctance about this particular war. He smoked large cigars, spitting out little flecks of tobacco from time to time. He was heavily patronizing towards the other western ambassadors, behaving in ways that they, older men brought up in more conventional diplomatic traditions, found annoying: putting his feet on the table, reading while they were speaking, laughing loudly at things no one else thought were funny and – no doubt they found this the most irritating of all – assuming he had the right to speak for all of them because he was American.

The can of videotape he was carrying was to be taken to the headquarters of Iraqi television. It contained George Bush's address to the Iraqi nation about the crisis. There was something faintly unreal about the idea that each leader should address the other's citizenry: an attempt to gain a moral foothold in each other's camp. It signalled a lack of understanding on the part of both men. Bush was presumably unaware of the enormous gap between Saddam's rhetoric and the interests of ordinary Iraqis, yet seemed to believe that public opinion was a serious force in Iraq. Saddam, who plainly had no idea that his people were reluctant to support him (presumably because no one, including the Mukhabarat, had dared to tell him) felt that his powers of persuasion would be great enough to convince the American public of the strength and justice of Iraq's position. It was a dialogue of the mutually uncomprehending.

We chose an open-air café beside the Tigris in which to watch the Bush message. The metal tables were rusty and there was a smell from the kitchen as though something had died there. The waiters were scurrying round with glasses of tea as the hookahs bubbled away and there was a pleasant atmosphere. Our minder, a faithful Baathist, had assumed a serious air and warned us to stay with him because the mood in Baghdad now was one of increasing anger against the West. I told him, tongue in cheek, that I thought we were prepared to take the risk of stirring up the wrath of the populace and he nodded judiciously. He managed to get the time of the Bush broadcast wrong by half an hour and eventually we had to shout at him and the café proprietor before they would turn the television set on. Most of the regulars were playing dominoes or backgammon and at first paid little attention to us; so much for their anger. But directly Bush started talking they abandoned their games and drifted over to watch the television set, which was perched on a ricketty chair standing on an even more ricketty table.

Bush was less than enthralling. He talked a great deal about peace and the need for Iraqi forces to withdraw and the united will of the world community that they should do so. It was not a long performance – a little more than eight minutes – and the overlaid translation into Arabic was the one the White House had sent with the tape. Immediately afterwards, though, a spokesman for the Iraqi President told the audience what to think about it. Bush, he said, expected that the whole world would do what the United States wanted. All honest Arabs and Muslims were joining the struggle against Mubarak of Egypt and King Fahd of Saudi Arabia. The rebuttal by Saddam's spokesman lasted more than twice as long as the original. Directly it started, I noticed, the café regulars went back to their dominoes and their backgammon.

We spoke to some of the customers on camera. Immediately, what I later came to think of as the Iraqi public face came over them: there was nothing new in Bush's broadcast, Iraq wanted peace as well, Saddam was their leader. One lawyer refused to comment at all. 'You're being very cautious,' said an American journalist who was with us. 'I have to be,' he said. He had the kind of look, nervous and yet almost cynical, which I soon learned to spot among those who did what they were told, but maintained an unassailable inner chamber of their minds into which Saddam Hussein could not penetrate.

There were supposed to be some major demonstrations after Bush's message, but they were over so quickly that they were finished before we reached them. As we drove back to the Al-Rasheed I remarked to our Baathist minder that the anger of the people had been remarkably restrained, considering he had warned us of its savage intensity. He was a decent enough man, the kind who was always surprised when security men stopped us doing the easiest and most natural things. He wore a watch decorated with a slightly pop-eyed Saddam in a purple robe.

'That is because they are hospitable, and you are our guests.'

'So why warn us?'

'Ah, Mr Simpson, Mr Simpson, you are always trying to trick me.' I was suddenly angry.

'I don't think most people here do believe in Saddam or what he says. I think all they want is a quiet life.'

His face took on a distressed look, as though something he really liked had been damaged. Weakly, I couldn't continue: he was too nice and it would be a form of sadism to argue with him any more. I changed the subject and soon he was telling me with his usual enthusiasm that the United Nations sanctions were a positive benefit to Iraq. It had depended too much in the past on oil; now it was having to devote its energies to agriculture. He sat there, thinking about all the good things that were going to happen to Iraq under Saddam Hussein's leadership. I said nothing.

I never went to the television station when we satellited our reports now: my colleagues said I only got into arguments. It was as painful to me to watch our material being censored as it was for the poor minder to be told that people might not love Saddam. The tough but incorruptible Madame Awatif performed the function of censor less often now and a new man had arrived. I rarely met him but I detested him all the same. His moods, I realize now, followed the changing pattern of events in Iraq. He began by being arrogant and officious; then, as the war came closer, he ceased to pay attention to what we did and allowed everything through. Finally, once the war was over, he positively grovelled. If ever he committed worse offences, it is impossible to detail them at the time of writing without risking serious trouble for him.

He prided himself on his English which was, in truth, only adequate. 'I know what Mr Simpson is trying to say here. He is very wrong, very bad. When he says "President's palace" he means that President Saddam Hussein has the palace for himself, but in fact it belongs to the whole Iraqi people. He must say "presidential palace". This part goes out.' And the plugs would be pulled on that sentence. I complained about such things and, to my delight, he was diverted to other duties for some weeks. His ear was lamentably insensitive. Sometimes I was able to turn it to our advantage, by slipping in colloquial expressions he failed to understand. At others he censored things that would have been, on balance, to Iraq's benefit.

An example of this arose after we visited the Mansour Melia Hotel, arguably the best in Baghdad, which had been turned into a staging post for Westerners being allowed home from Kuwait and Iraq. The Information Ministry organized a trip to the Mansour Melia so that we could see a group of British women who had arrived from Kuwait. They were bemused by the sudden change in their lives and deeply worried about the husbands they had been forced to leave behind. Many had no homes to go to in Britain and no certainty about their future income. Now they were surrounded by the sweating photographers and cameramen of 50 different newspapers and broadcasting organizations.

Most of them reacted well. They spoke about getting back to nice cups of tea and the English countryside, as though nothing had changed since the Blitz. They fought the tears for their children's sake and busied themselves with their luggage so the cameras couldn't pry into their emotions. Others complained. Their meals were cold. They couldn't use the swimming pool. It had taken too long to reach Baghdad from Kuwait by coach. 'My little boy is used to proper food – burgers, fishfingers, chips, things like that. All this rice and vegetables upsets his tummy.' The children, taking their tone from their mothers, started crying, or making a noise, or turning on their brothers or sisters.

There was a long list of grievances about the reasons for their being there. Like the Palestinians, they blamed Britain for much of it: the embassy in Kuwait had told them to do the wrong thing and they had got into difficulties as a result. Many seemed to regard Saddam Hussein as an act of God, like a drought or a flood, and felt the British government should compensate them for him. 'Why didn't the embassy do more to help us? I think it's disgusting.' Mrs Thatcher was a particular target. 'I don't see why we should suffer because of her and President Bush,' said one affronted woman. Another agreed: 'If she's going to call Saddam a dictator, why didn't she wait till we were safely out of Kuwait?'

In the background there was muzak, an incongruous soft medley of English folksongs, in which 'Dance to your Daddy' melded into 'Greensleeves'. It was an expensive and luxurious place to be, far from unpleasant, even though it was a prison. The women were confined to the upper floors for most of the day. The more independent-minded of them, like the British Airways stewardesses from the flight that landed in Kuwait just after the invasion, rarely complained and did their best to get round the guards and escape to the coffeeshop. They were brave and lively and managed to enjoy themselves in spite of everything. A few lost all control. 'I'm speaking for the children,' wailed a blonde from the Midlands in a voice loud enough to attract a dozen camera crews. She wheeled round in the circle they made, egged on by their attention. 'Someone's got to speak for the children. They're ill. They've got dysentry.' She meant diarrhoea.

In our report that night I went through the different reactions: the ones who were making the most of it, the ones who thought somebody else should have looked after them better, and the ones who blamed it all on Mrs Thatcher. The censor loved them in particular. But when it came to the blonde who had lost her grip on reality, he decided she had to go. He pulled the plugs on her and her wailing was in vain.

A little later I was driving with our Baathist minder down Abu Nuwas Street towards Tahrir Square, watching from the back seat as his hands moved nervously, his neck jerked, his head shook. 'There must be a good reason. We just don't know what it is, that's all.' I grinned to myself; I had been working on his susceptibilities in the most indecent way. 'Whatever reason

190

can there be to keep a dying man prisoner here, so he can't see his children?'

We had just been visiting the man's wife, who was sitting in a depressing room in the Palestine Hotel, waiting for her next visit to her husband. Tony Wilbraham had been diagnosed as having terminal cancer, but the Iraqis still wouldn't let him go. Maureen Wilbraham was a handsome, amusing, brave woman of about 50. She could have left the country and gone back to her native Lancashire, where she had a guest house on the Golden Mile in Blackpool. Instead she stayed on to be with Tony. I told her the story I had heard on the BBC World Service about an English girl who had just returned to London from Kuwait via Baghdad. Her father had been in hiding in Kuwait, but she had led the Iraqi soldiers to where he was – because, she explained brightly to the cameras at Heathrow Airport, the Iraqis had warned her she wouldn't be able to leave unless she handed her father over to them. So of course she did.

Maureen Wilbraham's face, when I told her that, was a study in national character. Much the same look must have passed across the faces of Boadicea, Elizabeth I and Florence Nightingale. 'She never did!' said Maureen Wilbraham. Her eyes went down to the biography of Sir Winston Churchill which lay on her lap. 'What we need is a few more like him,' she said firmly.

Back in Amman at the end of my trip I stood listening to another British woman who had been obliged by the Iraqi authorities to leave Baghdad. A British tabloid journalist was asking her how she felt and she told him she couldn't wait to get back.

'Silly bitch,' he said, under his breath. She didn't fit the pattern: everyone knew Iraq was a hellhole ruled by an evil butcher and populated by fiends. He turned instead to a woman who complained that if she hadn't taken plenty of bottled water with her on the coach trip from Baghdad to Amman her little boy might have been thirsty. That was more like it. He had his story: he could have been doing an exposé of some shady tour operator who failed to live up to the promises of its brochures.

Soon afterwards in the Jordanian capital I saw how these 'tour operators' dealt with other people – people who were not white and whose governments were of no account to Saddam Hussein. My colleagues and I, having just got out of Baghdad ourselves, were walking back to our hotel after a celebratory dinner in a nearby restaurant. A crowded bus drew up beside us. There seemed to be more people standing than sitting down inside it. The driver started pushing and kicking them out and they spilled onto the pavement, where they settled down among their cardboard boxes. Children began to cry. Many of the mothers were no more than 16 or 17 themselves and just as much in need of comfort.

'Where are you from?' I asked one older woman. 'Please,' she said, looking up at me, 'we are from Philippines.' The bus had brought them nonstop to Amman from Kuwait via Baghdad. It had taken more than 30 hours and they had only once been given food and water. They were skinny and feeble and quite incapable of fending for themselves. Some had been locked up by their employers in the houses where they worked as servants. They were nature's victims; and yet although they were several stages down the economic ladder from the British in Kuwait, the same attraction had drawn them there: the Kuwaiti dinar.

Now there was nothing for them to do, nowhere for them to sleep, no food to eat and no water to drink. The only available reception centre was already full to overflowing and the only place for them to sleep was the front garden. There was no one from their embassy to look after their interests. Virgin Airlines, which had volunteered to bring the British women and children home, wasn't laying on a charter flight for them. The Reverend Jessie Jackson, who had flown to Baghdad and Kuwait to get the American hostages out (and whose business manager told us when we asked if we could have seats on his plane: 'We aren't into chequebook journalism, but that'll be $100,000') wouldn't be coming to rescue them. The television cameras weren't waiting for them and the British tabloid press wasn't polishing up its adjectives to describe what they had gone through.

The 50 or 60 Filipinos sat in the warm darkness, quiet now except for the occasional whimpering of a tired child. My friends and I hung around awkwardly. All we could do was fetch our camera and film them, in the hope that some foreign government might feel obliged to intervene and help. As we walked off to get the equipment I looked back. They were still watching us, but no one complained that we seemed to be deserting them. Life had taught them that there was no one they could complain to.

The Build-up of Forces

We see now US and western armies deployed to occupy the land of the Arabian peninsula, which is sacred to Arabs and Muslims alike, in such a harsh, degrading and arrogant fashion as has never been witnessed, except through the story of the attempt made by Abraha the Abyssinian to invade Holy Mecca some 15 centuries ago.

Saddam Hussein, television speech, September 1990

Even the best camouflage never looks good from close up. Perhaps regular blotches of brown on a dun-coloured background do take on the appearance of rocks in the desert from a distance; they looked pretty unconvincing as a detachment of American marines marched across a sandy parade ground in Saudi Arabia, floppy hats shading brown faces and non-regulation sunglasses. To a British eye the troops didn't look particularly good: a little sloppy, a little slow, a little unfit. Perhaps it was the September temperature of 118 degrees in the shade, only there was no shade. But the US Marine Corps had what Americans are better than anyone else in the world at providing: equipment. It had come off the ships in staggering amounts back at the docks: tons of tents and blankets and tables and chairs and filing cabinets, entire containers filled with ice cream, steaks, prawns, a mile of frankfurters, a lake of soft drinks, coffee. There was less in the way of vegetables and fruit because fewer marines demand that, but there were entire vans, called roach coaches, which could stop anywhere and provide a platoon of men with a three-course meal or all the soda they could drink. Armies are like the nations they come from, reduced to their essentials. Here in the Saudi desert the US forces were a consumer society.

A colonel showed the cameramen around his field hospital. It was better than many capital cities could boast: 500 beds, 800 staff, four intensive care units, a beautifully equipped operating theatre with overhead lamps. NCB suits, for protection against nuclear, chemical and biological weapons, were piled neatly in the corners in case the surgeons had to operate in conditions of unconventional warfare. The air conditioning hummed quietly, the camp beds were ranged in neat lines, the plasma bags were hanging ready. After the stunning heat outside it was so fine and cool and new that it almost made you want to be ill.

Helicopters rose like pheasants in a field, clattering nervously into the air. In the heat they had no fixity of shape and swelled or contracted randomly as they moved away. The rotors seemed to draw the sand up towards them and it blew across the landing strip as a gauze curtain blows across the window. The sand was colourless, creeping effortlessly into the most intimate crevices of the body, working its way between the tongue and the roof of the mouth, the upper and lower molars, the waistband and the skin, the places where anything rubbed. It studded your soap and infiltrated the controls of your Walkman. It covered you as you slept. It was the medium in which you lived and moved.

The marines were, however, getting used to it, and they were cheerful. They also anticipated action. In the words of their general:

> I think the signal's very clear. [Saddam] has lost his opportunity if he wanted to do something. It is long since passed, and I think he ought to be reading that very, very clear. We want about three to five minutes, and we're going to give him the most violent three to five minutes that he's ever seen.

It was early days, but it was noticeable that while the politicians back in Washington were talking about what might happen, the Marine Corps general was talking about what would happen. From time to time everyone found themselves looking northwards to where the Iraqis were dug in.

It was the precise opposite of the cliché: everything the generals and politicians did was designed to avoid fighting the last war. Vietnam was the analogy on everyone's lips. 'Whatever else we do, we are not going to do it the Vietnam way,' President Bush was quoted as saying at the end of August 1990. The American military establishment and, particularly, the chairman of the Joint Chiefs of Staff, General Colin L. Powell, believed that the Vietnam war was lost because of the slow build-up of forces over months and years. The very word 'escalation' was coined and came into general use in 1966–7 as American political jargon to describe the process by which the military slowly increased the scope of their activities and demanded ever-greater levels of manpower to carry out the new tasks they had set themselves. The plan was therefore to estimate – if necessary to overestimate – the forces and equipment which would be required and then to provide them in full.

There would be no limited offensives. In Vietnam the constant repetition of relatively small-scale attacks far from the enemy capital had, so the thinking in Washington went, made the slow process of escalation inevitable. This time the attack would be massive and intended to smash the heart of the enemy's decision-making and communications. It would play to American strengths, especially technological superiority in the air. 'Smart' weapons like the Tomahawk cruise missile would be used to ensure great accuracy, and avoid the heavy civilian casualties which had revolted public opinion throughout the western world and beyond in the Vietnam war. The expression 'surgical strike' was frequently used by planners.

The memory of Vietnam and of the clumsy, botched attack on Libya in 1986 made some people deeply sceptical of the notion that bombs and missiles could be so precise. US pilots who bombed Hanoi in the 1960s and 1970s found it hard to hit even the biggest targets like the Paul Doumer Bridge accurately. In early September the *New York Times* quoted a naval pilot who had flown dozens of missions over Hanoi and Haiphong as saying: 'Surgical strikes exist only in think-tanks and mental institutions.' Experience supported that view, but the Joint Chiefs of Staff, knowing the test results of weapons like the Tomahawk which had never been used in action, took the idea of precision bombing seriously. They also believed it would avoid casualties on the scale of the 1973 Arab-Israeli war when 20,000 men were killed and injured in two weeks of heavy desert fighting.

The Pentagon was fortunate that Saddam Hussein had no intention of invading Saudi Arabia and no desire to take on the United States in battle. Had he wanted to, he could have inflicted serious military defeat on the few thousand soldiers of the 82nd Airborne Division who were sent in to Saudi Arabia as the advance guard of operation Desert Shield. Their only weapons against Iraqi tanks would have been TOW and Dragon missiles, whose effectiveness was thought to be questionable. But in the three weeks that followed 40,000 American soldiers and marines poured into Saudi Arabia. They brought with them a million tons of equipment and the first M1A1 Abrams tanks.

The build-up revealed serious deficiencies in American logistical planning. There weren't enough C-141 Starlifter and C-5A Galaxy transport planes, elderly and in need of replacement, to do the job; most of the troops and a quarter of the supplies had to be brought in by chartered civilian aircraft. The tanks and helicopters had to be delivered by sea, and the US Navy had only eight SL-7 logistics ships to carry them; two broke down at sea in the early stages. During the Iran-Iraq War, the US Navy had reflagged and escorted Kuwaiti tankers only to discover that it had no effective minesweepers in a sea full of mines. Minesweeping had been too unglamorous and low-tech to attract the necessary money and attention. Now the same difficulty had arisen with the workaday business of transporting men and equipment.

Twenty-two of the world's most advanced fighter-bombers, the F117 Stealth warplanes which could fly undetected through all known Iraqi radar systems, were sent to Saudi Arabia. Since they had no obvious defensive role the assumption at the time was that they were ready for deployment if the Iraqis attacked the Allied build-up of forces with chemical weapons. The F117s had been used only once before in action, during the American attack on Panama in December

1989. For the most part, though, the emphasis at this stage was still on defending Saudi Arabia. In the event of an attack by Iraqi tanks, Britain announced at the end of August that it was sending in 12 GR1 Tornado aircraft based in Germany. They were armed with BL-755 cluster bombs for use against tanks, but could also be used to attack deep into Iraq. For that purpose they were equipped with JP-233 airfield attack systems for use in cratering runways.

Naval forces were also assembling. The battleship USS *Wisconsin*, commissioned in the 1940s, was the most robust ship afloat whose 12-inch armour was thought capable of withstanding a hit from an Exocet or a Silkworm missile. The carrier battle group headed by the USS *Independence* stayed outside the restricted waters of the Gulf for the time being, as did the USS *Eisenhower*. The French carrier *Clémenceau* had had a troublesome voyage and underwent emergency repairs at Djibouti. A Nimrod based at Seeb in Oman became the first RAF plane since the end of World War II to receive instructions from a friendly Soviet warship. Flight-Lieutenant Malcolm Ridley, the Nimrod's captain, was called up by the *Admiral Tributs*, a Udaloy class destroyer 592 which headed the small Soviet squadron in the Gulf. The *Admiral Tributs* had spotted a tanker which it thought might be trying to break the UN sanctions against Iraq and suggested the Nimrod should investigate. Flight-Lieutenant Ridley said:

> We said it would be a pleasure. The Russian spoke very good but somewhat old-fashioned English. He gave us the vessel's name, course and distance as 75 cables [7.5 nautical miles]. We soon found the ship, the Panamanian-registered *Maersk Nautilus*. She was 'clean', but in spite of that the Russians were very appreciative.

The Royal Navy's Armilla patrol in the Gulf had had ten years' experience of cooperating with the Americans and the French there, but some of the naval forces which were beginning to gather were complete newcomers. Soon, aside from the British, American, French and Soviet navies, there would be ships from Norway, Denmark, the Netherlands, Belgium, Spain, Italy, Greece, Turkey, Argentina, Canada and Australia.

The number of countries supporting the coalition with troops or aircraft was even greater: the United States, Saudi Arabia, Britain, France, Egypt, Morocco, Turkey, Syria, United Arab Emirates, Bahrain, Pakistan, Bangladesh, Canada, Italy. In terms of the politics of this confrontation, Syria's involvement was particularly important. President Hafez al-Assad had joined the alliance partly because of his personal feud with Saddam Hussein and his wider strategic opposition to Iraq, but also because he saw it as a short cut to a better relationship with the United States and the West generally. American support would make it possible for him to reestablish full Syrian control in Lebanon by defeating the Christian general Michel Aoun who had been receiving covert support and arms supplies from Iraq and Israel. As it turned out, the international embargo on Iraq cut off Aoun's Iraqi supplies and he surrendered on 13 October 1990.

The years of diplomatic isolation during which Syria was regarded as a safe haven for terrorists ended when President Assad joined the Allies. Nothing seemed to change: the Palestinian terrorist groups that had settled in Damascus remained there and the Syrian ministers and officials who had used them for Syria's political purposes remained in their posts. Assad had a human rights record which was at least as bad as Saddam Hussein's, if not worse. He ruled Syria, as Saddam ruled Iraq, on the basis of terror, relying on a particular group of military men and politicians which paralleled Saddam's Takritis. The main difference between them was that Assad was far more cautious — Lebanon apart — about foreign adventures. All in all, though, it now suited American policy to adopt Assad as an honorary member of a club dedicated to upholding the rule of international law.

On 23 November 1990 in Geneva Assad received the ultimate seal of approval for his sharp change of direction: a meeting with George Bush. It was the first time the Syrian President had shaken hands with an American president in 13 years. There were signs inside Syria that his new alliance was unpopular, but Assad sent 3000 men to Saudi Arabia and promised to follow them with a 9000-man division normally deployed near the Golan Heights, his disputed border with

Israel. Given the sensitive state of public opinion inside Syria, the division he selected was entirely composed of men from his own minority Alawite sect whose loyalty was assured.

President Ozal of Turkey took a sizeable risk by giving forthright support to the coalition. According to opinion polls, 55 per cent of people in Turkey supported Saddam Hussein. Ozal still pressed ahead, blocking Iraq's oil pipeline, allowing American and other NATO forces to use their bases in Turkey to attack Iraq, and implementing the various Security Council Resolutions in full. There were, in Ozal's view, strong foreign policy advantages in doing all this: it would, for instance, make it even harder for the European Community to turn down Turkey's application for membership; and it would win strong American support. But it was still a gamble.

Egypt's rewards for taking part were more basic. The United States and the Gulf states quite simply wrote off half Egypt's debt. During the early part of the crisis nearly $14 billion was written off and by the end, another $10 billion was to be phased out by 1994. Of the $25 billion which was left, most was converted into long-term repayment at low interest with long grace periods. Egypt's annual repayments were cut from nearly $6 billion to $1.5 billion.

As early as the beginning of September the United States showed anxiety about the commitment of the other members of the coalition. Britain, which had deployed more forces than any other country in the alliance except Saudi Arabia and the United States itself, was criticized by the Democratic leader of the House of Representatives, Dick Gephardt, who said the Royal Navy and Royal Air Force contingents already in place should be strengthened. The chairman of the Ways and Means Committee, congressman Dan Rostenkpowski, widened the demand for greater participation:

> We're going to have to expect more cooperation from the 22 countries that are participating, and get more people on the ground.

Margaret Thatcher responded quickly. Two days after a Congressional delegation reported to President Bush that more needed to be done, she told the House of Commons, which had been recalled for an emergency debate about the Gulf issue on 6 and 7 September: 'We believe some additional forces will be needed and their composition is under consideration.' She appeared to mean that ground forces would be committed, though it was unclear who, precisely, had been doing the considering about the composition of the extra forces. Her statement took the chiefs of staff by surprise since some days earlier the British foreign secretary, Douglas Hurd, had said there were 'not at present' any plans to commit ground forces. The official position until Mrs Thatcher spoke had been that Britain's best contribution would be to send aircraft and ships. The RAF had been highly active. Each of the British squadrons based there had flown 200 sorties during the previous month, and the C-130 Hercules transports had flown over two million miles, more than during a comparable period in the Falklands war. Mrs Thatcher's response was a political one. She was not prepared to see Britain listed among the countries the United States regarded as failing to pull their weight.

The complaint aired by Gephardt and Rostenkpowski is an habitual one in the United States. Opinion polls tend to show that a sizeable majority of Americans believe it to be true and they are provided with little evidence to help them make an informed judgment. In the Gulf crisis, as in most other things, American television coverage concentrated to the exclusion of almost everything else on the activities of the United States. Throughout the months of August, September and October none of the main television networks seems to have devoted a report on its news programmes to the British or French response. Not surprisingly, people assumed that what they were not told about was not happening.

A number of the countries involved in the Alliance were irritated by this pressure. Many believed that whatever level of commitment they adopted, the United States would not allow them any serious involvement in decision-making. Even Britain was informed rather than consulted on some important decisions. The Americans were naturally reluctant to slow down the process of managing the crisis by canvassing its

201

Allies' opinions on everything, but many European governments felt that criticizing them was an easy and cheap way of keeping American public opinion happy. The Italian foreign minister, Gianni de Michelis, said acidly after a European ministerial meeting in September that the United States had based itself on the principle of no taxation without representation. It seemed to him that the Europeans were taking a considerable share of the Gulf operation, yet had no serious representation when it came to the strategic or tactical decisions Washington was taking.

Germany and Japan were most strongly attacked in the United States. The administration itself was polite but chilly; the backwoodsmen in Congress were noisy and sometimes openly insulting. A Republican senator, Alfonse D'Amato, accused the Japanese of being motivated by 'profit, greed and avarice', called their attitude 'really repugnant' and accused them of enjoying the benefits of the American military response while not being prepared to do their part. As for the Germans, D'Amato asked:

> Where are they? It is nice they have got East Germany and unification. It is wonderful they have got a strong economy. But what about their participation in a meaningful way economically?

Senator William Cohen, a Republican, said Germany was offering little more than pocket change to defray the expense of refugees in Jordan while the 'jugular vein of the US military is sitting out there exposed in Saudi Arabia'. The chairman of the House Energy and Commerce Committee said he would introduce a bill levying a 20 per cent import duty on goods from countries which 'didn't pay their share'.

American newspapers were quick to point out that although the Germans were paying the largest share of a $2 billion package from the European Community to help the countries contributing to the build-up, even Portugal had made a greater commitment to the coalition forces than the Germans had. The German government, faced with the heavy expense of supporting the collapsing East German economy, decided on 5

202

September that it could not subsidize the American build-up in Saudi Arabia because it was not, strictly speaking, covered by the various UN Security Council resolutions. Instead, the Bonn government offered to transport American troops to the region in German planes and ships.

Japan, for its part, had offered $1 billion to help the effort against Iraq and was considering aid of $2 billion more for Egypt, Turkey and Jordan. Its constitution formally prevented the sending of forces outside Japan. The government of Toshiki Kaifu, under heavy pressure from Washington, agreed to send members of its armed forces to the Gulf armed with pistols and other small arms for self-defence only. The debate in the Japanese Diet followed something of the same, faintly ludicrous line, but there was such opposition to the bill that on 6 November it was withdrawn by the government in some embarrassment.

It was difficult to find anyone in the American Congress who was prepared to sympathize publicly with the notion that either Japan or Germany should adhere to the constitutions which the US, together with the other wartime Allies, had helped to frame for them. The Japanese aroused more anger even than the Germans: 'They have proved once again,' said a Republican senator, John McCain, 'that they have the world's most flexible constitution.' In truth the precise opposite was true. After 1945 Japan had been provided with one of the world's least flexible constitutions and it had succeeded in making the Japanese some of the most peaceable people on earth.

France's Gulf contribution was afflicted by the same problem that the Americans had experienced. The French military interventions in Zaire in 1978 and in Chad in 1986 had both been compromised by a lack of transport planes. In both cases France had had to borrow civilian planes or US Air Force transports. Now the Defence Ministry toyed with the idea of buying troop carriers from the Soviet Union. On paper the French effort was greater than Britain's in the first few months of the crisis: 14 warships and 13,000 men; but the Foreign Legionnaires and the armoured regiments being sent to the Red Sea port of Yanbu were only a small fraction of the

Force d'Action Rapide, 47,000 strong, which had been set up to fight a limited overseas war.

The French were earning American irritation by refusing to supply details of the radar and surface-to-air missile systems they had sold to Iraq. There was a distinct anxiety in Paris that the future of French arms sales would be threatened if it became known that France was prepared to reveal information about the weapons it sold. The French government had, however, given Britain much useful information about missiles such as the Exocet which had been bought by Argentina and the British quickly passed this on to Washington. Soon the French realized that they were in as difficult a position as they had been in 1982 over the Falklands and told the Americans as much as they needed to know. There were other problems too. If it came to an air war, French pilots would have to face Iraqi squadrons equipped with French Mirage jets and Iraqi pilots trained in France on French missile systems. The Iraqis knew the battle tactics which the French air force used and had tried them out against Iran.

For these reasons, as well as for wider political ones, President François Mitterrand did what he could to promote a peaceful settlement to the crisis. Towards the end of September he told the UN secretary-general, Javier Perez de Cuellar, that all Iraq would need to do would be to release the hostages and evacuate Kuwait. Saddam Hussein, however, failed to oblige and Iraqi troops pushed France closer to the other Allies by raiding the French ambassador's residence in Kuwait on 14 September. They arrested a French military attaché, Edouard Crespin, and three Frenchmen who had taken refuge there. M. Crespin was later released but the other three were held as hostages. Diplomatic premises belonging to five other countries – Canada, Belgium, the Netherlands, Tunisia and Bangladesh – were all entered illegally by Iraqi troops on the same day.

The government in Baghdad denied vehemently that the raid on the French embassy had taken place, though it did not bother to deny the other raids with the same intensity. It seemed to have been done on the initiative of the local Iraqi military commander. Saddam Hussein still had hopes that

France, together with the Soviet Union, would persuade the Americans that a deal was possible. Meanwhile the French defence minister, Jean-Pierre Chevènement, was a strong critic within the French cabinet of the build-up of military forces. He argued the case for the French arms manufacturers: that Iraq had been a good and reliable customer and that future sales of arms would be jeopardized if France gave the Americans secret military information about the equipment it had sold.

President Mitterrand bided his time, as usual, and worked to weaken Chevènement's position without actually ordering the prime minister, Michel Rocard, to sack him. The day after the raids on diplomatic premises in Kuwait, Mitterrand said they seemed to be a test of the solidarity of Iraq's opponents and he announced that 4000 extra troops, 48 heavy tanks, 30 warplanes and 48 attack helicopters were being sent to the Gulf. At the time it seemed a decisive shift – the moment when France chose sides. As the months passed, though, the other coalition governments were to have cause to wonder whether France might still have hopes of rescuing the country which had become its best market in the Gulf.

The *Christian Science Monitor* published a cartoon in September which showed one American soldier in the desert reading a message to another:

> In the case of attack the US will confer with French, British and other Allied force commanders, coordinating with Soviet contacts, then jointly confer with Gulf states, the Syrians, the Egyptians, King Fahd and all 250 of his immediate family, the Emir of Kuwait, Senator Nunn and General Schwartzkopf. You may then fire at will.

It was never, in reality, the Bush administration's intention to let anything like this happen. The United States wanted to manage the entire crisis and it consulted its allies only as much as was necessary to keep them happy. Saudi Arabia had proposed that King Fahd should be the overall commander of the Gulf forces with the senior US officer, General Schwartz-kopf, as one of his deputies and Prince Sultan bin Abdul Aziz, the Saudi defence minister, as the other. President Bush disagreed and the resulting memorandum – only three pages long – which was to govern the stationing of hundreds of thousands of foreign troops on Saudi soil was revised to allow separate but parallel commands: the United States and its NATO allies in one, Saudi and Islamic forces in the other. The American command was assigned to a sector along the Gulf and south of Kuwait, the Saudi command was deployed to the west. There was also a thin line of Saudi troops separating the Americans from the Iraqi and Kuwaiti borders.

H. Norman Schwartzkopf (the H is simply an initial, it doesn't stand for anything) scarcely looked like a sensitive man or a good diplomat. He is six feet three inches tall, and weighs 17 stone. His neck is exceedingly thick and his hair exceedingly short. He had been nicknamed Stormin' Norman and The Bear at West Point military academy. There is a volcanic element in his nature and he isn't always very popular with his staff. But there is another side to him which fits neither the appearance nor the background. He is passionately fond of opera and he likes Bob Dylan; he speaks French and German reasonably well. He was born in 1934 and spent two years after World War II in Iran where his father, a general before him, had helped to set up the Iranian national police. He also lived in Italy and Germany. In Vietnam, where he served as a major from 1965–6 and as a lieutenant-colonel from 1969–1970, he learned the lesson that simply setting out to annihilate an opponent doesn't work. Unlike many American officers in Vietnam he was good at looking after his men. After he was appointed to head the Gulf force he told an interviewer: 'In a lot of ways I am a pacifist, though that may be too strong a word.' It probably was, but it demonstrated a sensitivity to concerns other than purely military ones. General Colin Powell, the chairman of the Joint Chiefs of Staff, had been promoted over Schwartzkopf's head, but he had been impressed by Schwartzkopf's ability to grasp the changes which the Soviet collapse and the end of the Cold War would mean for the US military. He proved to be surprisingly diplomatic in his dealings with the politicians and generals of the various countries involved in Desert Shield and Desert Storm and his press conferences earned him a reputation with journalists for being both intelligent and relatively open.

206

Saudi Arabia was a place that required diplomacy. The Saudi government was deeply sensitive to radical Muslim accusations that it was endangering the holy places of Islam by allowing western forces onto its territory. The American troops posed a special problem, since 15 per cent of them were women. Iraqi propaganda played on this, often lewdly. Women soldiers were under orders to cover their hair as Saudi women did and had to be careful when going out in public. No alcohol was allowed and the soldiers of all the different national groupings were restricted to soft drinks and water. Christian and Jewish religious services had to be carried out in an almost clandestine fashion. Many of the restrictions caused anger among the troops. The Americans were particularly incensed by orders they received to take off the small American flags they wore on their sleeves. The rumour went round that this was on Saudi orders; it turned out to have arisen from American commanders who were nervous that the flags would make their men a particular target.

The desert conditions made things difficult too. Helicopters, which are usually able to fly for 50 hours between services, were breaking down every two or three hours because of the fine desert sand. F-15 and F-16 fighters were also particularly vulnerable. The frontline M1A1 Abrams tanks suffered too and used up more than 12 gallons of fuel per mile. In the desert their average range was less than 100 miles. On those figures the Pentagon had seriously underestimated the amount of fuel required and there were not enough petrol bowsers to keep them going in case of attack. There were more doubts about the British Challenger tanks, which were to take up forward positions with the 7th Armoured Brigade – the so-called Desert Rats. The Challenger, one of the world's heaviest tanks at 62 tonnes, had been designed for desert fighting, originally in the 1970s for the Shah of Iran. Its reliability was questioned, though, and each of the 120 Challengers had to be fitted with sand filters and other modifications.

In the desert and in the southern Saudi city of Dhahran – which became a cross between a frontier town, an international capital and an armed camp – the military spewed out neologisms, acronyms and euphemisms. At the big press conferences the briefers would speak of HARMs, JAATs, TADS, SLAR, SLAMs and SLIPARs when they meant, respectively, high-speed anti-radiation missiles, joint air attack teams, target acquisition and designation sight, side-looking airborne radar, stand-off land attack missiles and short light-pulse alerting receivers. Everyone talked of NCB suits, such as the ones that I had seen stacked in the field hospital operating theatre, meaning their protection against nuclear, chemical and biological warfare which had to be carried round at all times. Later many journalists took to wearing them, if they weren't wearing army camouflage to match the verbal camouflage they slowly copied from the military: MIAs (missing in action), WIA (wounded in action), KIA (killed in action). The KIAs were provided with HRPs which earlier wars had called body bags; the new public relations title translated as 'human remains pouches'. Then there was the famous 'collateral damage', a term which came to mean civilian casualties though it was coined to refer to the effects of a near miss. Some of the military men, franker than the rest, spoke of 'civilian impacting': it meant the same thing.

We also learnt about target-rich environments where the enemy was massing. There was something called circular error probability, which simply meant the area where a bomb or a missile was likely to fall. No one spoke of body counts, partly because it was too reminiscent of Vietnam and therefore not acceptable in a war which intended to sweep away that legacy, and partly because they didn't need to: there were three or four ways of saying the same thing less bluntly. These linguistic inventions were remarkable, yet they had an opposite effect from most new coinings: they obscured reality instead of expressing it in some more vivid way. As preparations for war continued, it became taboo to talk about it in public. On 17 September 1991 the chief of staff of the US Air Force, General Michael Dugan, was relieved of his duties for declaring in an interview that it was the American intention to bomb Baghdad, and, perhaps, to kill Saddam Hussein himself.

No Blood for Oil

Mr Bush wants to bring back the sorrows of the United States and humanity by repeating the Vietnam experience – only this time the ordeal will be more violent, demanding greater sacrifices and bigger losses.

Saddam Hussein, quoted by the Iraqi News Agency, September 1990

It had once been the house of a Turkish official. Now it was an antique shop, and carpets and camel bags hung over the balcony that ran around the four sides of its central atrium. There were showcases of silver, glass and jewellery and scimitars hung on the walls. Ancient gramophones with brass horns like the trumpets of giant daffodils stood on top of dusty cupboards. Four or five years earlier it had become officially acceptable in Iraq to speak about life before the Baath Party and people brought out the political memorabilia of the past which had been hidden away: medals with the head of King Faysal I or King Ghazi, teapots with the face of President Qassem, entire tea sets with Faysal II on them.

This was the place in which I discovered that the superloyal had been decorating their watches – both the wrist and the fob variety – with the faces of their leaders since the days of the Ottoman empire. I bought a handsome Constantinople-made watch with the Sultan's face to go with my growing collection of Saddam timepieces. For the amateur of political kitsch the shop exerted a powerful attraction. I spent a great deal of time and some money there as for most of the period I was in Baghdad, from August to January, it was possible to wander around the city entirely on one's own. The assumption in the

West that after the beginning of September foreign journalists were closely monitored by the authorities was a fiction.

By October I had come to regard several Iraqi officials as personal friends. Even so, few talked to me with any great openness about Iraqi politics or the way they lived their lives. I discouraged those who did so, in their own interest.

'I know perfectly well what you're trying to tell me,' I said, more than once, 'so there's no point in putting yourself in danger to put it into words.' The fact was, most people wanted to say exactly the same thing: how they hated the system in Iraq and the man who had created it, how wrong they felt the invasion of Kuwait had been, how crazy they thought the decision to oppose the West was. Some of them felt it with such intensity that it did them good just to express themselves.

One such friend wanted to go to the antiques shop with me. I introduced him to the owner, but I could see that he was wary of him. In Iraq you learn early in life not to trust people at first sight. We drank a glass of sugary tea and looked at the Qassem-decorated cigarette lighter which I was always trying to persuade the owner to sell me. We wandered off as the proprietor talked to another group of customers. He kept the china in an upstairs room. The faces of kings and presidents looked at us from teapots, from plates, from cups and saucers. My friend looked around listlessly, then sank down on a pile of Persian *kilims*. We could hear the owner's voice down below: no one would overhear us.

'This man has got to be dealt with,' he said, after a moment or two. I knew which man he meant: if you criticized Saddam Hussein you didn't refer to him by name. 'If the West doesn't deal with him, then God help all of us. I don't care now what we have to suffer. They will bomb our cities, they will blow up our army. It doesn't matter – it couldn't be as bad as what we will have to suffer if he carries on. I only hope you realize that.' We heard the sound of movement downstairs and started examining the showcase with the blue and white china exported from England in the nineteenth century for the Persian trade.

I thought of him that night as I watched the television news. After the 20 minute lead item on Saddam Hussein's doings that day there was a round-up from western capitals of recent antiwar demonstrations: people marching along Kensington High Street, sitting down by the railings in Pennsylvania Avenue, chanting slogans in the Boulevard Saint-Michel. 'No Blood For Oil', said the slogan they carried and chanted. The protest was highly effective: the way it spread from country to country showed that. It arose from the feeling that the United States and its allies were concerned about Kuwait simply because it was an oil producer. The British Labour MP Tam Dalyell, a dogged and thoughtful critic of the Thatcher government's record in the Falklands and later, put it with great precision:

> [I]f Kuwait had been famous for its carrots, the US would not have lifted its proverbial finger.

This, however, does not seem to have been the case. On 11 September, in a speech to Congress, President Bush expressed his idea of the American role as follows:

> To deter future aggression. . . to help our friends in their own self-defence. . . and to curb the proliferation of chemical, biological, ballistic missiles and above all nuclear technologies.

Bush had another set of imperatives as well. He wanted to expunge the feeling that had lasted ever since Vietnam that the United States was incapable of fighting a successful war; and he wanted to establish a more peaceable order in a world which had finally emerged from the Cold War. The Iraqi invasion of Kuwait gave Bush the opportunity to reassert American power in the world – and, he would add, to create the kind of international system which would prevent one country from attacking another as Iraq had attacked Kuwait. Saddam Hussein gave him his opportunity, therefore; whether Kuwait had produced oil or carrots, Bush would have moved in to defend it. No doubt it mattered greatly to the United States, to Western Europe and to Japan that Kuwait did produce oil, but it wasn't the prime reason for acting against Iraq. If it had been an ally of the West which had invaded a small neighbour, things would probably have been different.

In this case, it was one of the nastiest régimes in the world, with few friends. That made Bush's task a great deal easier.

Kuwait's was not a particularly attractive society, as we have seen. It had an unimpressive human rights record and was run more like a family business than a country. After the ceasefire when the al-Sabah government was restored, a campaign of revenge started against Palestinians and others accused of collaboration which was nothing less than a crime in itself. A motion tabled in the House of Commons by the Labour MP George Galloway in January 1991, soon after the outbreak of war, neatly established the unattractive nature of the state which the Allies were fighting for:

> That this House notes that British forces are currently fighting, some perchance to die, for the restoration of the legitimate government of Kuwait: and notes that this legitimate government, viz: The Amir Jaber As-Sabah, the Crown Prince Sa'ad As-Sabah, the Prime Minister Sa'ad As-Sabah, the Deputy Prime Minister Sa'bah As-Sabah, the Foreign Minister Sa'bah As-Sabah, the Minister of Amiri Diwan Affairs Khalid As-Sabah, the Minister of Information Jaber As-Sabah, the Minister of the Interior Salim As-Sabah, the Minister of Defence Nawaf As-Sabah, the Minister of Oil Ali As-Sabah, the Governor of Ahmadi Province Ali Sabah As-Sabah, the Governor of Jahra Province Ali Abdullah As-Sabah, the Governor of Kuwait Province Jaber As-Sabah, the Governor of Faranawiya Province Ahmad As-Sabah, are an unelected government who appear to be related: further notes that the Kuwaiti National Assembly, which had a limited franchise and even more limited powers, was suspended by the Amir's decree in 1986, and wonders if this war aim of restoration can be justified.

The American senator, Daniel Moynihan, agreed:

> They're going to send our men and women into battle for those Kuwaitis who have taken over the Sheraton Hotel in Taif and are sitting there in their white robes, drinking coffee, and urging us to go to war. What is the matter with George Bush?

These, however, were more in the nature of good debating

points than moral arguments; Kuwait, however family-run and however undemocratic, was an internationally recognized sovereign state which had been snuffed out by its even more family-run and undemocratic neighbour. The international community had shown that it was not willing simply just to stand by and watch. The real question was therefore, what action should be taken?

In many countries, Germany in particular, this question divided many of those who had supported pacifist or leftist causes in the past. The songwriter Wolf Biermann supported the notion that it was necessary to go to war against Saddam Hussein. So did the writer Hans Magnus Enzensberger, who followed the example of George Bush and Margaret Thatcher in describing Saddam as a new Hitler. The novelist and controversialist Gunther Grass took a different view:

> It is absolutely right to protest against the Iraqis' brutal action. But [. . .] I'm on the side of the youngsters who have taken to the streets to demonstrate against the war. They may not be able to articulate very clearly why they are against it, but how can you expect them to? I disagree with those veterans of 1968 who believe they had the right arguments at the time and who now refuse to argue and instead rail against these young protesters. I was certainly shocked by the essay in which Biermann bluntly declared 'I support this war'. And I was shocked to see Enzensberger indulging in this silly equation of Saddam and Hitler, a line of reasoning which clarifies nothing and only obfuscates the real situation. Biermann and Enzensberger argue from very different standpoints of course, but they are both intellectuals who in their heyday coined radical slogans and produced sharp analyses. I cannot understand what has got into them.

Grass laid heavy blame on the countries of the West which had sold large quantities of weapons to Iraq in order to counterbalance Iran. He was particularly angry about the activities of German companies in supplying the Iraqis with chemicals from which to make weapons. He regarded the war as one of the first armed conflicts waged by the industrial countries against the countries of the Third World for economic and energy interests. He believed, finally, that not enough had been

213

done to search for a political solution. It emerged after the war was over that German companies had delivered about £340 million worth of arms and technology to Baghdad between 1982 and 1989 with the permission of their government, despite an official ban on exporting arms to 'areas of tension'. On 21 August, 1990, less than three weeks after the Iraq invasion of Kuwait, the German economics minister Helmut Haussman told a parliamentary committee:

> The dangerous proliferation has already taken place. Our country's international reputation, on which we are so dependent, has already been damaged.

The German authorities were later to investigate 110 cases of alleged attempts by German companies to break the UN embargo on goods to Iraq.

Many people in Europe and the United States agreed with Grass's view that the West had made the invasion of Kuwait possible. A poster printed by the Campaign for Nuclear Disarmament and handed out at demonstrations in London read:

IRAQ OUT OF KUWAIT

SANCTIONS NOT WAR

GIVE PEACE A CHANCE

The United States and Britain, however, were plainly determined to ensure that Saddam Hussein was not given the opportunity to escape; and continuing the sanctions indefinitely would, in the judgement of London and Washington, provide him with a way out of his difficulties without having to relinquish Kuwait. This was the view in Iraq as well. A senior government official assured me that if the United Nations relied on sanctions alone, Iraq was certain to win the battle of wills. After six months, he said, only Britain and the United States would still continue with sanctions, and even British and American companies would be making secret contacts with Baghdad to join all the companies from other countries which were trading with Iraq.

The fact is Iraq was not a suitable case for the imposition of long-term sanctions. For one thing, its oil was too valuable a commodity to have remained unsold for long. For another, Saddam Hussein's control over the population was so great that people would have been obliged to put up with shortages almost indefinitely. There was no serious shortage of food throughout the entire period of the crisis: prices were high but the vast quantities of food seized in the warehouses and storage centres of Kuwait kept the population of Iraq supplied for months. The country's economy would undoubtedly have been damaged by a long-term embargo on spare parts and new equipment, but Saddam Hussein showed, during the war with Iran, that he was prepared to risk serious damage to the Iraqi economy rather than risk his prestige by settling on humiliating terms. He would without question have done the same thing in the confrontation with the West. A United Nations policy of lengthy sanctions was very much what Saddam was hoping for.

The Bush administration rejected the sanctions strategy, without apparently being too clear at the start of the crisis what its precise reaction should be. The version put out by the more excitable and jingoistic newspapers in Britain (and echoed on the British left for reasons of its own), that Bush was undecided and Margaret Thatcher persuaded him that war was the only possible outcome, simply won't do. The main characters within the Bush administration seem to have taken different positions at different times but, at the risk of oversimplification, it seems that: Bush himself felt there would have to be war if Saddam Hussein did not humiliate himself by withdrawing from Kuwait beforehand; the Defence Secretary Richard Cheney was determined that a military solution was unavoidable; the Secretary of State James Baker wanted to find a diplomatic solution if one were available; the Chairman of the Joint Chiefs of Staff Colin Powell, following the example of Dwight Eisenhower, thought it better to pursue peace than war.

Bush's own objectives – a tougher-seeming presidency and a new world order – could only really be achieved by war. By the end of October James Baker, his friend and ally since the 1950s, fell into line. On 29 October he told the Los Angeles

World Affairs Council: 'We will not rule out a possible use of force if Iraq continues to occupy Kuwait.' From that point, it seems reasonable to assume, war became likely unless Saddam Hussein himself were prepared to compromise. He wasn't, of course.

There was nothing inevitable about the war, however. If Bush had wanted to avoid it at all costs it would not have been difficult. It was essential for him that the United States should emerge from the crisis with its power enhanced and that meant the humiliation of Saddam. Saddam himself believed that the precise opposite was possible and, indeed, likely: that he could humiliate the United States and establish Iraq under his leadership as a regional superpower. A peaceful settlement would, as the peace activists in country after country pointed out, save thousands of human lives and avoid an ecological disaster. Although it was often expressed in exaggerated terms, the warning proved later to have been justified. But to have compromised would have meant some measure of victory for Saddam Hussein and that was unacceptable not only to the United States but to the leaders of most of the countries which had joined the anti-Saddam alliance.

In the United States the debate about Iraq and its invasion of Kuwait followed the lines of most such debates there: that is to say, it was all about the United States and only rarely about anywhere else. Curiously, the opposition to Bush's policy came first from what might be called the loony right. Patrick Buchanan, a newspaper columnist, insisted that the American people were against Bush's decision to threaten the use of force against Iraq, but it emerged that this was because Buchanan felt that the United States should not become entangled in foreign adventures. There was little opposition to Bush's approach in Congress; like the leadership of the Labour Party in Britain during the Falklands crisis, most Democrats had no alternative but to support the administration. At first, as in Germany, some important figures from the 1960s protest movements came out in support of Bush. Todd Gitlin, a former president of Students for a Democratic Society, praised the decision to act in concert with the United Nations and made the point that 'Not only do all generals fight the last war, but antiwar people fight the last war too'. Another one-time peace activist, the Reverend William Sloane Coffin, praised the decision to work with the UN and said he had come out 'marginally in favour of Bush'. In their case, however, the support did not last long. Some formerly hawkish figures such as Zbigniew Brzezinski, who had played such a lamentable part in dealing with Iran at the time of the overthrow of the Shah and later, opposed the use of force against Iraq on the grounds that the casualties and the risk of political instability in the Middle East would be too high. The men and women of the Reagan era, like Richard Perle, took the Reagan era line: if Saddam were not dealt with firmly now, he would be even harder to deal with later. Some American politicians and newspapers, faced with the problem of deciding how they should react, left it to the President to tell them and then complained when he didn't seem to tell them clearly enough. One superbly named senator, Malcolm Wallop, said: 'I'd be happy to support the policy, if I knew what it was. But it can't be "jobs" one day and "I've had it up to here" another day.'

The Catholic bishops warned that a war with Iraq might contravene the notion of a just war, which St Augustine identified as one which was fought for the sake of the tranquillity of order, but in which only proportionate means of force could be used. The liberal Protestants of the National Council of Churches went further, condemning 'the illogical logic of militarism and war'. All of it, on both sides of the divide, was about America. Saddam Hussein crept into the argument only occasionally. For the right, he was the man whose actions would enable the United States to demonstrate its strength and leadership; for the left ('Saddam at his worst is merely following our historical example,' said the Nation, referring to Vietnam) he showed up American pretensions and hypocrisy. Few people, not even the Catholic bishops or the NCC, showed much interest in the position of ordinary Iraqis in all this. For the most part, they seemed to accept the word of the few American journalists who were allowed into Baghdad: that Saddam had the support of his people.

There was little recognition among those in Europe and the United States who opposed the war that Saddam Hussein might be a different kind of leader. The policy of sanctions could, for instance, have considerable effect on a country with a rational, self-interested policy. There is a good case for saying that eventually sanctions even succeeded in changing South Africa. But Saddam Hussein was not rational in that particular sense. Having set himself and his country a target, he would not stop until he had achieved it or was forcibly prevented from achieving it. It is probably true that no measures short of war would have got him out of Kuwait. Refusing to fight a war is an honourable position to take, but it could not easily be presented as a solution to the problem of what should be done about Saddam's invasion of Kuwait.

Europeans characteristically showed more concern than Americans about the practical effects of the build-up of forces in the Gulf. In Britain the widely-respected author and journalist Robert Fisk wrote an article for the *Independent* newspaper which proved very influential and gave many supporters of the Anglo-American policy of threatening the use of force a good deal to think about. Printed on 9 August, it was entitled 'History haunts the new "Crusaders"':

> Young foreigners have come here before in their tens of thousands – to Syria, Palestine, Egypt and Arabia – and almost all have departed in shame and ignominy. There are still old men alive who remember the last time a western army invaded Iraq, when the British marched in victory up the valley of the Tigris and died in their thousands at Kut al-Amara, of heatstroke, sickness and Turkish massacre. Their phantoms may have briefly reawoken yesterday.

Fisk recalled the debacle at Suez, when Britain and France attacked Egypt without the support of the United States, and pointed out that in his speech the previous day Bush had likened Saddam Hussein to Hitler, just as Eden had likened Nasser to the German leader in 1956.

> [I]t might be as well for the West to remember that history in the Middle East rarely rewards the just. It never favours the foreigner and it always takes its revenge upon those who see the region through their own eyes. Not once has a foreign military

adventure in the Middle East achieved its end. For it is also an irresistible trap: what else could Mr Bush have done in the face of Iraq's aggression? And what else can the Arabs do but support Iraq in a future war? Mr Bush urged his people yesterday to go to church and pray for the young Americans who are on their way to the Gulf. It was a wise precaution.

The article was intelligent, well written and accurate about the past. If it proved to be wrong, at least in the terms Robert Fisk set out, this was because history chose not to repeat itself. For the first time in such a situation, Arab unity collapsed and 'the Arabs' were not after all obliged to support Saddam Hussein. For most Arab governments, Saddam had behaved too badly for them to be able to support him. As a result of that deviation from the historical pattern, none of Fisk's eloquent forecasts came true. There was a certain amount of spiteful triumphalism about this on the part of other British newspapers when the war ended. It sprang from a sense of relief: most people who read the article in the first place found it disturbingly likely that the new Crusaders would indeed come to grief.

Other forecasts look bad when measured against the outcome. I myself, writing in the *Spectator* at about the same time as Robert Fisk, declared that the Americans were in danger of losing Soviet support for their actions in the Gulf and warned that ordinary people throughout the Arab world would come out in support of Saddam Hussein. I also anticipated that Iran would come out in support of the Alliance.

Predicting the future is, of course, a mug's game. Zbigniew Brzezinski got it more wrong than most when he gave testimony before the Senate Foreign Relations Committee in December 1990:

> In the region itself, it is probable that fundamentalist Iran will become the dominant power in the Persian Gulf, and that terrorist Syria will inherit the mantle of leadership among the Arabs. It is also possible that the destruction of Iraq by America and the resulting radicalization of the Arabs might leave Israel, armed as it already is with nuclear weapons, more tempted to use its military force to impose its will in this volatile region. How will all this affect the area's sensitive balance of power?

Fortunately we were not to find out.

Brzezinski's obsession with Iran, which was shared by many western commentators, had obviously coloured all his other perceptions. In fact, the Islamic Republic had ceased to be aggressively fundamentalist at least three years before the death of Ayatollah Khomeini in June 1989. By 1990 it was ceasing to be particularly fundamentalist even in its domestic policy, let alone its foreign relations. But the effect of all those television pictures of hundreds of thousands of black-clad demonstrators in Tehran takes a long time to wear off. Worse, it affected western perceptions of Islam as a whole. When Saddam Hussein, merely as a ploy, began using the language of militant Islam, people took it seriously in the West. It was as hard to persuade them that Iraq had not become a funda-mentalist state as it was to persuade them that Iran had ceased to be one.

Having assumed that Saddam was opening up a *jihad* against the West instead of being merely cynical and opportunistic, western opinion set the whole affair in a different and more threatening context: a kind of postcolonialist version of the anger that Mahatma Gandhi, Jomo Kenyatta and Archbishop Makarios had once aroused in the British. Saddam was perceived to be threatening the entire order of things; there was a temptation to see him as part of a process. People who believed that Islam was indeed on the march against western interests thought he represented the crest of the wave.

Some Arab writers saw this response as racist. The Palestin-ian writer Edward Said believed the West's response to Saddam arose from ancient prejudices and wilful ignorance; and it was obvious that what he had read in American newspapers and watched on American television had goaded him beyond endurance:

In the US most of what passes for journalistic and expert commentary has been a repetition of appalling clichés, most of them ignorant, unhistorical, moralistic, selfrighteous and hypocritical. All of them derive unquestioningly in one way or another from US government policy, which has long considered the Arabs either as terrorists or as mindless stooges to be milked for their money or abundant and inexpensive oil. . . Not a single report has mentioned that the population of Kuwait is largely – indeed overwhelmingly – non-Kuwaiti, or that with a few exceptions governments in the area have had little historical legitimacy; that they have derived their status from colonialism, force or sheer buying power; and that this situation has long been traded on by the major powers, especially the US.

All of which is true; but published only 10 days after the invasion of Kuwait, it sounded like the general Palestinian complaint that it was all the fault of someone other than Saddam Hussein.

There was something akin to hysteria in the reaction of many people and institutions in the West which should have known better. Sections of the British, French and American press had little to be proud of. The same was true of parts of the British government and civil service. The Palestinian writer Abbas Shiblak was arrested in London on 17 January and served with a deportation order alleging that he was a threat to national security. The Home Office had not managed to spell his name or the name of his street correctly on the deportation order. He had lived in Britain since 1973 and was opposed to Saddam Hussein and the invasion of Kuwait, but no enquiries were made about this. Shiblak spent the night at a police station, under conditions which he describes as appalling, before being taken to Pentonville prison where he met the other detainees. Most were Iraqis, mostly postgraduate students. It is certainly true that the Mukhabarat and Estikhabarat had plenty of agents among the Iraqi community in Britain, and no doubt many of them were students. Others, particularly the Palestinians, appeared to be there to make up the numbers. A British newspaper reported that the security services had arrested seven Palestinians who were plotting to carry out explosions in Britain. Shiblak read that and realized that there were six other Palestinians there and that he made the seventh.

One, Mahmoud Ayyad, was completely apolitical, and had worked for a Gulf embassy in London; another, Ali al-Saleh, had given up politics 12 years before and gone into management. The authorities never questioned them or searched their houses: it reflected very badly indeed on the security services.

After a considerable outcry and active lobbying by individuals and organizations, Shiblak and several of the others (including Ayyad and al-Saleh) were released and the deportation orders revoked.

These men were fortunate to have friends to help them. Under the 1971 Immigration Act and the 1974 Prevention of Terrorism Act a person accused of being a threat to national security will not know the nature of the accusation against him or her, nor have an automatic right even to a translator. In one case in the mid-1980s a Romanian who had escaped to England was deported to Romania on the grounds that he had entered the country illegally. Home Office officials provided him with an Italian interpreter because they thought the language he spoke sounded like Italian. Some of the rules were changed after that, but the system is still an encouragement to official sloppiness and inadequate police work. Shiblak wrote later that he was

> sad to have discovered the other face of a system I had always assumed was just and fair. This was a terrifying experience for my family and myself. After losing two countries, Palestine and Lebanon, Britain has been our home for the past 17 years. It is a country which gave me an education, shelter, and a sense of freedom. . . [Y]et suddenly I found myself completely helpless and defenceless, held in prison and threatened with the destruction of my future without any reason being given, without any legal defence. It is a terror I do not wish on anyone.

In June 1990, while travelling to Tehran, I found myself on the same plane as a Kuwaiti who had been deported from Britain under suspicion of having plotted to kill the writer Salman Rushdie. As we talked on the plane he insisted that he was innocent and that the real reason for his deportation had been his involvement in the campaign for human rights in Kuwait. 'Don't you think,' he said, 'that if I had wanted to kill Salman Rushdie I would be boasting about it, now that I'm being sent to Iran?'

The years of hijacking, murder and hostage-taking have built a powerful association between terrorism and Islam in the minds of many people in the West. Saddam Hussein's decision to play the Islamic card only strengthened the association. During the crisis the British journalist Peregrine Worsthorne wrote in the *Sunday Telegraph* that Islam 'has degenerated into a primitive enemy fit only to be sensibly subjugated'. Worsthorne is not known for his understanding of the Muslim world, but many of his readers no doubt agreed with such wild sentiments. For someone like him, terrorism, Islam and Saddam Hussein had merged into one great incomprehensible whole, irredeemably hostile, which could be dealt with only by fighting and subduing it. It could not be understood or approached on a more rational basis; nor could Saddam's posturings be distinguished from the reactions of other Muslims. To many people in the West they were all the same: in Worsthorne's words, a primitive enemy. As October wore on and the likelihood of war grew, many people ceased to want to know anything more about the enemy they confronted. They just wanted him subjugated.

Peace Proposals

If we see that war is not imminent and that the American officials are now beginning to think about alternatives, then all [hostages] will be allowed to enjoy their full freedom. But in this case we hope that while the Americans are concerned about the small number of Americans who are present in Iraq, they will also remember that the US administration has prevented 18 million Iraqis from travelling, has imprisoned them and deprived them of food and medicine, not dozens as is the case with the Americans.

Saddam Hussein, speaking to American television, November 1990

On 27 October 1990 the weather broke in Baghdad. As I looked out from the twelfth floor of the Al-Rasheed Hotel towards the western part of the city, rain clouds covered the green trees of the park, the crossed scimitars, the attractive new guest palace Saddam had been building, the Baath Party headquarters, the vast white building which housed the Mukhabarat close to the racecourse in Mansour. Great warm drops of rain fell and the dusty ground gave out an unfamiliar odour, sweet, pungent and musty. Puddles had formed on the hotel tennis courts. The surface of the hotel's excellent swimming pool grew choppy. Cars slithered about on the slick roads. Ripe dates, knocked from the palm trees by the rain, made walking dangerous. I watched it all with a certain frisson: a leading Palestinian had told me after speaking to Saddam Hussein that the Iraqi forces in Kuwait and elsewhere had been told to expect an attack by the Americans soon after the first rains. Lightning flickered on the horizon and my bedside lamp flickered in sympathy.

Hassan, Bob Simpson's detested driver, turned up in a black suit with stripes like railway lines to mark the end of the summer. It didn't go with his plastic sandals or his brown tie. He kissed my shoulder in Iraqi fashion when we met in the car park: a soggy experience for him, since I was soaked with the rain. But at least he was standing outside waiting. Mr Hattam, number one driver, had taken shelter in his red Toyota Crown. He too could afford expensive suits now that he was in fulltime employment and he didn't want to ruin them.

Next to him was Ramadan's car. I had sacked Ramadan the night before because he had been too drunk to take the producer and editor to the television station and they nearly missed the satellite. Ramadan saw me now and got out to shamble over to me, shoulders down, looking as though the rain had melted him. No doubt he had a terrible hangover. Mr Hattam, who had turned against him, told us that Ramadan had spent several years in prison for running someone over and killing them when he was drunk. He also told us that Ramadan had driven his family all the way to England in the 1970s with a crate of Johnny Walker in the back of the car. According to Mr Hattam's account of this picaresque journey, Ramadan had drained the last bottle as they rolled into London.

Looking at him now, it wasn't impossible. 'I say to you, Mr John, I am very sorry. It never will happen again.' 'This is the third time, Ramadan, and I've sacked you twice already. This time . . .' 'One more chance, sir.' To the amusement of my colleagues I took him back, of course, and made him my own driver since no one else wanted to go with him. It would happen again at any time; we both knew that. 'Hello, sir, thank you, hello,' he said, meaning goodbye. Working with us represented serious money to Ramadan and times were hard. I walked back to the hotel entrance in the rain and the electronic glass doors opened for me as though I were a rather damp coffin and it really was a crematorium. '*Bonjour*,' I said, absently.

It was an important day for news. Yevgeny Primakov, President Gorbachev's special envoy, was arriving in Baghdad.

His visit seemed the best – perhaps the only – hope for a peaceful settlement, now that stories were starting to seep out of Washington about the possibility of an air attack on Iraq on the first moonless night of November. When I went round to the British embassy to see if they had heard anything, someone told me he thought there could be war within the next couple of weeks or so. From the way his eyes glinted as he looked out of the window at the sluggish waters of the Tigris, I got the impression it couldn't come quickly enough for him.

Something seemed to be in the wind. My contacts at senior levels within the PLO were saying that Yasser Arafat had been encouraged the previous day by Saddam Hussein's reaction to his proposal for a withdrawal of Iraqi forces from all but the northern third of Kuwait. As if to give official credence to this, Iraqi embassies all over the world that day issued a new map which placed a boundary a third of the way down Kuwait. The lower two-thirds were marked as being the nineteenth province of Iraq; the northern third became part of Basrah province. Someone, it seemed, was laying the groundwork for a deal – if the price was right.

On that night's satellite I reported the various straws in the wind: Yasser Arafat's optimism and the new maps that had been issued. It seemed reasonable to expect that Iraq would go on insisting that there would be no change in its position until the very moment when a withdrawal from Kuwait was announced; official denials couldn't necessarily be taken at face value. The camera crew and I went out into the damp grounds of the Al-Rasheed that evening and recorded what is known in the trade as a piece to camera. Large insects, summoned into life by the damp and attracted by the camera lights, flapped into my face. I did a lot of swearing before we got a complete, insectless take:

> Tonight the Iraqi government continues to deny strongly that it has any idea of withdrawing from any part of Kuwait, which it maintains is permanently integrated into Iraq. Still, there's a distinct feeling here among officials and civilians alike that it won't now come to war. The next two weeks may show if they're right.
> John Simpson, BBC News, Baghdad.

It wasn't exactly the most outspoken piece I had ever done, but it was becoming very hard indeed to read the signs, and my friends in the Iraqi ministries and newspapers were not finding it any easier than I was. I was wrong, of course, in suggesting that we would know within the next two weeks whether there would be war or peace – it was halfway through January before we knew that – but something was definitely going on that day at the end of October.

Yevgeny Primakov was a bulky, tough-minded man, the kind who was always hostile and suspicious to westerners until the advent of Mikhail Gorbachev brought glasnost and perestroika. People like Primakov then felt able to be relatively open and very enterprising. Primakov is less open than many even now, but he is keen to take advantage of the new opportunities. After his experiences as a go-between in the Gulf crisis, he wrote a book with an eye to the western market called *The War Which Need Not Have Been*. For many years he worked for *Pravda* and was its Middle East correspondent when he first met Saddam Hussein. He found him impressive, but saw the signs of cruelty and ferocity and remarked on the exaggerated notions of honour and national dignity which obsessed him even then.

Primakov had already come to Baghdad on 5 October, bringing with him a letter from Mikhail Gorbachev. He found the Iraqis bitter about the way they felt the Soviet Union had let them down. There was little sign that Saddam Hussein or Tariq Aziz had properly understood the changes that had come about in the Soviet Union. They had completely underestimated the imperatives which now made it impossible for Gorbachev to support a former client like Iraq which acted against the wishes of the international community and, particularly, of the West. Primakov, who could be expected to react aggressively to criticism, asked Tariq Aziz why Iraq hadn't informed the Soviet Union before it invaded Kuwait. Aziz sidestepped the question.

Sitting in the interview room in Saddam's palace, with its tasteless gilt and white furniture and the glass-fronted bookcase full of unread books, Primakov had to wait while Saddam read the letter. It was strongly worded and demanded that Iraq should obey the UN resolutions and withdraw from Kuwait. Primakov raised the question of the Soviet advisers and specialists who were on contract to Iraq, most of them on military or security projects. It had been a mistake for Saddam to have refused to exempt them from the ban on foreigners leaving the country. Now he told Primakov they could all leave, but that they couldn't all go at once because the projects they were working on would be affected. He suggested allowing 1000 to leave over the next two months. Primakov, who knew that more than that had asked to go, proposed 1500. Saddam agreed.

The two men discussed the whole question of Kuwait and Saddam launched into his justification for the sudden adventure: the conspiracy which he had detected between the United States, Britain, Israel, Saudi Arabia and Kuwait. Primakov was inclined to believe some of it. Indeed, shorn of the exaggerated language and the paranoia, there was a case for saying that the United States and the others had been tightening the screws on Iraq. But the Soviet Union, like the West, refused to accept this as justification for invading Kuwait. Primakov, according to his own account, put a telling question to Saddam, a question which touched the nature of the whole enterprise on which Iraq was embarked. Did he, Primakov asked, have a Masada complex 'just like the Israelis'? Saddam apparently nodded his head. Primakov followed it up: 'But then your actions will to a great extent be determined by the logic of a doomed man.' He says it seemed to him that Saddam agreed with that too, though he didn't answer.

These were harsh things to say to a man like Saddam Hussein and it is not easy to imagine that he would meekly agree with them. Primakov nevertheless showed more insight than the western statesmen who came to Baghdad over the next few weeks in the hope of freeing the hostages and easing the situation. He warned Saddam that there would be war if he didn't pull out of Kuwait and Saddam accepted that. If it was a choice between going down on his knees and surrendering or fighting, he would fight. But, he said, he was a realist and was prepared to ease the conditions he had made in his speech on

228

12 August, linking an Iraqi withdrawal from Kuwait to an Israeli withdrawal from the Occupied Territories, a western withdrawal from Saudi Arabia and a Syrian withdrawal from Lebanon. He seemed to say that the questions of when these withdrawals would take place and the process by which the Palestinian problem could be settled were matters for negotiation.

Taken in isolation from the issue of Kuwait, this might have been an interesting offer. But, when Primakov returned to Moscow and reported to Mikhail Gorbachev, it was clear to them that anything which seemed to reward Saddam for invading Kuwait was out of the question. At the same time, his remarks about being a realist but not going down on his knees suggested that he was looking for a face-saving device. If some way could be found to get Saddam to agree to withdraw from Kuwait in exchange for clear undertakings that the process of settling the Palestinian question would begin, that might well be enough. More than that – as Yasser Arafat had hoped when he first proposed the idea of linkage which Saddam incorporated into his 12 August speech – it could be a serious method of solving the Arab-Israeli dispute.

The bitter dispute between Iraq and Kuwait would also have to be sorted out, but that could be regarded as secondary if the international community were prepared to offer Saddam a way out of the crisis by opening up the prospect of a general Middle East peace. If it were done publicly, though, it would constitute precisely what no one, including the Soviet Union, was prepared to concede: a reward for aggression. Saddam could certainly be relied upon to claim it as such, since he was determined to come out of the crisis as the victor. There were other serious drawbacks: even if he withdrew, he would still be the dominant military power in the Middle East and would be able to threaten any of his neighbours with the same fate he had visited upon Kuwait.

Between them, Gorbachev, Eduard Shevardnadze and Primakov decided the plan could only succeed if they persuaded Saddam that his withdrawal would unquestionably be followed by a determined international effort to solve the Arab-Israeli dispute. But the invasion of Kuwait had not been undertaken in the first place in order to solve the Arab-Israeli dispute and that was not Saddam's priority now. He wanted to save face by getting some clear reference to a 'linkage' between his withdrawal of Kuwait and a peace process for the Palestinian question. That was the one thing the United States and its allies would not accept. Nor could the Soviet Union. From that point on, Soviet diplomatic efforts would concentrate on finding a formula which promised everything and nothing.

When Primakov went to Washington to discuss the Soviet proposal with the Bush administration, he was told at once by Dennis Ross, the State Department's leading Middle East authority, that Israel wouldn't accept it. The Americans were more interested in his assessments of the situation in Iraq and of Saddam Hussein's character than in his ideas for peace. Yet he had the impression that George Bush had still not made up his mind whether there should be war. He wanted Primakov to go back to Baghdad to see if there might be any chance of movement on Saddam's part, once he knew the United States was adamant.

From Washington Primakov flew to London and travelled out to Chequers to see Mrs Thatcher. He found her in a much tougher mood than George Bush. She wasn't simply interested in an Iraqi withdrawal, she wanted to 'break the back' of Saddam and of Iraq's military and – Primakov thought – industrial potential. She wanted Primakov to make it clear to Saddam that the international community would not retreat from its position. He asked her if she saw any alternative to war. 'No,' she replied. Primakov returned to Moscow and told Gorbachev he thought it looked like war.

When he came back to Baghdad, on the first rainy day of autumn, Primakov tried again. This time Saddam had the other members of the Revolution Command Council with him. He told Primakov that there were 'hawks' and 'doves' among them, but Primakov wisely assumed that only one man's opinion counted. If anything, he had the impression that Saddam was a little more flexible; this after all was the day the new maps of Iraq were issued, showing Kuwait divided. He did not reject the idea that Iraq should withdraw first and seemed prepared to talk about the conditions for such a withdrawal. Primakov warned him outright that war was inevitable if he did not do it. Saddam showed he had not given up hope of getting something in exchange: he seemed unable to accept that a withdrawal could take place unless he knew that western troops were to leave Saudi Arabia, or sanctions were to be lifted, or he were to get a bigger outlet to the sea or linkage with the Palestinian question: in other words, what Mrs Thatcher and President Bush would see as a reward. Without that, Saddam said, it would be 'suicidal' for him.

As he left the rainy tarmac at Baghdad airport and flew off, Primakov still seemed to feel there was a faint hope. It is hard to understand why. There was no sign of the kind of movement Bush had been looking for, apparently so that he could make up his mind whether or not to move towards war. Margaret Thatcher actively wanted war and would therefore accept nothing less than a withdrawal on exactly the terms Saddam thought 'suicidal'. The idea of linkage with the Palestinian issue was clearly dead; the Israelis, who wanted to break Saddam's back at least as much as Thatcher did, would ensure that there would be no movement towards a peace settlement, if only to ensure that Saddam received no reward. Even before I stood in front of the camera that evening, with the insects homing in on the lights, the issue had in effect been decided. Yet no one quite realized it at that point.

On 20 October 1990, the day that Primakov saw Mrs Thatcher at Chequers, her predecessor as leader of the Conservative Party arrived in Baghdad. There was a general suspicion in Britain that Edward Heath had gone to Iraq primarily in order to annoy her, since she was so strongly opposed to any form of negotiation with Saddam Hussein. In fact when he told her he was going and why, she answered: 'Oh, but you must.' His reasons were simple enough: he had been approached by the families of a number of British hostages in Baghdad, many of them elderly or sick, in the hope that he might be able to get them released. It may be, too, that he had private hopes of becoming a go-between, who might just manage to achieve the breakthrough which he, like many other people in Britain, wanted to see. Heath felt strongly that the crisis was entirely unnecessary and that it would be a crime to allow the situation to drift into war. Over the years since he had lost the Tory leadership to Margaret Thatcher he had shifted to the left in many ways; partly, no doubt, because her policies were so firmly of the right.

The Iraqis had been angling for some weeks to get Heath to Baghdad. In the absence of foreign governments with whom to negotiate, they wanted distinguished private figures to visit Iraq and thereby earn the Iraqi position some credibility. So far a motley collection had made the trip – Reverend Jesse Jackson, who had been followed by a television team making a documentary as a commercial venture; President Kurt Waldheim, who found it hard to find other countries which would accept him as a visitor; a group of Labour MPs unknown outside Britain; the British Muslim Yusuf Islam who, before his conversion, had been the pop singer Cat Stevens; a Japanese MP, Ms Wakako Hironaka, who failed to get the speaker of the Iraqi National Assembly to accept a petition for the release of foreigners which had been signed by other female Japanese MPs. With the exception of Waldheim, the Iraqis had no interest in any of them. They wanted big names: Heath, Brandt, Nakasone, Lange. Eventually these – and others – came to Baghdad and, as a reward, were allowed to take some or all of their citizens home with them.

The hopes of the British hostage community rose very high when Edward Heath, the first of the elder statesmen to make the journey, landed at Saddam International Airport. I had come to know some of the hostages well and liked and respected them. Julian McCullough was a London plumber who had lost his wife when she was in her early thirties. He had transferred all his care and affection to his sister and her son, and when they came to Kuwait to rejoin her husband who was serving with the UN in the Gulf, Julian came to look after them. They arrived in Kuwait on 1 August 1990, the day before the invasion. His sister and nephew had been allowed back to England long before while Julian, who suffered from a mild heart complaint, remained a prisoner. He was always good company, a funny and thoughtful man. The boredom would sometimes get him down but he never allowed himself to show it.

Dick Pagett was also a Londoner, a quieter man in his early sixties who would cut loose at parties and show an anarchic sense of humour which would keep people supplied with jokes and anecdotes for days afterwards. There was also a group of decorators from Liverpool who were working on Saddam Hussein's new guest palace and had been told they had to stay until the contract was finished. There was a group of British nurses working at the Irish-run Ibn al-Bittar Hospital, who were not allowed to leave because no one would come to Iraq to take their places. There was Ramsam Noormohammed, a British Muslim suffering from serious depression, who had been inexplicably left behind when his four fellow-pilgrims were allowed to leave. There was Maureen Wilbraham, who was looking after her husband Tony, diagnosed as having terminal cancer. There was an elderly couple from Scotland, Jim and Mary Wright, who were both suffering from various illnesses. The younger hostages were mainly concerned about their families and their mortgages; the older ones usually worried about their health. All of them – and many others – looked to Edward Heath to get them out.

At the airport Heath was monosyllabic, as always. Was he here to negotiate? 'I have no powers to do that.' Did he have any message from the British government for Saddam Hussein? 'I don't pass messages.'

Heath had brought his personal assistant and his doctor to help him negotiate the freedom of the elderly and sick. He had a long list, given him by the British embassy. The task before him was a delicate one: if he lectured the Iraqis they might not let him take as many people as he wanted, but if he were too soft on them his reputation in Britain would suffer. He went first to see the people he hoped to release: Barry Jones, who was suffering from a brain tumour though the Iraqis took him off a refugee flight to London all the same; Pat O'Brien, who had had a number of heart attacks in the previous few weeks and needed better care than he could get in Baghdad; Tony Wilbraham and the others. There was a distinct feeling that the

Iraqis had held on to all these people specifically in order to get Heath to come to Baghdad. Now he had come.

The following day I went round to the villa which had been made available to Heath's group. The driver was very nervous: 'Is danger house. Calaboosh, prison, just for top people.' He took his hands off the steering wheel and crossed his wrists as though they were bound. The decor was terrible: a depiction of Saladdin in stained glass, Chinoiserie tables and chairs, machine-made carpets. For no clear reason the Iraqis had cut the phones off. Late in the afternoon Heath came in. He had spent three hours with Saddam Hussein and had been impressed by the President's desire to find a peaceful solution. The key question – his refusal to withdraw unless the Americans and their allies made some concession – was not raised. Heath seemed unaware, as we were, that this was now the central issue.

At the press conference Heath later gave at the Al-Rasheed, he spoke quite highly of Saddam Hussein's grasp of the situation. He hadn't, he said, discussed with Saddam the criticism he had received from the pro-Thatcher newspapers in Britain. 'If I did that,' he said, his shoulders moving up and down with silent laughter in the way people used to joke about in Britain in the 1970s, 'my whole life would be absorbed by it.' He plainly believed that the Americans and British were completely wrong in their approach to the crisis. His considered view was that Arab states should be allowed to solve the problem by themselves: though which states, and how, was less clear.

That night he, his doctor and his assistant stayed up until 4 o'clock, working with Iraqi officials on the list of people who would be allowed to leave. They found it a degrading and unpleasant business and the Iraqis resisted almost every case, claiming that many of them were not as ill as they made out. Of the 200 or so names on the full list, it was becoming plain that relatively few would be released. In the end only 38 of the sick and elderly were given leave to go, about half the number it should have been. In the car on the way to the airport the doctor told me that some of the British people, including one man with a serious cancer, had kept quiet about their illnesses because they hadn't wanted to take the place of others.

Some hostages managed to get aboard Heath's plane simply by pushing themselves forward. One man with a mild knee problem had bombarded every foreign visitor with requests for help for two months; he was given a place. So was a man with piles. Dick Pagett, who was older than some of those allowed out on grounds of age and had a respiratory condition, wasn't going. Nor was Ramsam Noormohammed. Nor was Julian McCullough. Their hopes had been high and now I had the task of ringing them and telling them the news.

Julian took it with courage and dignity. 'Well, that's it, lads,' I heard him say to the others who were in the room with him. 'We're not going. Nothing for it but to take it on the chin.' He remembered phoning his sister in London that morning to tell her he'd see her in 24 hours. 'And now . . . Oh well, no point in making a song and dance about it.' Within a minute or two they were making jokes about staying in Iraq for ever but it was a bitter disappointment, all the same. Edward Heath's specially commissioned plane, equipped to look after a hundred or more medical cases, took off that night with two thirds of its seats empty.

Eight days later the former Japanese prime minister, Yasuhiro Nakasone, followed Edward Heath to Baghdad. Japan had many advantages in Iraqi eyes: it was not involved in the build-up of forces, there was a powerful anti-war movement there and Japanese business and industry had a long tradition of moving into countries which the western world preferred not to have dealings with.

Following Heath's visit the Iraqis seemed to be actively looking for ways of getting rid of the hostages. On the day Nakasone arrived the speaker of the National Assembly, Sadi Mehdi Salah, announced that all hostages would be released in exchange for a guarantee of non-aggression. It was an offer which could not, of course, be taken up: countries like Japan and Germany, which might have been prepared to countenance something of the sort, did not have the power to promise Iraq that it would not face attack. On the same day Saddam Hussein told a delegation of the Arab Trade Union Federation in vague terms that some European workers would be allowed to leave; and the National Assembly voted in favour of his proposal to free 700 Bulgarians. Conditions in Bulgaria were so bad that many of them chose to stay in Iraq.

Nakasone met Saddam Hussein on 4 November and, like Edward Heath before him, appealed for the release of all the remaining foreign hostages. He argued that there would be considerable political benefits for Iraq in this and that public opinion in each of the countries which saw its nationals released would swing round and oppose the use of force against Iraq. There is no doubt that the arguments which Saddam heard from his distinguished foreign visitors during this period played an important part in his eventual decision to let all the hostages go.

Nakasone did a great deal better than Heath. 74 out of nearly 300 Japanese were brought from Kuwait and outlying parts of Iraq and housed at the Mansour Melia Hotel, ready for their release. Four Japanese men, all of them senior managers, were given permission to go but refused. They felt that it would not be right to leave while some of their more junior employees remained behind.

As the hostages left the Mansour Melia to board the buses that were to take them to the airport, one couple was surrounded by Japanese television crews who fought and struggled to get pictures of them. They managed eventually to climb into the bus and sat there, side by side. They had lived in Kuwait for 30 years: all their married life. Now their business was ruined and they were returning to a country which had itself become foreign to them. The bus pulled out to go to the airport. Free of the attentions of the camera crews the woman rested her head on her husband's shoulder. At 57 they were alone in the world, with no money, no family, no home and no clear future.

The third of the elder statesmen arrived 12 days later. Of all the journeys to Baghdad, Willy Brandt's had become the most controversial. When he had announced his intention of making the journey, Helmut Kohl's government tried to head off problems by linking him up with the former Italian prime minister, Emilio Colombo, and the former external affairs commissioner of the European Commission, Willy de Clerq, on a more formal, semi-official visit. The plan failed and Brandt's decision was heavily criticized by the British government which saw it as a potential sign to Saddam Hussein that international resolve was weakening. Made sensitive by British and American criticism of its constitutional inability to become involved in military operations abroad, Germany rejected the complaint with some irritation. One Anglophile member of the Bundesrat said to a friend of mine: 'Whatever we do is wrong. If we send troops the British press will say it's the Condor Legion on the march again. If we don't, they'll say we're not doing our duty. And if Willy Brandt goes, they'll say he's consorting with the enemy.' It was said in jest, but it represented the baffled annoyance that many Germans felt at the lack of understanding abroad for their particular political problems.

All the same, Chancellor Kohl was embarrassed by the Brandt visit. Brandt himself regarded it all with his usual caustic wit. I had not seen him for more than a year and noticed that increasing age, though it had not blunted his intellect, had made him even less prepared to bother with other people's opinions of him. When asked a question he would consider it for a long time, rolling it around in his mind as a connoisseur of wine might sample a mouthful of the vintage, then give his answer almost when everyone had decided he must have forgotten. Was he, I asked after he had met Saddam Hussein, going to be taking German hostages back with him. He laughed, poured himself a glass of water, sipped it, looked at me again and said: 'I shall be taking home more people than I came with, yes.'

During their meeting on 7 November Saddam Hussein agreed to allow Willy Brandt to take 120 foreigners, most of them Germans, with him when he left. The talks had clearly gone well and there again seemed to be a faint aroma of compromise in the air: the appearance, at least, of a willingness on Saddam's part to make a move – but not the first move. He hinted to Brandt that there could be dramatic change in the Middle East if the West made it easy for him. If not, he would refuse to budge. Brandt did not, however, criticize the stubbornness of Saddam so much as the stubbornness of Bush and Thatcher, particularly the latter: 'I hate to say it, but there is more readiness on the side of the United States than the United Kingdom [to show flexibility].'

The following day he saw Saddam again and the talks went, if anything, better. For one thing, Saddam agreed to allow him to take 50 more hostages with him, without the unpleasant haggling which had characterized the Heath visit. But whereas Heath had come primarily for the release of the sick and elderly, Brandt was concerned with the wider issue. For a while he gave the clear impression that he thought he might be able to broker a peaceful settlement of the crisis. It would have been a superb achievement and he may have been looking for signs of movement that did not seriously exist. After his second meeting he gave another press conference. Someone asked if it looked as though Saddam Hussein had softened his stance. Brandt's answer, though scrupulously honest, gave everyone reason to assume that something had changed:

> Of course I can't compare what he said to me with what he might have said weeks ago. What I can do is I would say that I could discover certain elements of flexibility, but it is difficult to spell it out. I must tell the secretary general of the United Nations and some of the leaders involved. . . I would rather not spell it out and would not call it a peace plan. I think I need the weekend to put it together and perhaps draw some constructive conclusions.

As for Saddam himself, Brandt's conclusions were even more favourable than those of Edward Heath:

> I was impressed by the intensity of his engagement. . . This is a man who in spite of the burdens he has to carry has a mind which goes beyond the present crisis.

Again, like Heath, Brandt was probably reacting against the hysterical judgments of the western press and the familiar comparisons with Hitler and Stalin. Nevertheless Brandt did even less to help a true picture of Saddam to emerge than Heath. Brandt took Saddam seriously as a man with whom it would be right to negotiate a peaceful conclusion to a serious international crime. He did not seem to appreciate Saddam's intense attachment to concepts such as Iraqi national honour, nor did he apparently manage – as Primakov had – to get Saddam to admit that there was something suicidal about his approach. Primakov had spoken of a 'Masada complex'. If Brandt failed to negotiate a settlement, it was not because of the inflexibility of Thatcher and Bush, real though that was. It was because, even though the Iraqi President realized that Thatcher and Bush were inflexible, Saddam believed that Iraq's national honour required him to be more inflexible still. Brandt left Baghdad on 9 November 1990 with 180 Western European hostages, but nothing more was heard of his notions about Saddam's flexibility.

On 9 November the crescent moon seemed to lie on its back as it rose. Someone in the teahouse I went to in the Merchants' Souq told me this meant that soon many people would die. It was a sobering thought as Remembrance Sunday drew near. I was expecting to interview Saddam Hussein soon and I asked the BBC to send me out a poppy to wear when I met him. Misunderstanding my request the BBC sent me a box of two hundred. In the week before Remembrance Sunday I made sure that everyone who wanted one could have one and, on the Sunday itself, I even persuaded the minders to let me leave the box on their desk in the Al-Rasheed lobby and forced them to wear poppies themselves. They were nervous but put up with it with good grace and much politeness. When we went out to film the Remembrance Sunday service at the British church, of course, they put the box under the table and took the poppies out of their buttonholes. In the circumstances, with British troops preparing for battle against Iraq in the desert, it was hard to blame them.

St George's Anglican Church in Baghdad contrasts strangely with the palm trees and the mud-coloured brick around it. The Union Jack flutters against a background of government buildings: Aldershot gothic versus Saddam modernism. It was built at the start of the British protectorate as a memorial to the British Empire soldiers who had died in the 1917–18 campaign against the Turks which led to the creation of modern Iraq.

On this Remembrance Day the church was full. Except for the journalists, the diplomats and a group of British women who had come to Baghdad to obtain the release of their husbands, the congregation was made up of Saddam Hussein's hostages. Even the lay preacher taking the service was a prisoner. A photographer from the *Baghdad Observer* was there, a rough-looking character with a cauliflower ear, a glittering dark blue suit, patent leather shoes and a poppy stuck in his top pocket as a kind of compromise. He took pictures of everybody who turned up for the service. Although the photographs were offered for sale afterwards, the negatives no doubt ended up with the Security Ministry as well.

The service had the true apologetic note of the English. We sang the twenty-third psalm and 'Jerusalem', our voices wailing in the accepted manner at the end of each stanza, and we mumbled our way through the unfamiliar prayers. No one wanted to make a show of themselves by being too loud or too enthusiastic. And yet it was a tribal occasion. It had little to do with worship and everything to do with the rituals and habits which defined our national identity. The sun shone down through the stained glass, covering the congregation with the colours of the vanished units which had once fought here: Prince Albert Victor's Own Cavalry, 36th Sikhs, 32nd Lancers, 67th Punjabis, Norfolk Regiment, Dorsetshire Regiment, 104th Wellesley's Rifles. The Iraqi Levies, the regiment raised locally with Assyrian Christians as one of its main components, was prominently commemorated. I had recently discovered an Iraqi Levies officer's sword in the dusty back room of a Baghdad antiques shop, among the Qassem teapots and the royalist coffee cups.

The blare of the organ died away and the voice of the officiating clergyman eased into that mild braying tone, accentuating the wrong syllables, which belongs to every Anglican service. On the wall near me was an inscription:

To the memory of Henry Robert Conway Dobbs, High

Commissioner of His Britannic Majesty to Iraq, 1923–9. A man greatly loved, wise in counsel, faithful in friendship, understanding the things of nature and the works of men's hands and minds, modest, humorous and good . . .

It was the self-image of another world, and yet we all found ourselves willing prisoners of it, half a century later, as much at the mercy of our own past as we were of Saddam Hussein.

I looked across at the church doorway: three of our Information Ministry minders were standing there, watching the unfamiliar spectacle of the British at prayer, my poppies pinned to their shirts. It was more than an act of politeness on their part: it was genuine friendship.

I was expecting the interview with Saddam Hussein any day now. We had proposed a complicated arrangement to the Information Ministry which would allow us to edit the interview and broadcast it in the way we chose. Up to that point his officials had insisted that all his interviews were broadcast in their entirety. It is one of the BBC's fundamental rules that it doesn't let anyone – neither the British prime minister nor Saddam Hussein – tell it what to broadcast. Not all British governments have had the wisdom to realize that this is important in a democracy, but it was a principle that certainly couldn't be sacrificed just in order to obtain an interview with one of the world's premier dictators. I undertook that our editing would not distort his meaning. I would be in charge of the editing and would be coming back to Iraq: if the Iraqis had a complaint they could take it up with me in person.

The advantage for Iraq was a major one: Saddam would appear on each of the BBC's large variety of outlets in television and radio, with incomparably the largest number of people listening, watching, even reading the interview, not simply in Britain but across the world. An interview with the BBC would give Saddam Hussein access to something like 120 million people. By contrast an interview with one of the big American networks would reach only a small proportion of that number. As for the BBC's British opposition, Independent Television News, once superb but now going through a bad patch, its audience would be smaller still.

We were in daily contact with the Information Ministry about the interview. Our proposal was accepted by the minister himself and I waited for the call to come. I prepared the questions carefully, balancing hostile ones with those which he would find it easier to answer. I planned a few trick ones as well and asked Julian McCullough, Ramsam Noormohammed and Dick Pagett to write letters to the President asking to be allowed to go home to England. I planned to give them to Saddam once the cameras were switched off, knowing his habit of making grand, generous gestures on the spur of the moment.

The few people who had already interviewed him taught me some tricks and told me what to expect. We might have to spend 24 hours at some government guest house while we and our equipment were exhaustively checked. We would probably have to wash our hands in some special solution before shaking hands with the great man, in case we infected him with some terrible disease. (I was reminded of Nicolae Ceausescu who believed the Russians had killed his predecessor by planting an atomic isotope in his office and always had visiting journalists checked by geiger counter.) Since I would be a good eight inches taller than Saddam, I should watch out for the moment of the handshake: with the Iraqi cameras on him, Saddam would hold out his hand at a deliberately low angle so it would look in the photographs and on Iraqi television as though I was bowing; that I was determined to avoid. He was not used to being interrupted and the way his interpreter translated only at longish intervals made it hard to take command of the interview as one normally would. Saddam's idea of an interview was a monologue with questions. It would be very difficult, I was sure, but it would be an entertaining experience. At the end we would each be given Saddam's photograph in a silver frame.

Somehow it became difficult to get hold of the official I had been dealing with. He was busy, he was away, he would call me. He didn't call me, so I went round to see him. 'Ah, yes, John, we decided in the end it would be better to give the interview to ITN. They promised that they would use all of it, not edit it as you wanted to do.' I found that hard to believe.

242

Unrestricted access to the British airwaves is something British politicians have long ago given up trying to obtain; and now a man who threatened British interests and held British citizens prisoner would be able to say what he wanted for as long as he wanted. It sounded like the first demand of a hijacker – an hour's free airtime.

I argued for a brief slot on the end of the ITN interview. It was not possible. The order had apparently come from Saddam's office: the President's words could not be edited, it was all or nothing. The Iraqis even demanded the right to nominate two members of the panel which discussed the interview afterwards. The next thing, I thought, they will want to dictate the questions. Yet when ITN's interview was shown the questions were good and combative. Saddam didn't say much of interest in reply, but at that stage he rarely did. Like any bad loser, I gave way to the annoyance of the moment, writing a spiteful article for the *Spectator* about it. I called the interviewer, Trevor McDonald, 'a newsreader', despite his distinguished career as a reporter and the best of ITN's news presenters.

Still, even failing to get an interview with Saddam could exert an occult power. When the ITN team was taken off to prepare for the meeting with the great man, we decided to take the evening off and have a good meal in a Lebanese restaurant. Afterwards a Dutch colleague and I decided to walk back to the Al-Rasheed. Along the way we stopped on the Jomhuriya bridge to look at the Tigris. It was midnight. Within five minutes a couple of police cars swerved up and mounted the pavement. Men jumped out and arrested us for something that ranged from suspicious behaviour to espionage. We both refused to be arrested. Senior policemen were called and things got nasty. When I refused to get into the police car, be searched or take my hands out of my pockets one of the policemen wanted to throw me into the Tigris. The other policemen and I dissuaded him between us.

Then I thought of something. Choosing my words carefully, to deceive but not quite to lie, I said: 'British television is interviewing Saddam Hussein tomorrow. If I speak to him, I shall give him your names and complain about your violence and your rudeness.' No one noticed the 'if' and the effect was gratifying: one of them radioed his base and I heard the words 'television' and 'Saddam'. There was a pause. Then, at 3 am, an old, beaten-up Volkswagen Passat drew up and a tired-looking young man of around 24 got out. He wore a rumpled suit that might have been expensive. His tie was loose. The most senior of the policemen almost bowed to him: Iraq appoints its secret policemen young. 'Did you really tell these guys you'd complain about them to Saddam tomorrow?' he asked, in good English. 'Something like that,' I said. He thought for a moment. 'If I drive you back to your hotel will you promise not to tell Saddam?' 'A deal,' I said. We shook hands all round and the man who had wanted to launch me into the river placed his hand on his heart and said 'Hello'. Something, at least, had been salvaged from the fuss about the interview. But the next day I made arrangements to go home. It would, I decided, be bad for business if I stayed.

Last Chances

O comrades: May God's peace be upon you. Happy New Year
and may God return the years on our dear people, on our noble
nation and on you with a realization of our noble and
legitimate dreams, God willing.

Saddam Hussein's New Year message, 1991

By late autumn, in spite of the immense build-up in the desert,
it was reasonable to suppose that there would not be a war.
There seemed to be plenty of scope for compromise. The Saudi
defence minister, Prince Sultan bin Abdul Aziz, said on 21
October that Saudi Arabia 'sees no harm in any Arab country
giving its Arab sister [country] land, a site or a position on the
sea'. The suggestion of the possibility of Kuwait handing over
the islands of Bubiyan and Warba seemed inescapable, though
when the assumption was made Prince Sultan claimed he had
been misunderstood. Abu Iyyad, Yasser Arafat's deputy in the
Palestine Liberation Organisation, made it clear in that he felt
a deal along these lines was ready to be done. France was
strongly in favour. Chancellor Kohl of Germany said in
November that the time was right for negotiations on other
conflicts in the Middle East. The Soviet Union was doing its
best to organize a settlement which would make such negotiations possible and the problems that Yevgeny Primakov was
encountering over Saddam Hussein's refusal to make the first
move were not generally known.

On 10 November George Bush announced a doubling of
American ground forces in Saudi Arabia: 1000 more tanks and
200,000 more men. Both publicly and privately people found it

hard to know whether the American president actually wanted a war, as his defence secretary, Richard Cheney, appeared to, or whether he favoured the approach of his secretary of state, James Baker, in using the threat of war to force Saddam Hussein into a humiliating withdrawal. The assumption in Baghdad was that President Bush would avoid fighting if he could, and that the real strength of the war party lay in 10 Downing Street. The Spanish prime minister, Felipe Gonzalez, had accused Margaret Thatcher of having a 'passion for war'. She herself had made it clear that force should certainly be used against Iraq if necessary, that the forcible detention of westerners as hostages should not deter the Alliance and that Saddam Hussein should face prosecution as a war criminal. It was obvious later, when the war began, that George Bush was no less keen than Margaret Thatcher to see the enterprise through, but he demonstrated greater political skill in allowing it to seem as though it was purely Saddam Hussein's intransigence which brought about the fighting.

While perception remained that Mrs Thatcher was the toughest member of the partnership, it was obvious enough, even from Baghdad, that her power was waning. The Iraqi government revelled in the thought. It was an important element in their determination to persuade Edward Heath to visit Baghdad. The information minister, Latif Jassim, was privately exultant: if Thatcher went, he thought, the real power behind the coalition would disappear. Jassim believed what his president believed: and though Saddam Hussein might have a poor grasp of the workings of a parliamentary democracy, he knew when a political leader had been wounded and was fighting for life. He could smell it.

The immediate cause of Mrs Thatcher's downfall was the resignation of her longest-serving minister, Sir Geoffrey Howe, after being thrust aside and ignored by her. The speech he made in the House of Commons on 13 November 1990, though delivered in his usual unemotional, soporific tone, was a devastating indictment of the autocratic way she ran her government and the Little England nature of her policy. The timing of Howe's speech and the powerful support it evoked among many Conservative backbench MPs encouraged Michael Heseltine, her one-time defence and environment secretary who had stormed out of her cabinet in January 1986, to announce his intention to stand against her in the forthcoming leadership contest.

When the vote was held on 20 November, Heseltine lost by 152 votes to her 204; but her campaign managers had expected her to win by a good 25 more than that, and the result was a serious setback. She received the news during a visit to Paris for a European summit on security, and came charging down the steps of the British embassy to make a statement live on BBC television news. She undertook to contest the next round. Her characteristic words – 'I fight on. I fight to win' – were circulated to the press. In the consultations she held the next day, some of her most senior supporters (widely known as 'the men in grey suits') advised her not to stand against Heseltine in a second round since she would probably not win and would be seriously weakened even if she did. By one o'clock on the morning of 22 November her decision was half-made, but she decided to sleep on it. When she woke, at 6 am, she talked it over with her husband. Then she rang her closest advisers and assistants and told them she was standing down. She had fallen victim to a political coup of great savagery, in a manner which did little justice to the longest-serving British prime minister since 1827, a leader who had restored her country's international position and prestige.

I watched it all on television, thinking back on the 11 years I had followed her round the world: the moment in 1979 when she dived with superb courage down the steps of an RAF VC10 in Lusaka into a hostile crowd at night; the press conference at the 1980 Dublin summit where the European journalists turned out to attack her and ended up giving her a standing ovation at the end of a magnificent performance; the triumphant visit to Moscow as she jumped up on her car and waved to the ecstatic crowd. There was the less attractive side too: the sneer as she showed how little she had given way to Commonwealth pressure for sanctions against South Africa in the Bahamas in 1985; the bullying way her press secretary Bernard Ingham dealt with a question from a young woman journalist from Africa who said, as the tears ran down her face, 'He only talks to me like that because I'm black'; her selective interest in

247

human rights; the belittling of other people's idealism for social change or European union.

When her successor John Major took over the following week, it was a return to a less combative form of politics. The British have sometimes been prepared to put up with harsh government when necessary, but their preference is always for a quieter, more avuncular style. From the very beginning Major's policies were different from Thatcher's, on Europe, the economy, social affairs. But on the question of the Gulf there was no change whatsoever. In Baghdad the entire leadership challenge had been viewed from an Iraqi perspective. Naji al-Hadithi, the Information Ministry director general, said the Gulf crisis had 'buried Mrs Thatcher just like the 1956 Suez crisis ruined Anthony Eden'. His minister, Latif Jassim, believed her resignation was the direct result of her policy towards Saddam Hussein: 'Anyone who takes hostile positions against Iraq will go to hell.' There was genuine rejoicing in Baghdad where people assumed that the coalition would simply crumble now that its toughest member had gone.

A week later, on 29 November, it seemed clear that this wasn't so. The UN Security Council, at the urging of the United States, passed Resolution 678 authorizing the use of force against Iraq unless it withdrew from Kuwait. The Security Council

> Demands that Iraq comply fully with Resolution 660 (1990) and all subsequent resolutions and decides, while maintaining all its decisions, to allow Iraq one final opportunity, as a pause of goodwill, to do so;
>
> Authorizes Member States cooperating with the Government of Kuwait, unless Iraq on or before 15 January 1991 fully implements. . . the foregoing resolutions, to use all necessary means to uphold and implement Security Resolution 660 (1990) and all subsequent relevant resolutions and to restore international peace and security in the area . . .

There had been some argument about the deadline between, on the one hand, the United States and Britain who both wanted a deadline of 1 January 1991, and the Soviet Union on the other. But the British UN ambassador, Sir David Hannay, made the point that it was important not to seem to be pushing the Iraqis too hard and so lose the coalition diplomatic support. In the end, 15 January seemed a reasonable compromise. The accusation in Iraq and many other Arab countries was that the United States and its allies had simply steamrollered the other members of the Security Council into doing what they wanted. This ignored the endless debates that went on both formally and informally inside the United Nations on the question of the Iraqi invasion and the best method of dealing with it.

There was also a good deal of debate outside the UN as well as inside about the exact nature of its function as peacebroker. Many people, including a number of ambassadors in the Security Council, felt strongly that the UN position on the issue undermined the efforts of Arab countries to negotiate a purely Arab solution. It was certainly true that the United States put heavy pressure on a number of countries represented on the Security Council to support the tough wording of the various resolutions and to vote for them afterwards. Nevertheless, there was always a consensus that the UN was taking roughly the right approach towards Iraq; and the picture might not have been very different without the American pressure. But throughout the crisis the critics of the American position pointed out the clear difference between the urgency which the western powers gave to the UN resolutions on Kuwait and the lack of any serious pressure on Israel to conform to Resolution 242 and later resolutions on the Occupied Territories and the Palestinian issue. There was, as the critics pointed out, a clear double standard.

No sooner had the signal apparently been given for war, however, than the White House gave what seemed to be an entirely contrary one. On the following day, 30 November, Bush announced that he was asking Secretary of State James Baker to go to Baghdad for face-to-face talks with Saddam Hussein; and he announced that Tariq Aziz would be invited to Washington within two weeks. He called it 'going an extra mile for peace', but said he was not hopeful about the likely results. There would, he insisted, be no face-saving formula for Iraq and no concessions. The Iraqi ambassador in Paris, Abdul Razzak al-Hashimi, called the proposal 'good news and a big step towards peace'. In private Iraqi officials were delighted.

George Bush rang Margaret Thatcher's successor, John Major, to explain his proposal, which had originally been suggested by James Baker. The British knew that Baker had been anxious for a diplomatic solution rather than a military one, but on the transatlantic telephone Bush apparently insisted that there was no thought in his mind of climbing down. The advantage of the scheme was that in person Baker might be able to persuade Saddam that the United States meant what it said; which would mean there would be no need for force. John Major lacked what Felipe Gonzalez had called Thatcher's 'passion for war' and seems to have found George Bush's argument convincing. Diplomats from Egypt, Israel and Saudi Arabia found it precisely the reverse: 'You wait and see,' one said. 'Bush doesn't understand the Middle East. Saddam will think he's looking for a way out.' Another agreed: 'Bush has blinked first. There won't be any war now. He's looking for a way out.' And he added: 'Bush wouldn't have done this if Thatcher was still around.'

Leaving for difficult assignments is always a melancholy business: the shock of the early alarm call, the hasty, un-scientific packing, the sense of things left undone, the watery tea which hasn't stood long enough, the engine of the waiting taxi throbbing in the quiet London square. It was 11 December 1990, grey and cold. I stowed the luggage in the cab, then looked up at the window. We exchanged the last wave, the last smile, each of us wondering when we would see each other again. Then the taxi pulled away and I had my last glimpse of her as she turned back to a flat which was suddenly still and empty.

'Where's it to this time?' Usually the answer 'Baghdad' encouraged the taxi driver to explain in great detail what should happen to Saddam Hussein and how it should be done, while I stared out of the window, enveloped in a self-pity as sour as the Cromwell Road car fumes. This time I was luckier. The driver was a quiet, tactful Indian Christian. We talked a little about his family and the places where he had lived. It was very restful. As he opened the door for me at Heathrow he said: 'God have you in His keeping.'

I was touched. I knew the unexpected pleasures of Baghdad well by now and had no complaints about going back there. What was more, long experience of going off to cover unpleasant stories had shown me that whatever happened, nothing was worse than the moment when the plane touched down at the destination. After that, even in a war or a revolution, one is too preoccupied to worry. It's a comforting thought in its way, knowing that no matter what happens you will never feel quite as nervous as you did on arrival. Even so, as I pushed my luggage, with a heavy load of extra supplies and food for the Christmas which I would be spending in Iraq, I felt a certain nervousness. This would be the deciding trip. Unless the Iraqis threw me out, I would stay to the end: whenever and whatever it turned out to be.

I arrived back in Baghdad 12 days after Bush's offer of talks. Influenced by the feeling in London, I assumed now that the end would be a peaceful one. It was only when I went the rounds of some senior figures in the government that I realized this was unlikely to be the case. Saddam Hussein had interpreted the offer of a 'pause for peace' and of negotiations with the United States precisely as my Egyptian and Israeli friends had assumed he would. It confirmed everything he believed about the United States – that it had no stomach for war, that democracies could not accept casualties for long and that they had no fixity of purpose. And he thought Margaret Thatcher's resignation had removed the one really tough member of the coalition. He had already begun testing the American resolve by insisting that he would invite James Baker to Baghdad on 12 January, only three days before the UN deadline ran out. The Americans were resisting.

The information minister, Latif Jassim, was friendly and welcoming when I returned, perhaps still a little embarrassed about the missed interview with Saddam Hussein. ('Please don't be angry with us about that any longer, Mr John,' said one of the gentlest of the Ministry minders when I shook his hand; they all knew why I had left Baghdad three weeks earlier.) Jassim had once asked me: 'How many losses can an American president take before he falls? 5000? 10,000?' I tried to explain the workings of the American constitution to him: the fact that George Bush would remain president until 1992, whatever the outcome in the Gulf. It was no use; he believed Bush had offered talks because he was afraid for his presidency.

Iraq took a fierce line in the battle over dates for the Baker visit to Baghdad. The Iraqis maintained that Saddam was too busy to receive him before 12 January. The Americans replied that even if a meeting on that day were successful, there would be insufficient time for all Iraqi troops to withdraw from Kuwait by the time specified in UN Resolution 678. The latest date they were prepared to accept was 3 January.

It seemed to me that there was a disturbing new mood in Baghdad. Since Saddam thought Bush was weak, he had decided to push for victory, not merely compromise. He no longer seemed interested in a settlement which would get Iraqi troops out of Kuwait with honour and a certain amount of territory. Now he wanted to force the Americans to retreat from the Middle East altogether. It was a terrible misinterpretation of the position, but I knew as I talked to ministers and civil servants that it was no use trying to make them believe me. After a day of listening to them, I went back and put it all into that evening's piece to camera, in our familiar position in front of the Al-Rasheed Hotel, a few palm trees in the background to show where we were:

There's no mistaking the feeling here that President Saddam Hussein has got the Americans on the run. Washington used to insist it would never talk to him while his troops were still in Kuwait – and yet the two sides are arguing now about the dates for the talking to start. The Iraqis seem convinced that they can go further, and force the Americans to back down on the UN ultimatum to withdraw from Kuwait by 15 January.

I had been back to Baghdad for only a day, but I felt certain there was going to be a war. Everybody I met was taking their tone from Saddam, and Saddam was not going to yield. When we had finished editing and the others took the piece round to be censored, I went upstairs to my new room on the eleventh floor. In the fading light I looked out at the view towards the Tigris and the centre of Baghdad. I had smuggled an ineffectual Russian-made telescope into the country and now I opened it out and peered through it. An anti-aircraft post had gone up on the roof of a government ministry close to the hotel. The gunners were lounging round in the evening sun, sipping tea, laughing and joking. I tried to picture the circumstances in which they would be firing up at planes and missiles coming in over the city, but my imagination wasn't up to it. I snapped the telescope shut and hid it away.

The drivers' pecking order had changed. Mr Hattam, as spruce and efficient as ever, a little bantam cock behind the wheel, no longer had my favour. He had become subservient to the minders and was always running to them to make sure we had permission to go where we wanted him to take us. Often, of course, we didn't. He was pulling various financial tricks on us and on our other drivers. But what rankled was the way he had let me down when I flew into Baghdad with a correspondent from BBC Radio, Allan Little.

Allan Little later did some remarkable reporting in Kuwait, but at the time I was most impressed by his Scots canniness and his knowledge of single malt whiskies. The customs man searching my luggage took exception to my shortwave radio set and confiscated it. A new regulation forbade the importation of radios which could pick up the broadcasts of Radio Desert Shield in Saudi Arabia. I lost my temper and grabbed it back from him, saying I wasn't leaving the airport without it. I sat down and started reading. After half an hour everybody had gone – secret policemen, customs officials, minders, passengers. I was left alone with my luggage and my radio. Looking through the glass partition I could see Mr Hattam and Allan waiting for me. I looked round. Why not, I thought.

We were hastily stowing the luggage in the boot of the car when two soldiers, armed with rifles, came running up. They were very polite. So was the customs officer who showed me the new regulation and gave me a receipt for the radio before locking it in a safe. The safe, I noticed, was full of other radios. No one mentioned the awkward matter of my attempted escape. As we were driving into Baghdad – 'Capital of Arabs' Saddam', said the notice by the roadside, newly repainted – Allan explained to me quietly that Mr Hattam had tried to persuade him to leave me there and drive into town. I had felt rather differently about him ever since, and the apologetic and lopsided Ramadan and the shoulder-kissing Hassan seemed a great deal more decent by comparison.

The situation in Baghdad was very different from my last visit in one important respect. On 6 December the Iraqi News Agency had reported the contents of a message from Saddam Hussein to the Speaker of the Iraqi parliament: following representations from Jordan, Yemen, Morocco, Sudan and the Palestine Liberation Organization, as well as from European members of parliament, he was recommending that all foreign hostages in Iraq and Kuwait should be allowed to leave. He had taken this decision, he said, because Iraqi forces had now completed their mobilization to confront possible military aggression in the province of Kuwait. He apologized to all foreigners who had been held for any harm done to them and asked for God's forgiveness. Information Minister Jassim said the foreign 'guests' had succeeded in preventing war.

Just about every foreign notable who had come through Baghdad and seen Saddam Hussein – Jesse Jackson, Edward Heath, Willy Brandt, Yasuhiro Nakasone, Ramsey Clark from the United States, Jean-Marie Le Pen from France, David Lange from New Zealand, Tony Benn from Britain, Muhammed Ali, the former boxer, an enormous Japanese MP who had once been a wrestler, and various others – had argued that it was in Iraq's interests to let the hostages go. But the really convincing argument had come from Yasser Arafat.

As so often during these months, Arafat's was the rational, restraining voice in an absurd situation. He had done himself and his movement great damage by linking their fortunes with Iraq's, but he still had hopes of redeeming the position by persuading Saddam Hussein to behave in a more acceptable

254

fashion. Saddam needed Arafat to prove his pan-Arabist credentials; Arafat, like King Hussein of Jordan, was one of the few Middle Eastern leaders who had an electorate to answer to. He had no political alternative but to support the Iraqi position, once the Palestinians had shown their powerful wave of support for Saddam. Even so, Arafat would probably have supported Saddam Hussein anyway because he was certain that it was possible to link a settlement of the Kuwaiti crisis with a settlement of the Palestinian issue. There were strong rumours at this time that the United States was prepared to back a UN-sponsored conference on the Middle East to resolve the Palestinian issue. Arafat believed the rumours, partly because he badly wanted to. But the United States denied them and they faded away.

On 4 December Saddam Hussein held a meeting in Baghdad with Arafat, King Hussein of Jordan and the Vice-President of Yemen, Ali Salem al-Bidh. Arafat took the lead in arguing the case for releasing the hostages. King Hussein, who by now had little influence over Saddam, preferred to allow Arafat to do the talking, but he seconded him strongly. The Yemeni vice-president played less of a part.

It looked as though Saddam wanted to be convinced and eventually he agreed. The announcement followed two days later. When the war started Saddam was bitterly angry with Yasser Arafat, believing that the coalition forces would never have bombed Iraq if there had been hostages at each of the country's main military and industrial installations. He was wrong: the Allies had taken a decision at least as early as September that the presence of hostages at the installations would not prevent the bombing. But thereafter in Saddam's eyes Yasser Arafat was to blame for having persuaded him to give up a measure of protection against the enemy. Saddam Hussein was not one to blame himself for having been convinced.

So they were all gone: Julian McCullough, Dick Pagett, the Irish nurses, the decorators who had been working on the presidential palace, all the people who had been hiding out in Kuwait. I went round to the British embassy, an attractive single-storey proconsular building in yellowish brick. The pleasant grounds were empty: no large plump bodies in the swimming pool, no one charging around the football field. The area where a group of British employees from the American company Bechtel had pitched their tents, having moved into the embassy grounds in a fit of nerves back in August, was empty. There was no one now to threaten to thump the cameraman for filming them and – they complained – for putting their lives at risk. Some of the Bechtel people were very pleasant, but they were not always in the majority. As autumn turned to winter and the nights grew cold, the unwisdom of their initial spasm of fear became obvious. Many complained bitterly about the lack of help they had received from the embassy, forgetting that they had not been invited there in the first place. Most of the other hostages were quiet and stoical. The Bechtel men sat in their cold tents and whinged.

The hall where the British business community, themselves hostages, used to meet the ambassador once a week was empty too. Harold Walker said that only his mother called him Harold and everyone else called him Hookey. He was charming and unstuffy and seemed positively to enjoy the occasions when we invited him to dinner at the Al-Rasheed. He made a good and regular interviewee, sparing and precise with his words: a great boon for radio and television.

I sat waiting for him now, trying to work out if the termite trails on the walls had grown any longer since I was here last. I am not always an enthusiast for the staff at British embassies, who are often highly superior to mere passport-holders and treat the local population with breathtaking rudeness, but Hookey Walker was not that kind of diplomat and he didn't have the British civil servant's terror of journalists. Now, as he came out of an inner room, I realized that I had interrupted his preparations for leaving. He was going to England to spend Christmas with his family and consult with the Foreign Office. Without him – and without the hostages – Baghdad was going to be an emptier place.

That evening we filmed in the New British Club, a rough-and-cheerful kind of place which smelled of beer. The few habitués who were left gathered sentimentally round the bar to sing carols: stout men in their fifties, holding the hymn sheets

256

out in front of their stomachs; young men in T-shirts, grinning through the familiar verses. In a few days they would all be gone too. The hostages used to look wistfully at the journalists, knowing we could leave Iraq and they couldn't. This Christmas, I thought, they'll be at home watching television and we'll be here watching the crisis.

On 17 December there was cheerful news. The British ambassador in Kuwait, Michael Weston, and the consul, Larry Banks, had arrived in Baghdad. They had stuck it out until the end, the last diplomats to leave Kuwait. During their 18 weeks in the besieged embassy they had suffered from heat rash and skin complaints (one embassy employee coming through Baghdad had said privately he thought they might go mad with the discomfort) and had had to strain the mosquito larvae out of the water they used for washing. But they looked pretty good as they stood at the entrance to the Baghdad embassy. Were they heroes, someone asked? Michael Weston's reply was cheerful:

> Not in the least. The real heroes were firstly the British community who stayed on; secondly the people who helped us and them: the Irish, the Australians, the Canadians and the New Zealanders. And thirdly, our wardens and the local staff. The staff are staying on there, and I'm sure you will wish them well over Christmas.

In fact the two of them made very good heroes indeed, in an idiosyncratic and old-fashioned British way: Michael Weston in his pince-nez and Larry Banks the compulsive gardener who had grown all the vegetables they lived on. The previous day, 16 December, with the last British people gone from Kuwait, they had locked and barricaded the embassy and clambered out of an upstairs window by ladder. They were confronted by armed Iraqi soldiers who, illogically, ordered them back into an embassy which the Iraqi government had insisted months before that they should evacuate. Michael Weston said to the man who was pointing a rifle at his chest: 'You'll have to shoot me, I'm afraid.' Only then did the Iraqis let them go.

A British Labour MP, Bernie Grant, visited Baghdad on 17 December and was told that if Iraq were attacked British and American interests anywhere in the world would be attacked. Terrorism was one of the big unquantifiable assets which Saddam Hussein appeared to possess and it was something of a mystery why Iraq had not yet made use of it. One afternoon before Christmas I went round with my colleagues to a modern bungalow in the Baghdad suburbs. Directly we reached the street I recognized it: Edward Heath had stayed just round the corner. Armed guards rolled aside a mobile set of tyre spikes and we parked. It could have been a quiet estate in Romford if it hadn't been for the Republican Guard soldiers in their red berets. We walked across the forecourt of an unremarkable bungalow, the main residence of Yasser Arafat, chairman of the Palestine Liberation Organization.

We interviewed Yasser Arafat at length. He was his usual ebullient self, the voice ranging from middle- to high-pitched, the hands, bandaged and covered with ointment as a result of an overlong stay under a sun lamp, making the usual extravagant gestures. There would not, he promised me, be a war. I would see. The Americans would not be so foolish. Would there be terrorism? He didn't think there would. He didn't add that he was doing his utmost to ensure that the various Palestinian groups under his control did nothing which would rule out the PLO as a negotiating partner once the Iraqi crisis was over. Saddam Hussein seems to have demanded action from the PLO and Yasser Arafat, while not refusing outright, never quite agreed. As a result not a plane was hijacked, not a car bomb was exploded. Interestingly, the government of Iran was also using its utmost influence on the militant Shi'i groups in Lebanon which came under the umbrella of Hezbollah to ensure that they too took no action. The reasoning was the same: Iran, like Arafat, was looking to the future.

Arafat had come close to disaster by allying himself with Saddam Hussein. There were moments in our interview when I thought he recognized it. Now his only hope was to show that he had had a moderating effect on Saddam. If he could prevent an outbreak of terrorism and maybe broker a peace agreement, he might stand a chance of rehabilitating himself. After the interview was over, he held my hand as we walked in to a belated lunch. For a time there was silence. People reached across the luncheon table to spear bits of beef or chicken from dishes in the centre. As a vegetarian I would have preferred rice and lentils, but my host insisted on putting a large chunk of beef on my plate and I ate it.

At the end of the table sat a big, subdued man whose hand I had shaken when I first arrived at the bungalow. I could hear him ingesting from a distance. I might have taken him for someone's bodyguard, but it was Abu Abbas, the man behind the attack on the *Achille Lauro* and the more recent amphibious landings in Israel. In May 1990, when the landings took place, Yasser Arafat believed that Britain was just about to recognize the PLO as the legitimate representative of the Palestinian people. Directly news came through of the attack by Abu Abbas's men, the British apparently drew back. Arafat called in Abu Abbas and gave him a talking-to. It was, by all accounts, a ferocious occasion and Abu Abbas was, as a result, the meek figure I could now hear chewing a chicken leg.

Arafat's ability to spot optimistic signs was undiminished. He had, he told me, helped to mediate between Iraq and Kuwait in 1972 when Saddam's predecessor was threatening to invade. Arafat even walked over the sandbanks which were glorified on the map as the islands of Bubiyan and Warba. Eighteen years later he was still suggesting that Kuwait should lease them to Iraq and so regain its independence. Now he stabbed a piece of meat and chewed it absently, while a waiter splashed some water deferentially into his glass. 'There will be no war,' he said. 'Bush is not mad. He knows the dangers. They [the UN Security Council] will set another date, later than 15 January. Then there will be an arrangement – perhaps with the Europeans, perhaps with the Arabs. Someone.' Abu Abbas was leaning forward now, frowning with the effort of listening to the English words. As I watched I remembered interviewing Arafat in Beirut in 1982, with the Israeli bombs raining down, still full of optimism even though he was about to be expelled from Lebanon. He was just the same now. In Arab politics only the partners change; the dance remains the same. Yasser

Arafat was a conciliator, a maker of deals, even when everything seemed lost.

That night the pianist in the restaurant of the Al-Rasheed had just launched into 'My Way' when a heavy man in a poorly-fitting brown suit lumbered across and began to fill up again at the buffet with chicken, beef and some nameless, light-coloured meat. He passed the vegetables by: no room on the plate. Back at his table his wife, stout but handsome, went quiet as he eased his bulk into the seat. Three attractive daughters wearing make-up and bright clothes looked idly round the room. Two sharply dressed sons glanced at each other. No one said anything. By now their father was pushing food into himself as if he had a deadline to meet. Aziz Saleh Norman, the governor of Iraq's new nineteenth province, was having a night on the town.

Norman came from the area south of Kut and his unlikely name probably derived from a father or grandfather who was a prisoner of the British during the World War I battle there: there are plenty of Johns and Georges in Iraq, though Normans are fewer. His had not been a distinguished record of public service: he was demoted in 1987 from his position as agriculture minister for negligence and incompetence. After spending three years as a Baath Party boss in a Baghdad suburb Norman was chosen, for no reason anyone could think of, to succeed Saddam Hussein's cousin, Ali Hussein al-Majid, as governor of Kuwait that autumn.

The appointment seemed to imply that Saddam had little interest in civilian rule in the nineteenth province. He was a stopgap, occupying the post until the issue of Kuwait's ownership could be dealt with, either on the battlefield or at the conference table. Could we, I asked one of the minders that night, approach Mr Norman for an interview? 'Why not?' said the minder, so I knew that was no use. When approached in person Mr Norman raised his head from his overcharged plate and simply stared. That was no use either.

Christmas drew closer. Mr Norman's food was laid out now on a table decorated with robin-and-reindeer paper. In the lobby of the hotel, solemn-faced Somali porters had set up stepladders among the groups of plump Kuwaitis and strung up silver and green decorations. Piped carols were in the air, instead of the muzak which usually filled the place like the unobtrusive hum of machinery. In the busy streets outside there were shops where you could buy tinsel, Santa Clauses of varying sizes and spray-on snow which drifted in the corners of the windows; this in a city which had probably not seen real snow in decades. A shopkeeper whose extravagantly loyal Saddam Hussein clocks I had always admired had tucked a sprig of holly into the beak of a stuffed budgerigar he kept by the door.

Epiphany is Army Day in Iraq. In the morning mist, under Saddam's flying saucer monument, splendid figures in scarlet uniforms and white helmets sloped arms and stamped in the approved British style of 70 years ago. The defence minister, in red tabs and Sam Browne, saluted longest-way-up-and-shortest-way-down as the buglers played 'The Last Post'. It was he who saved the city of Basrah when Iran besieged it during the Gulf War and Saddam Hussein had chosen him to work out ways of saving the entire country from a considerably greater attack now.

A few hours later the President himself was on television giving his Army Day speech. He looked and sounded tired and the studio director was clearly under orders not to show any close-ups. His mouth seemed drawn down on the left hand side and his speech was thick and a little indistinct. But if the intense pressures of the past few months were having their effect, his message was characteristically unyielding: 'the mother of battles' would soon begin, it would widen into a greater war for the Holy Places and the rights of the Palestinians, and the soldiers of Iraq were privileged to be called upon to fight in a war as noble and as holy as the early wars of the Muslim faith.

On this occasion, Saddam's rhetoric had a distinctly phoney edge to it. On 21 December we were taken to witness the mass evacuation of a million people from Saddam City, the enormous and mostly working-class suburb in northeast Baghdad. They were to be picked up by bus from a number of assembly points and deposited 10 miles away in the desert. At first we believed it. The streets of Saddam City were entirely empty, the shops were shuttered, the curtains drawn. Only the sharpest eye would detect the occasional twitching of a blind as we drove past. At the village of Rashidiyah several thousand people had been deposited and were sitting round in jolly fashion, lighting fires and brewing tea. Children chased each other with sticks and goats roamed around eating what they could.

Rashidiyah was one of the seven evacuation points, and there were doctors and a field hospital by the side of the road. The interior minister who came bustling along as if by accident assured us that the whole of Baghdad, certainly the women and children, would be evacuated if a war started. But at Rashidiyah there was something wrong: one seventh of a million is just over 142,000 and there could be no more than 10,000 people here. Only gradually did it become clear to us that the whole thing was an elaborate deception. Later someone from Saddam City explained that most people had been told to stay indoors that day and a few of the poorest inhabitants were given a day out, just to impress foreign journalists with the degree of Iraq's preparation for war. There was no real intention of protecting people against missiles and bombs. It was all thoroughly characteristic of Saddam's system.

For the second time in two years I would be celebrating Christmas in difficult circumstances. The previous year it had been in Bucharest, at the height of the revolution. Next Christmas, I had promised myself, would be spent somewhere warm and non-Christian; meaning perhaps India. As wishes tend to do, it came true in a very different sense. Yet it was enjoyable enough in its way. My colleagues were a pleasant group: Bob Simpson, the cameraman Neville Wong and his sound recordist Monty Johnson (who were apt to discuss questions like the difference between a plebiscite and a referendum), Jason Blount, an Australian freelance picture editor who beat me humiliatingly at tennis, and Malcolm Switzer, a Zimbabwean from Visnews who beat Jason. Mike Robinson, the news editor, came out as producer and enjoyed being on the road again so much that he found it hard to go back to London. Our colleagues from ITN were good company too, headed by Desmond Hammill, one of the best of their reporters and an honourable and pleasant man. His producer, Angela Fryer, had made all the plans for a joint Christmas dinner, turkey and all, and we had each been supplied with hampers by Harrods in London.

I got up early for my usual morning swim. You could tell what day it was because a country-and-western carol was playing in the lift. The singer was spelling out 'Christmas' and had reached 'I is for your eyes that shine' by the time we got to the ground floor. I strode past a life-sized painting of Santa Claus in the lobby. He was carrying a lantern and wearing purple boots; I was wearing a Queen's Club tracksuit. It was hard to say which of us was more out of place in Iraq at a time of international crisis. The carol had reached 'S is for your sweet caress' as the door opened and the bright Baghdad morning hit me with the force of a cold shower.

Steam rose thickly from the heated waters of the big outdoor swimming pool; so thickly that, as I headed into my daily 20 lengths, I could see only a few yards ahead of me. And so, like some heavily-charged freighter in the English Channel, I found the wreathing mist opening to reveal an obstacle which I was too unwieldy to avoid. A couple of hotel porters were bobbing up and down in the warmish water, singing a jolly song and pointing their fingers in the air. I carved my way through them, trying to smile and seem Christmas-like while not actually slackening my pace. They yelped and were swallowed up in the mist. Later I could hear them faintly over the sound of my own splashing, still squeaking their song in bat-like voices, out of sight and out of danger in the farthest reaches of the shallow end.

In the lift back to my room the carol had changed. Now it was Tex-Mex: 'Dear Senor Santa Claus, I'll tell you what I think.' That morning I thought that there wouldn't be a war. The BBC World Service, cracking away in the corner of my room, told me that President Bush was hoping to bring the troops back from the Gulf without a shot being fired. Like the most senior officials here, like the diplomats and like the other journalists, I found myself changing my mind on the subject every few days. Saddam Hussein, watching CNN on his

263

television set, must have been delighted: further signs of weakness. Although I found it hard to be certain, it occurred to me at the time that these apparent swings in Washington's mood made war more rather than less likely, since they confirmed Saddam's view of it all.

All the same, powerful rumours, of the kind that the Security Ministry was adept at spreading, were going the rounds. On Christmas Day the word in the *souq* was that the government would call a vast nationwide demonstration for 12 January, at which people would say they loved their President so much that they would beg him to withdraw from Kuwait and so protect himself from danger: an appeal to which he would graciously assent. It had a certain plausibility to it, though within a day or two it was denied so fiercely that it seemed to have been ruled out altogether. And although the placards were said to have been prepared and were stacked up in Baath Party offices, the demonstration never took place.

That Christmas morning our current minder, a large fellow who had the general appearance of an Iraqi secret policeman but was, in reality, pleasant and rather thoughtful, found us a Christian who would allow us into his home to film the family Christmas. He was a driver named Jabril (though he preferred to be called Jim), well educated and with a pleasant, smart appearance. Like many of our drivers, Hassan in particular, he had had problems with the mafiosi who ran the car pools and who tried to hand out the lucrative contracts to their friends. He was a former civil servant, now retired, who found it hard to live on his pension alone. I had found him some work in the past and had come to appreciate his company.

Jim's was an old-fashioned house, built round an open courtyard. His wife and daughter laboured away in the freezing kitchen, while the father and his sons sat round and ate small pastries like mince pies. Outside a cage of budgerigars chirruped and preened. Eventually the Christmas dinner was ready. 'It is the head of a sheep,' said the father proudly. Something stirred in the pot: I caught a glimpse of teeth. A large white pudding was fished out and put on my plate: rice sewn up in a sheep's stomach lining. It was too late to explain that I was a vegetarian. Neville Wong, the cameraman, shrieked and asked for a mince pie; Monty Johnson and Mike Robinson split a pudding between them. I was obliged to eat the whole thing while the family watched me, nodding and smiling. '*Shukran*,' I said when I had finished and took a small cup of potent coffee from their little daughter in an unsuccessful attempt to get rid of the taste. '*Shukran* same-same thank you in English,' said Mr Hattam helpfully. He always came in with us if he thought there might be food.

Over the heads of the family hung a photograph of Saddam Hussein, several pictures of the Virgin Mary and five crucifixes: all of them icons to ward off trouble, especially the picture of Saddam. I looked at their pleasant faces, happy that they had entertained someone for Christmas, nervous that the consequences might turn out to be bad in some unspecified way. These people had no protection other than that provided by their pictures. I remembered Mr Norman crouched over his food at the Al-Rasheed and reflected that these people were herbivores in a carnivorous world. Jim gripped my arm as we left. 'Will everything be safe this New Year?' he asked. It was an appeal, as though I could do something to protect them from bombs and missiles. I looked at the decent, open faces. 'Absolutely,' I said, as soothingly as possible.

There were signs of nervousness now. People were openly talking about getting out of Baghdad and, like Jim, endlessly asking us if we thought there would be war. We found ourselves under closer surveillance. A light bulb wasn't working in someone's room and he shouted: 'Why doesn't anyone replace these bloody bulbs?' A few minutes later, without being asked, someone came to the door with a new one. Bob Simpson's alarm clock disappeared from his bedside so he left a note there: 'Please put clock back here.' At 2.45 the next morning (we had been working and drinking late) he rang me in the tone of voice you use to say you have just seen a UFO: someone had put his clock back. Later that day Sean McGuire, a bright and highly literate producer-cameraman with Visnews was filming a new radar and anti-aircraft position from the window of our office, something we were not supposed to do. Within five minutes of setting up the camera one of the most senior minders came storming into the room to

265

take the cassette away from him and give him a warning. They couldn't have heard Sean on the microphones as he hadn't talked about what he was doing. Had they seen him on their television monitors? Or were there people stationed outside in the grounds with binoculars? We discussed it endlessly.

There was one last splendid evening. New Year's Eve is the holiday that people in Baghdad enjoy most. We decided to go to a big restaurant in the centre of town. We arrived around 11 pm and found everything in full swing. The noise and heat were stupefying. People were clambering onto the tables and squirting each other with foam and taking endless photographs of one another. Older women made a lot of noise and flirted with everyone, especially us. Pretty women looked at the floor and giggled. Young girls danced with portly old men, other girls and, occasionally, with their boyfriends. The dance floor was the sweatiest and the jolliest part of the whole place. A man with a Face of God mask ran round the tables trying to catch girls. Waiters sweated and held trays with bottles of dreadfully bad champagne high over their heads.

A man stood on a table and announced that we were from the BBC. At that, people clustered around us, proferring glasses of champagne, handshakes, kisses. A man tipped his glass high above his head, poured a last reluctant drop of some colourless spirit down his throat and called out: 'BBC very good. England very good. Hello.' As always, he meant goodbye. He sank into a chair and took no further part in the proceedings. Midnight drew closer: the midnight which would bring in an unknown and, quite possibly, terrible new year. The gaiety grew wilder, the Face of God ran faster and caught more girls, the dance floor was crammed beyond any possibility of serious movement, musicians sweated over their instruments.

Then the lights went out. There was laughing and singing and the first candles were lit. I looked round the gleaming faces, the excited eyes glinting in the yellow candle flames, the hands reaching out across the table as people sang softly and smiled at one another and at us. Only 15 days away, I thought. An old man, bald and fat, was sitting silently by himself. Opposite him at the same table was a woman who was probably his daughter. She was plain and rather fat too, but her face was bright with the pleasure of the moment and she bounced a child on her knee, making it clap its pudgy hands in time to the music which had just started up again. The old man sat there in all the noise and jollity and watched time, the tears running unchecked down his fat grey cheeks.

On 15 January, the day of the United Nations deadline, the streets of Baghdad seemed very quiet as we drove along. Most of the shops were closed, their windows shuttered and taped against blast. The midwinter sun cast long shadows as we parked our car near an intersection. At the end of the road, on a big platform decorated with an absurd smiling Saddam face, a man was screaming into a microphone. As we drew closer we could see that the street was entirely empty, but the speaker didn't care. I asked for a translation from one of the officials who was standing around to make sure that the foreign journalists did nothing they shouldn't. 'Just the usual things,' he answered glumly and turned away.

I had long detected a lack of enthusiasm among Iraqis for what their President was doing in their name. Indeed, during nearly five months which I spent in Baghdad between the invasion of Kuwait and the beginning of the war, not a single Iraqi had defended Saddam Hussein to me in private, with the exception of two or three ministers and officials whose fate was closely bound up with Saddam's own. As the UN deadline came closer, various friends of mine grew more outspoken about the state of affairs in Iraq. Some openly welcomed the coming war as their only hope of getting rid of a régime they hated. No Iraqi had ever once reproached me for the coming war and only officials had been critical of the coalition powers. Once a western ambassador had told me he detected greater signs of hostility. When I asked him for an example he said: 'Just the other day a couple of Dutchmen were walking down the road, and when they hailed a taxi it wouldn't stop.' When I asked him if he had ever visited New York he laughed. The contrast between reality and the official presentation of a fanatical war-hardened nation united behind its leader could not have been greater.

Many of the people we dealt with seemed to have given up altogether. As war became more likely the old rules, the old duties, the old fears all become a little less exigent. Our Information Ministry minders seemed preoccupied, their eyes focussed on the middle distance, their attention harder to obtain. Supporters of the old system were suddenly showing signs of doubts about the future and small personal confidences abounded. A particularly stern figure whom I had seen every day for two months suddenly revealed he had a brother in London who was a journalist and knew me.

Corrupt officials became more reckless in their demands for money. If you wanted an extra satellite feed and were not on the official list, a $100 bill would sort out the problem. People stayed away from their offices and shops longer. The central telephone exchange sometimes failed to answer for 20 minutes at a time. The staff in our hotel were beginning to melt away. Laundry took two days instead of one, room service was dwindling, porters were harder to find. Each morning when I laboured up and down the hotel swimming pool the heated water was a little cooler and a little less clear with fungus spreading between the tiles. On the hotel lawn sewage appeared to be seeping to the surface. A nasty smell of decay hung around the front steps.

The man on the platform continued to bellow into his microphone. Pigeons fluttered up at the sound of his voice in the empty street. There were plenty of people up there alongside him now: photographers and cameramen, American, German and Australian peace campaigners, officials of the Baath Party in their olive-green uniforms. They were all staring down the road towards the approaching column of marchers. Faintly, above the roar of the man with the microphone, you could hear the sound of their chanting. It hovered over them like breath on a cold day: 'Down, down, Bush! Down, down, Thatcher! We give our lives and our heart's blood for Saddam!' The crowd was a big one. Twenty or more abreast, they stretched down the avenue as far as the eye could see, a compacted mass of people carrying banners and pictures of Saddam Hussein.

This was to be a march past, not a big public gathering. The

268

stewards hurried them along, the man with the microphone kept shouting at them to move faster. All over the country Challenge Day was being marked in this fashion: hundreds of marches by tens of thousands of people. From where we were standing it seemed like a powerful statement of support for President Saddam Hussein and for Iraq's control over Kuwait; even if you knew, as I did, that they were carefully marshalled and ordered out onto the streets by the Baath Party. The head of the crowd grew closer. There were, as always, large numbers of children in the vanguard. The plan to evacuate women and children out of the main cities before 15 January had been scrapped – if indeed it hadn't simply been a public relations stunt. There was more than a suspicion that Saddam Hussein might not after all worry too much if women and children were killed in the coming war: indeed, he would regard it as useful propaganda.

The Young Pioneers, wearing strange blue pyjama-like fatigues decorated with camels and palm trees, marched proudly ahead of the others: Saddam's spies in the home. Marching alongside them were hundreds of uniformed girls, all from the same schools, laughing and chatting with their friends and only occasionally remembering to chant the requisite slogans. They passed the platform where Saddam's face smiled its friendly smile at us all and the German and American peace workers had taken over the microphone to condemn the outside world's aggression against Iraq. They did so in English, so not many of the people marching in front of them can have understood what they were saying. No matter: every speech made on a public platform in Iraq invariably made the same points, over and again, and they all amounted to the notion that the entire country supported Saddam Hussein.

Once the children had passed and evaporated down the side-streets, giggling and laughing, a new wave of adult marchers arrived, stern, banner-waving, uniform-wearing. Some were in the camouflage fatigues of the army reserve, but most wore Baathist olive green. These were the true believers, men whose fate was entirely bound up with that of Saddam. For them, this was indeed a manifestation of loyalty. But they were not large in number; and slowly I began to realize the truth of what the BBC producer who was with me, Anthony Massey, had been telling me. An important confidence trick was being played on us all.

The Baathists were the core of the demonstration and were surrounded by thousands of ordinary Iraqis in everyday clothes. The ordinary Iraqis moved along quite quickly, as the children had done before them; but the Baathist core lingered in front of the platform, dancing, chanting, ripping up American and British flags, burning President Bush and some less identifiable figure (the little-known John Major, perhaps?) and generally catching the attention of the camera crews and stills photographers on the stage above them. But when we got down from the platform and ventured into the farther recesses of the crowd it became obvious that the great mass of demonstrators were not in fact demonstrating at all: they were standing around waiting for their friends to join them, or else heading off like the schoolchildren before them. 'I only came here because I was told to,' said one man in good English; and it seemed reasonable to assume that he spoke for thousands of the bored, rather resentful people who had been obliged to act out an enthusiasm none of them felt.

I looked back at the platform: all the other cameramen and photographers were still there, recording the evidence of the Iraqi people's fierce determination to follow their leader to death or glory. And yet there was no such thing. It was an illusion, a confidence trick, cleverly managed by people who must have realized that unless they staged something of this kind the cat would have been out of the bag. The fact was that only the Party members and those whose careers and lives were dependent on Saddam's continued power were backing him. He was about to take an almost entirely unwilling country into war.

Battle Stations

They asked us, 'Why are you not frightened, since 28 states are allied against you? We said: Their numbers do not frighten us. We depend on God the One and Only. Victory is near, God willing. It is as if we saw victory coming to us, balanced with the faith that is in our bosoms, because of our firm steps towards it.

Saddam Hussein, speaking to the International Islamic Conference, 11 January 1991

It is depressing to watch your diplomatic representatives, the people whose job it is to take up your case if you get into trouble, disappearing off to the border. No doubt the British ambassador and his staff would have stayed in Baghdad if they could, but they were under orders from the Foreign Office in London to get out quickly and without telling anyone. All the embassies of the coalition powers were closing down, partly for the safety of their staff and partly to put extra pressure on the Iraqis. Fortunately for us, our good friends at Sky Television had got wind of what was happening and told us. Our competitors from ITN had also heard: the embassy was looking after some of their equipment and had warned them. There was a certain embarrassment when we all turned up at the embassy at 5 am. Cocks were crowing on the nearby rooftops and embassy lights blazed into the surrounding darkness as we found the four-wheel drive cars being loaded up.

They left a few hours later. The cars turned the corner and disappeared from sight, hooting their goodbyes and their relief at getting out. Silence settled over the embassy. A few ashes whirled about in the wind: together with a heap of confetti on a rubbish heap, they were all that was left of the embassy's confidential papers. An evil old tomcat snuffled through the remains with the keenness of a security agent. In the inner courtyard the little World War I field gun still stood beside an inscription recording the British capture of Baghdad in deeds-that-make-an-Empire terms. Now the British had evacuated Baghdad. The consul general was staying on for an extra day to attend the trial of a British man, Patrick Trygg, who had shown great courage in helping hostages escape from Iraq and had been caught when he stayed behind to get some others out. I felt considerable guilt about him because I had reported the escape without realizing that he was staying behind. Fortunately Mr Trygg was acquitted and was free to go. The consul general went too.

We wandered round the quiet embassy, filming the locally-employed staff as they arrived for work and tried to come to terms with what had happened. They at least had been warned. A British woman, the wife of an Iraqi, turned up to collect something for the British Council where she worked. 'How could they just go off without telling us?' she said. A pleasant lady of a certain age said soothingly: 'Orders from the Foreign Office, dear.' As they spoke I noticed she was standing in front of a locker marked 'Ian Richter'. Mr Richter was a British businessman tried and imprisoned by the Iraqis when the mayor of Baghdad was executed for corruption: it had always seemed like an attempt to validate accusations that the mayor had been in the pay of foreign interests. Now Mr Richter was enduring an unjust sentence in a prison outside the city. There would be no one to visit him or take him the things kept in the locker which made prison life a little more bearable.

The Americans didn't try to make a secret of the fact they were leaving. Joe Wilson went round the Al-Rasheed the day before, trying out an electronic gadget that insulted people in a squeaky voice: 'Fuck you! You're an asshole!' We had problems editing out the sound. He also told those who planned to stay on in Baghdad that they were going to die. On the morning of the great American departure there was a good

272

deal of studied phrasemaking: 'We're leavin' because we don't want to be a pound of ground-round.' 'There's gonna be no more level terrain here. There's gonna be only rolling craters.' 'We're gonna pound these guys so far down you're gonna have to pipe in the sunlight.' The Americans didn't want any witnesses around when the bombs started to fall. It's even possible they were also trying to persuade us to leave in our own interest.

I had started to believe there would be war since the first few days of January. I kept in close touch with the stream of visitors who saw Saddam and pieced together a clear idea of his mood. My sources all agreed that Saddam was utterly confident. He knew as little about the nature of 'smart' bombs and missiles as the American chargé d'affaires and he assumed, like Joe Wilson, that Baghdad would be devastated by the allied attack. Instead of being worried about this, he welcomed it. His view of western – and particularly American – politics and society was profoundly contemptuous. He believed that President Bush's resolution and American public opinion would crumble directly the scale of the damage to Baghdad became obvious. 'We will only have to face two air strikes,' he told several people, 'then it'll be ended.'

As the UN deadline of 15 January 1991 approached the likelihood of war increased. I decided to nail my colours to the mast. I had satellited a report to London on 2 January which included a long piece to camera filmed in the *souq*. It was raining heavily and we had to choose a place where the roof didn't leak:

Like most Westerners here, I've swung back and forth during my months in Baghdad from one opinion to another: the Americans will attack, then they won't; Saddam will never withdraw from Kuwait, then he might. At present, though, it seems to me that Iraq won't make a move before the fifteenth, and the Americans will attack. The next 13 days will no doubt see a lot of heavy diplomatic activity: but short of something entirely unexpected, I think we're now looking at the likelihood of war.

The report caused a fuss in London where someone

described it as 'total crap'. The Foreign Office was unsure whether to believe it or not; there was growing nervousness there and in the State Department in Washington that instead of heading into war Saddam would pull out of part of Kuwait around 12 January and the West would be left without a policy. Both governments were inclined to believe the thing they most feared. Anyway, it seemed irrational that even a leader like Saddam Hussein would deliberately head into war; far more likely that he would simply want to give that impression. But Yevgeny Primakov had seen the signs of what he called Saddam's Masada complex and other people I spoke to reinforced this. One said Saddam was simply not talking in the kind of terms that gave any hope of a peaceful outcome. On the one hand he described a withdrawal as suicidal for himself; on the other he was still insisting that Iraq would face nothing more than two US air strikes which it could survive.

France tried some last-minute diplomacy. On 5 January Michel Vauzelle, a superbly-dressed figure in blue double-breasted suit and tie, his blonde hair exquisitely brushed, turned up at the Al-Rasheed. I had last seen him giving a press briefing at the Elysée Palace a year or so before. Now he was chairman of the foreign affairs committee of the Assemblée Nationale and was in Baghdad as President Mitterrand's special envoy. He spent nearly five hours with Saddam Hussein, much longer than any other western representative. It indicated a desire on Saddam's part to keep France on his side if possible. When he emerged and was interviewed over a satellite link by Georges Bortoli of French television's second channel, Antenne 2, Vauzelle said Saddam wanted guarantees both on the Palestinian question and on the future economic development of Kuwait:

The Palestinian issue is without doubt very important insofar as Baghdad – and naturally I am not making any judgments, I am making an observation – wishes to play a considerable role in the Arab world. And, naturally, Baghdad is leading a crusade in support of a cause which has failed to find a solution for too long. But I think that Iraq's occupation of Kuwait is also in response to concerns of an economic and political nature . . .

Vauzelle, in other words, had heard nothing more than was in Saddam's public statements. He still required the Americans to give him something before he would agree to withdraw.

Two days later, on 9 January, the US Secretary of State James Baker met the Iraqi Foreign Minister Tariq Aziz in Geneva. Much hope was invested in the occasion, yet Saddam was still insisting in private that Iraq would give way only if the United States made the first move by agreeing to implement the Security Council resolutions on Israel and the Occupied Territories. It gave me no pleasure to be pessimistic, but I began to wonder whether my information was correct when the first relatively positive indications came from Geneva and an ITN interviewee said he had good information that Tariq Aziz would offer a withdrawal from Kuwait. It didn't happen. When Baker gave a press conference at the InterContinental Hotel in Geneva he made it clear right at the start that the meeting had failed:

> Regrettably, ladies and gentlemen, in over six hours I heard nothing that suggested to me any Iraqi flexibility whatsoever on complying with United Nations Security Council resolutions.

The atmosphere had been polite and serious and the participants had each taken the time to put their views carefully so that there was no chance of missing some possibility for compromise. Tariq Aziz confirmed this at the press conference he gave a short while afterwards that none existed:

> Q: Would Iraq leave Kuwait if promised an international conference on the question of Palestine?
> A: I did not put it that way . . . I told the Secretary [of State] that if you are ready to respect and implement international legality, the principles of justice and fairness, as far as all the issues in the region are concerned, you will find us very cooperative.

It was the same obstacle as always: Iraq would do nothing unless the United States made the first move. Aziz refused even to take a letter from George Bush to Saddam Hussein. He opened it in Baker's presence and said it was not couched in the kind of terms that one leader should use to another. Someone at the press conference asked Aziz if it would come to war. 'If they decide to attack Iraq, we will not be surprised,' he said. Back in Baghdad, Saddam Hussein warned that American troops were falling into a trap. They would, he said, swim in their own blood.

Javier Perez de Cuellar, the UN secretary general, came to Baghdad himself and met Saddam Hussein on 13 January. Saddam was not in conciliatory mood. He regarded Perez de Cuellar as nothing more than an American stooge and was angry with him for failing to come to Baghdad earlier when he felt there might still have been a chance of genuine negotiation. Saddam kept Perez de Cuellar waiting for hour after hour to show his displeasure, while the UN officials in the party complained to each other that with war imminent this was no way to behave. When the meeting finally took place Saddam was cold and distant but not actually rude. Perez de Cuellar addressed the crowd of journalists afterwards in platitudes. Someone asked him if there would be peace or war. He answered: 'God only knows.' Then, with evident relief, he left.

Almost everyone expected war now. The BBC asked me to ask the group of people with me whether they wanted to stay. They all said yes. In the days immediately preceding the war there were seven of us: the two Simpsons, as we were known; Eamonn Matthews from 'Newsnight' who had been with me on my first official trip to Iraq soon after Farzad Bazoft's execution; Anthony Massey, a producer from the News programmes who had spotted the lack of enthusiasm at the big demonstration on the day of the UN deadline; Brian Hulls, an experienced cameraman who had covered wars before and was later to return during this one; Colin Jones, his sound recordist, who seemed to have an encyclopedic knowledge of weaponry and had trained as an engineer; and Jason Blount, the Australian picture editor.

I detected a certain irritation on the third or fourth occasion when I was obliged to ask them if they were still sure they wanted to stay. After that I stopped asking: I was glad to have their company. Our competitors at ITN had a particularly well-known cameraman in their group who had written a book about his exploits. He trained with weights and was usually in the swimming pool before me every morning. I was worried that when the war started he would pull some daring stunt which I would not have the imagination for. It was much easier to worry about that, than about what would happen to us when the war started. I noticed that one or two of us were showing physical signs of nervousness. I started to pick at my fingers again – a habit I thought I had given up. Someone else had a flare-up of eczema. But we stayed good tempered with one another.

There was no big, larger-than-life character like Derrick Collier – ex-petty officer, BBC cameraman and friend of Margaret Thatcher – who had come to Baghdad some weeks earlier hoping to cover the war and who instead had infiltrated the airport VIP suite with his sound recordist Matt and persuaded the taciturn Yevgeny Primakov to confess his disappointment at not having negotiated an agreement. Groups like ours have their internal dynamics. When Derrick and some of the others were there we played around a lot and were highly sociable. Now, as the deadline came and went, we were quieter and more self-contained. I found myself looking out of the window for minutes at a time, thinking about things at home.

Many other journalists had found their editors becoming increasingly peremptory. 'If you aren't out by the fifteenth I'll regard it as a personal betrayal,' said one. President Bush himself telephoned various American editors to urge them to evacuate their teams. That frightened a lot of people. Some journalists went round doing Joe Wilson's work for him. They knew they shouldn't really leave, but since they were determined to they wanted to get everyone else to go as well. People told us in graphic detail what 2000 pound penetration bombs do to the human body: what exactly happens to your eyes and your liver and to your insides. A large American said: 'Man, I wouldn't be in that shelter when one of those mothers comes out of the sky. I saw them used in 'Nam. You'll be dead meat, man. The vibration's gonna shake the fillings right outa your teeth.' I ran my tongue round my fillings, familiar and smooth:

how bad would the vibration have to be to shake them?

I found it hard to sleep that night. The hotel had emptied: on the night of 14 January there were 270 journalists in the Al-Rasheed. The next night there were 60, many of them also planning to leave. People were anxious to explain themselves: 'I came here to cover a crisis, not a war.' 'What's the point in staying, if you can't be sure of getting your material out?' 'Suppose the Israelis nuked this place?' The last possibility worried me too. I walked down the dark, empty corridors of the Al-Rasheed, wondering what damage a missile or a crashing B-52 would do to the structure. We had already moved our office from the twelfth to the fifth floor, on the grounds that I didn't want to climb so many stairs in the event of a power failure; it was really in order to feel less exposed.

I didn't want to stay but I couldn't bear to leave. I remembered what a CNN producer had told me. He was a tough but intelligent man, horribly overworked. Even through the dark glasses he had taken to wearing I could see three or four styes on each eye glowing out at me. He had been in Vietnam at the time of the American pull-out, he said, and he'd decided to leave rather than stay. 'It's a decision I shall regret till the day I die,' he said, and I could feel the intensity with which he said it.

A variety of things kept me in Baghdad: a sense of duty; the fact that I was writing a book; the knowledge that if I left others would feel obliged to stay behind and do my job; curiosity. But I remembered the CNN man too. I rather expected I was going to die, but equally I thought that if I survived I wouldn't be haunted by the feeling that I had let myself and others down. They were, perhaps, strange emotions for the last decade of the twentieth century, yet I found that they were shared by my other colleagues who stayed. A Latin tag came to mind, from Vergil's *Æneid*: *fato profugus*, driven on by fate.

Early morning mist blotted out the city. I walked over to the wall calendar and crossed off the date with a certain amount of feeling: 15 January. Then I put on 'Mars, the Bringer of War' from Holst's *The Planets*. We had reached the United Nations deadline for Iraq to evacuate Kuwait. I decided to go for a last swim in the outdoor pool. The water was cooler and dirtier now and there was a general smell of decay in the air. A small lake of sewage had seeped to the surface of the hotel lawn. The staff whose job it was to keep the pool clean had long gone, as had most of the others, with the exception of Mr Bagi, the philosophical Sudanese who cleaned our rooms.

There was news on the radio of a bitter blow to Saddam Hussein's chief ally. Abu Iyyad, the PLO head of security and intelligence, was murdered by a Palestinian security man who had defected from Abu Nidal's terrorist faction. Abu Iyyad was the leading influence behind the decision by the Palestine National Council in November 1988 to recognize the existence of Israel and negotiate a Palestinian state in the West Bank and Gaza. His voice was one of moderation and reconciliation and the murder did serious damage to the PLO and Yasser Arafat. Some suggested it had been engineered by Syria, as a first strike in the war to come. Others, more conspiratorial, observed that Abu Nidal's group had been responsible for the deaths of many Palestinian moderates and noted that Israel's secret service Mossad was believed to have infiltrated the group. Abu Iyyad's death meant that only Yasser Arafat was left of the four founders of the biggest group within the PLO, Fatah. The others had all died violently. Yasser Arafat now hurried back from Baghdad to Tunis and his restraining influence on Saddam Hussein was lost.

Baghdad had virtually closed down. People headed out to the countryside and most of the shops were shuttered. In Rashid Street you could walk down the middle of the road without having to look over your shoulder for cars. The *souqs* were deserted; pigeons strutted around in the empty halls. I went out to buy soap and found a solitary shop open beside a teahouse. The man behind the counter gripped my hand. 'You are from England? There won't be any bombing, I think?' 'I'm sure you'll be all right,' I said, ambiguously. '*Inshallah*,' he said, then: 'You are our friend. Welcome.' He put the soap in a special bag for me and tied it with a flourish. 'Hello,' he said and bowed.

For those with an eye for a bargain it was a good time. When his offer for an expensive carpet was rejected, a New Zealander working for NBC, Tom Aspell, told the shopkeeper: 'I'd accept it if I were you: the next person in here will be black, six foot six tall, and carrying an M16 rifle.' It worked. Bob Simpson and I went round to say our goodbyes, while trying not to give the impression that was what we were doing. 'It is time now for God to strike Saddam and give us peace,' one friend said loudly. He scarcely bothered to look round. 'You were always so discreet in the past,' I observed. He said: 'In the past we had no UN deadline.'

I went round to the television station for the first time in months on the assumption it wouldn't be there much longer. For all the vast amounts of money we and other television teams had poured into the place ($400 per satellite feed, with a receipt for $300; what happened to the extra $100 was unexplained) the place was tatty and depressing. The usual picture of Saddam Hussein hung crookedly on the wall and the clock was slow. The censor who had made life difficult for us for months didn't even look at the monitor when our tape was played. His eyes would wander to the ceiling as he fiddled with a paperclip. 'You aren't paying much attention,' I said irritably. I was obscurely annoyed that after the months of irritating, nit-picking complaints and excisions he shouldn't even bother to look at the screen now. 'What's the point?' he replied. 'The deadline is coming up.'

There was a last-minute attempt by the French to stave off war. Late on 14 January President Mitterrand had met the Iraqi ambassador and President Mobutu of Zaire, the country which currently held the presidency of the UN Security Council. The suggestion was that Roland Dumas, the French foreign minister, would go to Baghdad and discuss an agreement which would involve an Iraqi withdrawal from Kuwait, the introduction of a UN force there, and an eventual Middle East peace conference. Saddam, as always, would have to make the first move. The plan was discussed by the Security Council, with the British and Americans unable to hide their anger at France's behaviour. But it seemed as though Mitterrand wanted to show everyone that he had done his best before putting France's weight behind the Allies.

That evening President Bush rang Prime Minister John Major in Downing Street and, with his National Security Adviser Brent Scowcroft listening into the conversation in Washington and Sir Charles Powell, Major's foreign affairs adviser, doing the same thing in London, agreed the precise timing of the first military strike. It was to be at 2150 GMT the next day. No doubt the consultation was a formality: Major would scarcely have disagreed. At about the time they were speaking to each other I went to the Information Ministry to see the minister, Latif Jassim.

The Ministry was almost deserted and all its windows were taped up against blast. Jassim smiled genially and called me Simpson, as though we were members of the same club: I had interviewed him so many times I almost felt we were. 'Now, at last,' he said, almost playfully, 'we will prove to you that Kuwait is the nineteenth province of Iraq.' I asked about the last-minute French attempt to stave off war by diplomatic means. 'There is an end to diplomatic initiatives. We are fully prepared for confrontation.' He smiled again. As we drove through the empty streets afterwards the air raid sirens began to wail. Baghdad was preparing to be bombed.

We made our last preparations that night. Brian Hulls and Colin Jones had pulled off a remarkable coup when they came into the country a few days before: they had managed to smuggle an entire satellite telephone, complete with its umbrella-like dish, past airport Customs. It had taken team-work and considerable coolness to do it. When we told the Information Ministry they at first refused to believe us. We finally convinced them and came to an agreement that we wouldn't use the phone until such time as all communications were destroyed by coalition air strikes. We had also brought in a generator for which the drivers had found fuel. Without the satellite telephone the entire BBC effort would have been sunk. With it we had serious bargaining power with the Iraqis – and with the other journalists in Baghdad.

The Iraqis badly wanted the television people to stay. In particular they wanted CNN to stay. Saddam Hussein's strategy was dependent on having American television in Baghdad who could see – and transmit – the terrible scenes he expected would take place. This was why he anticipated only two air strikes on the city: CNN would show the results to the American people, who would put such pressure on George Bush that the air war would be called off. CNN was already Saddam's favourite channel and it was a status symbol for Saddam's ministers to have it in their office. It was pumped into Saddam's bunker and into the safe houses he maintained around the city. It was his window on the world; which explained, someone said caustically, why his view of the world was so weird.

CNN was given a permanent, 24-hour line to the outside world (a 'four-wire', as it's called) on a military communications network which ran in hardened gulleys to the Jordanian border. If all else failed – and Saddam expected that it would – the Iraqi president would still be able to appeal to the American people over Bush's head. Whether CNN knew it or not, Iraqi officials planned to use the four-wire to make contact with their embassies abroad and, if necessary, with their intelligence organizations. If Saddam Hussein had launched a widespread campaign of terrorism as he had promised he would, the orders would have been passed along CNN's 'four-wire'. I would have liked the kind of security a four-wire gave, but our satellite phone raised none of the moral questions which arose from doing deals with the Iraqi government.

We felt pretty well-equipped for a siege. We had plenty of food: powdered soups, large quantities of bottled water, tins of sardines and corned beef, some tinned smoked oysters which I kept for emergencies, and an unopened bottle of expensive single malt whisky for even greater emergencies. There were two uneaten Christmas puddings which Bob Simpson suggested we might use to drop on the heads of the Republican Guard if they came for us. Everyone had a big battery-powered electric lamp, plus a smaller torch. I also had a torch the size of my little finger which I had used in Afghanistan when I went to the lavatory in the mine-infested snow.

A doctor friend of mine, enthusiastically entering into the spirit of the thing, had donated a large quantity of morphine tablets. 'That's in case any of the people you're with get their arms or legs blown off,' he said earnestly. 'Give them a dozen if you think they're too badly injured to survive. That'll sort them out. And of course,' he added, in the tone of one offering a drink to a barman, 'take some yourself if you're badly injured.' I looked at them now and hoped that I'd be able to tell the difference in the dark between them and all the other pills and potions around.

At 6 o'clock on the morning of 16 January I was listening to the BBC World Service. The newsreader told us that the House of Commons in London had voted overwhelmingly in support of British government's policy towards Iraq when the radio cut out in mid-bulletin. 'Christ!' I shouted. We had always assumed that when the coalition planes attacked Baghdad all communications would be blotted out electronically. I grabbed the various things I planned to keep with me when the bombing started: torches, batteries, a razor, a selection of underwear, the morphine pills, Waugh's *Put Out More Flags*, my notebook, a supply of BBC pens and the radio itself. It was then that I realized it had cut out because it needed new batteries. We had a few more hours to go yet.

In a school in the pleasant, middle-class suburb of Amiriyah it was time for class, but some of the girls were coming in late because of the mist. The television camera caught the flick of the minute hand as it came up to the hour and the bell rang for 8 o'clock. Eight time zones away, at UN headquarters in New York, the deadline had just run out. The girls seemed unaware of it. They sat in rows in their neat navy blue uniforms, repeating the English words their teacher had written on the blackboard. The dark faces frowned in concentration: 'I am happy, you are kind, he is sad, they are good.' The teacher's voice was sharp: 'They are GOOOOD.' 'They are GOOOOOOOD,' the girls repeated obediently. Frowns intensified with the effort, brown eyes glanced up to see if the television camera was still on them.

According to the interior minister four weeks earlier, the girls shouldn't have been there. At the time of the phoney evacuation drill in Saddam City he had told us that women and children would be sent out of Baghdad before the deadline. If the order had ever been a serious one, it had since been countermanded. The speaker of the Iraqi National Assembly gave a press conference on the morning of 16 January to explain. A pleasant-faced man, he smiled politely: The Iraqi people know that Almighty God is responsible for their life or death. They wish to stay where they are.' The women and children too? 'These children are the sons and daughters of the heroes at the war front. Since their fathers are preparing to be martyrs, they are prepared to be martyrs as well.' He smiled again, in a particularly annoying way. I felt that if a missile landed on the school where our colleagues had filmed, he would regard it as excellent propaganda.

Hassan, our driver, was talking about leaving and was distinctly nervous. It did nothing for his driving. Jim the Christian had already gone, reminding me about his large family. Ramadan had announced he would be leaving for the country on 15 January but for some reason was still around. So was Mr Hattam, but he wanted much larger amounts of money and he wanted it in advance. I couldn't really criticize him – though I did. I also mentioned, for at least the fifth time, how his habit of checking in with the minders had meant that ITN had beaten us months before.

As we drove through the empty streets with Ramadan, I asked him if by any chance the Wednesday races were still on. 'Of course,' he said. 'They like racing too much there.' He disapproved of gambling, though it can scarcely have been on religious grounds; as usual I could smell the whisky on him. Bob Simpson did his Ian Paisley impersonation: 'This man has been partaking of the Devil's buttermilk.' Ramadan giggled and straddled the lanes. Behind us an army truck hooted angrily.

It was a beautiful wintry afternoon and the temperature was in the low 60s. Streaks of pink cirrhus lay across the sky. The sun slanted across the racetrack which had been constructed along British lines in the 1940s. There was a splendid electronic scoreboard which registered the complexities of the betting system which, in a field of 10 runners, seemed able to encompass odds from 8 to 1 up to 1675 to 1. By the time we settled in at the Baghdad Horsemanship Ground the 4.10 race was about to start. We had been refused permission to film it: the Information Ministry presumably thought that racing on the brink of war would not give the proper feeling of national dedication. We stayed for the pure enjoyment of the charming, sad, amusing occasion. Even at the time it had an elegiac feeling to it. I often thought about the 4.10 race in the weeks that followed. Anthony Massey, who had a fine turn of phrase, compared it to watching a game of deck quoits on the *Titanic*.

Led by a magnificent, absurd figure in hunting pink on a surprisingly small mount, the jockeys paraded round the paddock in the afternoon sun, splendid in their scarlet, gold and green. The horses were sharp and spirited, with their ears curled in the Indian fashion. There were several thousand racegoers, almost as many as usual. They were rakish, totally non-political and, as they drank their cans of Iraqi beer, totally non-Islamic too. Many of them wore flat caps and tweed sports jackets over their dishdashas, as though they had suddenly been transported to the Curragh or Kempton Park and hadn't quite had time to change. I had been to the races here several times before. Like the teahouses and the life beside the Tigris and the small shops in Rashid Street, it represented the side of Iraq I had come to love.

The betting was heaviest on Sheherezade at 5 to 1 with Lulu next at 9 to 1. People lined up boisterously to place their bets. 'You are from London? What do you think of the situation?' He was a big, greasy bookmaker with a pleasant smile and a large wad of 25 dinar notes. I told him. He shook his head, waving the wad for added emphasis. 'There will be no war. Nobody wants it.' Everyone who had gathered round to listen seemed to agree. In that atmosphere, I almost agreed too: things were so relaxed, so normal, so pleasant. Only the large white tower of the Mukhabarat headquarters, looming over the racetrack, was a reminder of a less attractive world.

By now the horses were rounding the final bend and heading into the straight. The late afternoon sun shone through the dust their hooves threw up and they raced towards us in a golden penumbra, heads straining forward, the whites of their eyes flashing. Everyone in the stands jumped up as though an anthem were being played, waving their racecards and shouting. There was a drumming of hooves, a blur of colour in front of us and Sheherezade duly won. At the Baghdad Horsemanship Ground the favourite always seems to. I spotted the big greasy bookmaker: he was counting out a few notes to a small group of people. Things had gone well for him today.

'Two points,' said Mike Robinson over the phone from London that evening. He knew me and he knew Baghdad from his time as producer there over Christmas. I knew him too: he could scarcely keep out of his voice the feeling that he ought to be in Baghdad. 'At the risk of unsettling you, the State Department says that from midnight Baghdad will not be a safe place to be. Second point, everyone there should know that if they change their minds about staying, they must be free to leave.' I agreed and went and told them all what he had said. We worked hard that evening, getting everything ready. I moved down from the twelfth floor to the fifth to be near the office. I also tried to have a word with friends at BBC Television Centre – John Mahoney the foreign editor, Mark Damazer the editor of the 'Nine O'Clock News' and others – to show we were there of our own free will. I didn't want anyone blaming themselves afterwards.

Now we were starting to hear from the Americans and the French teams that their governments were saying the attack would start in the next few hours. If you're British, you learn not to expect that kind of warning. We still had our telephone line through to London, which we tried to keep going permanently and always restored if it went down: the team of marvellous ladies (and a few excellent men) at Broadcasting House with their cool, well-modulated BBC voices ensured that. Bob was using the line to describe the situation in a city where the bombs would soon be falling. He remained as calm as ever, but his conversations with his bosses in between the broadcasts were obviously getting him down. His feelings were the same as mine: it was our job to be there and he wasn't going to allow the most famous broadcasting service in the world to pull out.

In the end I thought I'd better face up to things and rang the head of the BBC News and Current Affairs. Tony Hall is a good friend and he said he didn't want to see people being killed simply because they thought the BBC was forcing them to stay. He felt, therefore, that it would simplify everything if he ordered us all to leave. I was probably much too heavy-handed in my response; I usually am. 'You'll have to get yourself a new foreign affairs editor then,' I said. A coarser man would have said that if I stayed he'd have to get himself a new one anyway. Instead, Tony endeavoured patiently to talk me down, as one might talk down some potential suicide on a windowledge. But it wasn't going to work and I was strengthened by the feeling that the other members of the team wanted to stay too. In the end we came to a civilized compromise: the order to leave stood, but no disciplinary action would be taken against those of us who chose to disobey. Since I was half-expecting to be turned into Joe Wilson's pound of ground-round, the notion of disciplinary action by the BBC did not bulk large.

I was absurdly pleased with myself as I went back into the room where the others were waiting. Bob Simpson, who could see what was coming, told me afterwards it was like watching someone walk into an open liftshaft by mistake. I accept that it had its farcical side. The others had received strict orders from their particular bosses in London to leave and they had already agreed between themselves that they would obey. I was the only person in the room who didn't realize that. I announced that I had negotiated a deal which would allow us to remain there. Even as I was speaking, I could tell something had changed, but I couldn't make out what it was.

They heard me out. Then as I paused for their reaction one of them explained to me, quite gently, that he was leaving anyway. Like the members of a jury giving their verdict, others said the same thing one by one as they sat round our communal table. I had no right to criticize them: they had their instructions and, like everyone else, they thought they would be killed if they stayed. Two of them were married and had children. I had told them time and again that if they did want to leave I wouldn't put any moral pressure on them to stay. Even so, it was as bad a moment as I can remember: I had lost a vote of no confidence. The only people who hadn't yet spoken were

287

Bob and Eamonn Matthews. I found it hard even to look at them.

Then I heard Bob say: 'Well, I'm staying.' He made the statement as naturally as someone refusing a second helping at the dinner table. That left Eamonn Matthews, who was sitting opposite him. He nodded vigorously. 'So am I,' he said and nodded again a couple of times for emphasis. A minute or so before that was no more than I would have expected them to say: Bob had been through some of the worst times in Beirut and Eamonn had spent weeks in Afghanistan among the mines, the rockets and the mad fundamentalists. It was just that I had become uncertain about everything.

Three were staying and four were leaving. The trouble was, we were losing our camera crew and our editor. A couple of reporters and a producer alone aren't much good for television. The Visnews producer-cameraman, Sean McGuire, had also been ordered out. Apart from CNN, which regarded us as hostile, the only other American network remaining was NBC. They were close allies of ours, but they worked with different and incompatible equipment and there would be no way of converting the material once the war started. Eamonn remembered that a British cameraman, Anthony Wood, had been going the rounds trying to find work. He had been employed by TV-AM, though when he decided to stay on in Baghdad his contract was terminated. He didn't have a camera, but we hired him all the same. There was another British cameraman, Nick Della Casa, who had stayed on when CBS pulled out. His camera, like the BBC's was on the American standard. It was a slightly ill-assorted team, but at least it was a team. I would have felt rather better if I had known that our competitors, ITN, were having similar difficulties.

There was a shout of anger from the next room: the phones had been cut. Things would soon be happening now. I swallowed a little in anticipation, remembering Saddam's words to one of his visitors: there would be two strikes on Baghdad, which would be so destructive that the United States would be forced to stop. Now we had no means of communication: if we used our satellite phone without permission we

288

might be accused of espionage. Only CNN's four-wire was still in operation and, even if we had accepted getting tangled up with the Iraqi government, CNN had told us in the fiercest terms that they weren't sharing it with anyone.

Eamonn assembled everyone. Nick Della Casa was a pleasant-faced, extremely relaxed man in his early thirties, with an amusing upper-class drawl which belied his Italian name. Once he had fought with the Rhodesian special forces, at the time when I had covered the guerrilla war there. We had some friends and experiences in common. If he was worried, he certainly didn't show it. 'Won't be long now,' he said, with a certain satisfaction in his voice. Anthony Wood was younger, more earnest, and anxious about the lack of a camera. Fortunately we had a spare, and he started fiddling about with it under instruction from Brian Hulls. We decided that when the attack started Eamonn and Anthony and I should get out into the streets and film from there. There were only two flak jackets between the three of us; the other two belonged to Brian Hulls and Colin Jones. A flak jacket isn't really much protection, I tried to tell myself; but I knew from experience how much confidence it can give.

At some point during the evening I had remembered what a senior western figure who was passing through Baghdad – I don't want to be more precise than that – had told me at least a week earlier. We were standing by the reception desk at the time and he seemed to want to pass information to someone. I was the only person in sight. '3 am on Thursday the seventeenth, that's when the bombing will start. You'll see.' I had even used it in one of my reports, though only as one man's suggestion. I looked at my watch: it was 2.20. 'We may only have another forty minutes,' I said. Eamonn answered: 'Let's get going.'

Under the Bombs

All this [western] technological superiority, which is on paper, will eventually be tested in the theatre of operations. We are not people who speak on the basis of books; we are people with experience of fighting. We know what fighting is about . . . They will play Rambo in the air.

Saddam Hussein's speech to the International Islamic Conference, Baghdad, 11 January 1990

The moment had almost arrived: the moment we had prepared ourselves for and worried about yet tried not to think about for several months. And however slowly it had seemed to approach in the past, it came on us now with the speed of a missile. By the time we had got everything together, plus whatever we might need if we were arrested and gaoled, it was 2.32 am on 17 January 1991. We ran across the marble hall of the hotel lobby, scattering the security men and the minders. 'But where are you going?' a voice behind us wailed. We were outside by that time. The night air was crisp and everything seemed very silent. 'There's a driver here somewhere,' said Anthony. He had had the foresight to hire him for the entire night. The trouble was, the driver was an undoubted spook, a distinctly unpleasant person (he was always boasting about the number of Iraqi officers serving in Kuwait whom he had cuckolded) and a thoroughgoing coward. I was still swearing about it when Eamonn cut in, 'We'll have to use him; there's no one else.' A look around the empty car park showed that was true.

We hadn't had time to work out where we wanted to go.

That was a serious problem. The driver, whimpering with anxiety, shot out of the hotel entrance into the dark silent street and took the turning marked '14 July Bridge'. 'No bridges!' I shouted. Bridges were some of the most likely targets in the city and if we crossed one we might never get back to the Al-Rasheed. We all yelled different instructions, and the driver swerved alarmingly round a bend in the road, tyres squealing. At that precise moment the guns opened up all round us.

The darkness and silence exploded into violent noise. The car seemed to shake with the reverberations; some of the guns were close to us and the red and white tracer went shooting up in an almost liquid rush, like water from a hosepipe. The racket was tremendous and we had to shout. I looked at my watch again: 2.37. The war had started 23 minutes earlier than we had expected. Those minutes would have made all the difference. Anthony wrestled in the front seat with the camera, shoving its lens at an absurd angle into the sky. 'I'm getting this,' he grunted. It seemed to me that bombs were dropping by now, though it took us some days to work out the difference between the various types of explosion.

I could see our driver's face in the mirror lit by the red tracer; it gleamed with sweat. He was a badly frightened man and not entirely answerable for his actions. Another burst of cosmic fireworks, white this time, went off beside us. Eamonn and I shouted directions at the driver to which he seemed to respond at first. Not for long. 'Where's he going?' The car screamed round in a vast semicircle as the sirens started their belated, unearthly wailing. 'The bloody idiot – he's heading straight back to the hotel.' It was useless offering him money: his nerve had gone completely. He drove in fast through the gates and stopped, almost fainting in his seat. We had failed ignominiously to escape the control of the authorities and were back with everyone else in the one place I had wanted to get away from. I stood there and cursed myself and the unlucky timing which had caught us out, while the fireworks continued overhead. They were quite remarkable. Now, too, I could hear the full noise of the heavy machine guns: a stunning, appalling racket.

In the darkness of the lobby angry hands grabbed us and pushed us down the narrow staircase into the shelter. Immediately we were separated by the crowd. The smell of frightened people in a confined space was already starting to take over. Anthony held the camera over his head to get past the sobbing women who ran against us in the corridor. Children wept. Then the lights went out and there was more screaming until the emergency power took over. As an intense sufferer from claustrophobia, this business of being 50 feet below ground with 14 storeys of hotel over my head and the heat and press of bodies was stretching my endurance considerably. I tried to slow everything down, to keep calm, to establish control over the smaller things and extend it to the larger ones. In a way it helped that other people were panicking, because it showed me what might happen if I failed.

I was surprised, given the effort we had put into escaping from the hotel, to find so many journalists in the shelter. More surprising still was to see the cameraman whose skills and courage I had been so worried about and who had always been ahead of me in the swimming pool. He was standing in the entrance to one of the main shelter rooms, his camera pointing at nothing, watching the waves of frightened people with empty red eyes. I should have been sympathetic; as it was, I was relieved to see that ITN no longer had the advantage over us that I had expected. I found Anthony. He had neither cracked nor suffered a claustrophobia attack nor worried about anything except his makeshift equipment. 'I just can't be sure till I see the pictures,' he was saying. Outside the shelter the greatest military onslaught since World War II was going on and Anthony Wood was anxious that the electronics of his borrowed camera were different from those he was used to.

For the time being there was no getting out of the shelter. Guards armed with Kalashnikov rifles stood at the exits with orders to prevent anyone leaving, under whatever pretext. They seemed to think we wanted to go and signal to the incoming aircraft. By now the main shelter was almost too full to sit or lie full length in. Some people seemed cheerful enough and clapped and sang or watched Iraqi television which, somehow, was still broadcasting. In the general panic, normal patterns of behaviour were set aside. A woman in her thirties arrived from an upstairs floor wearing only a coat and a bath towel. In full view of everyone she took them off and put on the clothes she had brought down in a bag. No one seemed to pay the slightest attention. The heavy steel doors with their rubber linings and the great wheels which opened and closed them, stayed open. Even so I felt pretty bad. From time to time the structure of the hotel seemed to sway and shiver, as though bombs were falling around us. If they were, I wanted to be outside filming them, not a prisoner down here.

Anthony and I got through the submarine door and began to work our way up the staircase which led to the outside world. A guard tried to stop us but I waited until the next latecomer arrived and simply fought my way out, pulling at the door and pushing the guard aside. Anthony followed and we ran up the stairs before anyone could organize things to stop us. The windowless corridors on the upper floors were in total darkness. We laboured along the fifth floor, trying to work out by feel which was our office. Listening at one door which was not properly closed, I heard the murmur of voices. We were let in. Brian Hulls and the others were properly set up, filming the extraordinary show outside. They had no nightsight for the camera, a serious handicap for the BBC throughout the war.

Even so, the pictures were remarkable. Vast flashes lit up entire sectors of the horizon. The noise of the bombs landing thundered and rippled towards us as each new wave of aircraft, each new flight of missiles, came over. We were starting to get used to the noise and the sudden white and red light that erupted close to us. I recorded a piece to camera with Sean McGuire, waiting for a new attack to begin so there would be plenty of noises off while I spoke. We were both nervous that the appallingly bright camera light which shone on me as I knelt in front of the window would attract the attention of the security police or even a bullet. It was a relief when we were able to switch it off. Afterwards we went on whispering to one another.

Outside in the corridor there was a flash from a torch and the sound of my name being called. A security man had followed me up from the shelter. In order to shield the others from arrest I walked down towards him in the yellow beam from his torch. I had no idea what I was going to do; hit him, perhaps. Then I saw a partly open door to my left and slipped inside while he shouted at me. I couldn't believe my luck. The violent red and white flashes from outside showed that it wasn't a single room but an entire large suite which two of our colleagues had been using as an office. I worked my way round the furniture and ended up in a small bedroom. I locked the door and lay on the floor silently. The handle turned slowly. I gripped my lantern torch, ready to rear up and smash it over his head if he came in. The security man knew I was inside and started beating on the door and calling: 'Mr John! Mr John! Please!'

It is hard to hit someone who calls you by your first name and says please. My grip on the torch relaxed. But these doors were anyway built to withstand missile attacks and they were too much for a security man. He muttered in Arabic and wandered away. Close by, a 2000-pound penetration bomb landed, but contrary to everything I had heard my eyeballs did not explode and my fillings did not come out. I found a radio by the bedside and switched it on. President Bush was explaining to me what was going on. From where he was it sounded very rational and well-arranged. Here, underneath the planes and missiles, it was very disorienting. It was 5.45 and I fell asleep.

At 9 o'clock there was more banging on the door and an English voice calling my name. It was Eamonn, who had tracked me down to tell me he had got our satellite telephone to work, with the assistance of Colin Jones. To do it he had first got the generator up and running. I felt deeply embarrassed at my sloth, but I would have been little use at either operation. Eamonn and I had worked together in Afghanistan and his practical skills – and my lack of them – had been in great evidence there. He had begun his career as a nuclear physicist and had a formidable intellect. Throughout his wanderings in Afghanistan he had carried some densely-written work on philosophy. Eamonn had great charm and great toughness, in roughly equal amounts; I suspected that when the two clashed, the toughness would come out on top. If so, he managed to conceal it now. He even smiled. In a city that had taken greater punishment than anything since Hiroshima and Nagasaki, which was without electricity and without communications, we now had power and the means to speak to the outside world.

Eamonn moved the delicate white parasol of the dish around until it locked onto the satellite. Then he dialled the code and the number of the BBC. There, as always, was one of the pleasantest and best of the traffic managers, a Canadian called Jim. We exchanged pleasantries, just as though I was somewhere sensible and not on some stone steps sheltering beside a brick wall with a hedge along it, on a lawn with a spreading pool of sewage and puffs of smoke in the air from the latest ground-to-air missiles. I gave a brief account to the interviewer at the other end about the damage caused during the night, as best I could work it out: the telecommunications tower damaged, power stations destroyed. I had less idea what had been happening on the streets and felt bad about that. Some people, including Brent Sadler, the ITN correspondent, had already been out and seen what had happened. We had never been particularly friendly – his style of reporting is not mine – but we were brought together by the shared misfortune of losing the services of a camera crew.

I got hold of Anthony Wood and found a driver. Ali was an elderly crook, but over the months I had developed a kind of affection for him, mixed with contempt for his cowardice and annoyance at the way he had bilked me. 'Not good take picture now, Mr John,' said Ali, looking nervously at the camera. He was right, no doubt, but that was the job. I explained this curtly. 'Allah,' he said, putting a great deal of feeling into the word. We drove down to Rashid Street. It was quite extraordinary. The city was being stripped of its ability to function and yet it seemed undamaged. Apart from some broken glass outside the Trade Ministry, nothing much seemed to have happened. Those immense rumblings as the bombs and missiles struck, the flashes which lit up the horizon, the fires that were started: all of them seemed to be so precise in their aim that nothing around them was touched.

I found it hard to understand. The streets were almost

empty, except for soldiers trying to hitch a lift. Their faces were as strained and vacant as that of the cameraman in the shelter the night before. There seemed to be no talking now, not even in the groups that had gathered. People stood close to one another in silence. A woman dragged her child along by the arm, the child crying and knuckling its eyes; the woman's face was grimy and streaked with sweat, and her clothes were muddy. A few old men squatted with a pile of oranges or a few packs of cigarettes in front of them. An occasional food shop or teahouse was open; that was all. Anthony was filming it all as we drove.

'Allah,' said Ali with more feeling than ever. A white car was following us. 'He see you take picture,' said Ali. This could mean serious trouble: we had been warned about being caught without a minder in the streets, but of course no minder would have gone with us. I told Ali to swerve round to the right, but his nerve failed. He drifted to a halt by the roadside, paralyzed with fear. The security policeman got out of his car. I got out of ours. I made him shake hands and tried the kind of breeziness which sometimes works in Iraq. 'Just looking round,' I said, smiling away. 'I'm sure you don't mind.' He minded. 'He say you come with him,' said Ali, his voice trembling. I felt really bad for him and guilty at having involved him in our plan. 'Maybe,' said Anthony, his face taking on a particularly tough cast. He meant we wouldn't be going with the security man at all and I agreed.

We got back into our car and followed the security man over the bridge. We could see the Al-Rasheed now, beside the main road that lay directly ahead of us. It represented the only security there was. The sirens were wailing again and, as I watched, the Defence Ministry building beside the Tigris went up in a great column of brown and grey smoke. At the first turning after the bridge the white car signalled right and turned off the main road. 'Go straight on, Ali. Don't turn. Go there.' I pointed and hissed the words at him. His old face twitched, but he knew I was right. With a squeal of tyres the car lurched forward, leaving the security man turning in the side road, trying to get back on terms with us. Ali put his foot down for the first time in years and made it to the hotel, lurching up to the front door and then heading out again. The security policeman was only 30 seconds behind us, but he obediently searched for a place in the public car park. We ran into the hotel and lost ourselves in the crowd which filled the lobby.

In a windowless side office, where our minders sat for safety, I saw a face I knew: Jana Schneider, an American war photographer, completely fearless. She told me later she had been ringing her mother in Minnesota from the American embassy and had been walking back to the Al-Rasheed when the sirens went. Near the Sheraton she had photographed a 'smart' bomb taking out a Security Ministry building while the houses on either side of it were unharmed. As she told me about it now, I found it tied in with my own observations. As the day wore on Baghdad seemed to me to be suffering from a form of arteriosclerosis: it appeared unchanged and yet its vital functions were atrophying with each new air raid. I asked Jana what she was doing in the office. 'Oh, just arrested I guess,' she said. She had been kept in a police cell for most of the night and had managed to get the police to bring her to the Al-Rasheed by pure force of character. At that point the security man arrived in the office. I seemed to be under arrest too.

In the confusion I managed to get out into the garden where Eamonn was waiting. A little communications village had been established and four different satellite phone dishes had sprung up like parasols in a park: other people had been smuggling equipment in. ITN had set up theirs at the top of the steps; CNN had one a little away from everyone else; the French had established themselves on the grass itself. The phones were the subject of a great deal of competition and the Iraqis, with the approach to private property which had characterized their annexation of Kuwait, blandly ordered us to make ours available to everyone, regardless of our own requirements. The only organization which was allowed to keep its equipment to itself was CNN. So Eamonn became a telephone operator and I became his assistant. We spent a great deal of time organizing the small but anxious groups of people who needed to file their reports. If at any stage he felt nervous at standing out in the open he never showed it.

297

Eamonn was a man with remarkable self-control and he is not the kind of producer to tell his correspondents soothing untruths. 'He's a crap reporter,' Eamonn said now of one of our competitors, whose reporting he had been able to over-hear, 'but he's putting himself into it, and he's giving people a feeling of what it's like to be under the bombs as they come down. I don't think you're doing enough of that.' Having been brought up in the BBC tradition of keeping oneself out of one's reporting, I found it did not come easily to me; nor did I like it very much. But I was competitive enough not to want to be defeated by someone else: I started putting into my scripts the kind of thing I was jotting down in my notebook. The BBC tradition was being fully upheld, all the same. One British newspaper wrote a few days later of my namesake:

> Bob Simpson . . . filed some superbly calm reports, conspicu-ously more rounded and descriptive than the 'Holy Cow!' offerings of CNN.

Upstairs, meanwhile, the four who were leaving were getting their gear together. The night of bombing we had endured as a team turned out later to be the heaviest of the war, but since the damage was so concentrated we had felt reasonably safe. Nevertheless they still felt they should obey the orders they had received and I didn't want to plead with them to stay. I was talking to Anthony Massey who was looking out of the window which we had taped up heavily against blast: one of those pointless exercises, serving as a kind of therapy. His manner was normally calm and ironic and he used slightly old-fashioned speech forms. Now he said 'Good Lord!' in a manner that wasn't so calm or ironic. He had just seen a cruise missile go past the hotel, following the line of the main road and travelling from southwest to northeast. Later I saw one myself: we seemed to be on their route into town. I headed downstairs and got onto the phone to the interviewer, David Dimbleby, in London:

> I can hear quite loud sounds of gunfire or landings of rockets or missiles, I'm not sure quite what it is at the moment. The aircraft seem to be so high, and the missiles make remarkably

little noise. An extraordinary thing happened, I suppose about an hour ago now. We were looking out of the window of our fifth floor room in the hotel, and a missile of some kind, a Tomahawk – I don't know, I'm not very good at these things – passed by on the line of the road on which the hotel stands, at about the level of our windows . . . Where it hit, what it hit, what it was aimed for, I don't know. There was no great noise about it.

This is the first time anyone's seen a war like this. It wasn't what we expected, to be honest. I've covered quite a lot of wars in my time, but I thought this one was going to be horrendous – or at least I thought it was going to be last night. It turned out not to be so horrendous, and it's the accuracy of the missiles and the bombs which makes it less threatening than one thought. I've not spoken to very many Iraqis apart from taxi drivers and secret policemen this morning. But I think everyone is a little surprised because they assumed that the place would be flattened. And of course it hasn't been.

The Tomahawk (my amateurish guess turned out to be right) was a strange weapon, 18 feet long, shunting along the road at 500 mph, which is relatively slow: slow enough, certainly for an onlooker to be able to register everything about it: its blackness, its bluntness, its lack of markings, its rudimentary stubby wings, the absence of a fiery trail, a determined yet somehow not sinister appearance. It looked like some large but not necessarily dangerous sea-animal, ungainly but effective in its element: a walrus, perhaps, or a dugong. The appearance was seriously misleading: each missile carried half a ton of high explosive which could be delivered with extraordinary precision. But we felt, as we watched these things go by – one actually turned left at the traffic lights – that they were well enough directed for us to be moderately safe.

The accuracy of the attack was something of a relief. Situated between the Foreign Ministry, the Defence Ministry, the Baath Party headquarters and the airport used by top government people, overlooking every one of these natural targets, our hotel had seemed distinctly vulnerable. That was because we hadn't fully appreciated that missiles could go round buildings instead of slamming into them. On that first full day of the war we were reassured. The feeling did not last long.

By the afternoon of 17 January the hotel was even emptier. A big convoy had headed for the border, carrying everyone who wanted to go. Anthony Massey and the others took with them our first edited report on the war and managed to smuggle it past the customs point at the border where ITN's material was confiscated. That left about 33 of us, as far as I could tell. The British were in a majority, which reflected a greater determination to report on this side of the war than the Americans, Germans and Japanese showed. There were Patrick Cockburn of the *Independent* and Richard Beeston of *The Times*, as well as the BBC and ITN. That made 11. The French had, as far as I could make out, eight, though the old Anglo-French animosity, which I never personally feel, kept them apart from us and made it hard for me to count them. There were two Palestinians with Jordanian nationality, both of them women. There was NBC, with its New Zealander correspondent and its Turkish/Jordanian crew. There were CNN's three Americans (though one was a New Zealander by birth). There were three Italians from RAI. There were two Americans, Marie Colvin of the *Sunday Times* in London and Jana Schneider the photographer. There was an Australian newspaper man and there was Alfonso Rojo from the Spanish newspaper *El Mundo*. The various groups didn't always like each other and we competed stubbornly for what few facilities there were. Jana Schneider later sued the French photographer Fifi Demulder for something that took place. But it was an honourable company to be in and if it seems strange that I am not more certain about who was there and how many there were of us, it is because of the darkness and the confusion.

The hotel ceased to function. There was no power so there were no lifts, no lights, no heating and no water. By five in the afternoon we were lighting candles. It was necessary to keep all the things you wanted beside you, because they disappeared in the darkness. The most honest people seemed to regard torches as common property and would pick them up. Lack of sleep and an undoubted nervousness began to take their toll. Bob Simpson remained more buoyant than most and I knew why.

300

That morning, as we were looking out at the skyline and working out what had disappeared from it, he confided cheerfully to me: 'There's nothing like a good jump when the rockets go up.' Even before the war began he had been having an affair with someone in the hotel and the bombs and anti-aircraft fire of the night before seemed only to have enhanced matters.

That first afternoon, as yet another raid began, I was wandering around the hotel trying to find some equipment we needed. The air raid sirens started to go and, almost simultaneously, the first explosions came. We were already learning that the best time to get the satellite phone going was during the air raids because the minders and security men always headed straight for the shelters. It was the one time we were able to talk without being listened to or interrupted. Directly I heard the noise outside I ran down the dark corridor.

I wasn't worried about the darkness because at the midway point of the corridor, where it opened out by the lifts, there was always a light on beside the emergency stairs. This time, though, someone had closed the door and the light was invisible. I cannoned at full tilt into the heavy mahogany desk, like a pulpit, where the security staff sometimes stationed themselves. I took the corner in the lower ribs.

Half an hour or so later we were through to London with another air raid just beginning overhead. I heard someone in the gallery in London saying: 'We've just begun a 14-minute film on political reaction in Britain, so you'll have to wait, I'm afraid.' She'd gone before I could tell her what was happening. I listened to untold numbers of British politicians giving the viewers the wisdom of their opinions. In my jaundiced state, chest smarting, surface-to-air missiles shooting up and bombs falling quite close by, all their reactions seemed incredibly ignorant and foolish. It was as much as I could do, when the last opinion had died away, not to say so. The air raid had died away too by this time: there was nothing left in the sky but a few curls of vapour and the minders were emerging from their shelters to find us using the equipment, contrary to all instructions.

David Dimbleby, at the other end, asked me if there had

been any casualties from the day's attacks. Irritably, I said that I had cracked a couple of ribs and was the only casualty I knew of. This was apparently taken in London to be a coded message meaning that I had been beaten up. I was deeply embarrassed. Having long disliked the journalist-as-hero school of reporting, I found myself a minor celebrity for something which hadn't taken place. An entire country's economic and military power was being dismantled, its people were dying, and I was broadcasting about a couple of cracked ribs. Each time they hurt I felt it was a punishment for breaking the basic rule: don't make yourself a part of the story.

We were starting to get the hang of phoning in our reports. Apart from during air raids, the best time was when the minders and the security men were preoccupied in some way. Some of the minders were reluctant to stop us or censor us anyway. One sat beside me as I listed in some detail the buildings that had been hit. He looked up at the sky the whole time, as though to let me know he had not the slightest intention of interrupting me. The security people were more aggressive. Once, while pretending to be testing the phone and aligning it, I was talking to the live programme in London. I finished one answer and saw the large form of a security man coming towards me. He spoke no English: I had already established that. I tried to give him the impression I was fiddling about with the buttons on the telephone, while I continued talking to the programme. It was successful for a minute or two. Then he got suspicious. 'Can you help?' I asked him and he cut the line.

In the darkened hotel coffee shop, its tables bare, a neat but exhausted figure was reading from a thick sheaf of papers. Naji al-Hadithi, the Information Ministry director general, was wearing his Baath Party uniform. It gave him an unwontedly military air. Some people had always found him sinister. A *New York Times* reporter took shelter in the American embassy for four days after speaking to him. I thought he was splendid company. He was a considerable Anglophile and had a good sense of humour. When Mike Robinson and I went to see him just before Christmas he asked us where we'd been. 'We went to the ruins of Babylon,' I said, 'to see what the rest of the country will look like in a fortnight's time.' Oh God, I thought, I've gone too far. But al-Hadithi was rocking in his chair with silent laughter.

Now he looked close to exhaustion. He read out some communiqués and a long, scarcely-coherent letter from Saddam Hussein to President Bush. Afterwards, with the candlelight glinting on his glasses, his rings and on the buttons of his jacket, we argued about the new rules of censorship which were being imposed on us. Everything was going to be much more difficult from now on but I had taken a decision. Under most circumstances you usually hold some things back because they might offend your host country and make it difficult for you to return. This time, I thought, I'm going for broke, and I remembered the ancient journalistic adage: if you see it, say it.

That evening Brent Sadler, the ITN correspondent, rang me. CNN had told him they'd been warned by their office in Atlanta that our hotel was on the list of targets for the night. I thanked him and told the others. We discussed it fitfully among ourselves for a while, without coming to any conclusion. Bob Simpson, as calm as ever, said: 'I'm not going into that rathole in the basement. If we get bombed, I'd rather be up here in bed. At least I'd die comfortable.' I wanted to get pictures of the hotel being hit and suggested that we should do what we had tried unsuccessfully to do the night before and get outside. Our pictures of the bombing had a depressing sameness anyway, since they were all shot from the hotel windows.

I cleared out my safety deposit box, since I didn't want the large amount of dollars I had to be torched or looted, and gathered the necessities of my new life: identification in the event of arrest, money for bribes, a hairbrush in case I had to appear on television, a notebook and a pen. No razor: since there was no water in Baghdad, shaving was impossible. But we were unlucky again. That night the sirens wailed early and the automatic doors of the hotel jammed shut as we ran across the lobby towards them. We were trapped in a building that had been declared a target. Once again we were forced down into the shelter. Anthony and I debated whom we should tell about the possibility we might be hit. In the end we decided to tell the general manager and no one else. 'I know,' he said, 'one of your colleagues already told me. There's absolutely nothing I can do about it.' He was Indian – an amiable, easy-going man, as laid back as Bob Simpson – and he was right: there was nothing whatever to be done except go to sleep.

The shelters were more unpleasant than ever: fuller, smellier, noisier, more claustrophobic. Almost all the journalists were there, with the exception of Bob and Eamonn. So was the rest of the strange cast of characters who filled our world: Sadoun Jenabi, al-Hadithi's deputy, a large, easygoing man who had spent years in Britain and was an ardent lover of Scotland and the better things of life; an English peace campaigner, Edward Poore, who was a genuine eccentric, carried a cricket bat everywhere, wore a Romanian flag round his neck to remind himself of the time he spent there during the revolution, (he had occupied one of our rooms at my invitation until some of our people who had since left complained about the arrangement); most of our minders and security men; a large number of the hotel staff and their families. At some point in the night Anthony made his way upstairs by feigning an epileptic fit and then, when that failed, simply waiting for one of the guards to fall asleep, rifle on knee. I lay down on the dank carpeting on the floor and covered myself with one of the two flak jackets which were all we now had left: in spite of the large number of people there, the shelter was chilly. As I went to sleep it occurred to me, finally, to wonder why the Americans would want to bomb an hotel.

Outside something moved in the darkness: a shadow, succeeded by another and then by a whole group of shadows. Anthony and Jana, watching from the fifth floor, could just make out a man in a black balaclava and black fatigues directing others, similarly dressed, to positions around the shabby yard which lay behind the hotel. Occasional bursts of tracer and the flickering light from a big fire on the outskirts of the city made it possible to see what happened next. A truck with a highly sophisticated missile system mounted on it was backed into the yard, followed by a second. Soon the missiles were up and ready.

Moving their heads around constantly like Medusa's snakes, the missiles picked up the faintest radar signals from the sky, prepared to strike at any aircraft or object which might threaten the place they were guarding. But what *was* the place they were guarding? I had seen it a thousand times: it was just a deserted scrapyard at the back of the hotel. There seemed to be nothing there. Yet surely only something very important indeed would warrant the stationing of missiles of this sophistication under conditions of such secrecy. The black figures and their missiles remained on duty for more than seven hours. Then, half an hour before a sullen dawn broke on the horizon across the Tigris, the black figures and their missiles withdrew. The yard below was as empty and broken down as ever, edged by its wooden huts, their windows smashed. The sirens began to sound the all clear.

Some of the people I had spoken to in the last weeks after they had met Saddam Hussein had seen him in his command centre: the Bunker, as everyone called it. I had built up a fairly clear picture of it: 100 feet deep, as big as a small village, comfortable, lit by its own electricity and with its own water supply. There were about three dozen Soviet military advisers there, all in uniform. Saddam Hussein apparently liked to have them looking after him, because he felt he could trust them implicitly. They were all on special long-term contracts from the Soviet armed forces and came under his personal orders. They ran the Bunker and stayed there throughout the war. Nobody was able to tell me precisely where the Bunker was, nor the route they took to get in. In each case a special car would be sent for the guests. Its windows would be covered with curtains. Couldn't you, I asked one man, just pull the curtains aside? 'They would want to know why I should do a thing like that,' he said. The location of the entrances to the Bunker was a major secret.

Nevertheless it was possible to work out where at least one of them must be. At a special Islamic conference immediately before the UN deadline some television crews were waiting outside the conference centre immediately opposite our hotel in order to film Saddam Hussein arriving. He arrived, spoke to the conference and left without their seeing him. Since the building is free-standing, he could have got there only by some underground passage. The likelihood was that the Bunker lay in the area bounded by the airport (which had a special underground section, later bombed by the coalition forces), the Foreign Ministry, the Islamic Conference Centre and the Al-Rasheed Hotel itself. Since the Bunker was a good 50 feet deeper than the hotel shelter, it is possible that it lay beneath it.

What is certain is that since the Bunker was built by firms from Britain, Sweden, Finland, Germany, the United States and Japan, every detail of its construction was known to the Americans and the British. The decision not to bomb it may have been taken in order to spare our lives in the hotel. More probably Egypt, Syria and the other Arab countries in the coalition were opposed to the notion of targeting Saddam, just as they were later against the idea of capturing Baghdad.

Anthony had had a good night. Apart from spotting the missiles guarding the Bunker he had filmed the first pictures of a cruise fired in anger. It was heading along the road as usual, and its exhaust was a dot of brilliance in the darkness. The missile strikes which we had felt as faint quiverings in the shelter were spectacular explosions from the fifth floor. The hotel might not have been hit, but it was in the centre of the action. When I made my way upstairs at 7 o'clock the next morning, 18 January, I promised myself I would never be caught in the shelter again, no matter what I had to do to escape.

The first news I heard on emerging was that Iraq had fired Scud missiles at Israel. We looked at each other nervously. If Israel replied, its weapons would be a great deal cruder and the Israelis wouldn't care whether they hit the Al-Rasheed or not. For all we knew, they might respond with nuclear weapons. 'President Bush has praised Israel for its self-restraint,' intoned the BBC World Service in the corner of the room. 'Long may it last,' someone said.

It did. The Americans sent several batteries of Patriots, anti-aircraft missiles which had been converted for use against Scuds. Together with promises of financial help and – no doubt – the sense that the Americans would owe them something once the war was over and negotiations about the

Occupied Territories began, this was enough for the Israelis to promise not to retaliate against Iraq. They probably had no serious intention of doing so anyway. General Schwartzkopf said at one of his press conferences that the chances of being killed by a Scud missile in Israel were about as great as being hit by lightning in a Georgia storm. In the first six Scud attacks over an 11 day period, four Israelis died, two of heart attacks. An Israeli statistician pointed out that a better comparison would have been with the American murder rate. The chances of being killed by a Scud were 28 per million in a year; those of being murdered in the United States are 95 per million in a year.

Nevertheless Iraq scored an important political success with its Scud attacks on Israel and Arabs right across the Middle East admired the boldness of the strategy. Israel would not seem quite so invulnerable again. Few Arabs believed the low death figures. Few Israelis, by contrast, would forget the television pictures of Arabs on the West Bank standing on their rooftops and cheering the Scuds as they came over.

That afternoon there was a sudden call to go to the Information Ministry to see Latif Jassim. By the time he turned up it was almost too dark to film. We stood him under a single bulb in the main lobby: the only light which seemed to be working in the entire ministry. Al-Hadithi looked more exhausted than ever, but Jassim was chipper enough and claimed a victory because Iraq hadn't been defeated in the first two days. He spoke of having captured British and American pilots and, for once, it didn't just sound like a propaganda claim. He ended by thanking us for staying on in Baghdad in spite of the pressure from our governments and organizations. He was a fairly unpleasant character in his way, but he had been helpful enough to me. After the war, searching for a scapegoat for Iraq's collapse, Saddam Hussein selected his close personal friend Jassim. The idea was that the newspapers and television which he controlled had failed to inspire people sufficiently with the will to fight. He was shunted off to a nonexistent job as head of the international department of the Baath Party and a new minister was put in his place. Naji al-Hadithi, however, was promoted.

Eamonn was having trouble locking the dish onto the satellite when we got back. The reason seemed to be the jamming waves put out by the American AWACS aircraft which were protecting an attack on Baghdad by B-52 bombers. The security people and the minders started to panic, shouting at us to get inside fast while Eamonn and I preferred to make our calls during raids. We heard the familiar sounds: the distant batteries opening up against the planes. Then the rippling sound as each new anti-aircraft battery loosed off, coming nearer and nearer. Then the huge, disorienting sound of surface-to-air missiles going up, joining the red and white tracer which arched its way lazily across the sky. In the growing dusk I looked out for the handiwork of the man we called the Triple-A artist. He liked to weave patterns in the sky with his tracer, so that the lines of red dots rose sinuously upwards, crossing previous bursts as they faded away.

The bombing started with a rumble that shook the ground and agitated the stagnant pool of sewage that had formed 20 yards from our phone dish. The magnificent red beard of an Irish-Australian reporter appeared at an upstairs window: 'The power station! The power station's gone up!' There was a rush to see it and film it. Annoyed by the nervousness of the minders, I stayed by the phone to finish writing my script. 'Keep calm,' I called out to a security man, 'it's perfectly safe.' There was a thick whistling sound in front of my face and a heavy machine gun bullet flattened itself on the step in front of me. 'You see? You see? And you say it's safe?' I made a grab for the bullet, but missed. The security man wanted it as a souvenir.

Most of us refused to enter into any gentleman's agreements not to broadcast. 'You are prevaricating again, Mr John,' said Sadoun Jenabi. 'I know you. You are refusing to give me any undertakings.' His face was covered by three days' growth of beard and his eyes were bloodshot. 'It's my duty to broadcast, that's all. I'm not going to promise not to broadcast.' He walked away, still eyeing me redly.

That night Anthony Wood camped out in the hotel grounds with a camera. I eluded the security men and found him lurking near the swimming pool. I gave him my silver hipflask filled with Laphroaig whisky and helped him to settle on a bench from which he could film the night's attacks. As I walked away I could still see the faint glimmer from his torch. The sirens had already sounded and the night's raids were beginning. The hits were still a long way off, like sheet lightning on the horizon, flaring up and fading suddenly across great areas of the night sky. Then the SAMs went up with a yellow roar. The fighting came closer and the bombs started falling. They were close but I was too tired to worry. I laboured up to the fifth floor, ribs aching, took off my dirty clothes for the first time since the war began, arranged the necessary equipment in case my room was hit (painkillers, field dressings, torch) and read a little Evelyn Waugh by candlelight. The crump of a missile landing nearby made the flame flicker. I blew it out and went to sleep.

On 19 January I sacrificed two bottles of drinking water and washed. I changed my linen, but put my tracksuit on again. A very poor tennis player, I am nevertheless a member of Queen's Club and the tracksuit top bore a splendid crown on it. I wore it to irritate the Iraqis. Nevertheless I irritated the cameraman a great deal more by insisting on taking it off and putting it on back to front, so that the crown wouldn't show. I felt it would detract from the necessary objectivity a journalist should display. It was only later, when I was back in London, that I saw western television reporters appearing on screen in full battledress.

Sadoun Jenabi bustled across the lobby looking important. 'It has been decided that you should gather up your equipment and leave it in your rooms. Everyone will go to Amman for a few days, I will come with you to make sure you get visas to return.' 'We're being thrown out,' I said. 'Mr John, you always put the worst construction on everything.' 'Well, aren't we?' 'I swear on my mother, no.' But he agreed to let me pass a message to London – to alert the offices of everyone with correspondents in Baghdad. I said to Eamonn: 'I think we should tell this to Nicholas Witchell.' 'Make sure you tell him everything,' Eamonn replied. Witchell is the presenter of the BBC's 'Breakfast News'. He grasped the situation at once. 'Are you free to speak openly?' he asked. 'Absolutely not,' I said and winked at the minder who was sitting beside me. I went into the full details of the expulsion. Eventually the minder thought this was a curious personal message and told me to stop, but we'd got the news across.

We decided not to cooperate. I went to see the hotel doctor about my ribs and offered him $1000 if he would give me a note to say I couldn't travel. A sleek, grey-haired, feline character, he said: 'Why not?' I should have guessed. He wrote out on a sheet of headed paper:

TO WHOME IT MAY CONCERN. MR SIMPSON HAS TWO/THREE CRACKED RIB AND MUSLE SPASME. HE CAN NOT DRIVE IN CAR FROM IRAQ.

Underneath he wrote something in Arabic. Fearing a trick, I asked Ali, the driver, to translate. 'He say: "No problem. He can go."' 'Thanks a lot,' I said.

We did a little desultory packing, but as we were stowing the gear away there was a powerful series of explosions nearby. Anthony got his camera and started filming. Three cruise missiles were heading straight for the hotel and the anti-aircraft guns on the buildings round about were firing at them. Some of the fire was hitting the hotel. At the last moment the missiles turned along the front of the hotel, veered left around the shorter end of the block, then left again along the back. Two hit the conference centre opposite: one of the entrances to the Bunker. The third was hit by anti-aircraft fire and headed away out of control. I had started to record a piece to camera, shouting over the gunfire and the explosions. The biggest explosion of all came as I finished. I noticed the look on Bob Simpson's face: 'It went right behind you while you were talking. It was a cruise.' For once even his coolness had deserted him.

The missile that had been hit crashed into the hotel's staff quarters. Fortunately when the siren went they had all headed for the shelter. Because it was a 'smart' weapon, the warhead didn't explode: its computer told it that it wasn't in the right place. If it had, people in the hotel might have been hurt. Nevertheless it caused enough damage merely by crashing.

Foolishly I forgot to tell Anthony to take the tape out of the camera and put in a new one. We were arrested as we were filming the fire which the missile had started and, after a fight in which they outnumbered us, the security people got the tape with the cruise going past the window during my report to camera. Later one of the security men apologized to me for the violence that was used and handed me a small, stainless steel cogged wheel from the missile. I would have preferred the tape.

A big petrochemical plant was on fire on the horizon and we found a small window to film it from. Jana Schneider climbed out of the fifth floor window onto a concrete ledge three inches wide and five feet away from the window ledge. She was in full view of the anti-aircraft position as she took her photographs. 'Got it,' she said, and clambered back in.

Our efforts to stall were running out. Most of the journalists had already left. It was clear that CNN was to be allowed to stay, though the CNN people themselves and the Information Ministry officials all hotly denied it. Many of the rest of us found the deception tiresome.

Each day new features of the landscape were wiped out. The Iraqis I spoke to were sunk in the deepest gloom, from which only the firing of the missiles at Israel lifted them for a moment or two. Everyone thought Saddam was finished and that seemed to cheer them as well. Conditions in the city worsened by the day. It was the same in out hotel. As you walked along the corridors you could tell which rooms were occupied by the overpowering smell from the lavatories.

We thought we were leaving behind us one western correspondent, Peter Arnett of CNN. In fact we were leaving two. Alfonso Rojo from Spain managed to convince the Iraqis that Spain had such close links with the Arab world it would be to Iraq's benefit to allow him to stay on. He wrote a series of thoughtful and graphic reports for his Spanish newspaper, *El Mundo*, and for the British *Guardian*: some of the best writing done in the entire war. Rojo did not, however, find a friend in Peter Arnett. He needed to file his reports from CNN's satellite dish; Arnett refused to allow him to do so. It became a matter of bitter dispute between the two of them, left almost alone together in an empty hotel in an empty city. Arnett denied

Rojo's very existence, as well as denying him the means to report: the men in the CNN team were, he said in one of his broadcasts, the only western journalists in the country.

Arnett was a relative newcomer in Baghdad and I scarcely knew him. The day before we left I saw him pick himself up after being blown across the room by an explosion and thought: 'There's a man whose brains are going to be scrambled for a while.' With his bald dome and his hair brushed carefully over his ears he looked as though he were permanently surprised that the 1960s had ended. In an interview from Baghdad he said:

> I . . . am sick of wars, and I am here because my contribution will be to somehow lessen the hostilities, if not this time, maybe the next time.

It is unusual to find a foreign correspondent so aware of having a 'contribution' to make. For most of them, the act of finding out what is going on and then reporting it tends to be as much of a contribution as they want to make. It was Arnett who reported an American officer at a battle in the Mekong Delta during the Vietnam war as saying: 'It became necessary to destroy the town to save it.' It was a quotation which went around the world and made quite a contribution in its own right. It seemed to sum up the bankruptcy of American military thinking and it had a profound effect on the way many people regarded the war.

Arnett always refused to name the officer who said those words to him. Now the action against Saddam Hussein was explicitly being fought to rid the American mind of the legacy of Vietnam and here was Arnett reporting on that too, again wanting to make a contribution. And all the time poor Alfonso Rojo was trying to make *his* contribution too; and no doubt whenever he asked the Information Ministry if he could use the CNN dish an official would murmur: 'Why not?'

We were the last to leave, hoping that something might come up at the last moment to keep us behind. It didn't. The drivers acted according to their individual natures. Mr Hattam, number one driver, decided to drive someone else to the border because they offered him more money. Hassan persuaded us that we had booked a truck from him the previous day; and although no truck ever appeared we gave him a cancellation fee. He then announced it was too dangerous to drive us and went home, full of apologies and $100 bills. The man who appeared at 6 am with a tank full of petrol and three other drivers was Ramadan. He wasn't even swaying. Perhaps he had found it too hard to get his supplies of Johnny Walker.

I kissed Sadoun four times on his bristly cheeks and felt the wetness of the tears on his face. I was very fond of him in spite of our disagreements and told him he would always have a friend in me; which was, and remains, true. As the cars pulled out another raid was starting. I watched Sadoun waving until we turned the corner. Ahead of us lay innumerable problems: Sadoun had forgotten to put my name on the list for exit visas, though at Eamonn's suggestions one of the drivers wrote it in and no one noticed; the road to the border and from the border to Amman was exquisitely painful for my ribs, but I was in such a hurry to get to Amman to make the satellite that I kept quiet (not at all my usual reaction to pain); then, when I got back to London, the BBC doctor refused to allow me to return to Iraq. When he finally relented the Iraqis refused to give me a visa because Sadoun misunderstood something I had written about my experiences in the *Observer* – Farzad Bazoft's paper – and took weeks to get over his annoyance. Someone in the first wave of western journalists to get back to Baghdad gave a copy of the article to Sadoun and Naji al-Hadithi. A CNN reporter had done something similar to NBC a few weeks before. I didn't know it as we followed the road the cruise missiles had taken and drove towards the Jordanian border, but for me, as heavily-accented actors used to say in bad 1950s British films, the war was over.

War in the Air

The great showdown in the Mother of Battles has started, between victorious truth and defeated error. . . . . After the will of Satan has been destroyed in the White House, that den of evil and oppression, the basis of aggression in Tel Aviv will be destroyed as well.

Saddam Hussein broadcasting on Iraqi Radio, 17 January 1991

The Allies' first act of open war took place off the Saudi coast shortly after midnight on 17 January. Several hundred members of the crew of the refurbished World War II battleship, the USS *Wisconsin*, were drawn up on deck. The sea was still and the sky clear. It was chilly enough for the men and women standing there to have put on sweaters and jackets. They were waiting for the launch of the first Tomahawk cruise missile to be fired in anger. The route to a target several hundred miles away had been programmed into a tiny computer on board the missile. In the control room there was a brief countdown: 'Three, Two. One. Launch.' 'Missile away.' 'Yessir.'

At precisely 0050 hours the roar and blast of the ignition came from the missile battery at the *Wisconsin*'s stern. The darkness of the deck and sea were illuminated by a vivid, magnesium-white glare as the missile headed away from the ship, leaving a dense column of white smoke which quickly evaporated. The missile rose at a gentle angle and vanished northwestwards. The spectators cheered dutifully, then some of them wandered off to bed. The sea mirrored the missile's path like phosphor until the brilliant white dot faded in the night: 1100 pounds of high explosive and $2.5 million disappeared into the blackness. More than 100 cruise missiles were to be fired that night from the *Wisconsin* and other American ships. Five months and 13 days after the Iraqi army had moved into Kuwait, Operation Desert Shield had turned into Operation Desert Storm.

Ten minutes after the first Tomahawk missile had been fired, six AWACS 'command and control' planes, with their un-wieldy radar domes mounted on the body of a converted airliner, rumbled down the runway and took off into the night air. Their task was to protect the fighter-bombers that would soon take off by providing early warning of any hostile aircraft movements or missiles in the entire area of conflict: which meant Iraq and Kuwait. The AWACS aircraft would never need to leave Saudi airspace as their radar could 'see' well into countries to the north, west and east of Iraq. After the last of the six had left, their hunting partners, the F-4 Wild Weasels, began taking off. Their task was to destroy enemy radar installations which the AWACS identified for them.

There was a pause at Dharan and things were quieter. Then the racket started again and waves of the most modern aircraft in service anywhere in the world began heading down the runway: F-15E Eagle bombers with their strange double tailplanes and a thrust to weight ratio of more than one to one, making it probably the fastest climbing aircraft ever built; F-A18 Hornets, which had always looked old-fashioned to my inexpert eyes, a little like the aircraft that flew when I was a child in the fifties, but fast and effective as either fighters or bombers; A-6E Intruders, subsonic, low-level attack bombers which could drop 18,000 pounds of bombs on targets completely obscured by cloud or darkness; British Tornados, obliged to fly dangerously low to attack and destroy Iraqi airfields. Later the extraordinary F117A fighter-bombers, constructed according to what the defence industry called 'low observables technology' or Stealth, slid along the runways and headed for the missile sites and heavily-defended command centres which were their natural targets. They were almost completely invisible to radar, though the Royal Navy said afterwards that its ships had seen them perfectly well. They looked like stingrays in tropical water.

Many of the American and British planes which took off that night were heading for Baghdad, other cities in Iraq and Iraqi positions in Kuwait. The first attack lasted three hours and 18,000 tons of explosives were dropped: twice the amount that destroyed Dresden and almost the equivalent of the atomic weapon dropped on Hiroshima. Yet the one newspaper in Baghdad which still appeared carried the following report on 18 January 1991:

> In all cities, towns and villages in Iraq, women and children and old people have died.
> In Baghdad province, 2 were killed, 23 injured.
> In Wasit province, 9 were killed, 9 injured.
> In Saladdin province, 1 killed, 9 injured.
> In Meisan province, 4 killed, 2 injured.
> In Dhi Qar province, 7 killed and 23 injured.
> Total: 23 killed, 66 injured.

There was no reason for the Iraqi government to minimize the casualties and at this point the authorities in Baghdad were still able to keep in touch with the rest of the country. A check of hospitals in Baghdad itself indicated that the figures of two dead and 23 injured were likely to be true.

Captain Paul Andrews of the US Marine All Weather Attack Squadron 224 had been in the Gulf for six months, but this was his first time in combat. He and the other pilots had trained thoroughly for this moment. The American experience in Vietnam was that pilots who survived their first 10 missions had a much better than even chance of surviving their 13 month tour of duty. As a result, training for pilots was made as realistic as possible to give them the equivalent of 10 missions before the start of hostilities.

Captain Andrews climbed into his Grumman A-6 Intruder at the squadron's base in Bahrain. He was, naturally enough, very nervous; frightened even. But he had to lead the first strike and he was unwilling to show it. At such moments there is a kind of conspiracy of bonhomie: men slap each other on the back and boast a little, in a self-mocking way. No one wants to let a silence fall, yet everyone knows it's close. Waiting is unpleasant; an intelligent flight controller will try to compress everything into as short a space of time as possible, before the moment of take-off. Then someone says 'Kick their ass' and they walk over to the aircraft and climb in. Once on board habit begins to take over.

A British exchange pilot, Robert McCarthy, was flying with the squadron; it had never occurred to him when he joined the Royal Air Force that his first experience of war would be with the Americans. Both he and Andrews found that none of the succeeding missions was as frightening as the first, when they didn't know exactly how their aircraft or their weapons would operate in conditions of combat, nor how good the Iraqi defences would be. Their targets that first night were two airfields and a power plant between Basra and Baghdad. Eight British Tornados went with them. Both the airfields were well defended and there was massive anti-aircraft fire around Kuwait; but essentially the barrage was fired in their general direction, rather than specifically aimed at them.

Andrews felt a good deal better when he realized that. And when they fired their antiradiation HARM missiles, which searched out a radar beam and followed it down to destroy the Iraqi transmitters, they found them reassuringly effective. The radar stations which tracked them were either destroyed or shut down when they realized what was happening. Much of the Iraqi anti-aircraft artillery (or Triple-A for short) were radar-guided and supplied by the Soviet Union. The gunners operating them knew the danger from missiles like HARM and would switch off the radar directly there was an attack. They would continue firing, but with no real chance of hitting Andrews or his men. During the first night only one aircraft was badly hit and it managed to get back to Bahrain and was in the air again within six hours. The Intruders performed marvellously, Andrews said. In a technological war, he and the other pilots had the right technology. Everything worked. And the wider concerns?

I had no doubt I was fighting for a just cause. Saddam was like Hitler, and I guess I felt like the British and Americans must have felt when they were fighting the Germans in World War II. Nobody likes what they have to do, but we all had a strong sense of duty and we just hoped all the time that it'd be over quickly. It wasn't my job to be hateful or angry, and I wasn't angry with the Iraqis. But Saddam got what he deserved.

Out in the desert, British, French and American servicemen and women answered with regulation cheerfulness when they were asked about the prospect of fighting. 'Just another job, isn't it? Got to be done.' 'It's what we've trained for, and now the time's come to put the training into practice.' 'The President sent us here, we're the President's Own, so – anywhere, any place.' '*C'est le boulot.*' Even the Egyptians and Syrians caught the understated tone: 'Fighting is not something we enjoy. It is necessary.' Nevertheless a British correspondent who was with the Egyptians noticed their lightness of heart as they prepared to advance. When he asked the reason, one of the officers said they were happy because they were simply facing other Arabs and not the Israelis.

In their own way the downbeat, professional responses were the equivalent of the more absurd and flowery things Iraqi soldiers said on the other side of the line when they knew they were being listened to: 'Our heart's blood and our soul for Saddam,' for example. On their own, a British or American soldier might well confess to nervousness, just as an Iraqi might confess to having little enthusiasm for fighting. It would never do to say it in the hearing of their comrades. In the coalition lines it would get you laughed at; in the Iraqi lines it might get you gaoled – or worse.

There was a certain nervousness, it seems, among the Allied commanders. They had no serious doubts that they would win but they could not know the price they would have to pay. Every risk had to be determined on a worst-case estimate and the worst case of all was that the Iraqi army would prove as tough and experienced as Saddam claimed. Each night on Iraqi television a man with a bright blue microphone would interview groups of soldiers at unnamed locations which all seemed to be in the desert or in Kuwait. He would interview soldiers who would praise Saddam in song and warble sentimentally, while the rest of the group prepared messages for their wives and families. I used to feel there was something innocent and rather sad about them: they reminded me of Argentine soldiers who used to chant about the Malvinas and invoke the spirit of San Martín, before the Paras, the Marines, the Guards and the Gurkhas set about them. Before being expelled I wrote to the *Spectator* from Baghdad about the troops who appeared on television from the Iraqi front line:

> Their equipment looks badly maintained and they are sloppily dressed. They do not seem like conquerors, and my guess is they don't feel like them either.

It was one of the things I managed to get right.

From the Allies' point of view, there seemed reasonable grounds for anxiety. No matter how much they had trained for chemical warfare, the thought of it frightened people far more than the thought of bullets and shells did. There had been a good deal in the western press about Saddam's other weapons: the supergun, the Scud, the trenches full of petrol which would be ignited directly there was an attack, the Fuel Air Explosives, which spread petroleum vapour in the air and ignited it with, it was said, the force of an atomic weapon. And there were the rumoured nuclear weapons. No one could know for certain precisely what Iraq's arsenal did contain.

In many cases the capability of the weapons systems which Saddam possessed was described in full detail to Allied command by the company or the country that had made it. Saddam Hussein had tried to make his country an instant regional superpower by buying his weaponry off the peg. It was not a good idea to pick a fight with the countries who had sold him his armoury or who were on good terms with those who had. The Iraqis faced the most formidable array of weapons and several of the best equipped and trained armies and air forces in the world.

Saddam Hussein had boasted of being able to drive the Allied forces from the battlefield, of having weapons of vast destructive power, of teaching the invaders a lesson they would never forget in all their history to come. It is only with hindsight that this now appears empty rhetoric. Saddam did possess some highly-sophisticated weaponry, though he must have realized he could not approach the technological superiority of the Americans. The weapons the Allies worried about most were political ones: his potential ability to turn the conflict into an open war between the Arabs on one side and the Israelis and the western powers on the other, and his ability to sacrifice the lives of his soldiers on a scale the coalition could not tolerate.

The Allied commanders had to take Saddam's threats seriously. They knew he had the technology to mount chemical warheads on his Scuds and it was only after the third or fourth Scud had hit Israeli territory with conventional warheads that they began to realize he intended to play it safe. Saddam had told Yasser Arafat in August that he had expected the Americans to use nuclear missiles against Baghdad in revenge for the invasion of Kuwait. Perhaps he thought they would use them now if he hit Israel with chemical weapons.

Even before the air war began, American Special Forces and the British SAS and SBS were put into Iraq to try to pinpoint the Scud launchers. When the missiles began falling on Israel, the search was greatly intensified. Scuds are crude and imprecise weapons, but they can have a serious effect on civilian morale. They kill by chance and the lack of any pattern unsettles people. The Allied political leaders were always concerned that there would be a loss of life so serious that the Israeli government would come under considerable pressure to respond. The arrival of the Patriot defence systems made a considerable psychological difference. One of the main Patriot batteries was set up close to the sea in the northern suburbs of Tel Aviv. People could see them from quite close up in the daytime and if a Scud came over everyone could see and hear them being fired.

General Schwartzkopf's quip about the improbability of being killed by a Scud was matched by reality. By 27 January there had been six Scud attacks in the 10 days since the war began. One person had died from direct injuries and three had died of heart attacks. In the same period seven had died in traffic accidents. Even so, the Scuds were more effective than the Allied commanders had led their political leaders to believe and, in spite of the intense effort that was expended on taking them out, Iraq is thought to have ended the war with 30 launchers and between 20 and 40 missiles still intact.

The fact that all Iraq's Scuds were not destroyed was not regarded as a failure of the various groups of special forces deployed inside Iraq. It is reported that an SAS team captured an Iraqi ground-to-air missile at the start of the war and flew it out of Iraq by helicopter. The SAS has had long experience of warfare in the desert – it was founded by Colonel David Stirling for use in the Western Desert in World War II – and had trained extensively in Oman. General Sir Peter de la Billière, commander of British forces in the Gulf, had himself been a colonel in the SAS. That was a guarantee that the SAS, as well as the various American Special Forces groups, were used in the proper way. 'They were our eyes out there,' said General Schwartzkopf later and reconnaissance was an important part of their role. The Americans used big, fast, stripped-down vehicles nicknamed 'Dune Buggies'. They were heavily armed but carried no armour. The British used vehicles called 'Pink Panthers' with heavy Browning machine guns mounted on them, something in the fashion of the original SAS.

The relationship between the US Special Forces and the British SAS is usually said to have been good: the American Delta Force, which was also used behind the lines in Iraq and Kuwait, was founded along the lines of the SAS and several of the US groups had trained with the British. Together, their duties were varied. They were flown in by silent helicopter to blow up radar and communication centres. In northern Iraq, at Nimrod, I saw the heavy pockmarking of machine-gunning at ground level on a building which seemed to have been a chemical warfare plant and was attacked by the Allied forces; it is possible that some special forces group was involved there. They were used to pick up air crew who had been shot down and they were employed to attack Iraqi troops in full retreat.

The accuracy of some of the bombing in Baghdad and elsewhere owed something to the Special Forces and the SAS as well. They pinpointed selected buildings for the Allied bombers with small hand-held laser targetters. The Iraqis seemed to be aware of this. I was told by one senior figure after the war that they believed the SAS and, perhaps, the Americans had put people into Baghdad as delegates to the Islamic conference which Saddam Hussein called immediately before the expiry of the UN deadline. Many of the delegates were unable to leave because of the war and it would have been good cover if the suspicion were true. Five SAS men are known to have died during the war and several were captured. The figure for American Special Forces personnel who were killed or captured is not known.

Saddam Hussein was, as General Schwartzkopf said at his press conference the day before the war was brought to an end, 'neither a strategist, nor is he schooled in the operational arts, nor is he a tactician, nor is he a general, nor is he a soldier. Other than that, he's a great military man.' The Iraqi army was further handicapped by the fact that its generals were trained in the Soviet doctrine of massive static defences, which meant that they were highly vulnerable if the enemy achieved superiority in the air, of which the Allies were swiftly assured.

In the early days of the air war Iraqi pilots were under orders to avoid contact with the enemy. Saddam Hussein distrusted his air force on the grounds that its officers were mostly trained abroad and might well have become infected by western ideas or even have been turned into agents of the powers that trained them. His notion of battle was a ground conflict. His air force never therefore received its due proportion of the money that he spent on weapons.

It was on 26 January, the tenth day of war, that Iraqi Air Force planes began arriving at bases in Iran. The Americans said that at least 24 Iraqi planes had landed there during the day: 12 fighters, some of them Mirage-1s, and another 12 transport planes. The Iranians, always likely to be more cautious and perhaps less truthful on an issue that could embroil them with the United States, said only seven planes had arrived. A statement from President Rafsanjani's office said that any foreign military aircraft which landed in Iran would be impounded until the end of the war. Two days later, in an interview with CNN, Saddam Hussein said Iraq

322

respected Iran's decision. The number of Iraqi aircraft arriving there was growing rapidly. The following day, 29 January, the Israeli Defence Minister Moshe Arens said that all 25 of Iraq's Soviet-made Sukhoi-24 bombers were now in Iraq.

Within a few days about 150 of Iraq's fixed-wing planes were out of the war. There was puzzlement in the West and some deliberate disinformation from Iran. The Iranian ambassador to the United Nations said the pilots had flown there to save their lives and their aircraft, which made it sound as though they were defecting. It has been suggested that the first wave of aircraft did indeed defect, since four of them ran out of fuel and fell out of the sky before reaching the border, implying they had only enough fuel for local patrols. Iran was very nervous about the possibility of getting dragged into the war on one side or the other and was prepared to offer a certain amount of help to Saddam Hussein. It turned a blind eye to large-scale smuggling across their mutual border, for instance, so that UN sanctions would be less effective.

A highly-placed source close to Saddam Hussein at this time maintains that Iran offered to allow the Iraqi leader to send his air force across the Iranian border to protect it from destruction. The situation was becoming serious: Allied planes had destroyed more than 70 Iraqi hardened aircraft shelters and the choice was increasingly between putting them into the equivalent of storage and losing them altogether. According to the source the offer to allow the Iraqi planes to cross the border was not made by the Iranian government, since there was no telephone contact between Baghdad and Tehran, but by an intermediary.

As soon as the bulk of the aircraft had arrived on Iranian soil, Iran declared that it was impounding them. President Rafsanjani sent a reassuring message to the United States through a third party, probably France, to say that Saddam would not have the use of the aircraft at least until the end of the war and, the message hinted, after that as well. On 31 January Saddam sent Deputy Prime Minister Sadoun Hammadi to Tehran to ask about the aircraft. The Iranian foreign minister, Ali Akbar Velayati, showed the Iraqis the trap they had fallen into. He told Hammadi blandly that Iraq should have requested permission for its planes to enter Iranian air space. Since they had not, he said, Iran had the duty to impound them.

If indeed it was a deliberate plan, as the source insists, rather than a series of unconnected events, Iran did very well out of it. The planes would be a useful bargaining counter with Iraq in the future and to have impounded them was a useful act of revenge against the man who had done such damage to Iran in the past. It also meant that Iran had done the Allies a good turn, without being obliged to move away from a position of neutrality.

Even when General Schwartzkopf formally announced on 30 January that the Allied forces had complete air superiority, it didn't allay the anxieties about the coming battle. Everyone knew that Kuwait could be liberated only by soldiers on the ground; and for them, the Iraqis were still an enemy to be taken seriously. In the meantime, the air forces engaged in the bombing were still taking casualties. In the case of the British and Italian Tornados, whose tactics were to go in low, the chances of disaster were very real. Later there were accusations from some RAF personnel that their officers had ordered many more Tornado sorties than were necessary in order to show that Britain was playing a full part in the war and, perhaps, doing more than its share.

Tornados are high-risk aircraft; or at least the tactics they are obliged to follow are high-risk ones. The RAF had specialized heavily within NATO and had spent a good deal of money on the British-made weapon for attacking airfields, the JP233, which drops a succession of bomblets which crater the runway. It was much less well-equipped in the Gulf with the laser-guided bombs which, together with the cruise missiles, proved to be the most effective weapons of the war. The JP233s required the Tornados to fly very low over the runways they were attacking – perhaps as low as eighty feet – and to fly in a straight line for 10 seconds or even longer, making them vulnerable to Iraqi airfield defences. Within three or four days the RAF had to adapt its tactics.

While there was a good deal of discontent among the crews at the jobs they were doing and the way they were having to do them, within two weeks the Iraqi Air Force had either been destroyed or had flown to Iran and there was no further need to destroy airfields. The RAF had to call in its Buccaneers from Europe for greater flexibility. It was always a risky business to fly Tornados; in the Gulf, for instance, the elderly American F1-11s flew roughly the same number of sorties and yet not one of them was lost. Tornado pilots were accustomed to the risk: in the seven years between 1983 and the start of the war, 19 went down. One crashed on a low-level training mission four days before the war began. Seven others were lost during the fighting, but probably only three of them were shot down by the Iraqis. Two hit the ground when they were on low-level JP233 strikes; one developed technical problems and the crew ejected; one was destroyed when a 1000 pound bomb exploded immediately after it was released. Altogether seven Tornado crewmen were taken prisoner.

Saddam Hussein issued an order just before the war began that any airmen who were captured should not be harmed and that they should be handed over to the Iraqi military at once. The authorities paraded them on television in a way which caused revulsion not only in the rest of the world but among some people in Iraq as well. Several had received injuries when they ejected or crashed, but this did not protect them from being questioned on television. Flight-Lieutenants John Peters and Adrian Nichol were shot down in their Tornado GR1 close to the Kuwaiti border by a SAM missile on the first day of the war. Four days later they were shown answering questions. Peters' face was badly bruised and swollen and he was hunched down in his seat. His voice was faint and he said little more than that he had been shot down by a missile. Nichol sat up straight, a big stolid man with a Union Jack badge on his uniform, looking directly at the camera:

Interrogator:	What was your mission?
Nichol:	To attack an Iraqi airfield.
Interrogator:	How were you shot down?
Nichol:	I was shot down by an Iraqi system. I do not know what it was.
Interrogator:	What do you think about the war?

| Nichol: | I think this war should be stopped so we can go home. I do not agree with this war on Iraq. |

Other captured pilots were more forthcoming, Lieutenant Jeffrey Zaun of the US Navy, for instance:

Interrogator:	What was your feeling while flying over Iraq to launch an aggression against it?
Zaun:	Myself and the other pilots talked about what interest the USA had for going to war. And we could find none. This was before the war. And now we wonder whether American blood can be so cheap in the eyes of our government officials.
Interrogator:	What were the losses suffered by the US air force before you fell into captivity?
Zaun:	Our losses are very great. I can tell you that this was one of the main reasons for the fear of American pilots flying against Iraqi defences. We were talking together and we felt that Iraq has some of the best anti-aircraft systems and the losses to these systems in some aircraft have become very great and were leading to American pilots objecting to being in this conflict . . . I think that this war is unjust and I hope that I will be remembered for not wanting to participate in harming the Iraqi people.

Separated from the camaraderie of his unit and the need to maintain the outward appearance of toughness, Lieutenant Zaun cooperated considerably with his captors. It did not, however, seem to be necessary to go quite that far. An Italian pilot, Captain Maurizio Coccioline, who was shot down in a Tornado, appeared on television the same night as Lieutenant Zaun. When he was asked about attacking Iraq he said simply: 'I didn't feel very good because I knew the technology of the Iraqi Air Force and defences. I was very, very lucky to stay alive.'

The emotions of pilots who are trained to destroy installations on the ground are often mixed. They take a pride in their professional skills and try to avoid thinking about the casualties they may cause. One British pilot said after a successful mission: 'When you see the bridge go up and you know you've hit it, it's a wonderful feeling.' A radio conversation between a British pilot and navigator about the destruction of another bridge showed the same emotion:

A: 35.

B: Dog's knob. [A reference to the fact that the first bomb has hit the bridge on their screen.]

A: 40 – that one was a bit short.

B: Good job.

A: Let's get the fuck out of here.

B: Can you see it down there? [Their video camera is now panning along the bridge.]

A: Yes.

B: Is it gone?

A: I'm tied up with a Tornado. I can't see, mate. You look at the bridge.

B: A bit of damage. [The cloud from the explosion is drifting away.] Oh, nice, beautiful hole. A beauty.

A: Hm, not much left of the bridge there. Take off.

At press briefings the Americans and British were usually careful not to show film or photographs of casualties, civilian or military. There was a clear attempt to minimize the sense that people were being killed. One briefer showed a video of a bomb hitting a bridge immediately after a truck had driven out of range: 'The luckiest man in Iraq', he called him. There were several examples on video of unlucky men, but these were not shown. The British, however, understood better than the Americans the value of admitting an error when one was made.

As you drive to Baghdad from the Jordanian border, the bridge at Falujah, just outside the capital, has been destroyed. A group of RAF Tornados attacked it on 14 February. At the same time a bomb landed in the middle of the town about a mile away. The Iraqis have estimated the number of people who died at between 40 and 73. That night the British briefer in Dharan admitted the mistake. It did nothing to help the people who lost friends or relatives or those who survived but were injured. Nevertheless, it dealt conclusively with what had taken place and there was nothing more to say about it. A British reporter, Ed Vulliamy, went to Falujah after the bombing. He found that people there showed extraordinary good will towards citizens of the countries whose aircraft gutted their nation with bombs. There was even, he said, an England soccer shirt in the window of a shop.

Privately it is possible to find American officials who accept that the bombing of the shelter at Amiriyah, which took place on the previous day, the thirteenth, was a mistake as well. It was probably aimed at the topmost members of the Baath Party and their families who were thought to have been in the shelter. When it became clear that the 200 or 300 people who died there – an authoritative figure was never issued – were from families who lived in the area, a bewildering number of justifications started to emerge; it was an Iraqi command post; it was transmitting radio messages; the 'signature' of radio patterns from it indicated that Saddam Hussein might be there himself; Saddam might have taken 'a cold-blooded decision . . . to put civilians without our knowledge into a facility and have them bombed,' as General Thomas Kelly, director of operations for the Joint Chiefs of Staff put it.

In fact, the general lack of organization in Baghdad meant that civilians, particularly women and children, tended to just turn up at air raid shelters and were rarely turned away. In a war in which considerable efforts were expended to avoid civilian casualties, the advantages of bombing the Amiriyah shelter would have had to be very great to outweigh the loss of so many lives. It was, in any case, the twenty-eighth day of war, so it was hard to think that Amiriyah was given great priority as a target. By this stage some other buildings in Baghdad had been hit 20 or 30 times because of the limited number of targets available.

Jeremy Bowen, the BBC television correspondent who took my place in Baghdad, was on his own there with the freelance cameraman Rory Peck, a man with the aristocratic drawl of 50 years ago and the appetite for action of a nineteenth century cavalryman: without question one of the best combat cameramen in the world. Bowen and I share an office at Television Centre and I realized early on that his raffish appearance concealed a considerable sense of duty and a commitment to serious analysis; though it didn't stop him driving round in a sports car with the roof down. There are journalists whose reporting you never entirely trust: they show a proclivity to enhance or embroider, to dramatize themselves, or simply to be ignorant of the meaning of what they have seen; these things infect even their better work, making it inherently dubious. Jeremy Bowen is not one of them. He is an honest, sceptical and intelligent reporter of what he sees. It is necessary to make the point, because his reporting on the Amiriyah attack was greeted with scurrilous criticism in Britain. People didn't want to hear about big civilian casualties and they blamed him for telling them about it.

Jeremy and Rory were in the lobby of the Al-Rasheed at 8 am after a heavy night's bombing when they started to hear stories that an air raid shelter had been hit. They asked the minders if they could go there and a group formed up. As they drove up the main road to Amiriyah they could tell it had happened only a short time before. Large crowds were milling about, fire engines and rescue vehicles were drawn up and smoke was still coming out of the large white concrete building at the end. People were weeping in the crowds as they went through and for the first time in his – or my – experience in Baghdad they showed signs of hostility: 'Why did this happen?' 'Is this the way to win back Kuwait?' 'You animals, you sons of bitches.' Much of it was in English: this was a middle-class area where people were often well educated. One of the British tabloid newspapers said the next day that Saddam Hussein had brought in people who spoke English so that Bowen and Peck would be able to interview them.

As the two journalists reached the building they saw rescue workers bringing out pieces of body: torsos, thighs, shoulders, mangled and burned. Inside the building was hot and there was a great deal of smoke. The corridor was 18 inches deep in water and the workers were fishing out pieces of body from below the surface. A 2000 pound penetration bomb had cut its way cleanly through the 10 feet of reinforced concrete and steel of the roof. The building was on two levels. The upper level was a dormitory. Most of the people in the shelter had been here and they had died instantly. Others had died from smoke and burns.

The next day Bowen and Peck went back to the shelter. They arrived as a funeral of one of the people who had died was going past and, for a time, they were in some difficulty. Angry relatives were firing guns in the air and Jeremy Bowen said it was the only time in the month he spent in Baghdad during the war when he felt seriously frightened. Eventually they were saved by some armed security men. Inside the building it was still hot and the rescue workers were still finding bodies. Some were complete, others had been fused together by the heat and blast and lay crooked and absurd on the stretchers as the rescuers ran out with them, eager to finish the terrible job and get away. Sometimes there would be nothing but a great mass of flesh. Downstairs the surface of the water was an inch thick in melted human fat and Bowen and Peck had to throw away their shoes when they got back to the hotel.

No one directed them or stopped them going where they wanted in the shelter. Jeremy Bowen believes he saw 90 per cent of the building. He climbed onto the roof and saw the feeble efforts at painted camouflage. He examined the aerials which, he believed, were for television: all the specially-built shelters had them. He even found plans of the building, designed by a Finnish company. There was nothing in them to indicate that there might be a command centre hidden somewhere. The freedom they were given to wander around indicated that there was nothing there to find. Further stories circulated in Washington later: the Iraqis had moved out all the military bodies at the start of the rescue operation; a Swedish company had built a third level under the Finnish construction; a secret basement, fully equipped to communicate with generals at the front, had been flooded to prevent reporters from seeing it. Some stories contradicted others. To people who had not been there they probably sounded convincing.

When I finally returned to Baghdad in April, an American television reporter told me he had been back to Amiriyah and seen small spools of tape and film lying around on the ground outside, together with filing cards. He had been unable to get any pictures of this. I couldn't get close enough to see anything like that, if it was there. A sign still hung over the building: 'Department of Civil Defence. Shelter 35.' There was a wire fence round it and a soldier stood guard. Maybe the military had used it as a command centre. Maybe Saddam had visited it. Maybe it had generated radio traffic. But if it was so important, why wasn't it hit before? Perhaps after four weeks' bombing the Americans were running out of targets and were starting to take risks. They thought there was a chance of killing top Baath Party members and their families. Instead they killed ordinary women and children. Not even the British tabloid press denied that.

To the right of the wrecked building was a school. Our pictures on the morning of the UN deadline had come from there. I remembered the dark faces and the English lesson: 'I am happy, you are kind, he is sad, they are GOOOOOOD,' and the eyes wandering to see if the camera was still on them. Some of those girls would have been in the shelter when it was bombed.

The Bluff is Called

They will jam the command headquarters to cut off communications between the command headquarters and the fighters. As far as we are concerned, we will not need communication. . . . [F]or one year our army has been carrying out exercises and has been training on the premise that the fighters will be performing their duties when their communications are cut with headquarters.

Saddam Hussein, speaking on 11 January 1991

The ground war, as everyone called it, was one of the great anti-climaxes of modern times. The Pentagon's computer projections, which had originally predicted that Allied casualties would be as high as 40,000, had been scaled down to 5000 before the attack; the computers also estimated that the ground offensive would last between seven and ten days. But much of the data which the Pentagon was receiving was seriously flawed.

Intelligence estimates put the number of Iraqi troops in the theatre of war at 540,000. After the war was over it became known that, when the Iraqi army was at full strength in early January, there were fewer than half that number: approximately 260,000. Once the bombing began, the desertions began in earnest. Tens of thousands simply headed home. In the front line among the conscripted men the desertion rate was sometimes more than 30 per cent, according to General Schwartzkopf. The rate was less in the Republican Guard divisions where the men were better paid, morale was a little higher and the officers more experienced.

When the ground offensive began the coalition forces numbered almost 525,000, though by no means all of them took part in the final assault. The different contingents were as follows:

United States	350,000
Saudi Arabia	45,000
Egypt	38,500
Britain	32,000
Syria	21,000
France	12,000
Pakistan	11,000
Gulf States	10,000
Bangladesh	2,300
Morocco	1,700
Niger	500
Senegal	500
Czechoslovakia	200

By the time the ground offensive began the Iraqi strength must have fallen well below the initial figure of 260,000: possibly even below 200,000. The Allied Forces had an advantage of between two and two-and-a-half to one, depending on how large the Iraqi rate of desertion was. That was far more than the number required to do the job. US military intelligence, which had provided the grossly exaggerated Iraqi troop figures, was one of the main failures of the entire campaign. It wasn't only the quantity but the quality of the Iraqi army which was inflated.

Everybody believed that Iraq was a formidable military power. The fact that Iraq's army was the fourth biggest in the world was frequently referred to; it dignified the efforts that were being made to counter Saddam Hussein. No one referred to him as a tinpot dictator; he seemed a worthy adversary. Great powers do not like to feel they are not boxing their weight. A study carried out for the US Army War College warned:

Iraq is superb on the defense. Its army is well-equipped and trained to carry out mobile defense operations.

333

Another study written for the College, 'Iraqi Power and US Security in the Middle East', assured its readers that the Baath Party enjoyed significant support; the Kurds were crushed and that Shi'i opposition had long since disappeared; Iraqi troops were much better fighters than had previously been thought. Those who had experienced the fighting qualities of the Iraqi army and spent some time in Iraq might have told a different story. During the war with Iran the Soviet Union provided Saddam Hussein with some of the world's best defensive works. That would make any army 'superb in defense', as long as it was not required to go out and fight in the open.

The Iraqis possessed a mixed bag of equipment before the war, bought from half-a-dozen different suppliers. They had six types of tank: Soviet T-55s, T-62s and T-72s, Chinese T-59s and T-69s and British Chieftains. They had four types of self-propelled guns: American M107s, M109s and M110s, plus French GCTs. And they had the South African G-5 155mm gun. The difficulty of keeping such a variety of machines equipped and supplied would tax the abilities of far more efficient armies than Iraq's. The Iraqi military infrastructure was not efficient and found it hard to get basic equipment even for its footsoldiers. In Kuwait City the troops were often told to forage for their own food. The numerical superiority which the Iraqis supposedly had in tanks and artillery was not evident once fighting began.

The Iraqi population of 17 million was simply too small to be able to produce troops of sufficient quality in sufficient numbers to take on an army of the size, sophistication and training which the coalition had assembled. The Republican Guard, which journalists and politicians insisted on describing as 'élite', was increased by several divisions during the period of the crisis, largely by means of taking men from regular units and giving them red berets. Anyone who could march in step was considered eligible. The officers of the Republican Guard were usually better trained, but that generally meant that they too had to be taken from other units. The mass dilution meant that the Republican Guards' standards, which in the war against Iran had been above average, were little different from those of the rest of the Iraqi army.

A journalist with the advancing British forces noticed sourly that the Republican Guard weren't even very good at painting the red triangular recognition markings on their vehicles. When the ground offensive came, the 'élite' Republican Guard showed little more inclination to fight than the regular army divisions and the reservists. Robert Fox, one of the most thoughtful of the defence correspondents covering the ground offensive, went over the Iraqi positions with great care afterwards. His overall impression was that most of the Iraqi soldiers had come to the desert to get away from Saddam Hussein. It was certainly true that even the punishment squads positioned behind the lines with orders to shoot deserters had little interest in obeying. Many of them were themselves deserting.

By the third week of January, when the air strikes on Iraqi positions were at their height, you could buy a Kalashnikov rifle at the main Baghdad bus station for 20 dinars: three dollars at the black market rate. A month later, when the ground war was imminent, the price had dropped to 8 dinars. Soldiers were deserting in very large numbers and selling everything they had – equipment, weapons, uniform – in order to get their bus fare home. The war in the air, the daily and nightly attacks by bomb and missile on Iraqi positions and installations, destroyed Iraqi morale far more thoroughly than the Allies understood.

The West, which had failed to appreciate the nature of Saddam Hussein's bluff throughout the build-up to the war, failed to appreciate it to the end. He represented our worst fears and we showed a curious reluctance to give them up. At the same time there was an equally curious lack of interest in him or his motives. Western journalists who worked in Baghdad often complained that their editors were much more interested in the build-up of Allied forces in Saudi Arabia than they were in what was happening in Iraq. British correspondents in Buenos Aires during the Falklands crisis found much the same thing; so did American correspondents in Hanoi. In Baghdad, the team working for one television organization only received the nightsight it had requested two days *after* the ceasefire. Until that time all available nightsights had gone to

Saudi Arabia where it was assumed they would be more needed.

The clear evidence in Baghdad that there was no great support there for Saddam Hussein was mostly ignored. Indeed, by no means did all the news organizations represented in Baghdad report it; some were still talking in terms of mass rallies and fanatical crowds of supporters until the end. That was what viewers and readers expected, so that was what they got. For the most part politicians, soldiers and civilians alike found it impossible to believe that someone who spoke as fiercely as Saddam might not have a united people behind him. They assumed that the frontline soldiers must share Saddam's views; therefore they expected strong resistance.

Before the ground war began, everybody believed the Iraqis would use chemical weapons. President Bush expected it; British Defence Secretary Tom King agreed: 'We're ordering you not to open that window!' shouted CNN's anchor in Atlanta when one of the CNN correspondents in Tel Aviv, wearing a gas mask on air, suggested a simple test of whether the first Scud to land contained poison gas. Several British and American newspapers reported that it had and not many of them retracted the story the next day. Journalists and servicemen in Saudi Arabia carried gas masks wherever they went. The Israeli High Court of Justice ruled it was patent discrimination and a scandal that Jewish settlers in the Occupied Territories were issued with masks where Palestinians were not. Sales of gas masks were reported as far away from the scene of action as Germany.

Eventually, however, there was no reported use of any chemical weapon at any stage during the war. The advancing troops found not so much as a single canister of poison gas in the Iraqi positions they captured. A report that an American marine had become contaminated when shifting captured military equipment turned out to be wrong. Iraq had built up large stockpiles of chemical weapons of different kinds, but Saddam Hussein knew that if he used them the Allies would overthrow him for certain and put him on trial.

As for Gerald Bull's G-5 supergun, which was supposed to fire enormous projectiles huge distances, Robert Fox stumbled across one in the desert. It was, he said, utterly useless and had never been fired. In their more conventional weaponry the Iraqi forces were mostly inferior to the Allies (except for rifles: the Kalashnikov seemed largely unaffected by sand). The Soviet-built T-55 tank which the Iraqis had in large numbers was an updated version of the World War II T-34 and was hopelessly outgunned and outclassed by the American Abrams and the British Challenger. In the desert the T-55s were mostly dug in and used as artillery. Time and again advancing Allied soldiers came cross T-55s in well-prepared, rather comfortable positions, incapable of moving, their guns able to traverse only a few degrees. Often the batteries had been taken out to provide lighting, heat and music systems for the crew. The war in the air had been serious. The ground offensive was a mopping up of illusions.

It was miserable in the desert at the end of January. The temperature was almost down to zero and the streaming rain turned the sand to a nasty pale mud. The waiting was, if anything, worse. In the vastness of the desert it gave a sense of claustrophobia. The soldiers sat in their rainproof ponchos and went through the motions, faces reddened and roughened by the sun and the desert wind. There was plenty to do and no time to sit around and brood. But everyone knew that at some stage soon they would have to move in for the final ground attack. First, however, the Iraqis delivered a brief shock to the Allies.

CNN had shown pictures filmed by ITN which showed that the town of Khafji, 12 miles south of the border with Kuwait, was unoccupied. General Wadoud, who commanded the Iraqi 3rd Corps in Kuwait, was the one general Iraq seemed to possess with a truly offensive spirit. The others, wary of Saddam's known dislike of successful generals, sat and waited for orders. Wadoud, however, kept sending radio messages to Saddam Hussein in the Baghdad bunker warning him of the attrition rate his men were suffering under the bombardment and demanding to be allowed to counterattack. Eventually Saddam Hussein and, having seen the CNN report from

Khafji, he agreed that it should be the target: 1500 Iraqi troops, with tanks and armoured personnel carriers, moved into the town on 30 January.

Twelve US Marines died in the first 24 hours of the operation and there were casualties among the Saudi soldiers who were sent in to recapture the town. The job was done eventually, but the Iraqis had fought reasonably well and their tactics had caught the Allies napping. General Schwartzkopf dismissed it, rightly, as little more than a skirmish; but it seemed to show that there was more fight left in the Iraqis than anyone had expected. General Wadoud's part in it was played down in Baghdad. In Amman and other Arab cities where people supported Saddam Hussein in large numbers, people came out onto the streets holding up his portrait and chanting his praises.

The attack on Khafji was to be the only example of Iraqi initiative throughout the ground war. Wadoud was not foolhardy enough to suggest any more ways of winning glory. The soldiers in the trenches continued to take heavy punishment and, where they could, desert while preparations for an all-out ground attack continued. On 15 February, two days after the attack on the shelter at Amiriyah, it looked for a moment as though Saddam Hussein was surrendering. The Revolution Command Council met during the night and put out a statement speaking of Iraq's readiness to 'deal with' Resolution 660, under which the UN had demanded the withdrawal of Iraqi troops from Kuwait. It went on to demand that an undertaking to withdraw should be followed by a full ceasefire and linked with an Israeli withdrawal from the Occupied Territories. In Baghdad people thought it meant that the war was over and they came out into the streets and fired guns in the air, danced and sang, while the air raid sirens everywhere wailed.

The Soviet Union made one last attempt to head off the ground offensive. President Gorbachev invited Tariq Aziz, the Iraqi foreign minister, to Moscow to negotiate a ceasefire. On 22 February, to the surprise and pleasure of the Soviet side, the talks ended in success. The eight points of the agreement included a full and unconditional Iraqi withdrawal from

Kuwait, to begin on the second day of a ceasefire. The withdrawal would take place within a specified time and would be monitored by international observers. Economic sanctions would end after two-thirds of Iraqi forces had withdrawn and all UN resolutions would cease to apply after the withdrawal was complete.

President Gorbachev was probably as concerned with appeasing his conservative critics as with trying to settle the crisis. There was never any serious possibility that the Allies, at this late date, would accept terms which were relatively generous to Saddam Hussein. By now London and Washington were determined that nothing less than surrender was acceptable. In rejecting the Iraqi-Soviet agreement George Bush swallowed his irritation with Moscow but made it plain that there would be no time for anything other than full Iraqi acceptance of the UN demands before the ground war began. Speaking on Friday 22 February on the White House lawn he read from a prepared statement:

> In view of the Soviet initiative, which very frankly we appreciate, we want to set forth this morning the specific criteria that will ensure that Saddam Hussein complies with the United Nations mandate.
> The coalition will give Saddam Hussein until noon Saturday to do what he must do: begin his immediate and unconditional withdrawal from Kuwait. We must hear publicly and authoritatively his acceptance of these terms.

It was an ultimatum and it gave Saddam Hussein 24 hours to comply.

Every piece of British artillery in the Saudi desert, 72 in all, was fired that day, the gunners grunting and shouting their orders and responses hoarsely as the shells in their red cloth jackets were passed from hand to hand and placed in the breech. Self-propelled M109 guns on tracks like tanks fired their 95-pound high explosive shells on targets 12 miles away. The British Army's newest acquisition, the American M270 multiple launch rocket system, fired its long slender rockets too fast for the human eye to see properly, the vast columns of smoke they left behind them intertwining. The British said it was the biggest use of artillery since the Korean War: 1300 shells and 144 rockets. The gunners talked in the usual terms about having a job of work to do. One officer was quoted as saying: 'The lads have been feeling slightly frustrated. We have been here for 125 days. It's been a long wait and they are now glad to be involved.' On the other side the losses were frightening. Later, one Iraqi company commander said that M270 rockets had killed all but seven of his 250 men within ten minutes.

Gaps had already been bulldozed in the berms – the large banks of sand which marked the Saudi-Kuwait border. Markers with arrows and brigade symbols were set in the desert, marking the way to the gaps: everyone's big worry was having to queue up to get through the berms, with Iraqi tanks and artillery able to pick them off – perhaps with chemicals and gas. Iraqi deserters came across, hungry and scared, on most mornings. Many of them waved the leaflets which had been dropped in tens of thousands over their trenches. They brought with them stories of shortages and low morale. Many said they had no medical supplies and only a little rice and bread each day. 'When we showed him the roach coach,' one American marine said, meaning the mobile catering vans used by the US forces, 'I thought he was gonna lose it altogether. He just kinda stood there looking at it and crying.'

The forward Iraqi positions where these men came from had not for the most part been bombed. That would be a signal that the big push was coming. Still, American tanks and special forces were already pushing their way across into Kuwait in some places, rarely attracting more than a very occasional Iraqi shell in return. The assumption among the military was that this was because the Iraqis were husbanding their ammunition and waiting for them. It was an uneasy feeling, looking in the direction of the gaps in the berms, wondering what would happen when the tanks and armoured personnel carriers got there.

In a way the situation resembled World War I: you had no real idea who the other side were. For the allies, Iraqi soldiers were either deserters or bodies in the sand. There was something unpleasantly reminiscent, too, of the first day of the

Somme: the greatest artillery barrage in human history, which failed to wipe out the enemy; and men mown down in their thousands by machineguns as they queued up to get through the gaps in the wire. Everyone was confident enough but there was a salutory voice inside many of them that thought: 'Suppose we're being too confident?'

Some weeks later, in the comfortable Chelsea Arts Club in London, I talked to two of the television people who covered the war with the greatest success, Mark Urban from the BBC's 'Newsnight' and Steve Anderson, the producer who had worked with him. Mark Urban was a former army officer, young and confident, who specialized in defence reporting. When other people had been forecasting a war in November 1990, he had toured the Saudi desert and came back to report that fuel supplies simply weren't complete enough for the troops to attack.

Now, with the ground war imminent, he and Steve Anderson were having the time of their lives: instead of being restricted to the media pools as the better-known television names were, they were free to range around where they chose. Sometimes Urban would wear his Tank Corps beret and they would be waved through with a salute. They had entered Khafji just before the Iraqis attacked it and seen General Wadoud's forward observers watching them. Later they had watched the attacks on the Iraqi lines; 'As good a view,' Urban said, 'as watching the Crimean War from the Heights.'

When, eventually, the official media group got there, an NBC reporter called Brad Willis tried to get them and the other enterprising, free-wheeling journalists like Robert Fisk of the *Independent* ejected from Khafji on the grounds that they were there unofficially. Back in Dharan there was a problem with an American reservist officer called, absurdly, Captain Koko, an insurance executive from Kentucky in real life, who acted as a press liaison officer. He likened the 'rogue' journalists, as he called them, to cockroaches scuttling round a tenement building. He wanted to make life miserable for them, he said, and he certainly made it more difficult.

The irregular reporters, or 'unilaterals' as they called themselves, tended to look down on the official pool system

341

and often felt it did no good to the journalists who belonged to it and who, therefore, were closely associated with the military. The unilaterals felt that living the army life and wearing uniform for its own sake rather than as a disguise to get around – which is what the unilaterals did – blurred the necessary distinction between the reporters and the people they were reporting on. It certainly wasn't true of everyone in the pools, but in the end the unilaterals had the best of it: they were free to do the more adventurous and, often, the more informative reporting, and they often saw more action. The ground offensive was over so quickly that the British troops and many of the best American units were not as involved as much as they had hoped. As a result many of the journalists who were attached to them had disappointingly little of the war to report on.

The virtual sidelining of the British and others came partly as a matter of chance and partly from a decision which the British themselves took. When General Schwartzkopf began his plans for Operation Desert Sabre it was intended that the British 7th Armoured Brigade, with its Challenger tanks and its Warrior armoured fighting vehicles, should provide the heavy armour for the US Marine force which was to attack southern Kuwait and head up the coast. Slowly, though, the much inflated intelligence reports of Iraqi numbers changed General Schwartzkopf's mind for him. The Americans decided they would have to double their troop strength; the British also sent in a divisional command, another armoured brigade, more artillery and so on.

The commander of the British 1st Armoured Division was a youngish man with a formidable intellect, Major-General Rupert Smith. He had been badly burned in 1978 when he saved the life of one of his men in a car bomb explosion and was decorated for gallantry. Smith decided that his division would be more effective if it worked alongside the American VII Armoured Corps. They had taken part in NATO exercises together and many of the officers knew each other and had cooperated well. But that altered the relative balance of forces. A British armoured division is a great deal better equipped than the American Marine Corps, but is about half as powerful in terms of weaponry as an American armoured division. It also altered the direction the British would take. If the Iraqis had made a fight of it, the British would have been involved in some of the heaviest action. But what was to have been a battle turned into a race, and the British were not in a position to be up with the winners.

To fight a tank war in a desert is to play Nelson at Trafalgar. The sand is like the water, a medium through which the battle fleet progresses rather than a series of objectives which must be captured. This allows of the bluntest tactics: great arrows pointing into the heart of enemy territory, rather than cautious probes. General Schwartzkopf knew this. His model was the Battle of Alamein, a much smaller affair in terms of numbers (1200 British tanks against 520 German ones; the Allies had 3500 tanks against Iraq's 2000) but, as it turned out, a serious fight rather than a rout.

Schwartzkopf decided to telegraph to the enemy that an entirely different type of battle was about to be fought. The US Marine Corps was ordered to carry out a series of exercises designed to give the impression that part of the coalition forces would storm ashore and capture Kuwait from the sea. This was very much what Saddam Hussein's generals would have liked them to do: the coast was fairly well defended and there were thousands of mines close in to shore; 10 Iraqi divisions guarded the coastline against just such an attack. The main body of the coalition troops had spent four months along the southern border of Kuwait and the Iraqis assumed that this must be where the main Allied punch would come from. If they had invested $2.35 in a copy of the previous week's *Time* magazine they might have learned that the threat would come from the west; though by that stage it was probably too late anyway. Nevertheless the thief in West London who stole a lap-top computer from the car of an unfortunate RAF officer, Wing Commander David Farquhar, on 17 December had in his or her hands the entire outline of the Schwartzkopf plan. Wing Commander Farquhar was staff officer to Air Chief Marshal Sir Patrick Hine, the joint commander-in-chief of

British forces in the Gulf. He left his car for a matter of a few minutes in Acton, West London, to look at a car showroom. In that time the computer was stolen. The British Ministry of Defence and the Pentagon believed it was too much of a coincidence and decided that Iraqi agents must have been following Farquhar's car and seized their moment. The thief later sent the computer to the police, together with a note which presumably said no information had been given to Iraq. The incident ruined the career of the poor officer involved, but Saddam Hussein remained in ignorance of the plan to deceive him.

Schwartzkopf had been shifting his forces westwards along the Saudi-Iraqi border ever since the war began. Special forces had been infiltrated into Iraq almost as far as Nasiriyah, gathering intelligence and making sure the bridges were all down so that no supplies could reach Kuwait from Basra and no retreat was possible. A quarter of a million men and thousands of tanks, together with the enormous quantities of supplies they required, had taken up position well west of Kuwait by 23 February. In any other conflict it would have been quite impossible for such a deployment to go undetected. But the Iraqi troops in Kuwait were blind. They had no way of seeing what the Allies were doing because one way and another they had lost their air force and had no other form of intelligence available. Soviet satellites passed over the area at least twice a day but, in spite of the suspicions of some of the Cold War Warriors in the American intelligence community, Moscow did not pass on what it saw to Saddam Hussein. The Iraqis were trapped.

At the press conference he held when most of the fighting was over, on Wednesday 27 February, General Schwartzkopf made the entire plan clear, deception and all, in front of a large map:

Our plan initially had been to start over here in this area [the southern border of Kuwait], and do exactly what the Iraqis thought we were going to do, and that's take them on, head on, in their most heavily-defended area. Also, at the same time, we launched amphibious feints and naval gunfire in this area [the

Kuwaiti coast], so that they continued to think we were going to be attacking along this coast, and therefore fixed their forces in this position [a little inland from the coastline]. Our hope was that by fixing the forces in this position, and with this attack through here in this position [from the south], we would basically keep their forces here, and they wouldn't know what was going on out in this area [southwest of Kuwait]. I believe we succeeded in that very well.

The first move came shortly before dawn on 24 February. Saudi, Egyptian and Syrian troops, together with the US Marines, advanced all along the border into southern Kuwait. The Iraqis assumed this was the main thrust and their 3rd Corps moved slowly to meet it only to be driven back by the American Marines. The American 1st Cavalry division was also part of the deception, feinting into southwest Kuwait with orders to wheel and engage elements of no fewer than four Republican Guard divisions: the Hammurabi, the Faw, the Medina and the Tawakalna.

Meanwhile the real thrust was developing as the American VII and XVIII Corps moved into the undefended Iraqi desert. The XVIII Corps headed northwards, above and behind Kuwait, to make sure that the Iraqis' escape route would be blocked; the French captured the desert town of Al-Salman. The VII Corps, accompanied by the British, carried out a Guderian-like wheeling movement and took the Iraqis in the flank in the approved cavalry manner. As they smashed into Kuwait from the west they found the Iraqi tanks were often dug into positions facing entirely the wrong direction.

The best television pictures of the entire war were late in coming to people's screens. They were shot by a freelance, Vaughan Smith, who is part of a group of cameramen who were formerly in the British Army and specialize in covering wars. Rory Peck was another of the group. Vaughan had tricked his way into Saudi Arabia and hoped to be able to trick his way further by joining the regiment in which he had once served. Vaughan was wearing his old captain's uniform, which was a little out of date, and he felt very conspicuous because he was the only soldier in the entire theatre of war who didn't seem to have a weapon of any kind. He satisfied most people by saying he was an official army cameraman.

There were problems, however. When he reached one British base he found himself in a queue of men waiting to be checked into a computer and given orders. He made an excuse before reaching the head of the queue, escaped and hitched a lift on a truck which took him to the base of the British 4th Brigade. There he found a tank which took him to the front. His luck held. He talked his way onto an M270 multiple launch rocket system and got some remarkable pictures as the rockets were being fired: including the final low-tech moment when someone has to get out and check that all the rockets have really gone. That night, with the ground offensive about to begin, Vaughan Smith went in to a briefing where everyone was getting their orders. At the end of it the commanding officer said they should all be careful because there was a journalist who was masquerading as a captain in the army. Vaughan laughed dutifully with the others, and pushed his camera bag further under his seat.

Finding the British too inquisitive and too restrictive, Vaughan decided to try the Americans. He caught up with a US brigadier and told him angrily that he had had a road accident which was entirely the fault of the Americans. He had, he said, lost his Land Rover and his rifle and he wanted to know what the brigadier was going to do about it. The brigadier said he could send him into battle in a Bradley armoured vehicle. As captain, Vaughan outranked the Bradley's commander and gave the orders part of the time. When the gunner wasn't firing he went up and filmed from the turret as the Bradley headed into the Iraqi lines. With Vaughan filming, they destroyed two Iraqi T-72 tanks and one in a bunker. The vehicle beside them was hit and three or four Americans were killed. Nobody else had such good television pictures.

For Robert Fox, with the 14/20th King's Royal Hussars at the head of the 4th British Armoured Brigade, the battle began at 2 am on Sunday, 24 February: nine hours after President Bush's ultimatum had expired. It was raining and everyone seemed slightly nervous. Privately, Fox felt, most of them

346

half-expected that as the armoured vehicles were lined up to get through the gaps in the berms the Iraqis would hit them with chemical weapons. Instead it was an anti-climax: the Americans had bulldozed all the Iraqi positions on the other side into the ground. There would be no opposition there. Further on, he said, the Mother of Battles had turned into the Mother of Traffic Jams as they were forced to give way to the supply columns of those who had got through before them. They waited for hours. The rain came down in heavy, greasy drops thickened by the soot from the blazing Kuwaiti oil wells.

The men Fox was with saw a certain amount of action, but not the hand-to-hand kind that many of them had anticipated. As they drove through Iraqi lines they often came under fire, but the British Challengers picked off the elderly T-55s with ease as they and the Warrior fighting vehicles moved from one objective to the next. There were blazing tanks everywhere. By morning the Iraqis were giving up in their thousands. Elsewhere on the vast battlefield, Richard Dowden of the *Independent* found a group of Iraqis surrendering to him: a superb moment.

The worst casualties any British unit suffered during the entire war came that morning, when two Warriors were hit by Maverick missiles fired by American A-10 Thunderbolt aircraft. Nine soldiers died and 11 more were wounded. Three of the dead and wounded were hit when they ran over to try to rescue the men in the first Warrior. It was the single biggest loss of life in the war and there was considerable bitterness about the incident afterwards. The British Ministry of Defence did not reveal the full circumstances of the men's deaths. The Americans have a long-standing reputation in the British armed forces for carelessness and excitability on the battlefield dating back at least 50 years. When we were in Baghdad, Bob Simpson's father sent him a message congratulating him on coming under attack from the Americans. 'It happened to me twice in World War II,' he said.

By the evening of Monday, 25 February the Iraqis had effectively given in. The Soviet ambassador in Baghdad, who had remained there throughout the war, reported to the Soviet

Foreign Ministry that Saddam Hussein had told him he was prepared to comply with all the UN resolutions. A statement was issued on Baghdad radio at 10.35 London time which went some of the way towards that:

> Orders have been issued to our armed forces to withdraw in an organized manner to the positions they held prior to 1 August 1990. This is regarded as practical compliance with Resolution 660. Our armed forces, which have proven their ability to fight and stand fast, will confront any attempt to harm them while they are carrying out the withdrawal order.

American signals intelligence had intercepted a number of radio messages from Iraqi generals in Kuwait to Saddam Hussein asking – and sometimes pleading – for permission to withdraw. It must have become unpleasantly plain to him as early as Sunday, 24 February that the war was lost. Indeed, he may well have realized much earlier that directly the Allies attacked he would have to order a withdrawal. His bluff failed once it became clear that the coalition was using weapons which were not causing mass destruction in civilian areas, and would not therefore result in the kind of international revulsion he had been counting on.

Saddam Hussein had repeated to Yevgeny Primakov two weeks earlier, during the final attempt by the Soviet Union to negotiate a peaceful end to the crisis, that it would be suicidal for him to show weakness. Now, with his generals reporting a military collapse all along the line, he must have realized that the moment of real weakness had arrived. His army was the one protection he had; it was more important to surrender in Kuwait than to risk being overthrown in Baghdad. The statement on Baghdad radio was intended to minimize his personal humiliation while in effect asking the Allies to stop destroying his forces. It failed. President Bush wanted Saddam Hussein to say the words himself.

As early as January, according to officials in Baghdad, Saddam had issued a set of outline orders to his generals in Kuwait. He had anticipated the disruption of his communications and he gave them instructions in the event of a withdrawal. Those instructions included setting off explosives at Kuwait's main oil installations. At the end of January Iraqi soldiers, acting on orders received from Baghdad, opened the valves on the oil pipeline leading to Kuwait's Sea Island loading terminal, offshore from the Mina al-Ahmadi complex on the coast south of Kuwait City. The millions of barrels of crude oil which gushed out into the sea formed a slick 35 miles by 10 miles, moving at a speed of about 15 miles a day: the biggest oil spillage in the history of the world.

Now, with the war already lost, there was a new assault: the first of 500 fires were started by explosions at Kuwait's oil installations, setting fire to the gases mixed in with the oil. Flames sprang up all along the horizon, turning the sand dunes grey and black for miles around and darkening the sun at noon. In Saudi Arabia people drove in daytime with their headlights full on and aircraft found it impossible to land or take off. It was an act of pre-meditated vengeance on the instructions of a man who guessed his gamble might not pay off and who wanted to make everyone pay as a result.

By Tuesday, 26 February, two days into the ground offensive, the advancing Allies had taken 23,500 prisoners and the worst enemy was the weather. The number of American casualties from enemy fire was only as great as the number who had been injured or killed by accidents to their vehicles. The Iraqis were heading up the road to Basra in large numbers and the Apache helicopters were picking off the vehicles at leisure. As the rain grew worse it protected the Iraqis a little: the only protection they received.

The 1st Cavalry division was still engaged on the longest march American soldiers have ever made to engage an enemy. They swung into the north of Kuwait, near the Rumailah oilfield which had brought the Iraqis into the country in the first place. It had taken them 30 hours to get there and they were starting to close in on the Republican Guard divisions which were their target. Then they heard news of the ceasefire. Some of the men were pleased and relieved; others felt cheated. 'We came all the way over here,' said one. 'We should have done something.' The ground war had run out before their extraordinary advance could come to anything.

It was partly the 'turkey-shoot' on the road to Basra that did it. The BBC correspondent, Kate Adie, came across the hundreds of wrecked cars and trucks, with no noise in the entire place except the wind blowing through the shattered windows and the litter of stolen goods – handbags, toys, cheap jewellery – lying in the sand. Robert Fox thought there were probably no more than 400 deaths there – a massacre, certainly, but not the bloodbath on the scale many people in the West assumed. But the pictures on television apparently played a part in President Bush's decision to call a halt to the war then and there. It had lasted 100 hours and had achieved everything he had intended. He seemed anxious not to turn the public mood from one of relief and rejoicing into one of revulsion. There were other reasons too. Egypt and Saudi Arabia were unwilling to see Baghdad captured and Saddam taken prisoner or killed by the Allies. There was even some question about the willingness of Allied troops to go on attacking an unresisting enemy. Altogether, it seemed the best time to stop – even though General Schwartzkopf believed they should have gone on for another couple of days.

On Tuesday 27th a CBS correspondent, Bob McKeown, liberated Kuwait City some way ahead of the first Allied troops. It was an act of considerable enterprise, achieved because he and his crew were not part of the official pool system and were therefore free to venture out on their own. They received an ecstatic welcome from the Kuwaitis as they drove into the city. But what he saw in Kuwait appalled him too:

> Beyond the jubilation we felt there is desolation. Buildings have been destroyed or partially destroyed. There are hulks of automobiles and Iraqi vehicles, and there is a sense of desertedness . . . I took a ride with the captain of the Kuwaiti national football team who was taking his BMW for a spin for the first time in seven months. He had kept it in hiding because he was sure the Iraqis would take it. A lot of homes have been appropriated, a lot of the hotels along the seafront have been burned. The streets have been barricaded. There is a Beirut-like sense to parts of downtown Kuwait.

But now people were flooding out onto the streets to

welcome in their liberators. Mark Urban and Steve Anderson of the BBC and their camera crew made it to Kuwait City the day after McKeown. Other BBC teams had been less lucky and were beaten to Kuwait and its capital by ITN. The US Marines tried to stop Urban and his group getting in because they wanted Arab troops to have the honour of taking the city first. But Urban and Anderson had some extremely good maps and found a way in across waste ground. People poured out to greet them as well. They stopped to ask a man what his feelings were when he saw the first Allied soldier. 'You're the first we've seen,' the man said. 'I've stayed indoors for four months and I've just come out.'

Urban and Anderson made for the British embassy and joined the others who had arrived ahead of them. The television satellite dishes had already been set up. That night, after sending their report, Mark Urban slept in the sand outside the embassy.

> The next morning we're cooking breakfast and I'm shaving and loving myself and being cheerful when a couple of lads from the Sports and Social [the SAS] turn up. I recognize them by their weapons, Armalite carbines, and because they're older. A moment or two later, they bring back a bloke from MI6 in the full Monty – green quilted jacket, walkie-talkie. After he's asked who we are, he says: 'If I were you, I'd keep on filming, because something rather spectacular's going to happen.'

A helicopter arrived and several more SAS men came swarming down a rope. They went through their building-clearance routine and blew the embassy door in shortly before the janitor arrived with the key. Then the ambassador, Michael Weston, was brought in laughing and joking to take control of the embassy where he had held out for so long under siege before the war began. It was another dark morning and the tall buildings on the skyline were outlined against the burning oilfields. It looked as though all the worst predictions about the war had come true. In some ways, perhaps, they had.

Vaughan Smith, the cameraman who commanded the American Bradley in action, ended up catching a US army plane to Sicily in order to get his pictures out uncensored. At the American base there they almost rumbled him and a sergeant began to telephone the British military authorities in Germany. Vaughan snatched his completely unofficial credentials from the sergeant's hand and stormed out, planning the hire a car in order to drive to Frankfurt. He stopped a little way out of town at a beach. He had lost his only pair of socks long before the battle started and some of the skin from his heels had become detached after sticking to his boots. As he was paddling in the water he heard a sound and saw four men stealing his camera equipment from the car. He ran on his painful bare feet to the police station, tracking blood across their carpet. The police adored the drama.

The chief of police was very sympathetic when Vaughan told him why the cassettes were so important. He replied that his men could start a big search, which might not produce anything, but if Vaughan paid him $8000 he would definitely get the cassettes back. The next day the cassettes were returned, though not the equipment. The chief of police summoned the local press and there was a photocall for Vaughan Smith – who had filmed some of the best pictures of the Gulf War – and for the chief of police who got them back.

THE HOUSE OF PEACE

Uprising

> Those who were misled by saboteurs and rioters have nothing to fear ... Only murderers, rapists and those who stole State or private property will not be pardoned. We have nothing against people who were forced to attend demonstrations and who shouted just to satisfy the saboteurs.
>
> Saddam Hussein, speaking in Kurdistan after the uprising, 14 April 1991

Three tents had been fitted together to make one large enough for the ceremony. For the sake of security they were unmarked. Hard chairs were set round a plain table and a row of seats was arranged behind. There were notepads on the table in front of each place, bottles of water, white coffee cups. Little bowls contained hummus and chips. Outside tanks, field guns and even a battery of Patriot missiles had been assembled: the Republican Guard were only a few miles away. At 11.30 two US Army vehicles, escorted by Bradleys bearing large white flags with red crescents, came driving up to Safwan air base in southern Iraq. Two Apache helicopters flew low overhead, keeping to the speed of the convoy. The base had been captured by the Americans less than a week before. Now it was Sunday, 3 March, the culmination of the careers of the men who were waiting. For those being escorted in it must have been both painful and dangerous.

General Schwartzkopf was polite and punctilious as the eight Iraqi officers arrived. They were introduced to the other leading figures: Lieutenant-General Khalid bin Sultan, the Saudi commander, Lieutenant-General Sir Peter de la Billière,

Major-General Jabir al-Sabah, the Kuwaiti chief of staff, and others. To those of us who had watched Iraqi television, one of the newcomers was a familiar figure: the bulky, pleasant-faced Lieutenant-General Sultan Hashim Ahmad, looking a little like Saddam Hussein himself. The other was also a lieutenant-general, less well-known, called Saleh Abbud Mahmud. Both of them had the right to kiss Saddam on the cheeks: we had watched it dozens of times. A major-general, Kahlid Hussein Ali, went into the tent behind them and did not sit with them; he would have kissed Saddam only on the shoulders.

The rest of the Iraqi group followed: four brigadiers, an air force officer, two naval officers, a colonel and an interpreter. It must have been a very uneasy group, each of them watching the others for any words or behaviour that would have to be reported back to Saddam Hussein himself. A word spoken out of place, a glance, might lead to their execution. Saddam had been strongly against sending his military commanders to what was, in effect, a surrender ceremony, but he was persuaded to take part by the Soviet ambassador in Baghdad. General Schwartzkopf ordered the cameras not to film the Iraqis being searched. 'I don't want them embarrassed in any way,' he said and submitted himself to a search before them. The meeting in the tent went on for more than an hour and the Iraqis agreed to everything. Saddam wanted everything dealt with fast; a little humiliation now would protect his position later. The ten points of the agreement included:

> The immediate release of Allied prisoners of war;
> the return of goods taken from Kuwait after the invasion;
> the return of abducted Kuwaiti citizens;
> the clearance of mines planted in Kuwait;
> and the clearance of booby traps inside foreign embassies in
>   Kuwait City.

By 1.20 the agreement was signed and everyone trooped out. Then something unexpected happened. General Schwartzkopf invited the Iraqis into his tent where they stayed for about 20 minutes. American sources indicated later that he had told them in plain terms that it was up to them as military men to get rid of Saddam Hussein and that Iraq would not return to normality while he was in power. Yet in making up the team Saddam must have anticipated something of the sort and must have regarded each of the officers with intense suspicion as a result. He was under more threat now than he had been at any time in his years in power. He would survive only by showing the strongest nerve.

The Iraqis had undergone a horrifying experience and no one yet knew how they would react. As the agreement was being signed at Safwan, soldiers were still streaming back to Basra and beyond. With them went what remained of the execution squads, Baath Party members for the most part with nothing to lose. Those execution squad members who hadn't deserted had been shooting people to the end and the best hope for most ordinary soldiers had been to surrender to the advancing Allies. They had grabbed eagerly at the leaflets which Allied planes and helicopters dropped over their trenches. They knew they had to wave them at coalition soldiers as a ticket to safety. In some trenches the leaflets were bought and sold; in others they were used as a form of currency. 'We counted the hours when we would see the Americans coming,' one officer said. 'If only I could live until they came, and then live long enough to see the soldiers face to face,' said a man in Basra, 'then I knew I would be all right. I would see my family again.' His face creased up, the tears came to his eyes and he couldn't speak any more.

Many of the Republican Guard divisions had been held back from the front line and they had stood firmer at the end despite their heavy casualties. Saddam Hussein had not committed them to battle, knowing that they would be needed to protect his government in the event of defeat. It was becoming clear that the destruction of the Republican Guard had been exaggerated. Several Guard divisions had already been withdrawn to Iraq by the time the ground offensive ended. Of the 29 Iraqi divisions which had been destroyed, the majority were from the regular army. It was the ordinary conscripts who had suffered the most.

In the week before the peace agreement was signed the retreating Iraqi soldiers were all mixed up together, caught in the terrible undisciplined column that withdrew from Kuwait towards Basra. Until the fighting stopped on 28 February the coalition insisted on regarding them as a retreating army, warning that they would be safe only if they abandoned their weapons and their vehicles. Even when they did, many Iraqis died. The action of the Allied forces did not contravene the Hague Convention of 1907, which forbids the attacking of soldiers who have already surrendered. These men mostly wanted to surrender, but had no way of showing it. They were attacked from the air and the Allied pilots who killed them can have had no idea whether they were armed or unarmed, willing to resist or desperate to give themselves up.

The horrors the Iraqi troops faced on the Basra road matched those which some of them had committed in Kuwait City: the random killings as they pulled out, the burning of buildings, the seizure of people as hostages. In the Nayef Palace the intelligence men had abandoned everything and run, leaving the tools of their trade behind them: electricity cable, electric fans, buckets of water, bloodstained hunting knives. Men and women had been slowly tortured to death for enjoyment here. Western reporters who saw Iraqi prisoners herded into cells in Kuwait found it hard to associate the terrible things which had been done with the pitiable figures they saw before them. Robert Fisk couldn't help but feel sorry for 'these defeated teenagers with their sad smiles'; but, he asked himself, what kind of men had raped Kuwait?

The aggressor-victims headed into Basra, hungry, frightened and bitter, their loyalties and their sense of values in turmoil. Many were openly blaming Saddam Hussein and cursing him for what had happened. At about the time General Schwartzkopf was advising the Iraqi generals in Safwan to overthrow Saddam, a group of Shi'i activists from Basra crossed the Allied line to deliver a plea for help. On the night of Friday 1 March, the day after President Bush called a halt to the Allied attack, a major uprising against Saddam Hussein had broken out in the city.

The uprising was not begun by soldiers, but the chaos they brought with them as they crowded into the streets of the city, jamming the roadways with their vehicles and firing their guns, showed how catastrophic the defeat had been. Basra had suffered more during Saddam Hussein's wars than any other Iraqi city. It is almost 100 per cent Shi'i and the old resentments against the rule of the Sunni Moslems gave a focus to the mood of anger and bewilderment. It was a revolutionary moment.

Crowds stormed through the centre of the city, attacking everything connected with Saddam Hussein and the Baath Party. The governor's palace was burned, the Baath Party headquarters ransacked, the security offices looted and the files destroyed. There were road blocks on all the entrances to the city to prevent loyalist soldiers getting in. At first the leaders of the revolution were local people whose hatred for Saddam Hussein's rule was largely unfocused but who knew that he was critically weakened and that now was the time to move against him.

Within a day new leaders and a new set of aims arrived. Shi'i fundamentalists, the followers of Mohammad Bakr al-Hakim, began arriving in sizeable numbers from across the border in Iran. Al-Hakim was a long-standing opponent of Saddam Hussein and his group, the Supreme Assembly of the Islamic Revolution in Iraq, was based in Tehran. It had the strong backing of the Iranian government which supplied them with transport into Iraq when the moment came. It was that, more than anything else, which ensured that the uprisings which were starting to take place spontaneously in the other Shi'i towns and cities in southern Iraq, would not succeed.

In Basra a fundamentalist crowd stormed the Sheraton Hotel, burning the bars and the casino. In the centre of the city another large group, largely composed of men and women who had arrived from Iran, started to proclaim the establishment of a Shi'i Islamic Republic. This immediately divided the soldiers who had come up from Kuwait. Many of them were themselves Shi'i and half-inclined to go along with the revolutionaries. But many of the others were Sunni and the officers in the Iraqi army are largely drawn from the Sunni area around Mosul. If the revolutionaries had concentrated on the overthrow of Saddam Hussein and the Baath Party, they might well have gained the support of the shattered remnants of the army and given it an objective to fight for. The demand for a

Shi'i republic, however, held no attraction for them what-soever. It seemed to promise only sectarianism and the break-up of the country. The army has traditionally seen itself as the one institution which holds Iraq together. The officers began to rally their men against the revolutionaries. Yet the uprising had such strength among the ordinary citizens of Basra as well as the committed exiles that the fighting was bitter and lasted several days. When I went to Basra a month later with Bob Simpson we found the evidence everywhere. On a piece of waste ground an armoured personnel carrier had been attacked and blown to pieces. Helmets and bits of equipment still lay beside the roadway. Every portrait of Saddam had been shot at, smashed, burned, attacked with paint.

The revolutionaries had expected help from the Allied troops a short way away. The group who had headed for Safwan came back empty-handed. They had been unable to see any senior Allied officers. The coalition insisted in the ceasefire agreement that there should be no movement of aircraft in Iraq without permission; later, two aircraft which took off north of Baghdad were shot down. But the agreement did not specify that there should be no movement of helicopters, tanks or artillery. Later there was a good deal of controversy over whether General Schwartzkopf should have continued the war for two more days and headed straight for Baghdad; he had to apologize to President Bush for suggesting the possibility in public. To have gone to Baghdad would have been unaccept-able to the Arab members of the coalition and would have gone well beyond anything sanctioned by the UN resolutions. It would also have landed the United States in precisely the quagmire which President Bush wanted to avoid.

But the Allies could certainly have forbidden Saddam Hussein to use tanks and helicopters in Basra and elsewhere and this was not done. Partly, it seems, it was the natural caution of politicians who had won a great victory and were wary of putting it at risk. There were also strong fears that Iraq might fall apart along religious and ethnic lines. It was easier to do nothing. There were hints afterwards in Washington that senior Iraqi military officers had made it clear that if the United States gave them a sign of support they would throw their weight behind the uprisings against Saddam Hussein. In a speech which many Iraqis would soon hold against him, President Bush spoke on 1 March of the need to get rid of Saddam Hussein. Referring to the economic hardship Iraq was suffering, he said:

> The Iraqi people should put him aside, and that would facilitate the solution of all these problems.

Britain agreed. On the same day the Foreign Secretary, Douglas Hurd said: 'Iraq cannot expect to be readmitted to the community of nations while it has a delinquent régime.' But within a few days that approach seemed to have changed. No clear signals came from Washington to reinforce what General Schwartzkopf had told the Iraqi delegation in his tent at Safwan: that the army should overthrow Saddam Hussein.

Meanwhile the Shi'i uprising spread and seemed to prosper. Apart from Basra, seven provinces fell under the control of the revolutionaries: Nasiriyah, Amara, Kut, Simawa, Diwaniya, Najaf and Kerbala. In some cases they held on for almost a week before the Republican Guard moved in to crush them with tanks and helicopter gunships. The pattern was more or less the same: anger and bitterness against the government, followed swiftly by the Islamic fundamentalists. In many places the popular uprising was accompanied by a settling of old scores. People were accused of being government informers and attacked or murdered; sometimes, it was later said, the government informers got in with the first accusation to save themselves. There was no proper control over what was done and little thought was devoted to guarding against the inevitable Republican Guard counterattack.

In Kerbala, the second holiest city of Shi'i Islam, it took six days of constant shelling by tanks and field artillery to subdue the revolt. An unknown number of people died and bodies littered the streets for days. The Army had orders not to move the dead in order to frighten people and to punish them as well. In Kerbala and elsewhere many Party and Security officials were hanged because they had escaped rather than staying to deal with the outbreak. If they had stayed, of course, the revolutionaries would have killed them; serving Saddam was never an easy option. When the loyalist forces regained power, some of those who were shown to have taken part in the uprising were executed by being forced to drink petrol which was then set alight.

I went to Kerbala in April, a month after the uprising. Little had been done to clear up the devastation which the army had caused. It seems likely that we were allowed to go there only because there was still a general uncertainty about the political future of Iraq and the Information Ministry officials were unclear what they could and couldn't allow people to see. Later it became impossible to go to either of the holy cities. Even in Kerbala we were not allowed to see one of the shrines because the damage was too bad. The rebels had withdrawn there, assuming they would have some measure of protection. But the Republican Guard units which were attacking them were Sunni and had no compunction about using artillery to shell the shrines.

When I talked to the crew of a Chieftain tank parked outside the shrine of Al-Abbas it was plain that Saddam had their total loyalty. Like him they were Sunni Moslems and they didn't like Shi'ites much: one said they were dirty animals. Saddam Hussein's picture smiled out at me from the tank's driving compartment, where other soldiers might have put a pin-up. Their tank was established right in front of the entrance to the shrine. To right and left buildings had been knocked down to create a field of fire. Property-owners had been given three days to leave the area and find somewhere else to live. 'Long live the Islamic Revolution under Imam Bakr al-Hakim' said a slogan on the wall of the Baath Party headquarters. No one had yet started painting out the graffiti.

When we reached Najaf we found the same contempt among Sunni soldiers for a Shi'i holy place. The soldiers had parked their motorcycles in the courtyard of the most sacred mosque in Shi'i Islam. It was as though an army of Calvinists had taken over St Peter's in Rome. The golden dome of the shrine had been hit several times by artillery fire and the outer walls had been badly damaged: we were not allowed inside. In the shops opposite the shrine the shutters were closed but the shopkeepers were locked up inside them.

We were taken to see the leading cleric of the Shi'a faith. Grand Ayatollah Abolqassem al-Khoei is 93 and was in a pitiful state. There was only one person to look after him and flies settled incessantly on his face as he spoke to us. He chose his words as carefully as he could, but it was clear he had been taken from Najaf against his will and made to broadcast an appeal to people not to support the uprising. The broadcast had confused many of the revolutionaries and seemed to have weakened their support for the uprising. Since then the Grand Ayatollah had been under house arrest. Armed soldiers were on guard outside his door, though they were removed for our visit. When he started to complain about all this we were told we had another appointment and had to leave.

In the past Saddam Hussein had always tried to deal even-handedly with the different religions in Iraq. He had been filmed praying at Najaf and had donated large sums of money to beautify and enlarge it. Now that approach had changed. Saddam must have approved a series of six articles in the Party newspaper, *Ath Thawra*, which strongly attacked the Shi'i faith. Gossip said he had written them himself. One article implied that Shi'i weren't proper Iraqis, but had been brought from India. If you look at their faces, it said, you can see they look like monkeys. Another questioned their religious rites and their morals: 'Their wives leave home every day, and their husbands don't know where they go.' A third doubted the validity of Shi'i marriages because the ceremony is borrowed from ancient Persia. The implication was that the children of any Shi'ite marriage would be illegitimate.

Much of the centre of Najaf had been levelled and people were kept away from us in case they might speak. A little later, in the deserted, desolate, ruined neighbourhood around the shrine of Ali, I faintly heard a call to prayer. The Shi'i call includes a mention of the dispute which separates Shi'a from Sunni Islam: 'There is no God but God, and Mohammed is His Prophet – and Ali His Deputy.' It was now forbidden to proclaim the essence of the Shi'i belief in the position and religious significance of Ali.

The new governor of Najaf, appointed immediately after the end of the revolt, was a singularly unpleasant man called Abdul-Rahman al-Douri. He had previously been director general at the Security Ministry in Baghdad, making him privy to the workings of the Iraqi state. In Najaf he was probably called on to do even worse things. He was thoroughly unprepossessing: oleaginous, soft-footed, his hair a miracle of the trichologist's art, combed and plastered sideways and forwards to cover his bald patch. There was too much flesh on his face and it lay in folds along the line of his chin. He praised Saddam Hussein so intensively and so long when we went to see him that it became necessary to interrupt in order to ask him some questions. He confirmed that a sizeable proportion of the population of Najaf had taken part in the uprising, but would say nothing about the methods used to end it. In the streets no one wanted to talk about what had happened either. It was said that hundreds of thousands of people had fled to the marshlands near the border with Iran. The conditions there were terrible, but in the vastness of the marshes they at least felt safe from Saddam's army.

The sufferings of the Shi'i people attracted little sympathy in the West. In the public mind they were associated – wrongly, since the Shi'i in Iraq have a long tradition of quiescence and moderation – with terrorism, hijacking and hostage taking. They were also associated with Iran and the involvement in the uprising of the Supreme Assembly of the Islamic Revolution in Iraq, with its headquarters in Tehran, strongly reinforced that. With different people, under different circumstances, the United States might have decided to help the rebels. Now there was no incentive at all. The White House envisaged the possibility of a break-up of Iraq, with the southern Shi'i part being taken by Iran.

American anxiety about what was happening in southern Iraq was probably misplaced. It was highly unlikely that Iran, which had often showed a high degree of nervousness about its small Arab minority in Khuzestan, would want to increase its Arab population by a further eight or nine million Iraqis. In fact, once the rebellions had started, Iran's anxieties ran strangely parallel to those of the United States. Its Foreign

Ministry warned that if Iraq started to break up, Saudi Arabia would move in and establish a régime favourable to itself. Iran was happy to weaken Saddam Hussein by sending in the volunteers from the Supreme Assembly, but it did not want to see him – and Iraqi unity – disappear. President Rafsanjani sent messages to Saddam urging him to negotiate with the rebels in order to prevent a collapse of the national structure of Iraq.

And so the United States began to row back. On 5 March, only four days after President Bush had spoken of the need for the Iraqi people to get rid of Saddam Hussein, White House spokesperson Marlin Fitzwater said: 'We don't intend to get involved . . . in Iraq's internal affairs.' It was a clear signal to the Iraqi military that Washington would not intervene to help them if they attempted to overthrow Saddam Hussein. The following day, 6 March, the Republican Guard finally succeeded in taking Basra. Tanks moved in and cleared the city of opposition street by street. The damage was worse than anything suffered during the war with Iran or the Allied bombing. Dogs ate the bodies of the dead, left where they fell as a warning to the population. The executions began.

By 3 March there was revolution in the north of Iraq too. It attracted much greater interest and sympathy in the outside world than the Shi'i uprising had. The Kurdish rebels had more cohesion and purpose than the Shi'i and the Patrotic Union of Kurdistan (an umbrella grouping which included seven different Kurdish parties) kept in touch with the bands of insurgents who had risen up to attack the Baath Party organization and the security police in each of a dozen or more Kurdish towns and cities. Later, when they felt the Americans had betrayed them, the Kurds tended to give the impression that they had risen up against Saddam Hussein because President Bush called on them to do so.

At first, as in the south, everything went their way. When the guerrillas of the Kurdish Peshmurga attacked the headquarters of the Iraqi 24th army division near the town of Dukan on 5 March, hundreds of soldiers surrendered to them and some joined the fight. The remarkable aspect was that the 24th was composed of Iraqi Arabs who, it had been assumed, had little sympathy for the Kurds. There was even better news for the Peshmurga that day. Units of the Jash, the fiercely pro-government Kurdish militia which Saddam Hussein had set up to keep control of Iraqi Kurdistan, were defecting to the rebels.

The sympathy for the Kurds in the West was often tinged with guilt. At the end of World War I, President Woodrow Wilson of the United States promised the Kurds their own state in the break-up of the Ottoman Empire. The treaty of Sèvres in 1920 enshrined the promise. But Britain's decision to give the oil-bearing region of Mosul to the new country of Iraq made that an impossibility and subsequently the Kurdish lands were divided up between Turkey, Syria, Iraq, Iran and the Soviet Union. When the Kurds staged an uprising in what was just becoming northern Iraq, the RAF carried out a campaign of air bombardment against Kurdish villages. It was the first time air power had been used against a civil population in peace time.

As descendants of the Medes and the Scythians, twenty-five million in number, the Kurds are the largest nation on earth which still lacks the right of self-determination. Curiously, it was only in Saddam Hussein's Iraq that the Kurds achieved a degree of autonomy. The Kurdish language, which was illegal in Turkey and hardly encouraged in several of the other countries where they live, was given official status by the Iraqi government. Yet when the Kurds of Halabje showed their desire for independence from Iraq in 1988 and sided with Saddam's enemies, his retaliation was savage. Elsewhere thousands of Kurds were rounded up and, presumably, murdered. 'The Kurds have no friends but the mountains,' runs one of their proverbs. History had borne it out many times and was about to bear it out again.

Even when 12 out of Iraq's 18 provinces were in the hands of rebels, Saddam Hussein kept his nerve. There seems to have been some truth to the rumours that he contacted the government of Algeria to see if it would give him asylum. The rumours began on 27 February, the day before the ceasefire was agreed. By 1 March *Le Monde* reported it as fact, though it was strongly denied by the Algerian presidential office. It was probably an insurance policy on Saddam's part. The man who had once shown pictures of Ceausescu's body to his colleagues was not going to enter a period of serious unrest without a little forethought. He is said also to have allowed his generals and anyone else to know that if anyone tried to overthrow him and failed, three entire layers of their extended family would be destroyed: that could have meant well over 100 men, women and children.

Saddam's instinct was to crush the rebellions, not to run from them. On 6 March he appointed a new interior minister, Ali Hassan al-Majid, one of his cousins from Takrit. In the past al-Majid had done some of Saddam's dirtiest work for him, as minister in charge of internal security for example. Now, however, he was out of a job: he had most recently been governor of Kuwait. In the 1970s al-Majid had been in charge of the 'Arabization' of parts of Kurdistan, an operation which had destroyed 3000 Kurdish villages. In 1988 it was he who gave the orders for the use of chemical weapons against Halabje. In Kirkuk, where he had a house, the local people called him 'Ali Chemical'. By appointing him interior minister, Saddam Hussein was making the strongest possible declaration of intent: he was determined to hold on to power by any means whatever.

Other gestures were made to show that Saddam was planning to stay on. The Republican Guard was given a cash bonus of 100 dinars, followed by another of 25 dinars. Much as the later Roman emperors secured their legions' loyalty at times of rebellion by paying them donatives in debased silver, so Saddam Hussein's Finance Ministry printed hundreds of thousands of new 25 dinar notes on photo-copying machines. These were the notes which prudently omitted his portrait.

The war had not changed life in Baghdad to anything like the extent seen in the rebellious Shi'i towns and cities to the south. Although there was little water or electricity – of the 1195 megawatts Baghdad required for domestic and industrial purposes, it was unable to provide more than 120 two weeks after the war ended – the government was plainly in control and it was not difficult to persuade people that it was going to remain so. There were no television broadcasts for Saddam to

367

appear on, but Baghdad Radio had ordered a series of new songs to be composed in praise of him and his decision to throw the country into a hopeless war:

> By standing alone, O Iraq,
> The whole world will regard you
> With pride and dignity
> Until the end of time.

And:

> Sir, don't worry,
> With you Iraq is safe.
> Only God knows how much we love you,
> O Saddam.

Even Saddam's playboy son Uday reappeared. The story had spread that Uday had been killed in the Shi'i uprising, but in the 6 March edition of a new newspaper, *Al-Baath*, of which he was chairman of the editorial board, he wrote a signed editorial to say he was back. The rumours that he was dead were, he said, 'crows' croaks and dogs' barks.' The style was unmistakeably Uday's.

There are few more heady experiences than being with people who have liberated themselves by their own efforts from some hated regime. Everyone is a brother. Revolutionary crowds cease to be a collection of cowardly, fallible individuals and become, for a brief moment, something grander and more generous. Portraits of the tyrant are smashed, words are spoken that no one has dared speak before, the air of liberty is breathed. It has an intoxicating effect and, once free, it is hard for anyone to imagine that they could ever again become enslaved. From Prague in 1968 to Tiananmen Square in 1989 and on to Kirkuk and Basra in 1991, people believed that because what had happened was so right and because so many good and decent people wanted it, the revolution could never be reversed.

This feeling was everywhere in Kurdistan. People danced in

the streets. They broke into the offices and torture-chambers of the Mukhabarat. They savoured the experience of being able to say what they wanted for the first time in their lives:

> You don't know what it's like, not having to think about what you are saying or who you are saying it to, not having to think about who is watching you or who is following you. It is wonderful, wonderful . . . Saddam is finished. We are free. We have got rid of fear.

It was the beginning of March. The mountains of Kurdistan were still covered with snow, but the valleys and the meadows were green and spring torrents were starting to flow fast down to the chilly lakes. It would soon be Now Ruz, the Kurdish new year. In Zakho and Kirkuk, Erbil and Suleimaniya a new era had already begun. It was, people said, the first time they had been free in 71 years and the yellow flag of Kurdistan was everywhere. A squat, heavily-built bear of a man, Massoud Barzani, the second generation of his family to lead the Kurdish Democratic Party, toured the liberated area and addressed enormous crowds in the towns and villages. Again and again he expressed his delight at being able to appear openly in places where he could scarcely have come in secret before:

> One second of this day is worth all the wealth in the world.

The sheer pleasure on people's upturned faces as they listened to him showed that it wasn't just rhetoric.

Barzani had long been a realist. He knew that a Kurdish state which would take in all or even most of the Kurdish people was an impossibility. He was not looking for independence but for autonomy within the Iraqi system. To British correspondents he would say he wanted it to be like Scotland. As they crowded round him, reaching out their hands to touch him, the people looked different from Arab Iraqis. Their hair was lighter and many of their children were blond; many had the green eyes and the fiercely hooked noses which indicated an Indo-European rather than a Semitic origin. The Arabs tended to look down on them. 'They are dirty and primitive,' a

369

cultured friend of mine said in Baghdad. The Kurds felt a certain hostility to the Iraqi Arabs, but it was not intense. Their real hostility was centred on Saddam Hussein.

People who had been away from Iraq for years were coming back to the Kurdish towns and villages from Turkey and Iran and from much further afield: Britain, France, the United States. They wanted to be in at the beginning, to create a new Kurdistan from scratch. Even the old inhabitants of Halabje were returning from Iran. They had escaped there when Saddam Hussein's cousin, Ali Chemical, destroyed their homes and their relatives. It was a painful experience and some of them even now found the decayed and hidden bodies of people who had died in the poison gas attack. But it represented something important to them: a sign that Kurdistan could live again.

The feeling endured for exactly three weeks. Then, on 26 March 1991, Ali Chemical came back. In Kirkuk the helicopter gunships appeared over the horizon without warning. In Zakho and Suleimaniya the Republican Guard moved in with heavy artillery. It was carefully judged: the weaponry used against the Kurds was purely conventional. Saddam Hussein pushed everything to the limit, but not beyond. If he had used chemical weapons against the Kurds a second time, Allied forces would have intervened. As it was, they did nothing. President Bush warned the Iraqis not to attack the Kurds, but nothing was done about it when the attacks took place. The Iraqi leadership played the game with the greatest subtlety; it knew that the guiding principle behind all United States action now was the desire to avoid any more fighting or any open-ended commitment to keep ground forces in the area. It was a matter therefore of pushing the Americans insistently but never quite hard enough to force them to retaliate.

In the mountains of northern Iraq, as in the marshlands of the south, the people who a short time before had believed that Saddam was finished and that they would never be his prisoners again were setting out in pitiful refugee convoys, leaving everything in order to escape his army. At least four Republican Guard divisions which had escaped from Kuwait are thought to have taken part in the recapture of Basra, Najaf and Kerbala, then moved northwards to the Kurdish towns and cities. They joined other Republican Guard divisions there. Sometimes they attacked the refugee columns on the roads to the mountains, but mostly they left them alone; too many attacks on civilians might attract the attention and anger of the United States. Hundreds of thousands of Kurds found no means of transport and had to walk over the mountains: eastwards towards Iran, northwards towards Turkey. It was well below freezing at night and there was no food on the way. The mountains – supposedly the Kurds' only friends – were their enemies now.

Many Kurdish people felt a bitter fury at what they saw as the Allies' betrayal. On the border with Iran, the BBC correspondent Charles Wheeler found a family who had walked the hundred miles from Suleimaniya. It had taken them two weeks. At first the husband did the talking and the wife said she was too exhausted to say anything. Gradually, though, the anger welled up in her and the words forced themselves out in English.

> Five million people are in this coldness and this rain. Who is responsible for this? Our house is destroyed. Some of us – we don't know where they are. But only we go to Iran. Maybe we see them.
>
> Mr George Bush is responsible for all this. He could destroy Saddam and his army but he don't try. All this because he don't want Kurdish and Shia to be the leader in Iraq, to run Iraq. Why did he do that? He could destroy that army. We could live in peace. The war is finished. He [George Bush] destroyed Kuwait. Kuwait is one million people. He do all this war for one million people. We are five million. Saddam Hussein bombing, helicopters destroy us. They saw this. They did nothing. Why? We are human, like you. *Why?*

Iran, whose revolutionary government had once persecuted the Kurds as much as the Iraqis, did what it could for the refugees on the border. Iran's frontiers were open and it provided them with camps, though these were little more than collection-points on the hillsides. Turkey, where it had been

371

illegal to speak Kurdish or wear Kurdish national dress, was harsher. In some places Turkish soldiers opened fire on the refugees. In others they stole relief deliveries in order to sell them to the refugees. At the Isikveren camp near Uludere, which was a sea of mud and filth and where the stench of excrement was strong enough to be smelled long before you entered the camp, the refugees said that if a parcel dropped from a supply plane landed near the Turkish army quarters the soldiers would claim it. The refugees could have it if it landed near them.

Soon Allied soldiers involved in the relief effort complained that the Turkish soldiers were being obstructive, often trying to stop supplies getting to the camps or stealing them once they did. At the camp at Sendimli there were no medical facilities and the Turkish officer who ran it refused to allow a group of French doctors and nurses to work there. The refugees claimed they were fed only once every three days. The anti-western feeling which had been growing for some months in Turkey increased greatly when the Turkish newspapers printed accounts of the reporting of these things by the *Independent* journalist Robert Fisk. Westerners who travelled around southern Turkey were often stopped at military roadblocks and asked if they were Robert Fisk. There was even greater anger when he slipped out of the country on an RAF aircraft bound for Britain.

There were no parachute drops of supplies in Iran at first; western countries and agencies seem to have felt that dealing with Turkey was bound to be easier than dealing with Iran. There were roughly half a million refugees in Turkey and a million in Iran. It took some days of negotiation before the Turkish authorities would agree to allow the refugees to come down from the inhospitable mountainsides to more acceptable areas lower down. Distributing the food supplies that were brought in was often an unpleasant and degrading business. Hungry people whose only loyalty was to themselves and their families would fight like animals as the parcels and tins were handed out. The strong were fed, the weak and the old were not. Among the Kurdish peasantry, men would expect to be fed before women and children. Now they used their greater strength to ensure they were. There was no way of keeping order; the refugees were so hungry that shots fired in the air did not deter them.

Slowly the horror of the camps stirred the conscience of the international community. John Major, who had been prime minister in Britain for less than five months, felt a personal duty to do something effective to bring the Kurdish refugees down from the mountains and back to the towns and villages they had fled. This could only be achieved by forcing the withdrawal of Saddam Hussein's men from the area. To the private dismay of some of his ministers, he proposed creating what he called a 'safe haven' in Kurdistan to allow the inhabitants to return. In a television interview he said he realized his objectives might well fail:

> I may end up with egg all over my face because they fail. But I will tell you this, I would rather end up with egg all over my face having tried and failed than not having put forward solutions to this problem.

Major was immediately criticized by some supporters of his predecessor, Margaret Thatcher, for mentioning the possibility of failure. This was not a word Mrs Thatcher would have used in connexion with herself.

Major's biggest problem was America's reluctance to put troops into another part of Iraq. On 14 April the last US forces in the southern part of the country had withdrawn from Rumailah. Everyone knew what would happen to the Iraqis who had first welcomed the Americans and felt free in their presence to express their opposition to Saddam Hussein. When people feel they have been liberated they are rarely as cautious as they sometimes need to be. Now the Iraqi security men were sitting in their cars by the side of the road, watching who went where and waiting for the Americans to leave. Then they moved in. When I reached southern Iraq a week later, all these places were thoroughly under Baghdad's control again. Those people who had come out openly against the Baathist system were presumably under arrest.

None of this was as important to the Bush administration as

the urgent need to get out. At first, therefore, John Major's proposal that several thousand US troops should move into northern Iraq was greeted with hostility in Washington. Less public attention had been given to the question of the Kurdish refugees in the United States where the emphasis was still on the military victory which had been achieved. The British pushed hard, arguing that the Kurds would come down from the mountains only if they were given the assurance of protection by Allied armed forces. They argued that the scheme fell clearly under the terms of UN Resolution 688, which had been passed in order to protect the Kurds from Saddam's army. Eventually Bush gave way. It was a considerable victory for John Major but the price that had to be paid was an acceptance of Bush's determination that the American troops would not stay there long.

The 'safe haven' scheme worked extremely well. The great majority of refugees came down from the mountains and went back to their towns and villages. The small print of the agreement, that the Americans were determined not to stay long, was not made evident to the Kurds. The hospitals were cleaned up. Malnourished, sometimes dying, children were brought in and lives were saved. The western doctors often had to single out those they could treat and shut the door on the others. They had problems with rich men who pushed their way in on the principle that wealthy people naturally received more help than the poor.

In Zakho and other towns the Americans, British, French, Dutch and others patrolled the streets and gave an ultimately deceptive feeling of security to the inhabitants. All but 50 of the 800 Iraqi soldiers in the town had pulled out. Those who remained wore black berets and the dark green fatigues of the Baath Party uniform. There were spies everywhere, watching to see who fraternized with the westerners and listening to what was said. Tira Shubart of 'Word Monitor' noticed that the only café with any food for sale was also the only café with a picture of Saddam Hussein on its wall.

Despite all this the sheer size and evident toughness of the western soldiers compared with the Iraqis gave everyone a sense of confidence. So did the way the Iraqi policemen deferred to them. When a television correspondent asked a couple of women in the town what they would do if the Allied troops left, they laughed uncertainly as if they thought it might just be a joke, then reached out their arms beseechingly: 'If they go? No, no, please don't go. We want you here. Please. Please.' Yet the more thoughtful people realized what was happening: Saddam's men were simply waiting until the Americans' interest and patience ran out. It wouldn't take long.

Aftermath

The past is the past. Let us start again . . . Each should return to his town, home and family and we should start anew. Thank God, we are used to starting anew and, God willing, this we will do.

Saddam Hussein, speaking in Erbil on 14 April 1991

The Iraq I returned to in April 1991 was a very different country from the Iraq I had come to know earlier. The rhetoric of aggression and power had been replaced by the rhetoric of meekness. Saddam Hussein had become a born-again democrat. 'If you get things right, you'll get the credit,' he told a group of Iraqi journalists to whom he was explaining the new liberty of the press. 'If you get things wrong, I'll take the blame.'

Everything was going to be new and different from now on. The old idea of turning Iraq into an instant regional superpower by buying military technology over the counter hadn't worked; the very companies which had sold him the weapons or the bunkers or the communications systems had delivered the specifications and plans to his enemies. He sent Tariq Aziz, newly promoted to vice-president, to Tunis to tell Yasser Arafat and the PLO leadership of his new idea for Iraq. The model would be Germany after 1945: a country which had lost a war but would go on, through its economic success, to win the peace.

After the war, as before it, the personality of Saddam Hussein was the central factor in the entire affair. His daemonic energy, his obsessive notions about the dignity and honour that was due to Iraq, his lack of careful, balanced planning, his willingness to sacrifice anyone and anything to protect his own position – these called down on his country the heaviest weight of military power since World War II. This is the only sense in which he was comparable with Hitler: if Saddam had been killed, no one would have carried on fighting.

What kept Saddam in power after the war was, partly, his extraordinary courage and, partly, his hunch about the United States. He had got it terribly wrong at the start of the crisis, assuming that the Americans would not have the fixity of purpose to fight; he had simply not anticipated the ability of the new weapons systems to destroy a country's capacity to fight a war without destroying its citizens. But his instinct was right once the war was over. The most important thing for the United States was to get out. Saddam had only to keep quiet and go along with everything that was asked of him and wait until the Americans left.

As I write this, at the end of June 1991, the troops which made northern Iraq a safe haven for the Kurds are being withdrawn. To the great alarm of the Kurds themselves, the only people taking their place are a small group of security guards from the United Nations building in New York armed with handguns. Saddam Hussein is hoping to hold presidential elections which will make him an off-the-peg democrat, much as he tried to be an off-the-peg superpower. His job description has already been composed. Little noticed in the crisis over Kuwait, Saddam's new constitution was published on 31 July 1990, two days before the invasion. The relevant passage reads as follows:

> The president is elected by general direct secret ballot which is regulated by the law. He should be an Iraqi by birth, and not of foreign origin. He should be known for justice, courage, wisdom, prowess and distinguished service to the homeland and the nation. The president should also be known for his loyalty to the principles of the 17–30 July Revolution and his active participation in the Gulf War [against Iran]. He should also have a deep conviction that this war was inevitable to preserve Iraq's territorial integrity. Furthermore, he should be an advocate of socialism.

If it was a central war aim of the British and Americans to overthrow Saddam, it failed; even though it seems clear he was terribly weakened by the war and will never again be what he once was.

So what did so much expenditure of money and weaponry achieve in fighting Saddam? Firstly, Kuwait was liberated and its government duly restored as the UN resolutions required. The basic rule of international behaviour, whereby one country does not attack a smaller neighbour and swallow it up simply because it is smaller, was reasserted.

Secondly, the war was an exhibition which showed how powerful the United States and, to a far lesser extent, its European allies were. The superiority of Western technology over the Soviet brand with which Iraq was equipped was almost total.

Thirdly, no one could doubt that the United States would come to the aid of a stricken friend, at least if it were sited in an important strategic location. That, I take it, is the practical meaning of Mr Bush's grand words about a new world order: it means a world in which the United States – if possible with the assistance of the Soviet Union – is a force which everybody will have to reckon with; at least until its attention is distracted. George Bush is only a politician like others and those are three important achievements for a politician.

Yet nothing is ever quite the same after a war. Even a war aim which has been achieved does not turn out as expected. The Emir and the al-Sabah family were restored to power in Kuwait, but it had become a different place. Governments, like individuals, are liable to become what they fear. Kuwait was never a particularly attractive state before its invasion by Iraq. Following its liberation, Kuwait underwent a violent personality change. From being merely restrictive and selfish it became paranoid. The revenge which its citizens started to exact was in direct proportion to the terror they had suffered after the Iraqi invasion of 2 August 1990.

Eamonn Matthews, who was with me on my first visit to Baghdad and then stayed with me when the war started, went to Kuwait with Charles Wheeler who, at 68, is arguably the finest correspondent working in British television. They

378

arrived a few days after liberation. The city was full of road blocks run by Kuwaitis, Saudi soldiers and the shadowy new militias. They were visited in their hotel by a Palestinian; it had taken him 12 hours to get through the different road blocks. The story he told them was a terrible one, of torture and execution on a par with the Iraqis. The Kuwaitis were torturing and executing those they accused of collaborating. Eamonn went out with the Palestinian and met 20 people in a single afternoon who had been lashed, burned, given electric shocks or beaten. Slowly he realized that these people were the lucky ones, the ones who had been released.

A British-trained Palestinian doctor in his mid-fifties told them his story. He showed the classic symptoms of someone who has undergone the trauma of being tortured severely: breaking down in tears, frightened of being alone, alarmed by every noise. It seemed all the worse in such a dignified man. He had been picked up at a road block and taken to a police station. He wasn't too badly beaten because of his age, but he was put in a cell with younger men, all Palestinians. All had been badly tortured. Many had arms or legs which had been broken but not set. They were given no water and were obliged to drink their urine. During the night a Kuwaiti guard walked up to the door, poked his automatic rifle in and fired at random. A bullet grazed the doctor's scalp. He heard the guard remark: 'I wonder if I hit any of the bastards? I hope so.'

Eamonn followed up the man's story and visited the places where he and others had been held. They were mostly schools and each was guarded by machine gun posts. They started hearing stories that when people were almost at the point of death in these places, doctors would come for them. They were taken to one particular hospital where, one of the nurses told Eamonn, they were treated for their injuries. When they were starting to recover the doctors would send them back to be tortured again. According to the nurse the Saudi military as well as the Kuwaitis visited the hospital and knew all about it. The schools where the torture went on were run officially, so the Kuwaiti government knew. Charles and Eamonn went to the hospital and managed to get to the door of the ward where the torture victims were held. The doctor in charge screamed at them that they should have been there filming when the Iraqis were there.

In a way, the Iraqis are there still. In their loathing of what Saddam Hussein did to their country, the Kuwaitis have turned into Iraqis, trying to root out his memory by using his methods. One set of evils has generated another. The death squads, some of them reportedly containing members of the Crown Prince's family, roamed the streets looking for non-Kuwaitis to humiliate, torture or kill. Palestinians were sentenced to death by properly constituted courts for wearing a Saddam T-shirt or applying for a job in a pro-Iraqi quisling newspaper, *Al-Nida*. A group of labourers were lucky to be found not guilty of the capital offence of collaboration because they mended a lavatory in the newspaper's office. The state which never accepted Palestinians as citizens is exacting a ferocious price for their failure to behave like citizens. Kuwait hasn't rid itself of Saddam Hussein in other ways: the hundreds of oil-wells which carried on burning for months are his work; so is the tide of crude oil along the entire coast, killing everything it covers.

If these things are the price of victory, it is not surprising that so many people have wondered whether the victory was worth it. Yet what was the alternative? My months in Baghdad before the war convinced me that a country as fiercely controlled as Iraq could have lasted years under sanctions without being forced to withdraw from Kuwait. Once the invasion had taken place, it achieved nothing to say that the West should not have provided Saddam Hussein with many of the weapons he required to carry out his repression.

It was true, however. The West should never have supplied Saddam with such weapons; neither should the Soviet Union or the Chinese. Yet some of those who argued most strongly against the war had earlier argued in favour of doing something to stop Saddam attacking the Kurds and violating human rights. Taking action against him through the United Nations was at least positive and would not have led to war if Saddam had been prepared to compromise. George Bush and Margaret Thatcher may well have wanted to fight Saddam Hussein all along, but he could perfectly well have avoided it.

Twice in 10 years Saddam Hussein gambled on a quick victory and lost: two quick, almost flippant decisions. The first, in 1980, may have brought a million deaths. The second cost an unknown number, wrecked the lives of millions and convulsed an entire region of the world. The waste which this man alone has generated is incalculable.

I thought of that as I left Iraq in April 1991 for what will probably (after this book) be the last time; at least until Saddam Hussein leaves power. We had driven across the desert from Baghdad to the Jordanian border. A few desert dogs howled beyond the barbed wire fence which marks the crossing-point at Trebiel. Not far away was a large portrait of Saddam, painted on concrete. It had been so badly damaged by gunfire that the local officials had had to pin a blue cloth over the face, so no one could see the extent of the desecration.

The customs post was filthy with nine months' uncleared rubbish. Hundreds of thousands of refugees had passed this way in the summer, ejected from Kuwait by the Iraqis and heading for the camps in Jordan. A miasma of sand and muck closed in on us like a gritty, smelly fog, blown around by the wind from the desert. Desert winds should be clean and sterile; this one stank of petrol fumes and faeces. It gathered up the muck on the ground, whipping it into pointless circles: soft drinks cans, little rustling plastic bags, squares of toilet paper, pink yellow and white, plastic coathangers, empty blue plastic bottles which had once held mineral water, empty cigarette packets – Sumer, Monte Carlo, Gold Coast, Cedars, Top Twenty, cheap Third World brands – orange peel, carbon paper from old visa applications long since granted or refused, an air mail letter, neatly stamped and addressed to someone in France.

It all circled round me, the dust getting in my eyes, the little alert flies scarcely affected by it as they pounced on the dirt that lay everywhere. 'GOING PASSENGERS'S HALL' a sign outside the office where they stamped the exit visas read: I was a going passenger. I left the country where I had lived for almost six out of the previous nine months without looking back.

Chronology of Events in the Gulf Crisis

August 1990

2   Iraqi troops begin their invasion of Kuwait at 0200 local time and within hours take control of Kuwait City. The UN Security Council, meeting in emergency session, passes Resolution 660 condemning the invasion and calling for immediate and unconditional withdrawal. US President Brush and British Prime Minister Margaret Thatcher call for a collective international effort to force Iraqi withdrawal. All Iraqi and Kuwaiti assets and property in the US are frozen.

3   US Secretary of State James Baker and Soviet Foreign Minister Eduard Shevardnadze issue joint declaration in Moscow demanding withdrawal and call for all countries to impose an arms embargo on Iraq.

6   UN Security Council Resolution 661 is passed imposing economic sanctions on Iraq and Kuwait.

7   The US announces that it will be sending 82nd Airborne Division to Saudi Arabia.

8   President Bush makes televised address to the nation explaining his decision to send US forces to Saudi Arabia. Britain and France announce intention to contribute to multi-national force in Saudi Arabia. Iraq announces formal annexation of Kuwait.

10   Arab League summit in Cairo votes to send a Pan-Arab

force to Saudi Arabia but there are abstentions and Iraq, Libya and the PLO vote against.

18   Iraq announces it is to play 'host' to foreign citizens as long as there is a threat of aggressive war.

28   Kuwait is formally declared 19th province of Iraq and Kuwait City is renamed Kadimah.

September 1990

9 . In Helsinki President Bush and President Gorbachev announce their joint opposition to Iraqi occupation of Kuwait and its continuing hostage policy.

October 1990

2   London-based Amnesty International accuses Iraqi authorities in Kuwait of widespread killings and human rights violations since 2 August.

7   Israeli authorities begin distributing gas masks to civilians following threats of chemical attack by Iraq.

9   Saddam Hussein states that only an Israeli withdrawal from the Occupied Territories and the withdrawal of foreign forces from the Gulf will resolve the problems of the Middle East. President Bush rejects any such linkage.

28   Soviet envoy Yevgeny Primakov, on his second visit to Baghdad, holds further inconclusive talks with Saddam Hussein.

29   UN Security Council 674 makes Iraq responsible for war crimes and reparations.

November 1990

8   President Bush orders an increase in US forces in the Gulf.

19   President Bush and Prime Minister Margaret Thatcher denounce Saddam Hussein's offer to release foreign nationals over a three month period from Christmas day.

23 President Bush holds talks with President Mubarak of Egypt before leaving Cairo for Geneva where he holds talks with President Assad of Syria for the first time in thirteen years.

26 Tariq Aziz visits Gorbachev in Moscow and is warned of a tougher Soviet attitude.

29 UN Security Resolution 678 is passed authorising the use of military force against Iraq unless it withdraws from Kuwait by the 15 January 1991.

30 President Bush launches a new initiative – 'an extra mile for peace' – by announcing his intention to send James Baker to Baghdad to invite Tariq Aziz to the US for talks.

December 1990

1 Iraq accepts President Bush's offer of talks but says they must include wider issues. The US rejects linkage.

6 Saddam Hussein announces the release of all remaining foreign hostages.

20 Eduard Shevardnadze resigns following internal disagreement over the Soviet Union's Gulf policy. Saddam Hussein warns of the great loss of life if war breaks out; a loss which he claims President Bush cannot sustain.

24 In a further attempt to widen the conflict into an Arab-Israeli one, Saddam Hussein warns that Tev Aviv would be Iraq's first objective in a conflict, whether or not Israeli forces took part in the war against Iraq.

31 Ali Akbar Velayati, Iran's Foreign Minister, says that Iran will remain neutral in the event of war.

January 1991

6 In a televised speech to mark Army Day, Saddam Hussein calls on the Iraqi army to be prepared to make sacrifices for the battle to liberate Palestine.

9 James Baker, and Tariq Aziz, hold talks in Geneva. The talks fail when Baker announces that he has heard

nothing which suggests any Iraqi flexibility in responding to the UN call to withdraw from Kuwait by 15 January 1991. James Baker says that there may be a way that the UN Secretary General can use his good offices before the UN deadline.

11 Presidents Bush and Gorbachev discuss the Gulf crisis over the telephone and announce their complete agreement in their stand against Iraq.

12 Thousands attend anti-war demonstrations in Europe. President Assad of Syria appeals on state radio for Saddam Hussein to withdraw from Kuwait.

13 Javier Perez de Cuellar meets Saddam Hussein in Baghdad in a last attempt to avert war. Asked what the chances for war or peace were, the UN Secretary General replied, 'God only knows.'

15 UN Security Council meets to discuss a peace plan put forward by France which links the Gulf crisis to a Middle East peace conference. The plan is rejected. President Bush signs a national security directive authorising a military attack against Iraq.

16 At 2150 GMT the first cruise missiles are launched from warships in the Gulf at the start of 'Operation Desert Storm'.

17 Iraqi Radio broadcasts a message from Saddam Hussein saying 'the mother of all battles' has begun. US Defense Department officials say there were four hundred raids in the first three hours of air attacks.

18 Israel comes under Iraqi missile attack (the first of a number that occur in the following days). Fears that the missiles contained chemical weapons were unfounded. A Scud missile launched on Saudi Arabia was shot down by a US Patriot missile – the first time it had been used in combat. According to Jordanian sources 750,000 refugees from Iraq have begun trekking towards the Jordanian border.

19 Chairman of US Joint Chiefs of Staff, General Colin Powell, states that disabling of Iraqi airfields and air defences is complete and around the clock air attacks will now concentrate on Iraqi ground troops.

20   Iraq shows a group of captured allied pilots of television
      – some of them appear to have been badly bruised.
25   US accuses Iraq of dumping large quantities of oil into the
      Gulf. Iraq blames the oil slick on US bombing of Iraqi
      tankers.
26   At least 12 Iraqi Air Force aircraft arrive in Iran. Iran says
      that they will be held until the conflict ends. Over the next
      few days at least a hundred aircraft are reported to have
      flown to Iran.
30   Iraqi troops capture the Saudi Arabian border town of
      Khafji and hold it for one day before it is retaken by
      Allied forces.

February 1991

13   An Iraqi air raid shelter in the Amiriya district of
      Baghdad is bombed by US planes. Iraq claims as many as
      400 civilians died in the attack; the US claims the shelter
      was a military bunker.
15   Iraq's Revolutionary Command Council issues a condi-
      tional withdrawal from Kuwait but it is unacceptable to
      President Bush.
17   Tariq Aziz arrives in Moscow for talks with Gorbachev
      over Iraqi offer to withdraw from Kuwait. Gorbachev
      requests the US delay any ground offensive until after his
      talks with Tariq Aziz.
18   President Gorbachev announces Soviet peace plan.
19   President Bush rejects Soviet peace initiative as 'falling
      well short of what would be required' but sends Moscow
      a list of minimum terms that Iraq must accept if the war is
      to end – the list goes well beyond conditions set out in
      Soviet peace plan.
21   Iraq accepts Soviet plan but US states that it will only
      order a ceasefire on evidence of a massive Iraqi with-
      drawal based on its own timetable. Iraq begins a
      'scorched earth' policy in Kuwait, burning oil instal-
      lations.
24   Allied forces launch ground war into Iraq and Kuwait

following Saddam Hussein's failure to meet US deadline.

25 Allied forces reach suburbs of Kuwait City, having cut through Iraqi defences 'with ease' and taken more than 10,000 Iraqi POWs. Baghdad Radio announces that Iraqi troops have been ordered to withdraw from Kuwait.

27 Allied tanks recapture Kuwait City after seven months of Iraqi occupation.

28 Bush announces a Gulf ceasefire, one hundred hours after the ground offensive began and six weeks since the start of the air war.

March 1991

1 Iraq officially agrees to Security Council Resolution 660 and subsequent UN resolutions on the crisis.

3 Allied commanders meet with their Iraqi counterparts in a tent at Safwan airfield in southern Iraq and agree to a Gulf ceasefire. A Shi'a uprising begins in southern Iraq.

5 Revolt against Saddam Hussein spreads as Kurds in the north join in uprising.

7 Saddam Hussein orders his Republican Guard to crush the rebellions.

10 US states its determination not to get involved in 'Iraqi internal affairs'.

19 Large areas of northern Iraq come under Kurdish rebel control including the oil city of Kirkuk.

28 Loyalist Iraqi troops recapture control of the southern Shia city of Kerbala.

30 Iraqi troops recapture Kirkuk.

April 1991

3 Iraqi troops recapture the Kurdish city of Sulaymaniya .

7 As many as two million refugees are reported fleeing from the Iraqi army.

9   John Major proposes a UN protected enclave for the Kurds in northern Iraq.

11 Bush warns Saddam not to use air or ground forces in proposed safety enclaves as the West steps up its emergency aid to the refugees.

13 A ceasefire is declared between Kurdish guerillas and Iraqi army.

17 Bush and Major agree on need to police refugee camps.

24 Following negotiations between the Patriotic Union of Kurdistan (PUK) and the Baghdad government, provisional agreement on Kurdish autonomy is announced.

May 1991

7   Kurdish leader Massoud Barzani attends the second round of autonomy talks in Baghdad. Kurdish leaders state their desire for an international guarantee on any deal with Baghdad. Last US troops pull out of occupied southern Iraq leaving behind them thousands of refugees who dare not or cannot return to their place of origin.

10 Plans for a UN police force in northern Iraq appear in disarray as Baghdad rejects such a move – its acceptance being a UN precondition for implementation.

18 Kurdish leaders claim to have secured an agreement with Saddam Hussein. Trials begin in Kuwait of more than 200 alleged collaborators.

June 1991

1   Reports continue to emerge from Kuwait of acts of vengeance and torture – against Iraqis, Palestinians and Kurds.

2   Kurds in Zakho appeal to the Allied forces to stay on.

15 British and American troops, as part of their phased withdrawal from Kurdish safe haven areas, prepare to hand over protection of Kurds to ill-equipped UN security guards.

388

18   Human rights organisations express deep concern at the death sentences being passed on alleged collaborators in Kuwait.

21   US temporarily halts its withdrawal from northern Iraq following pressure from the European Community to allow more time to decide how best to ensure the future security of the Kurds. Kurdish leaders announce a draft agreement on autonomy with Saddam Hussein.

25   US announces plans to create a small allied rapid deployment force based in Turkey to protect the Kurds.

26   Kuwait announces that all death sentences passed in recent trials in Kuwait have been commuted to life imprisonment. Kurdish leaders in Baghdad decide not to sign an autonomy agreement with Baghdad following new conditions laid down by Saddam Hussein.

Bibliography

Bulloch, J. & Morris, H. *Saddam's War*, London: Faber & Faber, 1991

Bulloch, J. & Morris, H. *The Gulf War*, London: Methuen, 1989

CARDRI: *Saddam's Iraq*, London: Zed Books Ltd, 1989

Chubin, S. & Tripp, C. *Iran and Iraq at War*, London: I.B. Tauris & Co. Ltd, 1988

Darwish, A. & Alexander, G. *Unholy Babylon*, London: Victor Gollancz Ltd, 1991

Farouk-Sluglett, M. & Sluglett, P. *Iraq Since 1958*, London: KPI Ltd, 1987

Fromkin, D. *A Peace To End All Peace*, New York: Avon Books, 1989

Al-Hadithi, N. *Iraq 1990: An Official Handbook*, Baghdad, 1991

Hiro, D. *The Longest War*, London: Grafton Books, 1989

Karsh, E. & Rautsi, I. *Saddam Hussein*, London: Brassey's, 1991

Al-Khalil, S. *Republic of Fear*, London: Hutchinson Radius, 1990

Lassner, J. *The Topography of Baghdad in the Early Middle Ages*, Detroit: Wayne State Univ. Press, 1970

Mansfield, P. *Kuwait, Vanguard of the Gulf*, London: Hutchinson, 1990

Marr, P. *The Modern History of Iraq*, Boulder, Colorado: Westview Press, 1985

Matar, F. *Saddam Hussein*, London: Highlight, 1990

Niblock, T. *Iraq: The Contemporary State*, London: Croom Helm, 1982

Pelletiere, S. & others *Iraqi Power and US Security in the Middle East*, Strategic Studies Institute, US Army War College, 1990

Schofield, R. *Kuwait and Iraq: Historical Claims and Territorial Disputes*, London: The Royal Institute of International Affairs, 1991

Woodward, R. *The Commanders*, New York: Simon & Schuster, 1991

Index

devises 'democratic executions', 35–6; miscalculates over invasion of Iran, 40; apologizes to Pres. Reagan for attack on USS Stark, 44; fears US-British-Israeli conspiracy, 67; anger against Kuwait, 88; personal vanity 89; Caliph-like behaviour, 91–93; cult of personality of, 93–94; offices and functions of, 94; interviewed about April Glaspie, 105; anger as spur to invasion of Kuwait, 108; links withdrawal from Kuwait to Israeli withdrawal from Occupied Territories, 124; visits British hostages, 153–154; release of women and children, 158; fears nuclear attack, 158; negotiates release of some hostages with Willy Brandt, 237; techniques in television interviews, 242; tests US resolve, 251; believes US is giving way, 252; agrees to release all hostages, 255; on 'mother of battles', 261; lack of genuine support for, 267; contempt for democratic system, 273; belief that war would be short, 273; Bunker of, 305; weaponry of, 320; Gen. Schwartzkopf's opinion of military qualities of, 322; distrust and subsequent loss, of air force; unpopularity of, 336; orders withdrawal from Kuwait, 348; orders destruction of oil wells in Kuwait, 349; reports of plans to seek asylum in Algeria, 366; reasons for political survival of, 377; guilt of, 381

Hussein, Uday, 368

al-Hussein Rashid, Muhyi Abd 32–4

Ibrahim Izzat: 34, 35, 95, 104, 107

Ibrahim, Sabaawi (Saddam's half-brother): 109

al-Illah Prince Abd: 25

Independent Television News (ITN) 59, 241–243, 276, 292

Iran–Iraq War, 39–43

Islam Yusuf: 232

Iyyad Abu: 279

Jackson, Rev. Jesse: 192, 232

al-Jalil, Ghanem Abd: 33, 35

Japan: 123, 202–203

Jassim, Latif Nsayef: 65, 152, 251, 281, 307

Jenabi, Sadoun: 304, 308–309, 313

Jenkins, Susan: 113

Johnson, Monty: 262

Jones, Barry: 233

Jones, Colin: 276, 281, 294

Jordan Times, The: 143

Karadighi, Mustapha: 25

Kaunda, President Kenneth: 63, 65

Kealy, Robin: 63, 64

Kelly, Gen. Thomas: 328

Kerbala: 362

al-Khoei, Grand Ayatollah Abolqassem: 363

Khomeini, Ayatollah: 40–1, 46

Kohl, Helmut: 122, 237

Koko, Capt.: 341

Kurdish uprising: 365–367, 368–375

Kuwait: background and growth, 74–87; invasion of, 113–116; human rights and other abuses in, after invasion, 161–174; withdrawal of Iraq troops from, 348; destruction of oil wells in, 349; liberation of, 350; abuses of human rights after liberation, 378–380